World War I, Mass Death, and the Birth of the Modern US Soldier

Lexington Studies in Contemporary Rhetoric

Series Editor: Gary C. Woodward, The College of New Jersey

This series provides thought-provoking and accessible analyses of the uses of language and media from the middle of the twentieth century to the present. In particular, this series examines how modern discourse is constructed and communicated in our distracted times, focusing on specific settings such as health communication, crisis communication, changing norms of interpersonal exchange, political communication beyond the presidency, etiquettes of communication in the digital age, celebrity as a rhetorical form, changing norms in "reality" and narrative television, and altered patterns of address in computer-mediated discussion. These books will provide depth and clarity about discourse more familiar than understood.

Recent Titles in This Series

World War I, Mass Death, and the Birth of the Modern US Soldier: A Rhetorical History
By David W. Seitz

US Public Memory, Rhetoric, and the National Mall
Edited by Roger C. Aden

Rhetoric of Femininity: Female Body Image, Media, and Gender Role Stress/Conflict
By Donnalyn Pompper

The Rhetorical Invention of America's National Security State
By Marouf Hasian Jr., Sean Lawson, and Megan D. McFarlane

World War I, Mass Death, and the Birth of the Modern US Soldier

A Rhetorical History

David W. Seitz

LEXINGTON BOOKS
Lanham • Boulder • New York • London

Published by Lexington Books
An imprint of The Rowman & Littlefield Publishing Group, Inc.
4501 Forbes Boulevard, Suite 200, Lanham, Maryland 20706
www.rowman.com

Unit A, Whitacre Mews, 26-34 Stannary Street, London SE11 4AB

British Library Cataloguing in Publication Information Available

Library of Congress Cataloging-in-Publication Data

Names: Seitz, David W., 1980- author.
Title: World War I, mass death, and the birth of the modern US soldier : a rhetorical history / David W. Seitz.
Description: Lanham, MD : Lexington Books, [2018] | Includes bibliographical references and index.
Identifiers: LCCN 2018016791 (print) | LCCN 2018024702 (ebook) | ISBN 9781498546881 (electronic) | ISBN 9781498546874 (cloth : alk. paper)
Subjects: LCSH: World War, 1914-1918—Social aspects—United States. | Soldiers—United States—History—20th century. | War casualties—History—20th century. | World War, 1914-1918—Psychological aspects. | National characteristics, American. | Collective memory—United States. | Memorialization—United States—History—20th century. | Reconstruction (1914-1939)—United States. | Sociology, Military—United States.
Classification: LCC D524.7.U6 (ebook) | LCC D524.7.U6 S45 2018 (print) | DDC 340.3/73—dc23
LC record available at https://lccn.loc.gov/2018016791

Contents

Acknowledgments

I wish to extend my deepest gratitude to Nicolette Amstutz, Jessica Thwaite, and everyone at Lexington Books for their patience, guidance, and support over the past few years.

This book is dedicated to my students, colleagues, friends, and family, but especially Adrienne, Finn, and Quaide.

Introduction

The political, social, and material transformations unleashed by World War I (1914–1918) revealed what Celia Malone Kingsbury has termed "the peculiar sanity of war"[1]—an illogical scheme of contradictions, mass illusions, paranoia and jingoisms, superimposed upon the mass destruction of human bodies, minds, and spirits. Following the Armistice, the disjunction between the wartime perceptions of combatant nations' populations with the reality of the war's effects could no longer be satisfactorily accounted for by the vocabularies of religion, patriotism, militaristic gallantry, technology, nature, or political affiliation, precisely because such vocabularies had helped produce and prolong this seemingly mad international bloodletting. In short, the "Great War" produced a crisis of speech: traditional rhetorics that had been adequate and convincing before and during the war no longer were.

In the United States, the essential tasks of memorializing fallen soldiers, justifying soldierly death, and assuaging the personal and often gendered suffering of next of kin were highly problematic.[2] The nation had lost 116,516 soldiers in defense of territory that was not its own. Furthermore, threats to the American homeland and its interests were not as obvious, direct, or imminent as for European belligerents. Public doubts over the costs paid through casualties of conscripted U.S. citizens became common and eventually led to congressional investigations of wartime profiteers—the so-called merchants of death. Moreover, wartime rhetoric of preserving Western democracy against the "autocratic Hun" revealed lingering domestic contradictions. For example, African Americans who had bravely served their country returned home to find that any measures of social equality they had attained overseas meant little in the United States, with its continuing Jim Crow segregation and increasing racial violence.[3] In light of soldiers' bodies still lying in haphazard makeshift graves in battle-scarred fields and

forests throughout Europe many citizens rightfully wondered for what, and
for whom, had Americans died in what seemed strictly a European affair?
For Americans, the immediate postwar years provoked a "generative crisis,"[4] a crucial moment of exigence regarding the meaning of soldierly
death, ripe for rhetorical invention.

Drawing upon more than a decade of historical, archival, ethnographic,
interpretive, and scholarly research,[5] this book explains how World War I:
ruptured American conceptions of soldierly sacrifice commonly held since
the Civil War; triggered a turbulent national dialogue on the meaning of state-
sponsored war and soldierly mass death in the 20th century; and, spawned the
now-familiar ideographic construction of the U.S. soldier as *a global force
for good*. Per rhetoric scholar Michael Calvin McGee, ideographs refer to
words and phrases that serve as the building blocks of ideology—words and
phrases that condition people "not directly to belief and behavior, but to a
vocabulary of concepts that function as guides, warrants, reasons, or excuses
for behavior and belief." Historically, Americans have reacted "predictably
and autonomically" to ideographs like "law," "liberty," "freedom," and
"sacrifice," which are routinely found in political speeches, public discourse,
American war rhetoric, and the texts and designs of American war memorials and monuments. This book explains how after World War I, U.S. officials
established (both linguistically and visually) for the first time the "American
soldier" into an effective ideograph of near universal appeal.[6] Contextualizing
the postwar "generative crisis" within the broader American experience of
World War I (both domestically and abroad) and contemporary politics and
cultural practices, this diachronic study shows how collisions between divergent social forces (e.g., grieving families, famous military leaders, veterans
groups, immigrant communities, politicians harboring imperial designs, arms
manufacturers, "disillusioned" artists and writers, foreign dignitaries) within
public and private spheres wrought the generic and dubious yet rhetorically powerful image of the modern U.S. soldier and 'his' attending virtues,
motives, and willingness to fight and die across the globe for Americans and
non-Americans alike.

The conclusion of World War I may seem like a natural starting point for
this "rhetorical history."[7] But, as I will argue, the rhetorical 'birth' of the
modern U.S. soldier should be understood as a reaction to the vast distances
between Americans' wartime perceptions of the Great War and postwar
realizations of the conflict's human costs. Thus, the first half of this book
focuses on relevant political ideologies, public rhetoric, and material realities of the war years (1914–1918). The second half demonstrates how those
ideologies, rhetorics, and material realities subsequently shaped official and
vernacular projects of memory, framed public debates over the proper treatment and commemoration of the nation's war dead, and spurred the creation

of a necessarily ambiguous yet potent ideograph (the modern U.S. soldier) that could simultaneously: absorb anxieties over the federal government's newfound reach into the lives of private citizens; symbolically re-link the bodies of U.S. soldiers sacrificed on (and *buried in*) foreign soil with the American homeland; epitomize the supposed unity, equality, and shared interests of a radically heterogeneous and stratified American polis; and, validate the nation's marked transition from isolationism to interventionism. In other words, this book endeavors to provide a detailed genealogy of the iconic figure of the *universal* 'U.S. soldier' that emerged and circulated during the postwar years.

From the outset, it is crucial to emphasize (if briefly) just how transformative and disorienting the American World War I experience was. On an international level, America's participation in (and decisive impact on) World War I signaled (and confirmed) the nation's emergence as a new, major global force (economically, politically, and militarily speaking) with which traditional "Old World" powers would henceforth have to contend. As British politician David Lloyd George told the international press on April 6, 1917 (the day after Congress's declaration of war): "America has at one bound become a world-power in a sense she never was before."[8] Indeed, previous U.S. military interventions in foreign territories (e.g., the Spanish-American War) had been much smaller in scope, entailed comparatively few casualties, and had been fought by professional soldiers (as opposed to conscripted citizen-soldiers) in support of the young nation's own, relatively limited, imperial designs (rather than in defense of other countries or abstract 'American' ideals of "freedom" and "democracy"). And following World War I, the United States would come to play a leading role in the negotiations and crafting of the Treaty of Versailles—the controversial peace agreement that forced Germany to accept full moral and financial responsibility for the war and the devastation it wrought, redrew national borders around the world in favor of the Allied Powers' interests, and (unfortunately) set the stage for World War II. In short, World War I elevated the United States to a dominant position in geopolitics—a status that would only strengthen over time. Simultaneously, at the domestic level, World War I revealed the federal government's ever increasing (and, for many people, *unwelcome*) reach into the lives of ordinary Americans (evidenced first and foremost by the successful, unprecedented implementation of a universal military draft). Furthermore, it compelled citizens and communities (English-speaking or otherwise, natural born or naturalized, leftist or centrist or right-leaning, of every shade and color) to grapple with the new, disquieting, and undeniable (if seemingly irreconcilable) realities, traumas, and mandated personal "sacrifices" that 20th-century U.S. state-sponsored warfare entailed. As I argue in this book, such changes at the international and domestic levels help explain the genesis and the rhetorical contours and dimensions of the iconic, sacrificial U.S. soldier developed during and after World War I.

Written in the spirit of war-related cultural histories I greatly admire, such as Drew Gilpin Faust's *This Republic of Suffering: Death and the American Civil War* and Paul Fussell's *The Great War and Modern Memory*,[9] this book takes a decidedly 'bottom-up'[10] approach, albeit to rhetorical criticism and theory. While analyzing relevant dominant discourses of the era (such as those found in media reports, presidential speeches, official laws and policies, and Hollywood depictions of the Great War), it unearths and showcases "forgotten publics"[11] and "immediate testimonies"[12] discovered in previously untapped historical and archival materials (e.g., rare wartime diaries kept by U.S. soldiers along the Western Front, correspondence between traumatized widows and the federal government regarding the burial of fallen soldiers, opinion-editorials on questions of citizenship and soldierly sacrifice in local African-American, German-American, and Suffragette newspapers and pamphlets, behind-the-scenes communiqués between individuals responsible for the design of permanent U.S. World War I cemeteries in Europe)—publics and testimonies that directly influenced the rhetorical construction of the 'modern U.S. soldier' still in currency today.

CHAPTER DESIGN

This book—a genealogy of the rhetorical construction of the 'modern U.S. soldier'—is divided into four major chapters and a conclusion. Focusing on the rhetoric of contemporary newspaper and magazine reports and op-eds, popular cinema, governmental proclamations, public intellectuals, veterans of the Spanish-American War, and various social movement groups (e.g., African-American liberationists, Suffragettes, labor unions, anarchists, isolationists, German Americans, interventionists, nativists), chapter 1 brings forth, analyzes, and interprets American public discourse regarding the Great War and the attending issues of death, killing, sacrifice, burial, and commemoration during the period of American neutrality. This chapter shows how, between 1914 and 1917, a heterogeneous, fractured, American public came to perceive (through news reports reflecting both on-the-ground truths and competing British and German propaganda) the "War in Europe" primarily as something akin to a "human slaughter-house"—a mad, immoral, regressive, antidemocratic, and unnecessary mass bloodletting that: ruptured 19th-century conceptions of "good" soldierly death; harnessed the terrible destructive capacities of modern science and technology; and, had little to do with the interests of the United States (a relatively young nation still mending the social divisions and spiritual wounds wrought by the Civil War). To wit, in 1916, President Woodrow Wilson won his reelection campaign on the slogan, "He Kept Us Out of the War!" As this chapter shows, the apparent majority of Americans considered Wilson's victory to be a referendum against U.S. intervention in the World War. By tracing pertinent rhetorical action of the prewar period, this chapter contextualizes the unexpected, divisive, and epoch-shifting U.S. wartime policies (e.g., media censorship and propaganda, compulsory military service) and postwar policies (e.g., repatriation of the dead, the establishment of permanent overseas military cemeteries) that would soon follow.

Chapter 2 focuses on the turbulent and epoch-shifting period of American belligerence. In April of 1917, Woodrow Wilson committed one the swiftest about-faces in U.S. presidential history. Abandoning the staunch antiwar platform of his 1916 presidential campaign, he went before Congress and asked for a declaration of war against Germany. Members of the House and Senate overwhelmingly supported the president's idealistic call to make the world "safe for democracy" and plunged the United States into the Great War. Recognizing the antiwar and isolationist streaks that coursed through public discourse and consciousness, and comprehending the obvious incongruity between his pre and postelection stances, President Wilson helped develop a series of wartime laws, policies, and agencies that effectively made citizen (and noncitizen) support for the national war effort a matter of compulsion, not choice. Establishing an unprecedented national draft, a powerful propaganda and media censorship bureau, and a Justice Department hell bent on silencing and persecuting dissenters, as well as synthesizing premodern American war rhetoric with 20th-century propaganda techniques borrowed from European belligerents, the Wilson Administration attempted to control the "body and soul and spirit" of every American "in the supreme effort of service and sacrifice."[13] Within months, the people of the United States were legally and rhetorically transformed (through language, law, and force) into either "subversives" or "loyal," subservient and (at least in the case of able-bodied males) *expendable* components of the national war machine. By November of 1918, roughly 117,000 American men (and a much smaller but not unsubstantial number of women) would die "over there," on the other side of the Atlantic in support of "freedom," "democracy," and "justice." Utilizing rhetorical theorist Kenneth Burke's heuristic dichotomy of 'motion and action' to analyze Wilson's address and the nation's subsequent war effort, this chapter offers a rhetorical analysis of what I term the U.S. government and military's wartime "project of motion"—a program that sought to suppress dissent and symbolic action, and cast American intervention in the Great War as a matter of compulsion (motion), not choice (action). As the remaining chapters will show, this project fabricated for the American public largely false visions of the necessity, benefits, and human costs of

U.S. participation in the war. In the postwar years, U.S. officials would face the monumental task of rhetorically accounting for the incongruity between these false representations and the realities of American belligerence "over there"—a task that would, in time, spawn the rhetorical birth of 'the modern U.S. soldier.'

Chapter 3 examines the U.S. government's (often failed and/or ironic) attempts to justify mass soldierly death, assuage the suffering of those who lost loved ones in the war, and honor the fallen through various official speech acts and public memory projects during the immediate postwar years. This chapter focuses primarily on the federal government's unprecedented plan to establish a network of permanent overseas U.S. military cemeteries; constructed on or near the fields and forests throughout Western Europe where "Doughboys" had fought and perished, and sacralized as *American* sites, these burial grounds would (as figures like General John J. Pershing believed) help link America's fallen soldiers symbolically back to U.S. soil and the national purpose rooted there and, not coincidentally, express the nation's emerging prominent role on the world's stage to a transnational audience. Physical 'objects of motion' for the war effort in life, U.S. soldiers were meant to become metaphysical 'objects of symbolic action' in death.

Drawing upon extensive original research conducted in the U.S. National Archives and Records Administration, this chapter focuses primarily on the explosive and illustrative national debate over the government's controversial plan for overseas cemeteries, and brings forth the voices of citizens (and noncitizens) who, after the Armistice, responded to War Department inquiries regarding the final disposition of their loved ones' bodily remains. This chapter analyzes correspondence (c. 1918–1922) from a wide range of Americans: from those who relinquished the care of corpses to the government, to those who demanded, sometimes bitterly, the return of loved ones' remains, to members of the African-American community whose men had fought and died for a nation that treated African Americans as inferior citizens. Notably, this chapter shows how, through the process of communication it initiated with grieving families, the government learned to temper its highly bureaucratic and jingoistic speech with a more personal and sentimental vernacular appropriated directly from the letters of next of kin. In doing so, government and military officials were able to make a stronger, and ultimately, successful public case for the overseas cemeteries project. Moreover, I argue that through this process—and in light of the aforementioned "crisis of speech"—government and military officials came to recognize the opportunity (if not outright necessity) of manufacturing a new, generic characterization of the U.S. soldier as a model of unassailable virtue, strength, sacrifice, and righteousness that might have persuasive value for domestic and international populations from that point on. In sum, I argue that the ideograph of the "modern U.S.

soldier"—which would be manifested in the design and visual presentation of American overseas military cemeteries—can be traced directly back to the political vicissitudes of this historical, *kairotic*[14] moment and the intimate, unnerving negotiations between the War Department and grieving American citizens and communities between 1918 and 1922.

As indicated above, the immediate postwar years developed into a period of contestation and contingency in which prevailing meanings, understandings, and memories of the United States' participation in the Great War had not yet been settled, but were highly desired. It was an opportune moment for individuals and collectives—official, vernacular, or otherwise—to express publicly competing (and often directly opposing) statements about the perceived and real human, material, and spiritual costs and benefits of the national war effort. The torrent of letters sent from grieving American families to the War Department regarding the final disposition of dead soldiers, for example, had revealed a postwar crisis of official language, an exhaustion of state-sanctioned vocabularies that could no longer (if they had ever been able to) account adequately for the feelings and suffering of private citizens (and noncitizens) whose loved ones had been sent to fight and die in Europe.

Although the government eventually learned to appropriate the sentimental vernacular of grieving families into its own rhetoric (apparent in letters to grieving families, public speeches, decrees, interviews with newspapers, and official narratives of the national war effort) and successfully secured its plan to bury dead Americans in permanent overseas military cemeteries, the symbolic action of ordinary mothers, fathers, wives, sisters, and brothers (who were no longer bound by draconian wartime laws to remain silent) revealed just how difficult it might be for the government to shape, determine, and control public memory of the war. And amid a swirling sea of ad hoc domestic and overseas commemoration initiatives and practices, the bodily remains of roughly 80,000 soldiers were shipped back to the United States (by families' requests) during the early 1920s.[15] Delivered to next of kin in every state, to rural hamlets and giant urban centers alike, to every corner of the nation, these repatriated bodily remains presented 80,000 opportunities for individuals and communities to remember the dead—and perhaps more importantly, America's participation in the World War—as they best saw fit. Whatever political affiliations or feelings about the national war effort next of kin might have held, each dead soldier—lying silently and concealed in a government-issued coffin—represented a tangible and powerful reminder of the tragic (if theoretically noble) human costs and sacrifices of American belligerence. Each dead soldier, his life taken prematurely in the name of state-sponsored violence, bore witness to the death and destruction of the distant war. And each dead soldier required a proper burial ceremony of some kind, where individuals could give eulogies that might question the local, national, and international benefits of such a personal loss.[16]

While the U.S. government could not possibly have expected instantly to contain, dictate, or suppress this explosion of diverse postwar commemoration projects, it had successfully retained legal control over the bodily remains of 35,000 dead American soldiers—the decaying remnants of men's bones, tissue, and skin—that would, in short order, become the focus and symbolic capital of an unprecedented network of monumental U.S. cemeteries in Western Europe. Government and military officials hoped that the graves and tombstones of these 35,000 soldiers, displayed to international audiences in aesthetically pleasing, emotionally moving, and most vitally, *American* cemeteries, would constitute permanent visual and material arguments for the United States' righteous role in the Great War, and buttress the emerging and useful (if somewhat antagonistic) claim that the young nation had "rescued" Europe from itself. As G. Kurt Piehler indicates, those in charge of planning and creating these burial grounds approached the project with an overarching belief that each "individual soldier's grave would serve as an enduring monument to the cause of freedom for which they bled and died."[17] In communicating such sustained and loaded messages to the peoples of Europe (and elsewhere), these overseas cemeteries—if constructed properly—might also impact, or perhaps even trump, the meanings and rhetorical work of the countless domestic commemoration practices simultaneously taking place back home.

The central argument of chapter 4 is that the overseas cemetery project became an incubator for the ideographic construction of 'the modern U.S. soldier'—an icon that's message might reverberate back across the Atlantic to the homeland. Synthesizing, correcting, and expanding upon the arguments of the few scholarly works on U.S. overseas military cemeteries and monuments, this chapter utilizes visual rhetorical theory to analyze the aesthetic composition of the seven U.S. World War I cemeteries in Europe and reveal how the cemeteries—designed and constructed by the Commission of Fine Arts and the American Battlefield Monument Commission—came to display an unprecedented vision of the U.S. soldier as 'a global force for good.' Ultimately, I argue that it is within the visual display of overseas cemeteries and monuments that we can detect the birth of 'the modern U.S. soldier'— a potent, if intentionally elastic, ideograph in which, and through which, divergent emotions, memories, beliefs, and arguments of Americans and non-Americans alike could be satisfactorily poured, and satisfied, for years to come. The second part of this chapter shows how the ideograph of the courageous, selfless, sacrificial U.S. soldier established by the overseas cemeteries: (1) was swiftly normalized, sacralized, and circulated within American public discourse, memory, and consciousness; and, (2) became an invaluable, potent

Figure I.1 Attendees of a remembrance ceremony, Suresnes American Cemetery and Memorial, 2007. Author's own photograph.

rhetorical device that U.S. political and military officials used for a multitude of persuasive purposes (both at home and across the world) during the interwar period and beyond.

BOOK RATIONALE

Despite the international and interdisciplinary "memory studies boom" of the last thirty-plus years,[18] increased scholarly interest in how governments control and shape wartime discourse and postwar commemoration practices to construct and manage visions of national identity,[19] and the many cultural histories of European experiences during and after World War I,[20] few books have attempted to offer cultural and/or rhetorical analyses of the American World War I experience—let alone contextualize that experience and its legacy within broader U.S. history. In *Bodies of War: World War I and the Politics of Commemoration in America, 1919–1933*, archivist Lisa M. Budreau offers a military history of the complicated process American families went through to repatriate loved ones who had died in Europe.[21] Though it is certainly a valuable source for my own work, *Bodies of War* is relatively narrow in scope (with regard to topic), tends to let archival documents stand as unassailable vessels of historical truth, and (in my view) lacks the sophistication that a rhetorical scholar might bring to the analysis of political or vernacular discourse. Similar critiques, I believe, could be made of Steven Trout's *On the Battlefield of Memory: The First World War and American Remembrance, 1919–1941*.[22] To its credit, this book examines a broader range of cultural artifacts than *Bodies of War*, but devotes most of its attention to American postwar literature (which makes sense, as Trout is a professor of English). Historian Jennifer D. Keene's *Doughboys, the Great War, and the Making of America* endeavors to show how "the doughboy experience in 1917–1918 forged the U.S. Army of the twentieth century," but ultimately amounts to a straightforward if immensely insightful history of the establishment of the G.I. Bill during World War II.[23] Finally, historian Christopher Capozzola's *Uncle Sam Wants You: World War I and the Making of the Modern American Citizen* offers insights and arguments that dovetail with or support several of mine, but focuses exclusively on connections between World War I and the enormous growth of the U.S. federal government during the postwar years.[24] While the books mentioned above provide various sets of useful information and claims for my own project, no book (as far as I can tell) has yet to tell the story told here.[25]

Written with an eye toward the centenary of U.S. participation in the Great War, this book is designed to appeal to academic circles and general audiences alike. My hopes are that the book's application and development of rhetorical[26] theory attract scholars of rhetoric (particularly those who study intersections of public memory, nationhood, war commemoration, and visual/material rhetoric), that its insights to contemporary paradigm shifts and analysis of heretofore unknown and overlooked artifacts draw the attention of historians in various fields, and that its colorful and provocative subject matter, chronological narrative, and original thesis appeals to lay readers interested in World War I, military history, and/or U.S. history and culture. Emerging at the very moment when World War I should reenter mainstream American consciousness, this book is meant to be accessible to a wide variety of readers.

One final note: While I believe that the major arguments, ideas, and conclusions advanced in these pages are sound and revelatory, I do not wish to present this work as some *ultimate, definitive* treatise on the rhetorical construction of the 'modern U.S. soldier.' Since embarking on this project, I have always done my best to make reasonable, evidence-backed cases in support of my overall thesis. But in all likelihood, some readers and scholars will question and challenge aspects of this book. This, as they, is a good thing, and I would gladly welcome and consider all and any criticisms as I continue to research and write about this topic. For like many others in my field, I primarily conceive rhetorical scholarship as an ongoing, "endless" conversation in progress and rhetorical critics as conversationalists whose task is to advance discussion. That is, while rhetorical critics develop arguments, making cases for understanding some rhetorical phenomena one way or another, we do not necessarily strive for *unimpeachable* objective certainties. And we are judged, not by social scientific standards, say, but by the strength of the arguments we make and their contribution to the scholarly conversation. As Ryan McGeough observes, rhetorical scholarship should be judged by these two criteria (among others): "Does it offer something new?" and "Is what it offers interesting and/or insightful?" My hope is that readers of this book would answer *yes* to both questions.[27]

NOTES

1. Celia Malone Kingsbury, *The Peculiar Sanity of War: Hysteria in the Literature of World War I* (Lubbock: Texas Tech University Press, 2002).

2. David William Seitz, "'Let Him Remain Until the Judgment in France': Family Letters and the Overseas Burying of U.S. World War I Soldiers," in *Transnational American Memories*, ed. Udo J. Hebel (New York: Walter de Gruyter, 2009), 215–42; ibid, "World War I, Trauma and Remembrance: American Cemeteries and the Therapeutic 'Third Element,'" in *Speaking the Unspeakable*, eds. Catherine Ann Collins and Jeanne Ellen Clark (Oxford: Inter-Disciplinary Press, 2013), 71–102.

3. William E. Alt and Betty L. Alt, *Black Soldiers, White Wars: Black Warriors from Antiquity to the Present* (Westport, CT: Praeger, 2002), 70–85.

4. Paul Starr, *The Creation of the Media: Political Origins of Modern Communications* (New York: Basic Books, 2004), 274.

5. I began researching this topic in 2005 as a doctoral student in the Department of Communication and Rhetoric at the University of Pittsburgh. In 2011, I successfully defended my dissertation, *Grave Negotiations: The Rhetorical Foundations of American World War I Cemeteries in Europe*. As indicated on my curriculum vitae, I have published several essays on subjects covered in this manuscript. All of this work has entailed (among other things) three research trips to U.S. World War I cemeteries in Europe, six straight months of research at the National Archives and Records Administration, and countless hours collecting, analyzing, and synthesizing media reports, photographs, and a myriad of primary and secondary resources.

6. For more on the ideograph, see, Michael Calvin McGee, "The 'Ideograph': A Link between Rhetoric and Ideology," *Quarterly Journal of Speech* 66.1 (1980): 1–16.

7. In the introduction to *Doing Rhetorical History*, Kathleen J. Turner identifies rhetorical history as "social construction," a method of inquiry that attends to both the ways in which rhetorical processes have constructed social reality at particular times and in particular contexts and the nature of the study of history as an essentially

rhetorical process. Toward the first end, Turner claims, historical research provides an understanding of rhetoric as a process rather than as simply a product. Whereas rhetorical criticism—the term under which the majority of rhetorical studies seem to fall—seeks to understand the message in context, rhetorical history seeks to understand the context through messages that reflect and construct that context. Rhetorical historians know that single messages are rarely instrumental in and of themselves; for that reason, rhetorical historians are more interested in the perpetual and dynamic rhetorical processes of social construction, maintenance, and change that occur over periods of time. Turner tells us that the "rhetorical perspective" can contribute particular insights to an understanding of history, for the rhetorical historian ask questions different, but related, to those posed by colleagues in the humanities and social sciences. In an essay that follows Turner's introduction, David Zarefsky elaborates upon this point, arguing that what distinguishes the rhetorical historian is not subject matter but perspective. The economic historian might view human conduct from the perspective of the market, the political historian from the mobilization of interest and power, the intellectual historian from the standpoint of the evolution of ideas, and the rhetorical historian from the perspective of how messages are created and used by people to influence and relate to one another. In this sense of rhetorical history, the historian views history as a series of rhetorical problems, situations that call for public persuasion to advance a cause or overcome an impasse. The focus of the study would be on how, and how well, people invented and deployed messages in response to a situation. Countering a common presentist assumption that what happened had to happen, the rhetorical historian also directs attention to the roads not taken in certain rhetorical situations.

Turner's second general claim is that rhetorical history attends to the nature of the study of history as an essentially rhetorical process. Toward this end, the rhetorical perspective affects not only the questions we ask of history, but also what we consider to be "evidence," how we interrogate that evidence, and how we present our historical findings in our writing. As Turner points out, open any standard text in historiography and the first virtue of the historian will be defined as "accuracy." Yet, today, most historians regard historical discourse as emerging from an interaction between the historian and the record. Thus, the rhetorical perspective is concerned with the tropes, arguments, and other devices of language historians use to interpret historical sources, write history, and persuade audiences. For the rhetorical historian "accuracy" is only one elusive consideration in history writing. More important is the rhetorical power of stories and images historians use as symbolic constructions of the past—stories and images that need not necessarily be "accurate." Building off the seminal critiques of history advanced by Hayden White in the 1970s, the rhetorical historian sees the act of history writing as a fundamentally rhetorical act. Turner asks us to consider the popular metaphor: doing history is like putting together pieces of a jigsaw puzzle. Turner tells us that this jigsaw puzzle is of a distinctive kind in at least three ways. First, historians cannot look at the picture on the box top, for there is none; therefore, they are guided—at once, and fully—by the conceptions of their time and of themselves. Second, the jigsaw puzzle of history does not come with a clear and complete set of 500 pieces to be used in specific ways; thus, history is shaped by the pieces of the past historians choose to include in (as well as discard from) their writing. Third, the pieces of the jigsaw puzzle are not discrete, unchanging units; they are rather more like amoebas, changing shape and significance depending on the context in which they are placed. In this metaphor of the jigsaw puzzle, we clearly see that the "reality of the past" is shaped by the historian, rather than by some ultimate truths and facts.

Like Turner, Zarefsky concludes by arguing that rhetoricians are especially necessary to the study of history, for their efforts help to articulate the rhetorical climate of an age: how people defined the situation, what led them to seek to justify themselves or to persuade others, what storehouse of social knowledge they drew upon for their premises, what themes and styles they produced in their messages, and how their processes of identification and confrontation succeeded or failed. For more, see: Kathleen J. Turner, "Rhetorical History as Social Construction," 1–18, and David Zarefsky, "Four Senses of Rhetorical History," 19–32, in *Doing Rhetorical History: Concepts and Cases*, ed. Kathleen J. Turner, 2nd edition (Tuscaloosa: University of Alabama Press, 2003).

8. Bahman Dehgan, *America in Quotations* (Jefferson, NC: McFarland, 2003), 132.

9. Drew Gilpin Faust, *This Republic of Suffering: Death and the American Civil War* (New York: Vintage, 2009); Paul Fussell, *The Great War and Modern Memory* (Oxford: Oxford University Press, 1975).

10. In many ways, this book stands as a work of "new historicism." A legacy of feminist theory and the "linguistic turn" of the 20th century, new historicism is generally understood as a perspective of historical inquiry that pays attention "to objects, persons, and practices [...] that, until recently, have been understood as ephemera, secondary and inconsequential to the master narratives of Enlightenment historiography." In short, new historicism posits that a cultural text—whether a document, a speech, a national memorial, or anything else—should be considered a product of the time, place, and circumstance of its composition, rather than an isolated autonomous creation. Rejecting the 'top-down' approach to historical inquiry, new historicism privileges 'ordinary voices' and emphasizes the culture, power structures, and rhetoric of the historical moment in which a given text was created. See Hunter Cadzow, Alison Conway, and Bryce Traister, "New Historicism," in *The Johns Hopkins Guide to Literary Theory and Criticism*, eds. Michael Groden, Martin Kreiswirth, and Imre Szeman (Baltimore: Johns Hopkins University Press, 2005), 698–703.

11. Gerard A. Hauser, *Vernacular Voices: The Rhetoric of Publics and Public Spheres* (Columbia: University of South Carolina Press, 1999), 1.

12. Robert S. McElvaine, *Down and Out in the Great Depression: Letters from the Forgotten Man* (Chapel Hill: University of North Carolina Press, 1983), 5.

13. George Creel, *How We Advertised America: The First Telling of the Amazing Story of the Committee on Public Information that Carried the Gospel of Americanism to Every Corner of the Globe* (New York: Harper and Brothers, 1920), 5.

14. As opposed to the Ancient Greek conception of *chronos*, the scientific measurement and passing of time, *kairos* has been understood by rhetoricians as

the "right," "opportune," or "propitious" moment for symbolic action. Much more fluid, plastic, and ambiguous than *chronos*, *kairos* represents the moment (whether a second, minute, hour, day, year, or more) when one can use language to strike with maximum impact. For more, see, Jane Sutton, "Kairos," in *Encyclopedia of Rhetoric*, ed. Thomas O. Sloane (Oxford: Oxford University Press, 2001), 413–17.

15. Exhumations of American bodies for shipment to the United States began in 1920. The first exhumation was made at Gosport, England on February 3, 1920, the first transatlantic shipment of bodies on February 23. During 1921, repatriation of bodily remains was nearly completed, and the exhumation and concentration of bodies for burial in overseas cemeteries commenced. Nearly every dead U.S. soldier was laid in his final resting place—whether in the States or in Europe—by the end of 1922. See U.S. National Archives and Records Administration II, College Park, Maryland, Records of the Office of the Inspector General (Army), Record Group 159, Box 772, "Brief History of Organization and Operations of Graves Registration Service from Origin to July 31, 1930," October 24, 1930, 2.

16. Local newspapers often publicized the details of funeral services held for fallen soldiers who had been returned to the U.S. For example, in 1921, the *Philadelphia Inquirer* reported on a "solemn" burial ceremony that had been held for several men whose families lived in the same Philadelphia neighborhood: "Yesterday's solemn ceremonies closed the public mourning for our heroes who fell in France during the late combat. [...] There was no pride, pomp and circumstance of glorious war evident; there was no intention of magnifying military operations. The silence for a few seconds when the city's pulse seemed to stop while prayers ascended to make war impossible was a finer tribute than all the fanfares which might have been made." See "Taps for Our Soldier Dead," *Philadelphia Inquirer*, October 24, 1921, 12. The ability of these dead bodies to bear witness to the atrocities and devastation of the Great War relates to communication scholar John Durham Peters's insightful analysis of "witnessing." Peters writes: "Aristotle noted that witnesses in a court of law testify at risk of punishment if they do not tell the truth; he considers dead witnesses more trustworthy than living ones—since they cannot be bribed." See John Durham Peters, *Courting the Abyss: Free Speech and the Liberal Tradition* (Chicago: University of Chicago Press, 2005), 251.

17. Kurt G. Piehler, *Remembering War the American Way* (Washington, D.C.: Smithsonian Institution, 1995), 96, 114.

18. The rise of this "memory boom" is often attributed to influential works like: Pierre Nora, "Between Memory and History: Les Lieux de Mémoire," *Representations* 26 (Spring 1989): 7–24; E. J. Hobsbawm, *Nations and Nationalism since 1780: Programme, Myth, Reality* (Cambridge: University Press, 1990); Benedict Anderson, *Imagined Communities: Reflections on the Origin and Spread of Nationalism* (New York: Verso, 1991); Michael Kammen, *Mystic Chords of Memory: The Transformation of Tradition in American Culture* (New York: Vintage Books, 1991); and, Maurice Halbwachs, *On Collective Memory*, ed. and trans. Lewis A. Coser (Chicago: University of Chicago Press, 1992).

19. See, for example, George H. Roeder Jr., *The Censored War: American Visual Experience During World War Two* (New Haven, CT: Yale University Press, 1993);

Thomas Doherty, *Projection of War: Hollywood, American Culture, and World War II* (New York: Columbia University Press, 1999).

20. See, for example, George L. Mosse, *Fallen Soldiers: Reshaping the Memory of the World Wars* (Oxford: Oxford University Press, 1991); Jay Winter, *Sites of Memory, Sites of Mourning: The Great War in European Cultural History* (Cambridge: University Press, 1995); Daniel J. Sherman, *The Construction of Memory in Interwar France* (Chicago: University of Chicago Press, 1999); and, Antoine Prost, *The Great War in History: Debates and Controversies, 1914 to the Present* (Cambridge: University Press, 2005).

21. Lisa M. Budreau, *Bodies of War: World War I and the Politics of Commemoration in America, 1919–1933* (New York: New York University Press, 2011).

22. Steven Trout, *On the Battlefield of Memory: The First World War and American Remembrance, 1919–1941* (Tuscaloosa: University of Alabama, 2012).

23. Jennifer D. Keene, *Doughboys, the Great War, and the Making of America* (Baltimore: Johns Hopkins University Press, 2003).

24. Christopher Capozzola, *Uncle Sam Wants You: World War I and the Making of the Modern American Citizen* (Oxford: Oxford University Press, 2010).

25. What explains this relative dearth of scholarship? Surely it is not a lack of interest in the intersections of American war rhetoric, public memory, and media/visual/material culture, for these intersections have become popular subjects of study in recent years. Perhaps one of the biggest factors is the Atlantic Ocean; while American scholars have relatively easy access to pertinent historical databases and materials held at the U.S. National Archives and other repositories, conducting on-site research at the eight cemeteries abroad in order to bring certain documents to life (for instance) is a costly and time-consuming proposition. At the same time, while European scholars enjoy immediate physical access to various World War I-related archives and U.S. burial grounds and monuments throughout England and the greater continent, crucial information (written in *English*) concerning the American war experience or (again, for instance) contextually the establishment and intended meanings of U.S. overseas cemeteries can only be found thousands of miles away in American archives and libraries. In other words, a truly thorough analysis of the sites requires much hard work, dedication, and investment of resources. I am fortunate to say that while pursuing my Ph.D. at the University of Pittsburgh, I earned several fellowships and awards (the 2006 Stanley Postrednik Nationality Room Award, the 2008–2009 Andrew Mellon Predoctoral Research Fellowship, and the 2009–2010 Cultural Studies Dissertation Fellowship) that afforded me the resources and time to conduct on-site research in Europe and archival research throughout the United States. And since attaining my doctorate, I have had the ability to return to Europe twice to conduct further related research.

26. This book not only draws upon and (for lay readers) explains relevant rhetorical theory, but also advances original theoretical contributions as well. For instance, in chapter 2 I repurpose Kenneth Burke's heuristic dichotomy of motion/action as a means for understanding how individuals, groups, and institutions tend to frame issues of choice, intention, and responsibility. In chapter 4, I present my concept of "the third element"—the implied if invisible relationship between any two things

(objects, texts, ideas) that appear within close proximity of each other—during my visual rhetorical analyses of World War I cemeteries and monuments. Whenever possible, this book offers rhetoric scholars new concepts and ways of applying traditional theory.

27. Ryan Erik McGeough, "Endless Talk: The Purpose, Practice, and Pedagogy of the Rhetorical Conversation," in *Purpose, Practice, and Pedagogy in Rhetorical Criticism*, ed. Jim A. Kuypers (Frederick, MD: Rowman and Littlefield, 2014), 97–107. See also: Catherine Helen Palczewski, "What is 'Good Criticism'? A Conversation in Progress," *Communication Studies* 54 (2003): 385–91.

Chapter 1

The "Uncensored" View from Afar

American Perceptions of the Great War, 1914–1917

Focusing on the rhetoric of contemporary newspaper and magazine reports and op-eds, popular cinema, governmental proclamations, public intellectuals, veterans of previous U.S. wars, and various ethnic communities and social movement groups, this chapter brings forth, analyzes, and interprets American public discourse regarding the Great War and the attending issues of death, killing, sacrifice, burial, and commemoration during the period of American neutrality. This chapter shows how, between 1914 and 1917, a heterogeneous, fractured, American public, by and large, came to perceive (through news reports reflecting both on-the-ground truths and competing British and German propaganda) the "War in Europe" primarily as something akin to a "human slaughter-house"—a mad, immoral, regressive, antidemocratic, and unnecessary mass bloodletting that harnessed the terrible destructive capacities of modern science and technology and had little to do with the interests of the United States. To wit, in 1916, President Woodrow Wilson won his reelection campaign on the slogan, "He Kept Us Out of the War!" As this chapter shows, the apparent majority of Americans considered Wilson's victory to be a referendum against U.S. intervention in the World War. By tracing pertinent rhetorical action of the prewar period, this chapter contextualizes the unexpected, controversial, and epoch-shifting U.S. wartime policies (e.g., media censorship and propaganda, compulsory military service) and postwar policies (e.g., repatriation of the dead, the establishment of permanent overseas military cemeteries) that would soon follow.

This chapter largely entails analysis of American mainstream newspaper coverage of the war—coverage that often blurred the line between truth and the propaganda of the European belligerents. By the outbreak of World War I, daily newspapers had become the dominant source of current information on local, national, and international affairs for most Americans.[1] As historian

David Paul Nord has shown, as early as the 1890s, the popular daily newspaper had become a fixture of everyday life for readers of every social class
and geographical region in the United States.[2] In a world without radio and
television broadcasts, newspapers were the first and only place to turn to for
the latest news. Sociologist Michael Schudson tells us that, despite a healthy
skepticism fostered by the "muckraking" and "yellow journalism" of the
late 19th and early 20th centuries, during the Great War period, American
readers and journalists were by and large "naïve empiricists" who believed
that facts could speak for themselves—that what appeared on the pages of
newspapers were "not human statements about the world but aspects of the
world itself."[3] This sentiment was surely enhanced by the fact that telegraphy
allowed correspondents to relay information from the battlefields of Europe
almost instantly, thus giving editors and publishers only a small window to
interpret or filter the war's narratives; in the race to provide the freshest information, American newspapers had precious little time to fiddle with reports.
To be clear, this is not to say that news that made its way to American readers
was ever completely pure, true, unbiased, and accurate, as some influential
newspaper editors had never pretended to pursue such standards.[4] Nor is it to
say that the validity of popular information was never called into question as
the Great War stretched on (as we will see below). But the almost real-time
speed in which reports came from Europe probably strengthened the general
assumption that readers were getting an unadulterated, "play-by-play," and
therefore authentic view of the war—something akin to early 2000s attitudes
concerning American "embedded" reporting of the wars in Afghanistan and
Iraq.

In short, during this period, American newspapers enjoyed an exclusive
authority over the mass circulation of news. By virtue of more or less controlling information that was based on firsthand reporting and quotes from
official and expert sources, newspapers exercised an agenda-setting influence
that told Americans not only what to think about, but also *how* to think—
a process Nord describes as "event orientation."[5] Eliciting and publishing
letters of response from readers,[6] newspapers of this era truly were, in the
words of communications theorist James W. Carey, sites of "information"
and "conversation" that "preside[d] over and within the conversation of our
culture."[7] Thus, contemporary U.S. newspaper coverage of the war provides
an excellent (if not entirely complete) glimpse of the American public's
understanding and imagination of the war in Europe—a monumental "event"
that was consistently portrayed in bleak, disturbing, and grisly (if *attention-
grabbing*) terms.

This chapter is divided into five parts. Each addresses a major recurring
theme within media coverage of the Great War and relevant public discourse
during the period of American neutrality. The first section examines how

war-torn Europe was portrayed as a vast killing field teeming with corpses, where few fallen soldiers received proper burials, and many went unburied altogether (and thus were exposed to further posthumous degradation). The second section reveals how the war was depicted as a "human slaughter-house"—a savage affair that was destroying soldiers' bodies and minds in previously unimaginable ways; negating the possibilities of heroic soldierly sacrifice and the noble "good death" upon the battlefield; and, infecting soldiers and civilians alike with a crazed desire for murder and destruction. The third section surveys reporting about the new and terrifying rules of "total war." The fourth explores the ways in which the media handled issues related to European mourning practices and the personal grief of civilians whose loved ones perished in the war. This section also shows how the media paid little attention to the many U.S. citizens who died fighting for European armies (a fact that indicates that, at this time, it was socially acceptable and unremarkable for Americans to pledge their allegiance to other nations), and addresses the notorious sinking of the *Lusitania* (a scandalous event that dominated headlines[8] and bolstered the position of the nascent pro-war movement).

The fifth and final section analyzes public debates concerning the pros-pect of American belligerence and the sacrifice of U.S. citizen-soldiers that intervention in Europe would entail. Here, I examine the star-spangled, jingoistic rhetoric of Theodore Roosevelt, presidential candidate Charles Evans Hughes, and other members of the military "preparedness" and pro-war lobbies who attempted to raise martial spirits across the country and cast the inevitable deaths of U.S. soldiers as a sacrifice that patriotic Americans would willingly make in a time of war. Next, I interpret the rhetoric of feminists, socialists, anarchists, labor unions, and other anti-war groups that cited the potential deaths of thousands upon thousands of U.S. citizen-soldiers as a prime reason not to fight. In turn, I discuss how Presi-dent Woodrow Wilson won the 1916 presidential election by occupying a political and rhetorical position somewhere between the ideologies of the pro-war and anti-war movements. To conclude the chapter, I argue that, ultimately, the "uncensored" media depictions of the Great War between 1914 and early 1917 made it patently clear to Americans that the war in Europe was an extremely deadly, horrific, and immoral affair that had little to do with the material interests of the average U.S. citizen. This "uncen-sored" view of the war contextualizes and explains many of the official policies and public debates concerning patriotic death, just killing, collec-tive sacrifice, proper burial, and public commemoration that would emerge during American belligerence and the postwar years—policies and debates that subsequently would lead to the rhetorical invention of the U.S. soldier as a 'global force for good.'

"ACRES OF DEAD AND DYING"

From its inception, the War in Europe was portrayed and understood in the
United States as a conflict of unprecedented levels of mass death and human
destruction. On August 31, 1914, the *New York Times* published a front-page
article by British journalist Philip Gibbs, who recounted an "immense slaughter of Germans" he had witnessed during an Allied retreat near Amiens,
France. One of the earliest firsthand in-depth accounts of the Great War to
appear in the United States, Gibbs's report indicated that this conflict would
entail death on such a grand scale as to make the loss of life almost indescrib-
able. "I find it difficult to piece together the various incidents and impressions
and to make one picture," Gibbs wrote. "It all seems to me now like a jigsaw
puzzle of suffering and fear and courage and death." Notwithstanding this
problem of representation, Gibbs continued with his tale of what he had seen.
He reported that despite the French "death carts trailing back from unknown
places" past teary-eyed women and children, the retreating French forces had
exacted a heavy toll on the advancing Germans:

> I will tell at once the story of the French retirement when the Germans advanced
> from Namur down the Valley of the Meuse, winning the way at a cost of human
> life as great as that of defeat, yet winning their way. [...]
> French artillery was up on the wooded heights above the river and swept the
> German regiments with a storm of fire as they advanced. On the right bank the
> French infantry was intrenched [*sic*], supported by field guns and militareuses,
> and did deadly work before leaping from trenches. [...]
> In justice to the Germans it must be said they were heroic in courage and
> reckless of their lives, and the valley of the Meuse was choked with their
> corpses. The river itself was strewn with the dead bodies of men and horses and
> literally ran red with blood.[9]

According to Gibbs, in this modern war of attrition, the rivers, forests, and
fields of Europe would be "strewn with the dead bodies" of victors and vanquished alike. Few fallen soldiers, it seemed, would receive proper burial or
a peaceful resting place.

Following the First Battle of the Marne and the German invasion of
Belgium, shocking descriptions of corpse-riddled battlegrounds made their
way onto the pages of American newspapers. On September 17, 1914, the
Washington Post reported: "Terrible stories are reaching the French capital
of the piles of dead and wounded which incumber [*sic*] the battlefields along
the Marne. At one place the Germans built a barrier 6 feet high of dead,
behind which to resist the French charges. This barrier finally was carried,
after a bloody struggle [...] and a horrible litter of 7,000 bodies now marks
this spot."[10] Another *Washington Post* article claimed: "At the Wavre and St.

Catherine forts alone (outside of Antwerp) the German dead may be counted by thousands. At several points the corpses lie in heaps. Entire companies have been exterminated."[11] The *New York Times* reported that Flanders, Belgium, had become "a vast cemetery." Quoting a British official "eyewitness," the *Times* wrote:

> All the ground near the front line is plowed up with shells and furrowed with the remains of old trenches and graves. [...]
>
> In a sheltered spot [...] there is a little graveyard where some of our own dead have been buried. Their graves have been carefully marked, and a rough square of bricks has been placed around them. In front of the trenches German bodies still lie thick. [...]
>
> At one point of the brickfields recently some thirty men tried to rush our line. At the head was a young German officer who came on gallantly, waving his sword. He almost reached the barbed wire and then fell dead, and lies there yet with his sword in his hand and all his thirty men about him.
>
> It is the same all along the front in this quarter. Everywhere still gray figures can be seen lying, sometimes several rows together and sometimes singly or in twos or threes.[12]

Such reports intimated, that due to the conditions of the fighting, few corpses were receiving proper burial, and that the majority of soldierly remains were being left to rot in muddy battlefields, where they became exposed to even further degradation. On September 23, 1914, the *Los Angeles Examiner* published the following gruesome testimony taken from a French soldier near Amiens:

> We have fought over and over the same old ground until now there are about ten miles of dead bodies. We go on fighting over corpses of friends and enemies until the road becomes impassable. [...] The dead bodies. The artillery is driven right over them, time and again, until a hundred have been crushed right into the ground. We never need to bury them.[13]

Eviscerated by modern munitions, then mashed into the earth by mobile artillery equipment, infantrymen fighting in Europe were being rendered into little more than actual, not metaphorical, cannon fodder and human fertilizer. Per the *Los Angeles Examiner*, the integrity of their bodies was wrecked until all that remained was fleshy pulp.

As decaying dead bodies became an integral and seemingly unavoidable dimension of the Great War battlefield, soldiers began using the festering corpses as defensive fortifications, much like trench walls. The evocative image of piles of dead soldiers serving as ramparts for desperate compatriots became a common meme in early coverage of the war. Describing a scene from the Battle of Verdun, the *Macon Daily Telegraph* (Georgia) reported in a front-page article: "French machine guns and rifles for two days have been pouring death into the ranks of the Germans attacking in mass the village of Douaumont. [...] Each time that the fortune of battle has changed more dead from the thick masses of German assailants have been added in the piles behind which their surviving comrades have sought brief protection."[14] In a lengthy exposé titled, "Acres of Dead and Dying," the *Washington Post* offered this firsthand account of the Battle of Gallipoli from British infantryman Clutha Mackenzie:

> While acres of ground were covered up with dead and dying, the dried-up water courses were piled high with mounds of corpses. [...]
>
> The fighting was of the most awful character. The Turkish rifles and machine guns were spitting millions of bullets at us, and let me tell you, the Turk knows how to shoot when he is under fire. He doesn't lose his head. [...]
>
> Our advance was marked by a trail of dead and dying. Those in the rear had to clamber over the piles of corpses as they moved forward. In the midst of this frightful tangle of maimed humanity the shells from the Turks' big guns were dropping with frightful accuracy. [...]
>
> There was an explosion right in front of me that knocked me senseless and covered me with blood and dirt. When I came to everything was dark, and then I was told that both my eyes had been blown out by an exploding shell and was blinded for life.
>
> My trip to the rear was an experience of such frightfulness that I yet shudder to recall. Suffering the most intense pain and in absolute darkness I had to crawl on my hands and knees over the corpses of brave fellows who had been killed the day and night before. I wondered at the time whether I could consider myself any luckier than they.

Mackenzie's chilling statement implied that the dead outnumbered the living at Gallipoli. Carpeting the battlefield, the "frightful tangle of maimed humanity" had become one with the topography. Blinded by a Turkish shell, Mackenzie survived only by clawing through the ghastly "trail of dead and dying" that marked the way back to the rear and safety.[15] Antithetical to the order and tranquility of typical cemeteries and burial grounds, say, the battlefields of the Great War were, according to the American press, hellish human sewage dumps.

Often the heaps of human flesh were viewed not as useful defensive walls but rather as obstacles that had to be cleared for advancing forces. The *Aberdeen Daily News* reported that French military operations near St. Mihiel had been driven to a halt because the trenches and surrounding woods had become "so choked with [...] huge stacks of dead soldiers. [...] The battles are of so furious a character that neither army is able to aid its wounded, much less bury the dead."[16] In such cases, high explosives were used to part the sea of mangled flesh so that fresh troops could mount new attacks. An English observer stationed at Verdun reported the following scene to the *Wall Street Journal*:

> I could clearly see through my field glasses the Germans moving forward in mass formation. Suddenly, the French guns opened and mangled humanity was piled in windrows.
>
> I thought the battle ended, but in a short time another line in solid formation was sent steadily forward and as they started to pass over the piled-up heaps of their dead and dying comrades, the French cannon again blazed and the pile of dead and wounded looked a solid wall.
>
> I have never dreamed of such slaughter: but the sight that followed I think no man ever before saw. High explosive shells began blowing into pieces the masses of dead and dying.
>
> It seemed fiendish: I wondered that the French were so insatiated: when, horror of horrors: I discovered that the high explosive shells were from the German guns, blasting the walls of dead and dying that another line of German troops might pass through and execute the German order "Forward."[17]

By all measures, according to this overtly anti-German report, the armies of the World War had jettisoned proprieties concerning the treatment and veneration of war dead (the fallen, it seemed, were simply physical matter void of symbolic value). In this strange war, belligerent forces were capable of viewing the remains of *even their own soldiers* as obstructive detritus that needed to be removed from the gears of war.[18]

This is not to say that the universal desire to identify and bury the dead properly had been entirely snuffed out within the theater of war. Occasionally, American newspapers reported on the (predominantly futile) efforts that armies took to treat the war dead with some semblance of respect. In April of 1915, the *Washington Post* announced that a "special sanitary commission has been appointed to disinfect and purify the battlefields of Western Poland on which many thousands of the dead lie either unburied, or else buried in dangerously shallow graves and trenches." Equipped "for their unpleasant work with rubber garments and masks which sterilize the air they breathe," the sanitary commission was charged with the task of opening "all the so-called 'brotherly graves' in which friend and foe were buried together, and separating them from one another."[19] Such measures to inter the fallen, let alone those to separate the dead according to national affiliation, were rare and depended on a lull in the fighting, for in the war zone, burying the dead entailed exposing oneself to snipers, machine guns, stray bomb shrapnel, and the distinct possibility of joining the ranks of the departed. As the *Columbus Enquirer-Sun* (Georgia) explained in a 1914 report from Belgium, infantry-men were often forced to abandon impromptu battlefield burials of their comrades: "The French dead, in all sorts of conveyances, were a common sight and squares and cemeteries with unfinished graves, mute evidence of a hurried French retreat."[20] Usually, those who risked their lives to bury the dead during battle were deeply religious people for whom the sacred duty overrode considerations for personal safety. Such was the case with the Irish priest Father Lane-Fox, who ignored bullets passing by, "hissing of death and terror," as he dutifully buried the dead in no-man's-land; or the "heroic" Christian Zouave (a North African soldier fighting for France), who, to the astonishment of the Germans, crawled his way to fallen comrades left between the lines and from his belly, dug shallow graves for them with his bayonet and fingers.[21]

To offset the danger associated with battlefield burials, belligerent forces occasionally requested brief truces so that both sides could bury the dead.[22] Such proposals for momentary suspensions of hostilities could be refused[23] or, even more disturbingly, intentionally violated. In one alleged episode, British forces at Gallipoli acquiesced to a Turkish request for a burial truce; as British soldiers descended upon the battlefield to tend to their fallen, the Turks "[abused] the white flag" and "opened fire, killing a number of men."[24] In any event, burial truces were short, often just a few hours long,[25] a fact that made identifying the dead correctly before interment an all but impossible task. And as American newspapers revealed, even when soldiers were able to carry out battlefield burials, their efforts were just as likely to be upturned and destroyed by enemy artillery as not.[26]

This chronic inability to bury the dead properly had a number of detestable and marked effects that were widely reported in American papers. First, and perhaps most obviously, it left large swaths of Europe completely covered with an unholy mix of sun bleached human bones and rotten human flesh; Europe's picturesque landscapes, it seemed, had been polluted by mass human death. The *Los Angeles Times* reported that in Neuve Chapelle, France, "German skulls lie about like cobblestones."[27] In Louvain, Belgium, corpses "filled the roadways," where "riderless horses, some of them wild from the pain of wounds, dashed across the ground, trampling the dead."[28] On a battlefield near Ypres, the grisly remains of 10,000 soldiers laid exposed to the elements. "The stench is pestilential," wrote the *Washington Post*:

> It is ghastly beyond imagination. Words cannot portray to the mind that picture by day and night—white eyes staring out of faces burned coal black by the sun. There are places where there are veritable piles of bodies. As the days and weeks go by they shrivel and shrink together until they look like little heaps of old clothes. These silent heaps are more weird by moonlight than by day.[29]

Unable to keep pace with the war's production of death, soldiers watched in horror as wild animals gorged on the seemingly endless supply of unburied human remains. Along both the Eastern and Western Fronts, rats feasted upon the eviscerated and bloated corpses that polluted the trench mazes.[30] The *New York Times* described the "rats, rats, tens of thousands of rats" that populated the battlefield at Ypres, "slinking from new meals on corpses [...] crunching between battle lines while the rapid-firing guns mow the trench edge—crunching their hellish feasts."[31] In Galicia (a contested region between Poland and Ukraine), crows, ravens, and dogs "running wild with hunger" ate the flesh of fallen Russian and German soldiers.[32] In the forests of Petrograd, wolves descended upon a veritable banquet of unburied human carcasses.[33] The living, it seemed, could do little but turn away as the dead became animal food (and excrement).

Second, the omnipresence of unburied corpses seemed to be fostering deep psychological distress for soldiers and other witnesses who were forced to fight and live among the vast human wreckage. In June of 1915, the *Washington Post* published a vivid letter from a French infantryman who, in a voice betraying both terror and distress, described going into "German trenches, walking and running over dead bodies. Some were old men, some looked not more than 16 years, some in such curious positions they looked alive."[34] It was reported that many British soldiers along the Western Front had adopted the paranormal belief that the "bewildered" souls of unburied corpses could not escape to the afterlife, but rather were condemned to "hang over the battlefield where they met their fate" and torment the living who cowered in the trenches.[35] If not actually haunted by the souls of unburied dead, living soldiers were surely tortured by the constant sight and ungodly smell of exposed corpses. Writing from a battlefield in Champagne, France, American correspondent E. Alexander Powell described decimated German trenches as "the most horrible sight that I had ever seen or ever expect to see. This is not rhetoric, this is fact." Powell recounted:

> Going through an abandoned trench I stumbled over a mass of rags and they dropped apart to disclose the headless, armless, legless torso of a man. I kicked a hobnailed German boot out of my path, and from it fell a rotting foot. A hand with awful, outspread fingers, thrust itself from the earth as though appealing for help for its dead owner. I peered inquisitively into a dugout, only to be driven back by an overpowering stench.

"No wonder," Powell concluded, "that hundreds of the German prisoners were found to be insane."[36] If such reports were true, who could blame soldiers for suffering fits of madness?

Third, it was clear that the incapacity to identify and bury war dead in a timely, accurate, and appropriate fashion meant that the bodily remains of many dead soldiers would be forever lost to the muddy battlefields and burnt forests of Europe, or, at best, deposited into anonymous graves. "Europe is daily becoming a vast cemetery of unmarked graves," remarked the *Macon Daily Telegraph*, where fallen soldiers "are buried in trenches like dumb brutes merely to get rid of the odors arising from the decaying bodies. Their relatives and friends could not identify their burial places if they wanted to."[37] According to the *Washington Post*, along the Western Front, both the Germans and the French were struggling to identify the dead by anything more than nationality: "The only distinction [between German and French battlefield graves] is in the color of the crosses. The French are white, and the Germans are black. And on each is printed a number, the number of the regiment to which the dead belonged. There is seldom anything else."[38] It was clear that the nature of the war was making it increasingly difficult to maintain the sacred coincidence between soldiers' identities and their bodily remains. American readers learned that in Courdemange, France, the graves of hundreds of French and German soldiers were marked only by "small crosses formed of two broken branches of trees [...] without name or number to indicate the occupants."[39] A reporter for the *Oregonian* pronounced the figurative "silence"—the lack of commemoration and care—that surrounded most soldiers' burials as "unspeakably pathetic." Describing the burial of two unknown French soldiers, the journalist empathized with the relatives of the dead, who surely craved information about the location of their loved ones' remains: "Somewhere there will be French mothers and wives and sisters who will wonder what became of those two men. Weeks will go by with no word from them. They will be reported missing, but whether dead or as prisoners will not be stated. They will lie in their shallow grave in the field near a little Belgian town, with grave unmarked." Still, the author reminded readers, identifying war dead properly could entail great, unexpected pain for grieving families:

> The son-in-law of the president of the upper Rhine provinces was killed at Liege. A notice of his death was sent to his relatives, and they went at once in an effort to recover the body, which had been buried in a trench. I saw the widow when she returned from this sad errand. Her eyes were red and swollen from weeping and her father and mother were trying to console her.
> They had found the body in a grave, lying at the bottom of a pile of six other soldiers, officers and privates, and the father had identified the face of his son-in-law.[40]

Though they had been lucky enough to find their loved one's body, the family members were staggered by the ignoble manner in which he (and his comrades) had been interred.

Fourth, the inability to bury the dead facilitated the spread of infectious diseases throughout Europe. In March of 1915, American newspapers began issuing reports that connected the human cesspools of the war zones to various epidemics that were devastating civilian populations across the continent. In a front-page article titled, "Red Death in Europe," the *Los Angeles Times* claimed that the conditions of the Great War had set the stage for a type of plague not witnessed since medieval times:

> With much of continental Europe in a highly unsettled state, with fields and trenches drenched with blood; with shallow graves of thousands of dead scattered throughout the war area; with vermin and filth on every hand; with hundreds of thousands of wounded men being cared for in a pitifully inadequate way, a vast number of them having infected wounds, and with the approach of warm weather, and attending flies and mosquitoes, Europe may well be gravely apprehensive—fearful that an unprecedented plague will sweep the Old World.[41]

In places like Serbia, where medical and mortuary supplies and staff were scarce, typhus, dysentery, and smallpox had created nothing short of an apocalyptic scene. "Uskub is a veritable valley of the shadow of death," claimed the *New York Times*.

> If the tired nurses leave the crowded hospitals for a little exercise and fresh air they are met by a long procession of bullock wagons carrying rude coffins to the cemetery. Sometimes three coffins with unfastened lids rest on the same cart and the bodies of the dead are exposed as the wheels jolt over the rough pavements. [...] Take a large Serbian Hospital [...]. Details of the interior cannot well be printed, but may be conjectured when one mentions that fouls rags and dressings and even portions of amputated limbs are thrown over a wall and left to the attention of crows and magpies and pariah dogs. Similar refuse has been thrown in the river.[42]

The frightening reality portrayed was that, in less than a year, the Great War had left Serbia overwhelmed with rotting human remains. As the *New York Times* wrote in follow-up article: "Scarcely enough people remain unstricken to dig graves for the dead, whose bodies lie exposed in the cemeteries."[43] Upon returning from a tour of war-torn Belgium, former Major Surgeon in the U.S. Army Dr. Louis Livingston Seaman told the New York Peace Society that soldiers were fighting and dying on soil that, for farming purposes, had been highly fertilized. In Seaman's expert opinion, the rotting, unburied dead and the fertilized earth were combining into an unnatural concoction that would surely produce lethal epidemics the likes of which had not been seen in modern history.[44] In seemingly every corner of Europe, the war had incapacitated nations' abilities to bury their dead (civilian and military alike) properly. In turn, the exposed corpses facilitated the spread of disease, thus ensuring that more bodies would be added to the piles. In this tortuous arena, death begot death. In contrast to the apparent hellish scenes of the "Old World," the "New World" (the United States) must have seemed downright sanitized, orderly, and, perhaps, even heavenly to American readers.

As reports of the Great War's immense tax on human life became increasingly common, strange ideas about death, the human body, and gender politics in Europe began to circulate in American public discourse. For instance, in May of 1915, newspapers reported that Albert Oppenheim of Marietta, Ohio, a leading member of the Western Nitroglycerin Manufacturers' Association, was advocating the use of the bodies of men killed on European battlefields for the mass production of glycerin. Oppenheim believed that the War in Europe was depleting the world's supply of glycerin, an essential element of explosives, and leaving various American industries in peril:

> If the glycerin is entirely used up, [Oppenheim] said, it will have not only an important effect on the war, but much work, such as the development of oil wells, will be stopped. [...]
>
> "No explosive aside from nitroglycerin has the shattering effect necessary for shooting oil wells," said Mr. Oppenheim.
>
> "Glycerin is produced from but one source—animal sinews—and there is no way of increasing the production unless we can make use of the bodies of the horses and men killed on the field of battle."[45]

At once profane, cynical, unemotional, and morbidly practical, Oppenheim's sober proposition to turn dead soldiers into explosives that could then be used on the oil fields of Texas and the killing fields of Europe reflected the perverse reality that the War in Europe was creating an excess (and untapped resource) of dead human flesh.

While people like Oppenheim were concerned with the impact that mass death was having on certain global industries, others speculated about its potential effects on gender roles and norms in Europe. Less than a year into the war, some belligerent nations had begun replenishing their depleted infantry forces with women, placing, as one newspaper put it, "Amazons in the field" of battle.[46] Others had begun "prostituting" their social institutions of marriage and motherhood in the "interest of repopulation": the *Miami Herald* reported that to "replace the men rotting in unmarked graves on European battle fields, Germany, France and England [are urging] women to marry. Marry; never mind inclination or affection; marry, and breed."[47] As the extreme loss of male citizen-soldiers became increasingly apparent, some speculated that women would come to dominate European politics and civic life after the war. Citing the "staggering cost" of human life in the Great War—a war in which casualty lists made the carnage at Gettysburg seem "paltry"—editors at the *San Jose Evening News* bluntly claimed that in postwar Europe "there will be left only the men inferior in physique, and the women." As a result, the newspaper argued, women would inevitably use "their superior numbers and superior powers [to] take over the management of the nations." Thus, the editors promised, "The spectacle awaits us of all Europe being in the hand of the women."[48] For Americans who opposed women's enfranchisement, this notion must have been troubling. "The noted psychologist" Dr. Hans Huldricksen publicly argued that this return to the "matriarchate" might be a positive development for the Western World: "In the most primitive literature there is no suggestion that woman was an inferior, treated with contempt and cruelty as she has been during a large part of our civilized history. [...] There is, therefore, good philosophical ground for arguing that a return to the primitive matriarchal condition would within reasonable limits be a victory for justice and morality."[49] Whatever lay ahead, such media reports indicated a general consensus of opinion that the war's tax on human life was plunging belligerent nations into bizarre and unfamiliar futures.

In time, the World War degenerated into a network of bloody stalemates along continuous fronts in France, Russia, Northern Italy, Northern Greece, northeastern Turkey, and even Mesopotamia and Palestine.[50] As millions of men from around the world perished in this total war of attrition, U.S. newspapers kept track of each nation's casualty reports and, like morbid scoreboards, presented the incredible figures to the American public. On March 12, 1917, just weeks before American entry into the war, the *Los Angeles Times* reported the "appalling" number of casualties suffered by the belligerent armies: "More than 10,000,000 are recorded as killed, wounded, captured or missing in the European war." In less than three years, at least five million soldiers had died in the conflict, while another five million had been permanently wounded, captured by the enemy, or lost in the havoc of war. "These figures are admittedly only approximate and in some instances necessarily several weeks old," the *Times* stated. "They are not called exact in any sense, but are known to be so nearly so as to give a fairly reliable picture of the war's results."[51] The picture painted was dismal indeed. As we will see, when the United States eventually entered in the war in 1917, the picture would to be erased and redrawn to suit the needs of the government and military and ameliorate the anxieties of soldiers' families.

"THE HUMAN SLAUGHTER-HOUSE"

In 1913, a German schoolmaster named Wilhelm Lamszus published a prophetic book that foretold the horror, madness, and savagery of the impending European War. Titled, *The Human Slaughter-House: Scenes from the War That Is Sure to Come*, the book chronicles the experiences of a young German soldier who, after witnessing the grisly effects of modern warfare upon the human body and mind, quickly goes insane. In one particularly haunting passage, the main character and his comrades come upon an enemy soldier who has emerged from a mine explosion:

> He stumbles upright into the trenches and tumbles, sobbing and howling, among our rifles. He strikes out at us with hands and feet. He is crying and struggling like a child, and yet no man dares go up to him, for now he is rising on his knee, and then we see! Half his face has been torn away, one eye gone, the twitching muscle of the cheek is hanging down [...] he is kneeling and opening and closing his hands, and is howling to us for mercy. [...] We gaze at him horror-stricken, and are paralyzed [...] then at length the yokel—and our eyes thank him for it—raises the butt of his rifle and places the muzzle against the sound temple. Bang! And the maimed wreckage falls over backward and lies still in his blood.[52]

In an act of "mercy," the fictive Germans execute the disfigured enemy soldier like a rabid dog. Following this encounter and a series of similarly disturbing vignettes, the German unit meets its brutal end on an impassable minefield. Showered with the bodily remains of his friends, the book's protagonist finally crosses the threshold into madness:

> I raise my hand to my eyes. It is red and moist. Blood is flowing over my white hand. Then I realize it, the white thing under me, is not a heap of sand. I have been sitting on a corpse. Horror-stricken, I rush about, and one is lying over there too, and there, and there! Merciful God! I see it plainly now; there are only dead tonight. The human race died out this very night. I am the last survivor. The fields are dead—the woods dead—the villages dead—the cities dead—the earth is dead—the earth was butchered tonight, and I, only I, have escaped the slaughter house.

With this final damning realization, the young German raises a pistol to his head and pulls the trigger.[53]

Shortly after its publication, *The Human Slaughter-House* was banned by German authorities, who claimed that the book "would tend to arouse a horror of war in the laboring classes and make them refuse to perform their military service." As the drums of war were beaten loudly throughout Europe, the conservative press in Germany denounced the author as "a peril to the public safety," and Lamszus was removed from his position as a state schoolmaster. Despite these acts of suppression, *The Human Slaughter-House* was celebrated by pacifist groups, was translated into English, and became an international bestseller. By the outbreak of the European War in July 1914, at least 300,000 copies of the book had been sold. On August 30, 1914, the *Washington Post* reviewed Lamszus's book and praised it as an accurate picture of the "dreadful" war in Europe.[54] Indeed, brutal realities of the Great War would prove to mirror—and in many ways *exceed*—Lamszus's apocalyptic visions.

From the beginning, the European War was portrayed to Americans as something akin to a "human slaughter-house" that mutated once noble and civilized soldiers into something like crazed savages who cared little for either the living or the dead. On October 8, 1914, the *Washington Post* published its conversation with Col. Webb C. Hayes of the U.S. Army (and son of former President Rutherford B. Hayes), who had recently returned from an expedition to the front lines in Belgium and Northern France. "When I left Havre," Hayes said, "the allies were fearful that they would not be able to penetrate the German line through the mass of dead men and horses on the battlefields, which, unfortunately, the combatants seem not to heed about burying." Describing the war zone as one big "sausage grinder," Hayes reported that "the stench is horrible, and the idea of climbing over the bodies must be revolting, even to brave soldiers." Hayes was a grizzled veteran of the Spanish-American War who was familiar with the tribulations and terror of combat, yet he was profoundly disturbed by the incoherent spectacles of death he saw on the European battlefields: "The battle front these days is far different from what it used to be. There are few men to be seen and practically no guns. All are concealed. Shrapnel flies through the air and bursts. That is the scene most of the time." When asked if he would return to the Front to continue observing military operations, Hayes responded: "Does anyone wish to visit a slaughter house a second time?"[55] His question required no answer.

As the conflict unfolded into a ceaseless war of attrition, the combatant nations stepped up their production and implementation of unconventional armaments and modern war machines in hope of breaking the enemy's will. In the United States, the press reported on the development, use, and physical and psychological effects of gas shells, "liquid fire," "monstrous sharks of steel" (submarines), and "man-made vultures of air" (fighter planes) with an almost perverse fascination.[56] On January 25, 1915, the *New York Times* described a French medical report on "soldiers killed by the wind of shells, shock of explosion, gaseous fumes, [and] nervous disturbance." Quoting a French military doctor, the *Times* wrote:

> Dr. Sencert states that a soldier, brought to the hospital affected by a big shell bursting within a yard, though unwounded presented signs of graves disturbance, face pale and anxious, nose pinched, eyes hollow, respiration rapid and superficial, pulse faint and frequent. [...] Despite treatment he died a few hours later. An autopsy showed the lungs and stomach full of blood, which came from a large rupture in each lung. These were due to air pressure, resultant from the explosion, which forced into the lungs a greater volume of air than was endurable.[57]

The *Washington Post* reported that the constant barrages of high explosive shells along the Eastern and Western Fronts were having a "demoralizing effect" on troops from both sides, whose nerves were "turning to water."[58] In March of 1915, the *New York Times* announced that the Germans had begun using "liquid fire" against French forces in the Argonne territory of France. Quoting a traumatized survivor of one of the first attacks, the *Times* stated that "the Germans squirted liquid flame into the French trenches," then set the Frenchmen on fire with "a rain of incendiary bombs, grenades and torches." At least one hundred and fifty French soldiers were incinerated in the unholy pyre.[59] German flesh was just as combustible: at Verdun, French flamethrowers rendered unlucky German victims into "formless heap[s] of blackened ashes, from which all vestige of humanity [...] departed."[60] An American who had served with a Canadian regiment in France described the experience of being gassed to the *New York Times*: "A crawling yellow cloud [...] pours in upon you [...] gets you by the throat and shakes you as a huge mastiff might shake a kitten [...] your eyes starting from their sockets [...] your face turned yellow-green."[61] The *Washington Post* remarked: "On both sides men are being shot into pieces of palpitating meat [...] blown into separate parts of what was once a human body; being stifled by poisonous gases; incinerated by liquid fire."[62] In this conflict, the act of killing the enemy—the immemorial purpose of war—involved not only taking the life out of warriors' bodies, but also subjecting their bodies to theretofore-unimagined levels of torture and dismemberment.

Such textual depictions of the war were reinforced and substantiated by countless fictional and documentary films shown in "motion picture theatres" across the country. In Columbus, Georgia, the Bonita Theatre screened "the special four-part war drama" *War is Hell*, which revealed to audiences "the horrors of modern warfare in Europe today."[63] The *Duluth News-Tribune* (Minnesota) reviewed a popular seven-part documentary that offered American moviegoers "real pictures of real fighting" from "every phase and feature of the war on land and sea and in the air." Released by the British government in an effort to drum up war relief funds, the uncensored film's harrowing images were "vital and vivid with a grim desperate realism which cannot be simulated":

As everyone who has seen them must know, they are amazingly frank. They show a charge out of the trenches, where a man falls as he reaches the parapet, tries to claw his way up and sprawls on his face. They show a rush through the barbed wire, at least three soldiers dropping as they run. There is, too, a picture of a wounded soldier—title admits that he died half an hour afterward—being carried out, all limp, with the passing of his soul.

According to the *News-Tribune*, the film was so viscerally disturbing that audience members at one screening had left the theater "midway of the second reel, unable longer to control their emotions."[64] Mass-produced and distributed to big cities and small hamlets alike, such films disseminated the idea that this disastrous war was rendering death in ways and at levels unparalleled by previous conflicts.

As the war in Europe progressed, American newspapers reported that both sides had begun firing "dum-dum" bullets at each other. Developed by the British in India to suppress "fanatical savages," but banned by The Hague in 1899, this soft-nosed, expanding slug was notorious for its ravaging effects upon the human body. The *Washington Post* revealed that the "dum-dum" bullet "refuses to go straight but slashes and tears its way through the flesh and vitals of whatever object it happens to hit." Instead of leaving a small clean hole that could be more easily addressed by field surgeons, the "dum-dum" bullet "plunges sideways," "ruptures blood vessels for a considerable distance around its wound," "[tears] up tissue and [breaks] bones," and "delivers a tremendous shock [...] men go down when hit as if struck by lighting." Often, soldiers who witnessed the ghastly effects of the "dum-dum" bullet upon the bodies of the dead and dying were traumatized at the sight. Thus, it was clear that the weapons used in the World War could inflict both physical and long-lasting psychological damage upon enemy combatants.[65]

The psychological terror associated with the dum-dum bullet, flame-thrower, and grenade, however, paled in comparison to the general fear surrounding the new, long-range "big guns," which both sides used to rain death upon the enemy at unprecedented rates.[66] An American doctor volunteering for the French Red Cross described the "awful" effects of heavy artillery to the *Washington Post*: "I saw hundreds of men torn to pieces in a few seconds. [...] It was like the work of an unseen hand. I could see the ranks filled one moment and the next a gaping hole had been torn out and 50 men had disappeared."[67] For infantrymen pinned beneath the scant protection of trench walls, the knowledge that one could be wiped from the earth without an instant's notice was maddening. A French Canadian veteran told the *New York Times*: "The soldier in the trench never knows when he may be blown into small pieces—and that is why we always preferred to risk uncertain dangers between the lines at night, instead of lying down in the wet trench, helplessly waiting for death."[68] The futility of such risks, the inability to confront or hide from enemy guns, and the random luck of surviving the enemy's ceaseless bomb attacks indicated that there was little possibility within this war for the average soldier (who was more or less rendered impotent by the long-range guns) to die *heroically* upon the battlefield—to experience the "good death" so valued by the American public during the U.S. Civil War.

The atrocious weapons, tactics, and circumstances of the Great War produced not only dead bodies, but also countless injured soldiers who required
immediate emergency medical care (and who, if fortunate enough to survive,
would permanently display their injuries as evidence of the violence that
had taken the lives of so many comrades). Throughout the first few years of
the conflict, American newspapers offered readers explicit descriptions of
the war's effects upon soldiers' bodies and dramatic accounts of the risky
procedures that doctors performed to save the wounded. On December 13,
1914, the *Idaho Daily Statesman* ran a story about American surgeons volunteering in German hospitals along the Russian border. The front-page article
described the general condition of disfigured German soldiers the Americans
encountered:

> Here are gathered men who were worn, haggard and suffering long before
> they were wounded. Many of them had not removed their clothing for four or
> five weeks, and had slept in mud and filth. Water was scarce and food scarcer.
> A large number lay on the fields for a day or two after being injured before
> receiving medical attention. Following then by journeys of a day or more in
> jolting peasants' carts and three or four days nerve-racking riding on railway
> trains until the base hospitals finally were reached. [...] These delays caused at
> least 90 percent of the wounds to become infected, making the problems of the
> surgeons more difficult.

The article stated that although the American doctors preferred to use bone
and skin grafting methods to save damaged limbs, the conditions of the Eastern Front had forced them to become butchers that spent their days lopping
off gangrenous hands, arms, feet, and legs (a terrifying phenomenon that had
been common during the American Civil War).[69] Of course, the act of ampu-
tating an injured limb was often perilous for soldiers, who could easily die
from shock. On January 8, 1916, the *Washington Post* published an article
on the death of "Gen. Serret, who was in command of one of the divisions of
the French army in the Vosges." Having suffered a leg wound in battle, the
general was taken to a French hospital. "It was necessary to amputate a leg,"
the *Post* reported, but "the general did not recover from the shock" of the
operation.[70] Thus, it was clear that even officers, who presumably received
the best medical care, could perish from the "shock" associated with battlefield surgery.

Doctors in the battle zones were also routinely confronted with a peculiar
type of injury that had no known medical cure: "shell shock." In a November
7, 1915, article titled, "What Shell Shock Is," the *Washington Post* described
the baffling epidemic that was incapacitating legions of soldiers along the
fronts: "When a big shell explodes it creates a sudden and very great pressure

in the surrounding air. This pressure causes 'shell shock'." The *Post* stated that victims of shell shock "become temporarily deaf, dumb and blind. In nearly ever case, indeed, the eyesight is affected, and does not become normal until months after. [...] There have been a number of cases, too, where soldiers have lost their memory owing to shell shock, and are unable to recognize any of their friends." The *Post* reported that although doctors were unable to explain the physiological effects of shell shock, "the cure is chiefly a matter of time, the body slowly coming back, as it were, to its normal state."[71] The technologies of killing employed in the Great War led not only to ruptured flesh, muscle, and bone, but also to unprecedented, frightening, and *invisible* interior injuries that had no known clinical explanations or treatments. It appeared that in this strange war a soldier could go deaf, dumb, or blind even if his ears, tongue, or eyes had not been damaged, shot, or lopped off.

Although makeshift hospitals throughout Europe provided some measures of healing, refuge, and hope for wounded and dying soldiers, even these temporary clinics were susceptible to accidental bombings or targeted attacks in what had become a total war without limits. Though lucky to receive any medical attention at all, injured soldiers became sitting ducks when their respective hospitals came under fire. In a particularly visceral account of the perils of wartime medicine, the *New York Times* published the words of a young German stretcher-bearer, who had tended to German and French soldiers alike in an improvised hospital:

A soldier asks for a drink; as he rises with hand stretched out for a glass of water, a bullet comes through the window and strikes him full in the heart. The poor fellow sinks without a sigh. Most of the wounded are taken away in a lull of the combat. [...] An adjutant, terribly wounded, begs to be put into the cart. [...] Scarcely is he laid there when shrapnel bursts over him, killing him. [...] A wounded man in the kitchen calls me. Struck by a ball in the chest, the poor fellow pants for breath. He is supporting himself by one arm, which slips on the bloody straw. [...] Raising my eyes to the ceiling, I see the plaster break into a huge star, and through the gaping hole the end of a great shell appears. The ceiling sinks funnel-wise; at the same moment the roof cracks and the shell explodes. Then all is dark. Presently, I come to myself, half suffocated with dust and the fumes of dynamite. The house is riven from top to bottom, and we can see the calm blue sky through the broken roof. Nearly all of us are bleeding. The poor [soldier] is dead, disfigured.[72]

What madness, that even the dying were not left to suffer in peace, to die in dignity. No, it seemed that in this war a dying soldier was just as much a target as a healthy one. It seemed in this war not even the process of dying would be respected.

The safest hospitals were those in major cities far from the war zones. However, for a soldier to be treated at an institution in Berlin, London, or Paris, it meant that he had suffered injuries of the most serious and (in all likelihood) gruesome of kind. Throughout the war's early years, American newspapers routinely offered detailed clinical descriptions of what occurred in such medical centers, often conveying both a sense of wonderment at the miracles of 20th-century medicine and a sense of unease over these Frankensteinian-like workshops. For example, on September 24, 1916, the *Washington Post* published a long article on English hospitals that specialized in "face mending" and treating "the mutilating effects of modern war." At Hammersmith Hospital, doctors tended to "'claw hand,' 'trench foot' and the innumerable limb deformities which are caused by gunshot wounds" by grafting bones, applying special steel splints, and administering "electrical treatment." The *Post* described how at Wandsworth Common, "Lietenant Derwent Wood exercises his ingenuity as a sculptor in patching up damaged faces with copper masks painted flesh-color, and when necessary, with imitation eyelashes and mustaches." Another London hospital specialized in experimental treatments of nerve damage:

A little while ago, there was a patient who had had part of his arm shot away, so that the nerve was missing over four inches. In these circumstances to pick up the ends of the nerves and unite them was impossible. The surgeon who had the case in hand made inquiries at other hospitals in London, and he found that at one of them a man was to have a leg amputated at 3:30 o'clock the same afternoon. Orders were issued so that the moment the limb was severed it was put in a saline bath and taken to the military hospital in a taxicab. The patient at the military hospital being under anesthesia, his damaged arm was opened and a piece of healthy nerve from the other patient's amputated leg was substituted for the injured portion. The operation was completely successful, the patient recovering the use of his hand which had been paralyzed.

Acknowledging the disturbing undertones associated with these vignettes of "copper masks painted flesh-color" and taxicab deliveries of freshly amputated body parts, the *Post* reassured the public that due to developments in anesthesia and pain relief, "modern science has robbed [these procedures] of most of their terror" and given the average patient a new lease on life.[73]

Still, such stories of human mutilation must have been at least slightly distressing for American readers who lived in regions where the rights and public presence of disabled people were actively suppressed by the so-called "ugly law." Established in 1867 by the San Francisco Board of Supervisors to prohibit injured soldiers of the Civil War from begging on city streets, the "ugly law" eventually spread to every corner of the nation: from Portland

Oregon, to New Orleans; from Denver to the entire state of Pennsylvania; from Cleveland to Lincoln, Nebraska. The "ugly law" is perhaps best represented by Chicago's version (passed in 1881), which decreed: "Any person who is diseased, maimed, mutilated, or in any way deformed, so as to be an unsightly or disgusting object, or an improper person to be allowed in or on the streets, highways, thoroughfares, or public places in this city, shall not therein or thereon expose himself to public view, under the penalty of a fine of $1 for each offense." Such ordinances classified disabled people as unsightly "objects" that were to be removed from "public view." Seemingly designed to decongest city sidewalks, the "ugly law" enabled the government and big business (in the words of scholar Susan M. Schweik) "to position disability and begging as individual problems rather than relating them to broader social inequalities." In an era devoid of social safety nets and compensation for injuries sustained on the job, such laws had helped condition the American public to judge maimed veterans, injured workers, and disabled beggars with condescension, repulsion, and fear.[74]

The reality that the European War was transforming countless young soldiers into disfigured "objects" surely presented a problem for American elites who envisioned the United States' eventual participation in the war. The American public was well aware of the war's destructive impacts upon soldiers' bodies. But the same polis had been conditioned to harbor prejudices against the disabled and disfigured. How, then, would the American public react if the government called their sons, fathers, brothers, and husbands to fight in Europe? How could the public be convinced to participate in a war that would surely leave so many American men maimed, broken, and "ugly?"

Perhaps in a concerted effort to cope with this dilemma preemptively, American newspapers began reclassifying the horrendous damage inflicted upon soldiers' bodies as (what I call) "patriotic injuries." On April 2, 1916, the *Philadelphia Inquirer* described an emotional reunion between wounded French soldiers and their families at a Paris train station in such terms:

At the door through which they pass stands a galaxy of officers and civilians of note, who salute and lift their hats to the homecomers. One fellow, wheeled along in a chair, with a leg and an arm missing, manages to hold onto a large French flag. It is frayed at the edges and much faded. It partly covers his body and the missing leg. He draws a solemn salute and a tear as he passes. [...]

A soldier holds his sweetheart, but sees her not, for he is blind forever, so he feels her faces and smiles. A woman rushes into a soldier's arms and suddenly recoils to make doubly sure of his identity. Part of his face has been shot away. But he can see, and he stands up and throws his arms about her. He can only mumble indistinctly from a semblance of a mouth. But he does his best. [...]

The speaker is a notable from the War Office and a well known patriot among the people. He arises at the end of a table in a far corner of the room and bows low before his compatriots. He comes to thank his friends, his brothers, he says, for their service to the country. Their sacrifices have been for France, for those they love, for others, and the thought is a just compensation. [...] Here and there are soldiers who smile as they wave the little flags. [...] They have sacrificed their all, but it has been for France, their country, and there is cause for pride in that! Such is the spirit of the French people.[75]

According to this account, the French had learned to accept the war's toll upon the soldier's body—to embrace maimed soldiers as living representations of patriotic sacrifice.[76] In a similar vein, the *Washington Post* published an article on September 17, 1916, that discussed Germany's efforts to rehabilitate its "war-maimed heroes." Reporting from the Oscar-Helene Home in Berlin, the *Post* detailed the hospital's efforts to train disfigured soldiers and reintroduce them into German society as useful workers. The *Post* wrote of one Sergeant Neumann: "The bone of his forearm had been completely shattered, but the surgeons had saved his hand and a leather case held arm and hand together and with his crippled hand he was weaving a beautiful sofa cushion." The *Post* chronicled how "young war heroes" were trained to use their newly affixed "ball-bearing working arms" to build tables and even their own bowling alley. "1916 will produce no more war crippled beggars," the *Post* opined. "The days are past when cripples have to beg for food, when they must dance for alms."[77] Such portrayals of the living wounded worked to reorient the American public's perception of permanently injured soldiers, not as frightful embodiments of destitution, but rather as symbolic representations of patriotic sacrifice. This transvaluation of the crippled soldier's body, arguably crucial to motivating American participation in the war, would eventually be advanced and codified by the establishment of the Purple Heart following the close of World War I (in essence, the Purple Heart would be an official coping mechanism for the wartime reality of bodily destruction).

As the "sausage grinder" devolved into a bloody, attritional deadlock along the Western and Eastern Fronts, it became ever clearer that soldiers in the trenches were suffering deep psychological wounds. Reporting from the Battle of the Somme, the *Washington Post* described a "man, mother naked" who "raced round in a circle" upon the battlefield, "laughing boisterously" until an "impartial bullet went through his forehead" and "he fell headlong to the earth."[78] Sometimes drawing upon the terminology of Freudian psychology,[79] American newspapers reported with great fervor the war's "marked neurotic effect" upon once sane men. In an article published in the *Idaho Daily Statesman*, French military surgeon Henri Bourget claimed that "nerve racking insanity [is] breeding nightmares that banish sleep" from soldiers living and fighting in the trenches. Bourget described one French soldier who had to be awoken from a violent night terror:

> I asked him what the dream was. [...]
> "I could see the country in front of me exactly as you see it now," he said. "About fifty yards from there is a dead German lying on his back with his right arm stretched stiffly up toward the sky, and around him are twenty or thirty bodies."
> "You mean you saw them in your dream?" I asked.
> "I saw them in my dream, yes," he said, "but they are there. They are part of a charge from the German trenches this morning. If you will look through the observing glass you will see them."
> I looked through the glass and sure enough there they were, a number of bodies with one corpse near their centre. This dead man's right arm was rigidly stretched upward in one of those uncanny, terrible attitudes in which the violent death of the battlefield fixes some of its victims. [...]
> "As I stood there, in my dream, I saw the dead German with the outstretched arm begin slowly to rise. He stood, dead, with his arm still stretched upward as you see it. And slowly all the dead men around him began to get up. Then they began to advance upon me, led by this man with the rigid arm. Some of them had their faces shot off. Some of them had no arms; their bodies were mangled. Still I could not move [...] I awoke to find you beside me. I will not sleep again."

Bourget claimed that this dream was common among troops from both sides. So too was the sight of "sleeping men wandering behind the lines with arms outstretched and terror depicted on their faces."[80] It seemed that by day soldiers butchered each other; by night they piteously struggled with the traumatic memories of what they had done and seen.

Participants in a ceaseless program of death, decay, and mutilation, soldiers of the World War were turning into monsters capable of inflicting the worst cruelties upon foes and allies alike. U.S. newspapers published lectures from prestigious American scientists, who, monitoring the conflict from afar, analyzed the "profound alterations in soldiers' characters and thoughts after they have faced the terrors of battle" and explained the European War's "'throw-back' to primitive emotions and ideas."[81] On October 26, 1916, the *Idaho Daily Statesman* published a vivid letter sent home by a "Boise boy" volunteering in the British Expeditionary Force. In one of the few letters from American volunteers that slipped past British censors, the young soldier described the Western Front as "several kinds of hell." He wrote: "I have faced death in every form. [...] Been talking to a man, and the next instant his head was blown off." The young man knew that such events had drastically altered his very nature: "I shall never be the same; my nerves are in a rotten state now—I don't mean I am frightened, but when I come through a charge I look like some hunted beast, and I look much older than when I first came out here." The traumatic circumstances of the war had also shattered the collective conscience of his unit: "We lived for days in a German trench we captured, with dead bodies all around us, and the smell was terrible. You can't trust [a German] one inch, even when he surrenders; and so I leave it to your imagination—we don't take many risks."[82] It seemed that the conditions of the European War could even transform apple-cheeked American boys into callous executioners.

Similar stories of merciless killing and feverish bloodlust appeared in newspapers across the nation. In March of 1915, the *Kansas City Star* wrote of a French victory along the Western Front. French soldiers came upon a "few remaining Prussians [who] threw themselves on their knees. 'Comrades! Comrades!' they cried, but the carnage was on, and the bayonets and rifles did their terrible work, butchering the last with awful cries."[83] In May of 1916, the *Los Angeles Times* published a report about a French reprisal attack against German forces near Verdun. Covered with the "horrible fragments of [their comrades'] torn flesh," a decimated French unit managed to overtake a German trench, where they bayoneted their helpless foes to death as they would "rats."[84] In this hateful war, no quarter would be given to the enemy. Kill or be killed was the way, according to the press.

Americans also learned that the war had driven soldiers to enact what seemed to be insane and barbaric practices against their own compatriots. For instance, on December 31, 1916, the *Duluth News-Tribune* reported that the British army had begun punishing derelict soldiers with "crucifixion." Applied to infantrymen for even the slightest offenses (such as losing one's gas mask), "crucifixion" entailed "tying a man to the wheel of a wagon or to a tree and leaving him there for some time, usually two hours." The article quoted British General Sir Horace Smith-Dorrien, who attempted to rationalize this abuse: "The civilian experiences possibly a sense of shock at learning that punishment of this kind has to be inflicted at the front, but were he in the army he would realize that the most essential thing of all in the face of the enemy is the absolute maintenance of discipline."[85] In other instances, soldiers from both sides had been known to kill fellow countrymen who had gone "crazy" in the trenches so as to "become a menace to their own comrades and officers."[86] In essence, American newspapers reported that soldiers were being treated as little more than cogs in the grand instrument of killing. Those who proved to be imperfect were barbarically refined through torture or, in some cases, simply put down like rabid dogs.

It was evident that the madness that had infected soldiers of the war had overtaken civilian populations throughout Europe as well. Just three months into the conflict, Irish playwright George Bernard Shaw felt compelled to publish an essay in the *New York Times* that railed against a growing public sentiment in England that the Allied Forces should try to kill every German woman so that the "Teutons" might be completely destroyed, once and for all. "It would be too horrible," Shaw asserted. "Life would be unbearable if people did such things."[87] In September of 1914, the *Columbus Enquirer-Sun* told the story of a mob of citizens in Rheims, France, who attacked a small group of wounded German prisoners. Having raised their rifles to shoot, they would have mowed the Germans down were it not for the intervention of "a little priest, the Abbe Andreiux." Standing between the French mob and the helpless prisoners, the cleric pleaded: "Don't fire. You will make yourselves as guilty as they are."[88] That same day, the *New York Times* reported that the German army had been "willed" to destroy most of the Belgian city of Louvain because local citizens would not cease shooting German soldiers from the windows of their homes.[89] In April of 1915, the *Times* described how "Serbian civilians cut off the forearms and legs below the knees of a Hungarian hussar and placed him on a horse, which was chased round amid the applause of the people." Perhaps worse than that, the same group "bored a hole in a soldier's chest, then [drew] a rope through it, and hanged him in this way on a tree, afterward lighting a fire under him."[90] In every corner of Europe, it seemed, basic social moralities had been replaced by the frenzied, state-sponsored pursuit of almost-orgiastic mob violence. Reflecting on such events, Father James McGolrick of the Cathedral of the Sacred Heart in Duluth, Minnesota, told his congregation: "Europe's present war would indicate that many of the so-called Christian nations had lost their spirit of Christianity."[91] This was putting it mildly.

By 1916, media reports indicated that an uncontrollable desire to kill the enemy had permeated European civilian life to such a point that a peaceful resolution of the war, spiraled so far out of control, seemed impossible. "It is said that if any man in London seriously proposed peace he would be hung to the nearest lamppost," the *Wall Street Journal* announced in a front-page article. "The French are crazy with war passion and demand not only success for their side, but revenge across the line."[92] On February 10, 1916, the *Philadelphia Inquirer* reported that editors at the *Manchester Guardian* were so disgusted by the violent attitudes of their fellow citizens that they had begun to publish entreaties against the "competitive butchery of women and children" and urged that "England and her allies refrain from barbarism and fight out the war along civilized lines." Sadly, the *Inquirer* stated, the *Guardian's* message represented only a "minority sentiment."[93] Fearing that such attitudes were leading to the "suicide of Europe," Pope Benedict exhorted Catholics of every European nation to "redeem the sins" of war and "appease divine justice" by rededicating themselves to "works of Christian piety."[94] Regrettably, Pope Benedict's appeals for peace had little effect, as civilians throughout Europe had become integral and willing participants of total war now capable of the cruelest of acts.[95]

The horror, savagery, and insanity of World War I's early years were perhaps best displayed in the writings of the few nongovernment-affiliated, international journalists who managed to gain access to the trenches. On December 10, 1916, the *Washington Post* published a long dispatch from reporter Granville Fortescue, who recounted an apocalyptic vision of the Battle of the Somme:

> Out on the battlefield the waste of war is framed in a still more desolate setting. Half the scene is shut in by a naked forest of rotting ghostlike trees. They rise as withered bracken from the sodden soil. As far as the eye can see this soil is ulcerated with shell holes filled with reeking, viscid slime. Mixed in that slime is all the debris of war, broken rifles, casques, shells, clothing, bayonets, hand grenades, cartridge pouches, winged bombs, buried and rotting in the mud.
>
> Other hideous things are buried here. I see a gray-green repulsive form sprawling at the bottom of a shell hole. Passing through the trenches, heavy boots stick out from the trench wall, half blocking the path. Skeleton hands snatch at me. In the end, here is the real business of war.[96]

Fortescue's distressing portrait of the "business" of the Great War was something akin to Dante's and Hieronymus Bosch's respective, well-known depictions of Hell. However, in Dante's *Inferno* and Bosch's *Garden of Earthly Delights*, violence is strictly ordered and regulated—punishments are designed to match the sins. In the battlefields of Europe, however, the ghastly, man-made carnage and immolation of human flesh appeared to exceed all previous images of a world abandoned by God.

In time, American citizen-soldiers would find themselves in the trenches, fields, and forests of this forsaken land.

THE RULES OF TOTAL WAR

As the American public monitored the war from the other side of the Atlantic, it became clear that the great "human slaughter-house" was quickly rupturing previously held notions of the moral boundaries of state-sponsored warfare. It seemed that as the Allied Nations and Central Powers became ever more entrenched in the conflict, the values of honor, decency, and compassion increasingly vanished from European consciousness. Throughout the first year of the war, authorities from both sides accused each other of facilitating the wanton torture and murder of wounded and captured soldiers. Germany provided evidence to the international press that French soldiers had mutilated prisoners by cutting off their noses and ears and filling the holes with sawdust. The Germans also claimed that "meat axe"-wielding Senegalese and Hindu conscripts fighting for France and Great Britain (respectively) had "brought with them savage practices of warfare of their native countries [...] severing the heads from bodies as war trophies."[97] Meanwhile, the French accused the Germans of slitting prisoners' throats, burning prisoners alive on makeshift pyres, and throwing wounded enemies into the Meuse River to drown. A French soldier described the following scene from the small village of Hannescamp: "Two of our wounded had been shot by the Germans. [...] They were strapped to ladders and the ladders placed upright against a wall and their brains blown out. [...] I saw the bodies. They were still strapped to the ladders." Similarly, the English claimed that German soldiers had crucified a Canadian soldier by thrusting bayonets "through the palms of his hands and feet [...] pinning him to [a] fence."[98] Along the Eastern Front, a marauding Russian guerrilla nicknamed "Earless Peter"—credited with killing a countless number of German soldiers—was equally celebrated by the Russians and feared by the Germans for his insatiable thirst for blood. "Both of Peter's ears exist and are painfully sound," wrote the *Washington Post*. "He is 'earless' merely because he is deaf to appeals for mercy. [...] He slaughters no prisoners, but he refuses to take them."[99] Reporting from a Russian camp at Petrograd in March of 1915, a British correspondent described a wounded German prisoner's disillusionment with the base nature of the War in Europe. Published in the *San Jose Mercury Herald*, the account read in part:

> He persisted that it is not a real war when a man can be shot down before he has at least a fair chance of shooting his enemy. Within seven days of arriving at some large unnamed town he marched along a road near [Lublin, Poland] "in fours, singing." Rifle bullets and shells came from an invisible enemy. "It was like an apple-tree being shaken down on you." The soldier did not know whether his hand was smashed by a bullet or by a shell fragment.[100]

For this bewildered German prisoner, the World War was "not a real war," for he had never had a "fair chance" to fight back against the enemy. His vivid personal testimony signified a disjunction between previously held assumptions about chivalrous wartime killing and the seemingly uncivilized practices of this modern war. By all appearances, the armies of Europe were operating without their moral compasses.

As the real and imagined rules of war disintegrated, civilian populations—which provided the human, economic, and material resources necessary to sustain domestic war efforts—became prime targets for attack, much to the disgust of American newspaper editors. On October 6, 1914, in an article simply entitled, "Unbelievable," the *Idaho Daily Times* reported that German zeppelins had bombed London with great destructive effect. "The officially-directed killing of non-combatants, of women and children, indiscriminately—that is not warfare excepting from a cannibal viewpoint," the *Daily Times* opined. "The whole bomb-dropping business is bad, but it is damnable and inexcusable on the part of civilized nations when the targets are citizens [...] who are not active participants in the war. [...] It can only be justified in the minds of the brutal and the degenerate."[101] Similarly outrageous accounts of German zeppelin raids upon Paris and Antwerp emerged throughout 1914.[102] On October 16, 1914, the *New York Times* published a German accusation against a Russian officer who had supposedly "forced [Belgian] inhabitants of the villages under his control to join the Russian troops in the trenches." According to the report, the Russians then "used women as shields for [their] machine guns" during a firefight with German forces.[103] In May of 1915, English historian George Macaulay Trevelyan, having returned from a harrowing tour of war-torn Serbia, told the *New York Times* of atrocities committed by Austro-Hungarian soldiers against local civilians. "There was an Austro-Hungarian proclamation to the soldiers saying the Serbs were a race of murderers, and great severity was to be shown them," Trevelyan testified. "The Magyars made an invasion and killed 3,000 or 4,000 Serbian civilians. Some of them they burned alive, others had their eyes gouged out, their ears clipped off, or suffered similar injury." As stated by Trevelyan, the attacks had forced half a million Serbians to flee to a refugee camp in southern Serbia, where many succumbed to typhus.[104] A month later the *Times* reported that German and Russian forces, battling for control of the territory between Lodz and Warsaw, had equally terrorized Polish civilians throughout the region.[105] In September of 1916, the *Washington Post* announced that Romanian soldiers had been sweeping through Bulgaria and executing every male civilian they found.[106] Whether harnessing the indiscriminate power of new technologies like the zeppelin, or falling back on timeless means of terrifying populations (such as ethnic extermination or the spectacle of torture), the belligerent armies of the Great War had cast aside all protocols and rules of war that had been previously devised to mask the state-sponsored destruction of human beings as a civilized phenomenon.

According to several newspaper accounts that read somewhat like anti-German propaganda, civilians were just as vulnerable to attack, perhaps even more so, when traveling on ships in what were supposedly neutral waters. As the subsequent German U-boat attacks upon the passenger ships the *Falaba*, the *Ancona*, and the *Sussex* proved, virtually no corner of the theater of war was safe for noncombatants. "There can be no military justification for opening fire with shells and torpedoes upon a merchant ship carrying hundreds of passengers," the *New York Times* angrily declared following the sinking of the Italian ship the *Ancona*. "They were absolutely defenseless. [...] The act can be explained only as one perpetrated in savage cruelty for the joy of slaughter, for the lust of killing, because of an unquenchable thirst for blood."[107] Thus, it seemed that like crazed, mechanized sharks on perpetual hunt, German U-boats had sent hundreds of innocent civilians to their cold, dark, watery graves.

In the spring of 1915, tales of the deliberate and systematic extermination of ethnic Armenians started to emerge from Turkey (an ally of Germany and Austro-Hungary). On April 26, 1915, the *Washington Post* issued its first report on the efforts of the Ottoman Empire (which was predominantly Muslim) to purge its lands of Armenians (who were Christians), stating that 30,000 Armenians had been attacked and driven from their homes. According to the *Post*, the refugees had begun a deadly exodus toward Russia, dying from disease and hunger, or at the hands of marauding Turkish horsemen, along the way. Desperate Armenian mothers drowned their babies in rivers to end the infants' suffering, while the elderly died "unheeded and unmourned" by their families. "In fact," wrote the *Post*, "those who died seemed to be envied by the living." The *Post* related the story of a young Armenian named Hackatur, who had escaped "from a well in which the bodies of the dead had been crammed [by Turkish soldiers]. He fell with others, and was tossed into the well, but he managed to wriggle through the bodies lying on top of him and escaped at nightfall."[108] Throughout 1915, reports of the ongoing "Armenian Atrocities" dominated the covers of American newspapers. A *Lexington Herald* headline dubbed the event "The Murder of a Nation."[109] The *State* of Columbia, South Carolina, called it an exercise in "demoniac cruelty." According to the *State*, Turkish Major Djevdet Bey had dispatched his "Butcher Battalions" to massacre the Christians of the city of Sairt and torture others in the Armenian village of Mush: "Two head men of the village had their finger nails and then their toe nails forcibly extracted; teeth were knocked out and in some cases noses were whittled down, the victims thus being done to death under shocking lingering agony. [...] The female relatives of victims who came to the rescue were assaulted in public before the very eyes of their mutilated men."[110] An American missionary named Rev. Father Dakras, who claimed to have witnessed the Turkish "holy war" against Armenian Christians, corroborated these "scenes of wholesale murder" in an essay for the *Washington Post*:

> The savage Moslem Kurds and Bedouins on horseback had already entered the city. Like wolves charging into a sheep herd, they dashed into the frantic, terror-stricken, helpless multitudes. Like the harvester with his keen-edged scythe, so the Moslem hordes on horseback waved their crescent-shaped swords and mowed down innocent men, women, and even infants, many of whom were only a few months old. [...] The godless invaders gathered around units of panic-stricken Christians [...] and drove them into wells. These wells filled

with humanity, were guarded while other Kurds dashed to the already deserted houses, produced kerosene oil, and poured it into the wells. [...] [S]imultaneously they were set on fire. Merciful Father! I can still hear the shrieks of the victims. But their tormentors watched the work of their demon acts with serene satisfaction. [...] At Diza [...] the Kurds buried more than 3,000 Christians to their chins. The following day many of them had already died, but still quite a number of them were half alive [...] when the main Bedouin troops arrived [and] rode over the skulls of the thus buried Christians.

Offering a graphic testimony of rape, torture, terror, and murder, "Father Dakras" claimed "between 600,000 and 800,000 Christians of Turkey—Armenian Gregorians, Roman Catholics and Protestants—had been killed." He described the whole Armenian territory between the Black Sea and the Mediterranean as "a vast graveyard" strewn with the "mutilated bodies" and "decayed flesh" of Christians, lamenting: "If the Christians of the western world would only realize how many thousand times unholy is this Moslem 'holy war!'"[111] Here, the American public was encouraged to think about the war in religious terms, as a battle between moral Christian forces and, in this case at least, barbaric Muslims.

Tales of the German "Rape of Belgium" (facilitated by clandestine British and French propaganda agencies[112]) did little to quell the notion that the wartime actions of the Central Powers—Germany, Austro-Hungary, and the Ottoman Empire—were neither guided nor restrained by "civilized" Christian principles of mercy, compassion, and piety. In August of 1914, German forces executed the infamous Schlieffen Plan, which called for a swift and devastating attack against France via the neutral nation of Belgium. Unfortunately, Germany's invasion of Belgium violated, among other things, the 1839 Treaty of London, which bound Britain to guard Belgium's neutrality in case of invasion. The German occupation of Belgium not only gave Britain an "official" reason to enter the war,[113] but also provided the Allied Nations a seemingly endless source of anti-"Teuton" propaganda. The countless reports that emerged from war-torn Belgium between 1914 and 1915 seemed to prove beyond a doubt that a godless German army and its allies were willing (even eager!) to commit the worst atrocities against citizens of enemy and neutral nations alike in order to achieve their "barbaric" military and geopolitical goals.

Citing vivid eyewitness accounts from Belgium, the *Washington Post* wrote of violated and mutilated "bodies of young girls lying by the roadside," "bodies of boys impaled on hedge stakes," and a "drunken orgy" in which German soldiers raped the women of a small Belgian village while their husbands "were forced to look on at the frightful spectacle."[114] In Mont-sur-Marchiennes, a German soldier had taken a child by the legs and crushed his head on the sidewalk; another had hacked a young boy's right hand off.[115] In Liege,

> 400 people lost their lives [...] some on the banks of the Meuse, where they were shot according to orders given and some in the cellars of the houses where they had taken refuge. Eight men belonging to one family were murdered. Another man was placed close to a machine gun which was fired through him. His wife brought his body home in a wheelbarrow. [...] A hair dresser was murdered in his kitchen where he was sitting with a child on each knee. A paralytic was murdered in his garden. [...] Many of the inhabitants who escaped the massacre were kept as prisoners and compelled to clear the houses of corpses and bury them in trenches.[116]

An unidentified merchant from Roulers claimed that German soldiers there had murdered women and children en masse: "One woman was shot as she was burying her baby in a garden. [...] The kaiser said that the Germans do not make war on women and children. By . . . they do not [...]. Their bodies are the kaiser's breastplate!"[117] Other alleged victims included Catholic priests, who "were shot by German soldiers under the pretext that the clergy were French spies in disguise."[118] In a town near Ransbach, soldiers of the predominantly Lutheran German army raided a priest's house, "dragged him from his study, placed him against his own garden wall and shot him summarily as a traitor and spy. [...] The priest was buried without a coffin at the end of his little garden plot."[119] In Spontin, a local priest "was first hung up by the feet and then by the hands and pierced with bayonets."[120] Viscount James Bryce, a former British ambassador to the United States, attempted to put these purported atrocities into historical terms, telling American newspapers that "riot, lust and pillage" were prevailing over Belgium "on a scale unparalleled in any war between civilized nations during the last three centuries."[121] Characterized as untamed barbarians capable of the worst obscenities, the Germans appeared to be securing their place in the annals of infamy.

In time, the "Rape of Belgium" became symbolized by one notorious and memorable event: the execution of British nurse Edith Cavell. Serving at a clinic in Brussels, Cavell had helped smuggle hundreds of Allied soldiers and Belgian men out of the country and to safety during the first year of the war. Placed under arrest by German authorities in August of 1915, Cavell confessed to her actions. In accord with German military code, a tribunal condemned her to death. On October 12, 1915, Cavell was riddled with bullets by a German firing squad. In the following weeks and months, American newspapers buzzed with accounts of the woman's death, which was presented as the ultimate example of German "butchery."[122] British authorities relayed the testimony of the Reverend Stirling Gahan, an Anglican chaplain who had been permitted to see Cavell and give her Holy Communion before her execution. According to British reports, in her final moments, Cavell uttered these moving words to Gahan: "This I would say, standing as I do in view of God and eternity: I realize that patriotism is not enough. I must have no hatred or bitterness toward any one." Gahan further claimed that Cavell "was brave and bright to the last. She professed her Christian faith and said she was glad to die for her country. She died like a heroine." American newspapers reported that, in order to add insult to injury, callous German authorities had refused to hand Cavell's body over to Gahan or anyone else.[123] The stark contrast between Cavell, portrayed to United States readerships as an angelic saint, and her merciless German executors provided excellent fodder for public figures who advocated American entry into the war on behalf of the Allied Nations. Shortly after her death, James M. Beck, former Assistant Attorney General of the United States, published a lengthy treatise in the *New York Times* in which he compared the "murder of Miss Cavell" to the Romans' execution of Jesus Christ. For Beck and many others, Edith Cavell represented all the "other victims of the rape of Belgium"—all the "innocent" people who had suffered the wrath of German belligerence.[124] In a letter to the *Oregonian*, Chehalis, Washington, resident E. W. Herald echoed Beck's assertions, claiming that "when [Cavell] fell as the seething, hissing bullets tore through her tender flesh, she fell a martyr [...] a victim of that Frankenstein monster of militarism of which the whole world now stands in dread and fear."[125] For Herald, as for many others, the execution of this innocent, peaceful, Christian woman symbolized the relentless inversions of morality that the Great War entailed.

The obvious fact that most reports concerning the "Rape of Belgium" were emerging from British and French sources led some people to doubt the veracity of the tales. In September of 1914, the *New York Times* published a lecture by Jerome K. Jerome, the famous English humorist and author of *Three Men in a Boat*, who believed that such reports were gross exaggerations designed to "build barriers of hatred" on both sides of the Atlantic. "Half these stories of atrocities I do not believe," Jerome wrote. "In every war each side, according to the other, is supposed to take a fiendish pleasure in firing upon hospitals" and other vile acts. Jerome urged the peoples of the world not to let the stories make them "[m]ad with fear, mad with hate, blinded by excitement."[126] Objecting to media portrayals of the Cavell case, Boise resident Gustave Kroeger wrote to the *Idaho Daily Statesman*: "Your editorial relating to the execution of Miss Edith Cavell, seems to me so extremely unfair and biased, that I would ask permission to shortly reply to it." Kroeger advised editors at the *Statesman* to avoid becoming mouthpieces for the war's belligerent nations. "It is an easy matter for the press to arouse the passion and indignation of unthinking people, and for that reason, it seems that a newspaper should be careful how it uses its power and in commenting upon a case, of which partial and imperfect reports have reached."[127] To offset such sentiments, many newspapers attempted to provide irrefutable evidence of the alleged German atrocities. The *Washington Post*, for example, provided as "proof of the contention that German soldiers have been guilty of barbarity" the testimony of Dr. Frederick S. Mason, an American doctor who had treated Belgian victims in Paris. "With my own eyes I have seen enough examples to show barbarity among the invaders was not confined to scattered cases," said Mason, who described in detail the mutilation of young Belgian girls. In January of 1915, the *New York Times* quoted from diaries found on dead German soldiers in Belgium: "The Belgians, at Dinant on the Meuse, fired on our regiment from inside the houses," one soldier's diary supposedly read. "We shot everyone we could see, or we threw them out of the windows, women as well as men. The bodies lay three feet high in the streets."[128] The *State* of Columbia, South Carolina, cited an official British commission that had interviewed 1,200 people who had witnessed Germany's sack of Belgium. "[The witnesses] were cross-examined by trained lawyers. So soon as their stories showed signs of the natural hysteria incident to a severe strain, they were thrown out of the record." From this set of supposedly ironclad testimonies, the commission had determined beyond all doubt

that civilians were shot down in numberless towns by squads, that villages were put to the torch, that people were tortured and mutilated by order, that children were not spared, that when a house was fired the amusement of the soldiers was to fire at its fleeing inhabitants as though they had been rabbits.[129]

Such suspect evidence proved to be strong enough for Americans like L. H. Slaw of Baltimore, who, in a letter to the *Philadelphia Inquirer*, argued that Germany's actions in Belgium constituted "the worst vandalism perpetrated in all history, manifesting to what means Germany will descend in her hatred of her enemies."[130] In Slaw's mind, Germany's attacks against noncombatants was not only a direct violation of the traditional conditions set forth by just war theory, but also a war crime that exceeded all others that came before in its depravity.

PROPER MOURNING AND THE
LOSS OF AMERICAN LIFE

As the war degenerated into a "human slaughter-house"—an endless series of atrocities that produced "acres of dead and dying" and "vast cemeteries of unmarked graves" in seemingly every corner of Europe—American newspapers occasionally examined the attitudes, psyches, and mourning practices of those who grieved for soldiers lost in the infernal conflict. Two opposing viewpoints regarding this matter emerged. The first suggested that civilians in belligerent countries had learned to accept citizen-soldiers' deaths as a necessary, if unfortunate, aspect of wartime sacrifice, and to grieve for loved ones in ways that would not hamper national war efforts. It was reported that in France, where government officials made highly publicized visits to unmarked battlefield graves to honor "the immortal victors of the Marne," mothers and wives "cheerfully see [their] sons and husbands go to be maimed or killed [so] that France may live." The *New York Times* published a note allegedly sent by a grieving Parisian mother to her dead son's commanding officer: "In this unspeakable sorrow a great consolation remains to me. During seventeen years I have fought over my son with all kinds of sickness. I have been able, by constant care, to keep him out of the clutches of death. It makes me very proud to have succeeded in saving him from sickness to give him a chance to die for 'La Patrie!'" This mother's attitude supposedly reflected the "brave spirit" that had spread across the nation; as one *Washington Post* correspondent put it: "No woman weeps in France."[131] According to similar reports, this was the case in England as well. For example, a *New York Times* journalist described the measured, "reverential spirit" exhibited by Londoners on Easter Day of 1915:

> No one seeing the spectacle of London's Easter day could say that the Londoner takes the war too lightly nor yet that London put on a gloomy face. That's not London's way. [...] It was noticeable that though in thousands of families sons have been killed no mourning was seen in [Westminster Abbey], nor for that matter, on the streets. London's afflicted families all bravely refrain from wearing it.[132]

Another *Times* correspondent described the "wonderful spirit" of English citizens, many of whom had lost men in the war: "I went to a family dinner party at the home of a widow all of whose three sons had been killed. Several of the relations who were guests had put in black, but the widow said: 'There is no mourning in this house; my boys only did their duty.'"[133] Other reports from the *Times* made it seem as though news of soldiers' deaths did little more than strengthen English resolve to win the war: "The English people [...] had been quite calm until the publication of the first casualty list, after which the men poured forward with wonderful enthusiasm and offered themselves for enlistment."[134] Whereas media accounts of the "Rape of Belgium" implicitly encouraged Americans to imagine themselves as helpless Belgians and, perhaps, experience emotions of rage and indignation, these reports provoked a different sensibility—one of tranquil Stoicism. It is possible that such articles prompted American readers to contemplate what their own reactions to the loss of loved ones in battle would be—to wonder if they, in a time of war, could replicate the unflinching, soldierly like courage and "stiff upper lipped"-attitude exhibited by French and British families. Would Americans accept such enormous sacrifices with the same kind of grace, dignity, and grit?

At the same time, various newspaper accounts offered the antithetical view that European citizens were, in fact, crippled by grief for loved ones lost to the war's carnage. According to Rosika Schwimmer, secretary of the International Council of Equal Suffrage and a peace advocate, the war's death toll had touched so many families that government officials in Austria, Germany, and France had effectively forbidden public acts of mourning so that martial spirits would not be dampened. Following an extensive tour of war-torn Europe, Schwimmer told the *Washington Post*: "Women on the continent are not permitted by the authorities to dress in mourning even after the bodies of their dead are brought home," as the "sight of black might depress the public mind. [...] Such a policy is mockery and sends more and more women to suicide graves."[135] By repressing the human need to mourn for the dead, officials in Europe apparently were pushing citizens over the brink of madness. In certain regions of Germany, the girlfriends of slain soldiers had (in what may have been an act of defiance) begun adopting their sweethearts' last names in order to symbolize their grief and fidelity to the dead.[136] Various media reports suggested that a veritable cloud of despair hung over all of England. According to the *Fort Worth Star-Telegram*, the Great War had "leveled all classes" in England by shedding the blood of "duke and commoner alike"; thus, grief had become democratized, extending from factories, shipyards, and urban tenements to all the "noble houses of England."[137] The *Washington Post* claimed that the war's death toll had "bereaved every royal house" in England and "turned the House of Lords into the House of Mourning."[138] According to various reports, throughout Great Britain and Continental Europe, countless families "suffering from poignant grief" over the loss of loved ones had turned to a booming, pseudo-scientific "spiritualism" movement in hope of somehow communing with fallen soldiers. American newspapers reported that leading proponents of spiritualism included Sir Arthur Conan Doyle (creator of the famous literary character and symbol of logical-positivism, Sherlock Holmes) and the physicist Sir Oliver Joseph Lodge, both of whom had lost close relatives in the fighting. It seemed that even the most rational thinkers in the world, once directly touched by the war's hand of death, were willing to abandon scientific reason and turn to clairvoyants and crystal-gazers in order to ease their emotional pain.[139] It was clear that neither class, nor wealth, nor levelheaded rationality, nor patriotic courage could protect families from the unbearable pain of losing their beloved young men to this mad war.

While nearly all reports regarding death and mourning practices focused on European victims of the Great War, newspapers occasionally addressed instances in which Americans were killed in the theater of war. Between 1914 and 1917, hundreds of Americans died as a direct result of the Great War. Many of these victims had voluntarily enlisted in the armies of their ancestral homelands and perished on the battlefields of Europe. During the war's early years, newspapers frequently reported the deaths of Americans fighting for the Allied or Central Powers. Typically, these reports were brief, unemotional, nonjudgmental, and matter-of-fact—indicating that, during the period of American neutrality, it was socially acceptable for a U.S. citizen to pledge allegiance to another nation (France, Germany, or otherwise). For the most part, editors and journalists across the country took a cautious, neutral position on the meanings of such deaths, and resisted commemorating the dead in any grand fashion (perhaps because the meanings of the deaths were so uncertain).[140] Some articles addressed the personal characteristics and talents that the departed had exhibited while living in the States; for instance, in December of 1916, the *New York Times* discussed the "remarkable achievement in verse" by Alan Seeger, a young American poet who was killed in Northern France while fighting with the Foreign Legion.[141] Others described "impressive ceremonies" that grateful European nations conducted in commemoration of American volunteers killed in battle.[142] But rarely did U.S. newspapers show any pointed interest in exploring the emotions and attitudes of Americans whose loved ones died in the fighting, a provocative topic that surely could have been alluring to many readers.[143] Newspapers took a similarly dispassionate approach to reporting the untimely deaths of noncombatant Americans who, while traveling to Europe to visit family, volunteering in hospitals, or pursuing business opportunities, had been ensnared in the war's web of violence. It seems the media had adopted the attitude that American victims of the conflict should have known the risks entailed by entering the expansive war zone.[144]

The glaring exception to this tempered attitude can be found in media coverage of the infamous sinking of *Lusitania*. On April 22, 1915, the "Imperial German Embassy" placed a notice in the *New York Times* that warned Americans, in no uncertain terms, of the perils of traveling to Great Britain:

> TRAVELERS intending to embark on the Atlantic voyage are reminded that a state of war exists between Germany and her allies and Great Britain and her allies; that the zone of war includes the waters adjacent to the British Isles; that, in accordance with formal notice given by the Imperial German Government,

vessels flying the flag of Great Britain, or any of her allies, are liable to destruction in those waters and that travelers sailing in the war zone on ships of Great Britain or her allies do so at their own risk.

Despite the Germans' foreboding advertisement, on May 1, 1915, the British ocean liner *Lusitania* departed from New York City for Liverpool, England, carrying 1,959 civilians, many of them American. Six days later, a German U-boat torpedoed and sunk the mighty passenger ship off the Irish Coast, sending 1,198 passengers to their premature, frigid deaths. Of these casualties, 124 were U.S. citizens.[145]

In light of the relatively high number of civilian deaths, the sensational nature of the U-boat assault,[146] and the fact that American celebrities had perished in the attack,[147] the sinking of the *Lusitania* quickly became a major story as the media grappled with the political meaning of the deaths. For weeks, the question on everyone's minds was: "Could the deaths of so many Americans draw the United States into the war?" On May 8 (the day after the attack), the *New York Times* reported that, although the nation's capital was "full of rumors" that Congress would declare war against Germany, "the Government [...] has shown no inclination toward excitement or taking hasty action." President Woodrow Wilson, for his part, was staying mum. "The news that many lives had been sacrificed [...] was given to him at the White House about 1 o'clock this evening, but no word came from him as to what effect this intelligence had on him." But despite Wilson's silence, the *Times* cautioned, "the situation is full of dangerous possibilities."[148] It seemed plausible that the country might go to war over the death of a hundred citizens—an act that, ironically, would entail sending thousands upon thousands of U.S. soldiers to their own premature deaths.

While the federal government took a measured approach to handling the crisis, many citizens, newspaper editors, civic groups, and notable figures across the United States vocally weighed in on the matter. Billy Sunday, the charismatic and popular Evangelist preacher who commanded audiences in the tens of thousands, denounced the sinking of the *Lusitania* as a "damnable" violation of Christian morality:

> It's damnable, damnable, absolutely hellish. Such work deserves the righteous condemnation of every God-fearing person in Christendom. I'd say the same thing if England did it instead of Germany. To think—only to think—that in these supposed civilized days any nation would endanger the lives of thousands of Christians simply because they were under the enemy's flag. Hellish.[149]

Judging the scandalous affair from a position of religious authority, Sunday explicitly called into question German civility and fidelity to Christian morality. Former President Theodore Roosevelt spoke from a more secular perspective, arguing that it is the nation-state's obligation to protect the safety of its citizens, wherever they happen to be. Roosevelt told the press that the attack constituted "warfare against innocent men, women and children traveling on the ocean and on our fellow country women who are among the sufferers." As such, Roosevelt implied, the event warranted a military response from the United States: "It seems inconceivable that we can refrain from taking action in this matter, for we owe it not only to humanity, but to our own national self respect."[150] Roosevelt's veiled argument for war was stated more bluntly by one Mrs. John Philip Schaefer, who, in a letter to the *New York Times*, urged her fellow citizens to demand American entry into the European War: "Where has the spirit of '76, of 1812, of 1860 gone?" Schaefer asked. "Time was when our forefathers did not hesitate to give up their lives unquestioningly for the honor of our country. [...] Let us do more than protest by words."[151] Dr. Alexander Smellie, chairman of the British Association of Atlanta, Georgia, described the *Lusitania* affair as a "horrible offense against humanity" and demanded American belligerence: "It is a terrible thing to plunge a country into war, but in view of the atrocious nature of this latest crime, it is the only logical thing that can be done."[152] The *New York Times* published an editorial from the *Toronto Globe* that asked whether President Wilson "propose[d] to let German submarines [continue to] destroy the lives of American citizens" throughout the future. "Does he still think the mad dog of Europe can be trusted at large? Is it not almost time to join in hunting down the brute?"[153] This cascade of provocative metaphors surely appealed to the imaginations of Roosevelt and likeminded Americans, who considered themselves defenders of civilization and hunters of beasts. Former U.S. Attorney General George W. Wickersham employed different language—the language of sex—when he publicly argued that Germany's "wanton killing of American men, women and children" had effectively neutered the country: "It is now for the American people to decide whether this nation has any virility left." Wickersham criticized President Wilson for maintaining a "sexless policy" of neutrality, and implied that a display of military might—an act of violent revenge—could reinvigorate the nation's sagging masculinity.[154] To instill casualties, it seemed, was to be masculine. To suffer casualties was to be "sexless."

Many citizens and leaders, however, opined against an impetuous rush to war. For them, the arguments to go to war were synecdochical by nature, constructed on just partial (and in some cases, intentionally falsified) information. In a rather eloquent letter to the *Oregonian*, a reader named William Donniges challenged the position taken by Roosevelt and other pro-war advocates: "The comments of Theodore Roosevelt following the sinking of the Lusitania are somewhat vague. Does the gentleman mean that the United States shall go to war with Germany? If that is his idea, he would appear to be suffering with a surplus of Shakespearean east wind and to be taking his usual conversation method of relieving himself." Clearly familiar with Roosevelt's rhetoric, Donniges reminded his fellow countrymen and women that "ample warning was given by Germany as to the dangers of entering the war zone around Great Britain." Besides, Donniges argued, if the nation went to war, "thousands of United States citizens would lose their lives. [...] What would be gained by all this sacrifice?"[155] The *Herald* of Lexington, Kentucky, published a letter from local resident J. J. Dickey, who suggested that, under the rules of war, the German assault on the *Lusitania* had been justified. "It seems to me," Dickey wrote, "American citizens should [be] apprised of the fact that the Lusitania had in her hold munitions of war, such as brass, copper, cartridges, powder of various kinds, and probably the tin to make poison gas for bombs. Such is stated by Dr. Fisher, an American, who was on board."[156] In churches throughout Cleveland Ohio, a city that boasted one of the largest German-American populations in the country, German pastors deplored the loss of American civilians, but defended their homeland's actions. The Reverend J. F. Frederick Keller of Evangelical Luther Christ Church, for example, told his congregation: "I hold Germany is absolutely justified in sending to the bottom a boat which carried nearly a half million dollars' worth of munitions of war. [...] War is war, and the passengers must take their chances just as do those men who go to the front to fight in Flanders."[157] It seemed that for Keller, at least, patriotic devotion outweighed fidelity to universal Christian tenets of nonviolence. The noted Socialist Eugene V. Debs opposed American belligerence, but was thoroughly troubled by the implications of the *Lusitania* affair. Debs argued that Germany's murder of so many innocent Americans indicated "that Prussian militarism has gone stark mad," and that if the Germans were able, they would gladly "overrun this country and set off their asphyxiating bombs, poison the wells, rape the women, mutilate the infirm and murder the children." But despite the *Lusitania* sinking, Debs urged the U.S. government to resist entering the War in Europe. "Moral self-restraint at this crucial hour requires greater courage and is more potent for righteousness and peace than a declaration of war."[158] Sensing that mounting public anger over the sinking of the

Lusitania might actually bring the United States into the war on behalf of the Allied Nations, the German Foreign Office issued a somewhat half-hearted public apology, which stated:

> If England after repeated official and unofficial warnings, considered herself able to declare that that boat ran no risk and thus light-heartedly assumed responsibility for the human life on board a steamer which, owing to its armament and cargo was liable to destruction, the German Government, in spite of its heartfelt sympathy for the loss of American lives, cannot but regret that Americans felt more inclined to trust to English promises rather than to pay attention to the warnings from the German side.[159]

In effect, the German apology deflected responsibility for the lives lost onto the British.

Three days after the sinking of the *Lusitania*, President Wilson emerged in Philadelphia to articulate publicly what course of action, if any, his administration would pursue. Speaking before an audience of 4,000 recently naturalized citizens, Wilson reaffirmed his commitment to maintaining American neutrality[160]—the country, he stated, would not be coaxed into battle:

> America must have the consciousness that on all sides it touches elbows and touches heart with all the nations of mankind. The example of America must be a special example, and must be an example not merely of peace, because it will not fight, but because peace is a healing and elevating influence on the world, and strife is not. [...] There is such a thing as a man being too proud to fight.

The *New York Times* reported that Wilson's speech was met with "a tremendous ovation," a sign that, despite the loss of American life, few citizens (naturalized or otherwise) wanted war.[161] The following day, Wilson released a public note addressed to Germany that declared the assault on the *Lusitania* "to be indefensible under international law." Employing a more acerbic tone than that of his Philadelphia speech, Wilson reiterated the United States' neutral position, but outlined a series of demands, including the cessation of U-boat "attacks on merchantmen carrying non-combatants." Wilson stated that the "usual financial reparation will be sought, although Germany is reminded in effect that no reparation can restore the lives of those sacrificed in the sinking of the Lusitania." In closing, the president extended a vague threat of violence: "It is made plain that the United States will leave nothing undone, either by diplomatic representation or other action, to obtain compliance by Germany with the requests that are made."[162] Wilson's principled and determined, if somewhat toothless, stance seemed to fit the bill. Praising

Wilson's "even temperament and quiet nerves," the *Lexington Herald* urged its readers to

> follow the example set before us by the President of the United States and members of Congress; "do not rock the boat," but sit still and patiently, with Christian fortitude [...] reverently bow our heads amid the shadow of sorrow that enfolds us [...] and breathe a prayer for the departed souls of the innocent victims of this cruel war, including those whom an unrelenting fate decreed should find a watery grave just as the Emerald Isle beckoned them."[163]

Readers in Kentucky were encouraged to practice Christian restraint and, like their president, suppress the urge for revenge. Editors at the *Charlotte Observer* echoed this tone and contributed to what appeared to be a growing cult of personality, writing: "The Observer is not given to irreverence, but [...] it is now strengthened in the conviction that has possessed it for some time that Wilson was a divinely appointed leader of the people."[164] Investors appeared to feel equally blessed to have such a "divinely appointed leader": stocks soared on Wall Street as skittish traders responded favorably to Wilson's prudent approach.[165] For now, at least, the gears of capitalism would not be wrenched by war.

The loss of 124 Americans in the sinking of the *Lusitania* failed to draw the United States into the Great War. The world would not witness American belligerence until two years later. This infamous event, however, had several immediate and significant effects on American attitudes toward the war. First, the imagined scene of American and British civilians dying at the hands of German aggressors surely nudged American sentiment one bit closer to the side of the Allied Nations and one bit further away from the Central Powers.[166] Second, the sinking of the *Lusitania* was, as much as anything, a spectacle of German dominance over European seaboards—a spectacle that revealed the real and disturbing dangers that would be entailed in shipping American soldiers overseas, and their corpses back, should the United States enter the war.

THE PROSPECT OF WAR AND DEATH

The American presidential election of 1916 hinged primarily on the question of U.S. participation in the Great War. On one side was Democratic nominee Woodrow Wilson, who promised to keep the nation out of the war for as long as possible. Reaching out to Midwest and West Coast voters (the majority

of whom opposed the idea of American belligerence) and independent progressives (social workers, sociologists, and intellectuals), Wilson built his
reelection campaign around the slogan, "He Kept Us Out of War." On the
other side was Republican nominee Charles Evans Hughes, who fervently
preached the gospels of military preparedness and U.S. intervention on behalf
of England and its allies. Supported by the always-hawkish former President
Theodore Roosevelt and various pro-war groups (including munitions makers
that jockeyed to cash in on American participation in the conflict), Hughes
sought to raise enthusiasm for war to a fever pitch, and then capitalize on
voters' emotions at the polls. The dynamics of the 1916 election reflected the
conflicting attitudes—one anti-war, the other pro-war—that, for two years,
had dominated American public discourse regarding the possibility of U.S.
belligerence. This section briefly examines the rhetorics of the anti-war and
pro-war movements of 1914–1916, and reveals how both sides addressed the
very real prospect of American soldiers fighting and dying on the apocalyptic
battlefields of Europe.[167]

The pro-war movement originated with the actions of several so-called
"preparedness" lobbies, which saw the distant war in Europe as an opportunity to advance conservative and corporate interests at home. The strongest
of the preparedness groups was the National Security League (NSL), an affiliation of prominent corporation lawyers, Christian preachers, military brass,
bankers, and mega-rich capitalists like Cornelius Vanderbilt, Henry C. Frick,
Simon Guggenheim, and J. P. Morgan. Although the NSL privately supported
the cause of the Allied Nations, the group did not publicly argue for American
intervention at first. Instead, it pushed for measures to "prepare" (i.e., militarize) American society, such as shoring up national defenses by expanding
the army and Navy, instilling a system of universal military training, and
promoting patriotic education and a spirit of national service—measures that
translated into coordinated and successful campaigns opposing the election of
various Congressmen who favored labor unions and government ownership
of the railroads. Progressive reformists like Amos Pinchot were not fooled
by the efforts of the NSL and its ilk, and publicly declared that American
elites were "using the preparedness campaign as an excuse for preaching
the sanctity of American industrial absolutism." Despite Pinchot's warnings,
conservative and jingoistic civic groups like the Veterans of Foreign Wars
(VFW) responded favorably to the patriotic flavor of the NSL's message; in
August of 1915, the VFW issued a public demand that President Wilson steel
the nation for the potential "catastrophe of war."[168] The National Security
League's call for national "preparedness" was gaining traction.

"Preparedness" quickly became a productive term for Republicans, conservatives, and pro-war advocates of all kinds, who, like the NSL, used it as a vehicle to accumulate and mobilize political, social, and financial capital. While the motives of these groups may have varied, their arguments for "preparedness" tended to revolve around two emotionally charged ideas. The first was that the United States was ill equipped to defend itself against foreign invasion. Hudson Maxim, for example, the inventor of smokeless gunpowder and other war technologies, claimed that an enemy invasion of Boston or New York would decimate American forces within a day. "Nothing under heaven we could do would prevent the invaders from capturing the entire country between the Alleghenies and the sea within two weeks," Maxim counseled.[169] Editors at the sensationalist daily rag *New York American* argued that the government should create a military big enough to protect American civilization, "ruled by white men and white thought," from what they described as the "Asiatic hordes being led by Germany" into Europe through Constantinople. "It is our business to prepare this country for attack from every source, from the nations of Europe, from the brown men of Japan, and if necessary from the whole of Europe overrun by Asia."[170] Film studios released profitable, melodramatic, and suggestively titled "photoplays" that made overt arguments for national "preparedness." Movies like *The Battle Cry of Peace* and *The Fall of a Nation* depicted in graphic detail the horrors that a German invasion of the United States would entail.[171] Meanwhile, Major General Leonard Wood, the former Chief of Staff of the U.S. Army and an unofficial spokesperson for munitions makers everywhere, testified before the Senate Committee on Military Affairs that the homeland would not be secure from enemy attack until a system of universal service was adopted to strengthen the size and readiness of the U.S. armed forces.[172] Wood challenged Congress and the president: would they leave the nation in such risk?

The second commonly proffered idea was that military "preparedness" would somehow foster "Americanism," an amorphous, patriotic quality that the nation's ethnically heterogeneous population supposedly lacked. In October of 1915, the National Defense League, the Navy League of the United States, and the National Rifle Association linked "preparedness" with "Americanism" in a publicly issued resolution: "The American people, in order to provide for their needs at home and abroad, for their security from foreign aggression and for the maintenance of the ideals which have inspired the republic from its foundation, must create an efficient [military] sufficient in size to keep the national honor unstained." These associations—which stood to gain mightily from American entry into the Great War—argued that, by increasing the might of the U.S. armed forces and providing military training in public schools, "Americanism [would be] raised above the mere level of politics, [become] a part of our governmental system," and reveal the immigrant "parasites" and "so-called Americans" whose sympathies still rested with their ancestral homelands in Europe.[173] Around the same time, the *New York Times* published a long letter from military expert Frederick A. Kuenzli, who claimed that increased military training in public schools would help forge young American boys into respectable men and citizens:

> Military training is nothing else but a branch of physical training, that gives the boy gait and posture, straightens his spine, throws his shoulders back, and makes him walk erect. In other words, it gives him the manly appearance that you and I appreciate in the common expression, "Isn't he a fine young man?"

Downplaying the potential violence and mass death to which a military build-up could lead, advocates like Kuenzli instead amplified the benefits that "preparedness" might have for ethnic communities, American youth, and the nation as a whole.[174]

As was probably originally intended, the "preparedness" movement morphed into an outright "pro-American intervention" movement. As it did, pro-war agitators set their sights on ideological opponents who stood in their way, publicly lambasting pacifists, Socialists, Democrats, and other groups that sought to avoid U.S. belligerence. The loudest of these pro-war advocates was former President Theodore Roosevelt, who claimed that the United States should fight to protect "our self-respect" and the rights of "France, England and the rest of the civilized world." The championed model of American virility, masculinity, and militarism (the *New York Times* routinely called him "Colonel" instead of "President"), the former "Rough Rider" toured the country to denounce the "mollycoddles," "sissies," and "cowards" (i.e., pacifists and Socialists) who wanted to meet Germany's "policy of blood and iron" with "a policy of milk or water." Roosevelt roared that "if the pacifists are not all poltroons, they teach 'poltroonism,' and if they had their own way would breed a nation of poltroons." Likewise, he urged Americans to "realize that the words of the weakling and the coward, of the pacifist and the poltroon, are worthless to stop wrongdoing."[175] Editors at the *New York Times* advanced Roosevelt's denunciations, decrying the "spineless pacifism" and "opposition to preparedness" that had spread to Midwest states like Kansas.[176] In a similar vein, a *Times* editorial pilloried the "Socialist-Pacifist" students of the City College of New York who had held an anti-war rally at the campus flagpole. "The flag is the symbol of the nation, of what American youths, fit to be

Americans are ready to fight for and to die for," the *Times* opined. "These misled boys should run away from a flagpole. The American flag is nothing to them. It was born, as the nation was born, of war."[177] By contrast, the *Times* was impressed with students at the University of Illinois who hanged an effigy of U.S. Senator Robert M. La Follette, one of the leading figures in the anti-war movement.[178]

As the presidential election of 1916 drew nearer, representatives of the recently allied Progressive and Republican Parties stumped for their candidate, Charles Evans Hughes, mostly by attacking President Wilson's commitment to American neutrality and charging him with softness in defending the nation against German aggression.[179] President Wilson, they claimed, was a man who possessed lofty language but few convictions. Dubbing Wilson's White House as an "Administration of words," Senator Henry Cabot Lodge told an audience of Republican voters in Nantucket: "Behind a great barrier of words, the President has sheltered himself, surrounded by a cloud of phrases; big words with no meaning." In a time of international crisis, Lodge claimed, the nation needed intrepid action, not empty language.[180] The Progressive National Committee released a declaration of principles, which served as a thinly veiled diatribe against Wilson's alleged inaction and lack of courage. "The Wilson Administration has suffered American men, women, and children to be slaughtered [...] on the high seas. [...] It has stood by while the law of nations disappeared from the earth without adequate protest or effective resistance." By resisting the "preparedness" movement and adopting the "futile, cowardly, and unrighteous" principle of "peace at any price," Wilson had "repudiated the faith of our forefathers" and brought the "contempt of the world" upon American citizens. "Our people are becoming impatient of leaders who hold that comfort, prosperity, and material welfare are above honor, self-sacrifice, and patriotism," the Progressives asserted. "They are demanding that principles and policies shall be proclaimed and carried out by a man who has the wisdom to formulate them and the manhood to fight for them."[181] Predictably, the bitterest polemics directed at Wilson came from Roosevelt, who told one receptive audience that the president's refusal to avenge Germany's attack upon the *Lusitania* had amounted to "kissing the bloodstained hand that slapped his face!" At an appearance in Manhattan, Roosevelt spewed that "there should be shadows now" haunting the White House lawn,

the shadows of the men, women and children who have risen from the ooze of the ocean bottom and from graves in foreign lands—the shadows of the helpless whom Mr. Wilson did not dare protect lest he might have to face the danger!

The shadows of babies gasping pitifully as they sank under the waves! The
shadows of women outraged and slain by bandits [...] the shadows of deeds that
were never done, the shadows of lofty words that were followed by no action,
the shadows of the tortured dead![182]

Roosevelt had revenge on his mind, and hoped that more Americans might
too. And just days before the election, Roosevelt told a packed audience at the
Brooklyn Academy of Music that Wilson's cowardice and anti-militaristic
attitudes had left the country "shamefully unprepared" and "helpless in [the]
event of war." Introduced as "a man who is not too proud to fight for his
country," Roosevelt once again tied militarism with Americanism, claiming
that Wilson's reluctance to fight had fostered treacherous sentiments among
the nation's various ethnic groups (particularly German Americans and Irish
Americans):

Thanks to Mr. Wilson, our unpreparedness in naval and military matters is
appalling and our dereliction in duty to humanity at large shocking beyond
description. But our spiritual unpreparedness, thanks to Mr. Wilson, is even
greater than our physical unpreparedness. Mr. Wilson, through his ceaseless
flow of graceful elocution, has bewildered the minds and crippled the sense of
honor of our people. The too-proud-to-fight doctrine is a cloak behind which
the coward hides. [...] It has been the chief cause responsible for the spread of
the spirit of disloyalty in the United States among those who openly or secretly
believe in a divided citizenship. [...] No man will be permanently loyal to a
country that is too proud to fight.

Roosevelt implied that Hughes, if elected, would offer more than words, lead
the country to victory on the battlefields of Europe, and correct the damage
that Wilson had inflicted upon the American people's honor and unity.[183]

Of course, Americans who had paid attention to media coverage of the
Great War's tax on human life knew that intervention would inevitably result
in the deaths of a large, if unknowable, number of U.S. citizen-soldiers. This
unpleasant fact hung over the "preparedness" and pro-war lobbies' exhorta-
tions like a dark cloud, but was rarely addressed head on, in concrete terms.
At best, those in favor of intervention shrouded the certainty of soldierly
deaths in a blanket of star-spangled abstractions and myths. For instance,
while campaigning in Bridgehampton, New York, Hughes preached to an
audience of potential voters: "It is because we had men who were willing
to suffer, to die, to venture and to sacrifice that we have the country, and it
is only by that spirit that we will ever be able to keep a country." Hughes
claimed that by nature, Americans "are not filled with a spirit of militarism."

Nor are they "anxious to get into trouble." But, Hughes declared, "If anybody thinks that the spirit of service and sacrifice is lost and that we have not got the old sentiment of self-respect, he doesn't understand the United States."[184] Hawkish editors at the *Washington Post* made similar allusions to national mythography, insinuating that *true Americans* would be willing to fight and die for their country, just as George Washington, Benjamin Franklin, and "the American revolutionists" had been "ready to make war rather than endure an unjust peace." The *Post* opined:

> We have no fear that the impracticable, illusory, un-American theory of peace at any price has become an obsession with any great number of Americans. The liberties and rights that were bought with blood will be defended by blood, if necessary. They will not be handed over in a dream to the spoiler and the invader. With eternal vigilance, Americans who have received these liberties will guard them and hand them down to their children. They will fight and die rather than surrender them.[185]

Dying, it was argued, was something American men would gladly do in the names of their forefathers and children. But what of the mothers, wives, and girlfriends of soldiers lost in Europe? How would they react to the deaths of their beloved? The "preparedness," pro-war answer to that question was perhaps best enunciated by Lucy Abbot Throop of New York City, who, in a letter to the *New York Times*, proclaimed her supreme faith that American women would exhibit a patriotic Stoicism in wartime:

> You will find that there are many women   in fact, I fancy the great majority of them—who believe men go to war with love of country, self-sacrifice, and true heroism in their hearts, knowing that suffering and death may be their share, but still going gladly. Many women realize that while war is horrible, more horrible than words can say, and that it brings ruin and devastation in its train, it is sometimes necessary, and when the time does come it must be met bravely, promptly, efficiently, and fought to the bitter end. Many—in fact, most—women realize that human life and suffering are the price which has to be paid for the onward sweep of civilization, and that the brave men who have the sorrow and the great honor to be making such tremendous history will not flinch until the task is done—until, at not matter what cost to themselves, they have beaten down the principle of cruelty and hate which is trying to submerge the world.[186]

The notion that American mothers and wives would gladly hand over their children and husbands to defend both a country in which they could not vote and a civilization that had done little to advance the welfare of women was dubious at best, propagandistic at worst.

Opponents of the "preparedness" and pro-war movements offered stiff resistance to the nation's march toward militarism. Some countered Roosevelt and his cohort's vague reasons for belligerence (such as defending the nation's honor and rights abroad, developing "Americanism" at home, and protecting the liberties symbolized by Ol' Glory) with similarly vague reasons as to why the United States should not fight. For instance, some alluded to the Christian doctrine of "turning the other cheek," arguing that it takes "courage not [...] to be bullied into a fight,"[187] while others (particularly those whose hearts were with the Central Powers) evoked the supposedly democratic ideal of "fair play" to oppose an international ganging-up on the already beleaguered German nation. "A few days ago the press of this country yelled for war against Germany," a Columbia, South Carolina, resident wrote to the *State*. "Oh, you gallant, brave boys, after five big nations are already on top of Germany, the chances for America to jump on Germany also, without getting thrashed herself, looked pretty good, eh? But where is the boasted American love of fair play?"[188] Many anti-war advocates, however, cited more tangible reasons for avoiding belligerence. For example, the Woman's Peace Party, a feminist coalition led by Fanny Garrison Villard, Carrie Chapman Catt, and Jane Addams, warned American women of the detrimental effects that mobilization would have on their quest for suffrage. As historian David M. Kennedy puts it: "They felt that war, which would glorify the material and virile virtues, posed a particular threat to the feminist movement, struggling as it was to minimize sexual differences and to discredit the spurious claim that male primacy in the sexual order derived from the primeval prowess of men as warriors."[189] Economics, not gender equality, was the crucial issue for automaker Henry Ford, who publicly insisted that American neutrality and the pursuit of peace in Europe was "not a sentimental proposition, but a business proposition." Ford advised his fellow magnates (many of whom were salivating at the thought of U.S. military contracts) that the Great War was suppressing innovation and international trade, and that "there is ten times as much prosperity in peace work as in war manufactures."[190] Meanwhile, less capitalistic voices in the anti-war movement argued for neutrality from a polar opposite perspective, denouncing the corporate profiteering and (in the words of Yale professor Irving Fisher) "prostitution of public interest to private interests" that militarism and belligerence would inevitably entail.[191] To unveil and confront these threats, Democratic Congressman James H. Davis of Texas, a self-proclaimed "Preparedness Foe," introduced a bill that mandated "that each corporation shall be forced to pay the cost of maintaining one soldier or sailor for each $50,000 of capital and surplus in excess of $250,000 and in time of war for each $25,000 in excess of $75,000." Likewise, immense wartime taxes would be placed on the personal incomes, inheritances, dowries, and incomes by foreign investment of the wealthiest American citizens. "Violators of the law, if it becomes one, Mr. Davis would punish by treating them as deserters," wrote the *Washington Post*. "In war time they would be shot." If Davis had his way, he would pop the upper class's bubble before it even expanded.

The anti-capitalistic strain of Davis's proposed legislation reflected both the media coverage of the Great War's carnage and the worldview of anarchists, the American Socialist Party, and the Industrial Workers of the World—radical, yet influential, leftist groups that vigorously opposed entering a war in which (as they saw it) the proletariat of each side had nothing to win and much to lose. Drawing upon popular understandings of the Great War's tax on human life, socialist and union leader Eugene V. Debs publicly argued that the ongoing World War had resulted from economic competition among European nations for international markets and was a conflict between two groups of capitalists that had little concern for the welfare of those who were called to fight and die. "Let the capitalists do the fighting," Debs wrote in an editorial for the *Nation Rip-Saw*:

> Do that and there will never be another war. Not even a skirmish. They are not fools enough to go out and kill one another and the fools they hire for that purpose they hold in contempt.
>
> The capitalists tell us it is patriotic to fight for your country and shed your blood for the flag. Very well! Let them set the example.
>
> It is their country; they own it and therefore according to their logic it is their patriotic duty to fight and die for it and be brought home riddled with bullets and covered with flowers as shining examples of patriotic duty to the youth of the nation. [...]
>
> You never had a country to fight for and never will have as much as an inch of one as long as you are fool enough to make a target of your bodies for the profit and glory of your masters.
>
> Let the capitalists do their own fighting and furnish their own corpses and there will never be another war on the face of the earth.

Debs's critiques of capitalism and nationalism were seconded by Morris Hillquit, founder and leader of the American Socialist Party, who cited "commercial rivalry, imperialism, and militarism" as the main causes of "the heavy tragedy of blood-stained Europe." Hillquit attacked Roosevelt and other proponents of "preparedness" for "cultivating the deadly germs of strife and bloodshed" through the abuse of Americans' sense of patriotism.

Anarchist Emma Goldman (dubbed "a professional lawbreaker" by the *New York Times*) attacked "the big interests [...] who are growing phenomenally rich by the manufacture of military supplies," and asserted that the Great War would have lasted only a few months "had the American munition clique and food speculators not been given the opportunity to supply warring Europe with the means to keep up the slaughter." Max Eastman and other writers for *The Masses*, a monthly periodical devoted to Socialist politics, composed scathing essays that denounced "bloodthirsty ministers," "war-mongering Christians," "unscrupulous patriots," and members of the "owning class" who would happily push the nation into war. In 1916, a popular sticker issued by the International Workers of the World advised members of the underclass:

DON'T BE A SOLDIER. BE A MAN

Join the I. W. W. and Fight on the Job for Yourself and Your Class

Journalist and communist activist John Reed was perhaps the most effective at putting the relationship between class and war into stark relief. In March of 1917, Reed published an essay in *The Masses* that appealed to sentiments against the war's savagery and asked:

> Whose war is this? Not mine. I know that hundreds of thousands of American workingmen employed by our great financial "patriots" are not paid a living wage. I have seen poor men sent to jail for long terms without a trial, and even without any charge. Peaceful strikers, and their wives and children, have been shot to death, burned to death, by private detectives and militia men. The rich have steadily become richer, and the cost of living higher, and the workers proportionally poorer. These toilers don't want war—not even civil war. But the speculators, the employers, the plutocracy—they want it, just as they did in Germany and in England; and with lies and sophistries they will whip up our blood until we are savage—and then we'll fight and die for them.[192]

It appeared that, if given the choice, many likeminded American workers would never willingly risk their lives in a war that had little or nothing to do with their own material interests.

Whereas those in favor of American "preparedness" and intervention in Europe addressed the prospect of mass casualties tangentially by casting U.S. soldiers' deaths as an unavoidable, but noble, sacrifice that patriotic citizens would be willing to make in time of war, those who opposed "preparedness" and intervention cited the prospect of soldierly death as *a prime reason not to militarize and fight*. Appeals for a greater consideration of the human cost of American belligerence came in different shades, from various corners of the anti-war movement. Some were delivered by socialists, union leaders, and radical leftists, who cogently argued that the majority of future U.S. casualties would be members of the large American working classes, not members of the so-called plutocracy. Anarchist Ricardo Flores Magón, for example, urged workers to think of the plight of their counterparts in Europe, "imbeciles" who "die fighting for the glory of their own exploiters." In a November, 1914, essay for his Los Angeles-based magazine *Regeneración*, Magón advised his readers to contemplate the daily reports of mass death, and to reject what would inevitably be their own "march to the slaughterhouse":

> How many have died in the present conflict? If one said that a million workers have died, that would be a low estimate of the number of lives lost. But let's suppose that the number lost in this evil war is a million; this would signify that a million families find themselves without protection because their men were so stupid that they preferred to march to the slaughterhouse to defend the interests of their exploiters rather than to go to war in defense of the interests of their class.[193]

For Magón and his cohort, the Great War was a rich man's war that should be fueled by the blood of the wealthy and "stupid," not the poor and wise. As James H. Maurer, president of the Pennsylvania Federation of Labor, told a joint Senate-House military committee in 1916, "The workingmen will refuse to be cannon fodder for [capitalists'] wars."[194] This notion was endorsed by none other than famed public figure and activist Helen Keller. In a 1916 speech at Carnegie Hall, under the auspices of the Women's Peace Party and the Labor Forum, Keller contextualized the prospect of American participation in the European War thusly:

> Every modern war has had its root in exploitation. The Civil War was fought to decide whether the slaveholders of the South or the capitalists of the North should exploit the West. The Spanish-American War decided that the United States should exploit Cuba and the Philippines. [...] The present war is to decide who shall exploit the Balkans, Turkey, Persia, Egypt, India, China, Africa. And we are whetting our sword to scare the victors into sharing the spoils with us. Now, the workers are not interested in the spoils; they will not get any of them anyway.[195]

For Keller, the facts and the stakes were clear: U.S. intervention in the war would benefit the rich and devastate all others.

Concerns over the inevitable loss of life that American belligerence would entail were also voiced by interested ethnic and professional groups. A coalition of German Americans from Toledo, Ohio, for instance, publicly urged government officials to reflect upon the devastating impact that mass death would have on American families: "The present crisis may plunge our nation into this world war, thus adding the lives of untold thousands of our men to the already long list of fathers, sons, and husbands who up to now have been sacrificed on the blood-stained battlefields of Europe."[196] Dr. Abraham Jacobi, the former president of the American Medical Association, was worried about the negative effects that "the tax of blood and brain" would have on American society writ large. "We see much talk in the newspapers of the number of men killed in present combat, but with the mere statement of their number the accounts stop," Jacobi told the *New York Times* in 1916. "When we see reports of property destroyed we are likely to see, also, estimates of its value. Such estimates never follow the accounts of human life destruction. That is puzzling." Borrowing from (what seems to the modern eye like) Social Darwinian thought, Jacobi warned that the destruction of American soldiers ("the best male part of [the] nation") upon the battlefields of Europe would result in "an even greater social loss": an increase in "physical and moral degeneracy and poverty," "spiritual deterioration," and "psychological and mental loss" here at home.[197]

While anti-war advocates like Jacobi discussed the inevitable effects of mass death in broad societal terms, others addressed the matter at the more personal and emotional level of motherhood. In a 1914 anti-war poem entitled, "Who Pays?" Edna Valentine Trapnell argued that only women "know by each birththroe the value of human life":

Cheers and shouts greet the headlines that tell of the battles won.
Who remembers the death-wrecked bodies motionless under the sun?
"Victor stood to our banners, only a handful lost—"
Only! We bore those bodies, and we know what bodies cost!
(Mothers and wives of the soldiers dead—who better can gauge the cost?)
[…] Counselors, kings, and rulers, ye take what ye cannot give.
Can ye say to the things in the trenches, "Be whole, rise up and live?"
Do ye know—who have killed your thousands by a word from a death-tipped pen—
One little pang of the cost to those who breed your fighting men?
(Who pays, dear Lord, for their bodies and souls
but the mothers and wives of men?)[198]

Trapnell's poem was meant to remind Americans that rapturous eulogies and military ribbons could never bring the departed back to life; that government officials who signed young men's death warrants could never understand nor experience the unique suffering of "mothers and wives of the soldiers dead"; that women, the bearers of human life, occupied an almost unrebuttable position from which to protest policies of death. Similar ideas appeared in other anti-war pieces of popular art, perhaps most notably in the 1915 song, "I Didn't Raise My Boy to Be a Soldier." Written and composed by Alfred Bryan and Al Piantadosi, this pacifist song purported to be the lament of a lonesome mother whose son has been killed in the Great War, and argued that if mothers around the world stood together in solidarity, they could bring an end to the fighting in Europe:

Ten million soldiers to the war have gone,
Who may never return again.
Ten million mothers' hearts must break,
For the ones who died in vain.
Head bowed down in sorrowin her lonely years,
I heard a mother murmur thro' her tears:
I didn't raise my boy to be a soldier,
I brought him up to be my pride and joy,
Who dares to put a musket on his shoulder,
To shoot some other mother's darling boy?

The song was a smash hit; over 700,000 copies of the music sheet were sold in the first eight weeks of its release, and recordings flew off the shelves.[199] The anti-war anthem became so popular that Theodore Roosevelt, in true fashion, felt compelled to curb its momentum. "As for the woman who approves the song, 'I Did Not Raise My Boy to Be a Soldier,' her place is in China," Roosevelt publicly snorted, "by preference, in a harem in China—and not in the United States. [...] Every woman who has not raised her boy to be a soldier at need has, in unwomanly fashion, striven to put a double burden on some other boy whose mother has a patriotic soul."[200] Thus, for this famous saber-rattler, pacifism was something akin to prostitution—an act that was diametrically opposed to traditional American values.

Seeking the votes of a populace that seemed evenly divided over the war issue, President Wilson strategically pursued a political middle ground where he could relax his neutral stance while simultaneously expressing his desire for peace. David M. Kennedy tells us: "By the late summer of 1915, moving to protect his vulnerable right political flank, he had begun to indicate his support for what he called 'reasonable preparedness.'" As the campaign season progressed, Wilson submitted to Congress a proposal for the expansion of the military and Navy,[201] and told an audience in Cincinnati, Ohio: "This is the last war that involves the world that the United States can keep out of."[202] At the same time, his election committee made widespread use of the anti-war phrase, "He Kept Us Out of the War," printing it in handbills and plastering it on billboards throughout the country. Wilson further muddied the political waters by co-opting the major arguments of the "preparedness" movement: he publicly agreed with his foes that the nation's armed forces were dangerously small and weak, and that there was a disturbing lack of "Americanism" among disloyal "hyphenates" (a disparaging term for Irish Americans, German Americans, and other ethnic groups).[203] Naturally, Wilson managed to outrage both progressive leaders, who fervently opposed militarism, belligerence, and xenophobia,[204] and conservative leaders, who considered him a hypocrite. "President Wilson appeals for support on the ground that he has kept us out of war," Roosevelt correctly argued, "and now [...] he says that never again is the United States to keep out of such a war. [...] What does he mean by promising in the future the exact reverse of what he has done in the past and is now doing in the present?"[205] It seemed that Wilson was not required to provide answers to such pointed questions, as his middle-of-the road, pro-"preparedness," anti-war position successfully appealed to enough centrist voters on both sides of the political spectrum. By promising to strengthen the nation's military might while simultaneously casting his opponent, Charles Evans Hughes, as a trigger-happy warmonger who was eager to send American boys to their muddy graves in Europe,[206] Wilson was able to win the 1916 election by a narrow margin.[207] While the race had been close, many considered his victory a referendum against war. As one British dignitary commented at the time: "The elections have clearly shown that the great mass of the Americans desire nothing so much as to keep out of the war."[208] Still, Americans should not have been completely surprised when, five months after the election, on April 2, 1917, President Wilson asked Congress to declare war on Germany. For on January 31, 1916, while speaking before 15,000 people at a campaign rally in Milwaukee, Wisconsin, Wilson had indicated his willingness to sacrifice American soldiers upon the battlefields of Europe:

> God forbid that we should have to use the blood of America to freshen the color of that flag. But if it should ever be necessary again to assert the majesty and integrity of those ancient and honorable principles, that flag will be colored once more and in being colored will be glorified and purified.[209]

Indeed, in less than two years the color of Old Glory would be freshened with the blood of young conscripted American men.

After consuming disturbing "uncensored" media coverage of the Great War for two and a half years, the majority of American citizens were dead set against the idea of entering this sordid, evil, and destructive affair. Who, in

Figure 1.1   Dog tag for U.S. Private Seymour Prestwood, killed in action September 26, 1918. U.S. National Archives and Records Administration, Record Group 92.

her or his right mind, would want to see the United States enter a war that had diminished the possibilities of patriotic death, just killing, collective sacrifice, proper burial, and satisfactory public commemoration? Who would gladly send American men overseas to be utterly destroyed or disgustingly maimed by terrible new war technologies? Who would idly stand by as American men were sent off to butcher the men of other nations? Who could support entering a war that had already claimed the lives of millions, and left countless families without any hope of reclaiming fallen soldiers' remains? The graphic reporting of the Great War's many brutal and negative aspects between 1914 and 1917 undoubtedly fostered deep and widespread anti-war sentiments, and shaped public imaginations about the calamities that belligerence would entail. As we will see in subsequent chapters, media coverage of the Great War and the public discourse it cultivated during the period of American neutrality would, in time, directly inform and shape official wartime policies (such as media censorship and compulsory military service), official postwar policies (such as repatriation of the dead and the establishment of overseas cemeteries), and American vernacular and ideology concerning the sacrifice, nobility, treatment and commemoration of U.S. soldiers killed in action.

NOTES

1. In a letter to the editor of the *State*, Columbia, South Carolina, resident Frithzof Knudsen spoke to the (easily abused) power newspapers had on the shaping

of public opinion: "In my opinion the present bad feeling between this country and Germany is entirely due to the gross ignorance of the American newspaper men with regard to European affairs. And as a majority of the American people derive their knowledge of current events from the newspapers, the American point of view relative to the present war is completely distorted." See "Is Perfectly Neutral," *State*, June 18, 1915, 6.

2. David Paul Nord, *Communities of Journalism: A History of American Newspapers and Their Readers* (Urbana, IL: University of Illinois Press, 2001), 225–45.

3. Schudson writes: "From the 1920s on, the idea that human beings individually and collectively construct the reality they deal with has held a central position in social thought." See Michael Schudson, *Discovering the News: A Social History of American Newspapers* (New York: Basic, 1978), 5–6.

4. For instance, two years before the war James Keeley, the chief editor of the *Chicago Tribune* and the *Chicago Herald*, famously told a group of journalism students at the University of Notre Dame: "In publishing a newspaper you endeavor to print what the people want to read." James Keeley, *Newspaper Work: An Address Delivered Before the Students in the Course of Journalism at Notre Dame University, Nov. 26, 1912* (n.p., n.d.), pamphlet in library of the Chicago Historical Society, 2, quoted in Nord, *Communities*, 249.

5. Nord, *Communities*, 280.

6. Ibid, 246–77.

7. "The Press and the Public Discourse," *Center Magazine* 20 (March–April 1987): 4, quoted in Nord, *Communities*, 6.

8. Reflecting upon Hollywood actor "Fatty" Arbuckle's rape scandal of 1921, newspaper magnate William Randolph Hearst remarked that sensationalized stories of Arbuckle's case "sold more newspapers than any event since the sinking of the *Lusitania*." See: Wanda Felix, "Fatty," *Review of Arts, Literature, Philosophy and the Humanities* (Fall 1995), http://www.ralphmag.org/fatty.html (accessed February 5, 2017).

9. Philip Gibbs, "Vivid Narrative of Great Retreat," *New York Times*, August 31, 1914, 1.

10. "7,000 Dead Where Bodies Were Used as Rampart," *Washington Post*, September 17, 1914, 1.

11. "Thousands Slain by Belgian Guns," *Washington Post*, October 3, 1914, 1.

12. "Flanders Front a Vast Cemetery," *New York Times*, February 27, 1915, 4. Note: I am not distinguishing between wire services, syndicated reporting, and original stories, for all three appeared in a swirling, inseparable manner to readers on a daily basis.

13. Quoted in David A. Copeland ed., *The Greenwood Library of American War Reporting, Vol 5: World War I and World War II, The European Theater* (Westport, CT: Greenwood Press, 2005), 46.

14. "French Machine Guns and Rifles Pour Death into the Ranks of Kaisermen," March 5, 1916, 1.

15. "Acres of Dead and Dying in Front of Trenches Along Dardanelles," *Washington Post*, October 17, 1915, 3.

16. "Terrible Battle Still Raging in France," *Aberdeen Daily News*, April 9, 1915, 1.

17. "Frightful Cost of the War in Humanity," *Wall Street Journal*, April 24, 1916, 1.

18. The notion that neither side considered veneration of the dead to be a priority was supported by the fact that battles could take place in even the most holy of sites: historic village cemeteries. On July 13, 1915, the *New York Times* reported that "a German gas attack, followed by hand-to-hand fighting with bomb and bayonet" at the Souchez Cemetery (in a critical zone between Lens and Lille, France) had left the Germans "masters of the shattered burial ground." See "Germans Capture Souchez Cemetery," 3.

19. "Sanitary Commission Named to Purify the Battlefields in Western Poland," April 25, 1915, 18.

20. "Wounded Left on Field to Die," September 12, 1914, 5.

21. "Somme Offensive Described in Graphic Terms by Irish Private Who Took Part," *Washington Post*, August 13, 1916, 1; "Braves Fire For Dead," *Washington Post*, March 28, 1915, 16.

22. See, for instance, "Truce on Dniester Front," *New York Times*, July 11, 1915, 5.

23. For example, see "Zeppelins Harry Fighters," *New York Times*, October 25, 1914, 2.

24. "Allies Gain Slowly Along Dardanelles," *New York Times*, May 17, 1915, 3.

25. See, for example, "Invasion Lags in Serb Passes," *New York Times*, November 12, 1915, 1.

26. See "A Young Frenchman's Narrative of Trench Horrors at Fort Vaux," *New York Times*, June 14, 1916, 12; "Story of War Told by Lines of Crosses," *Idaho Daily Statesman*, December 14, 1915, 7.

27. "Neuve Chapelle a Graveyard," *Los Angeles Times*, April 17, 1915, 12.

28. "Belgians Retire From Louvain Toward Antwerp," *Wall Street Journal*, August 21, 1914, 4.

29. "German Walls of Iron Hold 'Hell of Death' Battlelines between Arras and Ypres," *Washington Post*, June 28, 1915, 1.

30. "Grave Danger That Soldiers of the Disbanded Armies May Scatter Epidemics Throughout Europe and America," *Washington Post*, August 22, 1915, SM1.

31. "American Barber's Grim War Story," *New York Times*, June 4, 1916, SM1.

32. "Conditions in Poland Described as Terrible," *Los Angeles Times*, July 4, 1915, 12.

33. "Frost New Terror of War," *New York Times*, November 6, 1914, 4.

34. "Smoking Out Germans," June 27, 1915, 17.

35. "Spiritualism," *Washington Post*, December 5, 1915, E9.

36. "Cosmic Bestiality of War, a Phantasmagoria of Sin," *Los Angeles Times*, October 22, 1915, 11.

37. "Europe's Unmarked Graves," *Macon Daily Telegraph*, September 6, 1914, 4.

38. "Flags Fly in All Fields," *Washington Post*, August 8, 1915, R4.

39. "Villages in Ruins," *Oregonian*, December 5, 1914, 3.

40. John T. McCutcheon, "Pitiful Havoc is Left in War's Wake," *Oregonian*, October 2, 1914, 1.

41. "Red Death in Europe," *Los Angeles Times*, March 26, 1915, 1.

42. "Plague of Diseases Prostrates Serbia," *New York Times*, March 20, 1915, 4.

43. "What Lipton Saw in Stricken Serbia," *New York Times*, March 23, 1915, 2.

44. "Argue for Peace, But Back Wilson," *New York Times*, May 17, 1915, 2.

45. "War's Dead for Glycerin?" *Washington Post*, May 30, 1915, E4.

46. "Women, Too, Are at War," *Kansas City Star*, February 21, 1915, 9A.

47. "War Brides," *Miami Herald*, March 9, 1915, 5.

48. "Staggering Cost of War in Human Lives," *San Jose Evening News*, October 31, 1914, 4.

49. "Will Women Rule After the World War?" *Washington Post*, August 22, 1915, SM 2.

50. Gwynne Dyer, *War* (New York: Crown, 1985), 81.

51. "Ten Million Men Toll of World War," *Los Angeles Times*, March 12, 1917, 12.

52. Wilhelm Lamszus, *The Human Slaughter-House: Scenes from the War that Is Sure to Come* (New York: Frederick A. Stokes Company, 1913), 103.

53. Ibid, 112–13.

54. "'The Human Slaughter House'—The Supreme Horrors of Modern War," *Washington Post*, August 30, 1914, 48.

55. "Hayes on Battle Line," *Washington Post*, October 8, 1914, 2.

56. See, for instance, "War—On, Beneath and Above the Waves," *Washington Post*, September 20, 1914, SM3.

57. "Air Pressure Kills When Shells Explode," *New York Times*, January 25, 1915, 3.

58. Granville Fortescue, "Entire Fort Wiped Out by Shell," *Washington Post*, December 10, 1916, ES13.

59. "Liquid Fire Attack Failed," *New York Times*, March 6, 1915, 3.

60. "French 'Fire Curtain' Is Deadly in Effect," *New York Times*, April 11, 1916, 2.

61. "American Barber's Grim War Story."

62. "Plea to Wilson for Peace After Visit to Scenes of Slaughter on West Front," December 10, 1916, 3.

63. "Advertisement," *Columbus Ledger*, October 2, 1916, 8.

64. "Official Pictures Show Tragedies of War," *Duluth News-Tribune*, December 31, 1916, 6.

65. "What High-Speed Bullets Do," *Washington Post*, February 28, 1915, M4; "France Prepared to Use Gas Bombs as Reprisal for Dumdum Bullets," *Washington Post*, August 26, 1914, 4; and "What Dum-Dum Bullets Are," *Wall Street Journal*, September 14, 1914, 4.

66. The common postwar idea that soldiers of the Great War had been "cannon fodder" was not an exaggeration, as over seventy-five percent of battlefield deaths in World War I were caused by long-range cannon fire. See Albert C. Manucy, *Artillery Through The Ages: A Short Illustrated History of the Cannon, Emphasizing Types Used in America* (Darby, PA: Diane Publishing, 1994), 20.

67. "Men Torn to Pieces," October 9, 1914, 1.

68. "American Barber's Grim War Story."

69. "Wounded from Russia Suffer Hardships," *Idaho Daily Statesman*, December 13, 1914, 1.

70. "French General's Wound Fatal," 3.

71. "What Shell Shock Is," *Washington Post*, November 7, 1915, MS4.

72. "At the Front in France and Belgium," *New York Times*, August 8, 1915, 61.

73. "Face Mending New Science," *Washington Post*, September 24, 1916, MT4.

74. See Susan M. Schweik, *The Ugly Laws: Disability in Public* (New York: New York University Press, 2009), 1–5. For more on this topic, see Joanna Bourke, *Dismembering the Male: Men's Bodies, Britain, and the Great War* (Chicago: University of Chicago Press, 1996); Seth Koven, "Remembering and Dismemberment," *American Historical Review* 99.4 (1994).

75. "Agonized Throngs Await the Arrival of 'Forever Unfit,'" *Philadelphia Inquirer*, April 2, 1916, 2.

76. The *Washington Post* described similar scenes in France, where, supposedly, women were expected to accept their loved ones' disfigurements with grace and charity: "If her 'fileul' should be wounded, the 'marraine' devotes her best efforts to lightening the cares of his convalescence. And if he should come out of the hospital crippled or blinded or carrying the broken wreck of a once hale body, she it is who searches night and day to ease the broken soldier's path in life." See "Glory of France Revealed in Cheerful Heroism With Which Soldiers and Civilians Repel Teutonic Invaders," *Washington Post*, August 27, 1916, ES3.

American newspapers also reported that the Reverand Ernest Houghton, a rector in Bristol, England, had launched a "League for the Marrying of Broken Heroes." Pairing severely injured soldiers with "spinsters and widows," the program would help diminish in England the stigma of disfigurement. The *Los Angeles Times* wryly noted, however: "The allotment will be made by chance. Maybe when the one-legged man sees the lady he has drawn in the matrimonial lottery he will say, 'Oh, take me back to the hospital.'" See "Lame Marriages," *Los Angeles Times*, October 16, 1915, II4; "'League for Marrying of Broken Heroes,'" *New York Times*, October 14, 1915, 1.

77. "Germany Trains Her War-Maimed Heroes, as Well as Her Crippled Children, to Be Self-Supporting," *Washington Post*, September 17, 1916, A3.

78. "Somme Offensive."

79. See, for instance, "Unexpected Moral Changes Produced by the War," *Idaho Daily Statesman*, September 17, 1916, 6.

80. "What Soldiers Dream About," *Idaho Daily Statesman*, March 7, 1915, 3.

81. "Unexpected Moral Changes."

82. "Boise Boy Gets Trench Letter," *Idaho Daily Statesman*, October 26, 1916, 8.

83. "On the Paths of Glory," *Kansas City Star*, March 19, 1915, 3B.

84. Georges Le Hir, "German Verdun Drive Fails Woefully," *Los Angeles Times*, May 22, 1916, 12.

85. "Army Offenders Tied to Wagons," *The Duluth News-Tribune*, December 31, 1916, 10.

86. "American Barber's Grim War Story."

87. "Common Sense About the War," *New York Times*, November 22, 1914, SM1.

88. "France Protests Against Bombardment of Cathedral," *Columbus Enquirer-Sun*, September 22, 1914, 5.

89. "Louvain to Blame, Germany's Report," *New York Times*, September 22, 1914, 4.

90. "Austrian Red Book Charges Atrocities," *New York Times*, April 16, 1915, 2.

91. "War Appears to Be Butchery, Declares Rt. Rev. M'Golrick," *Duluth News-Tribune*, October 5, 1914, 2.

92. "Frightful Cost of the War in Humanity," *Wall Street Journal*, April 24, 1916, 1.

93. "Competitive-Butchery," *Philadelphia Inquirer*, February 10, 1916, 8.

94. "Pope Calls War Suicide of Europe; Again Appeals for Just, Lasting Peace," *New York Times*, March 6, 1916, 1.

95. This hateful attitude that infected European civilian life influenced public discussions regarding, among other things, the treatment of enemy soldiers' bodily remains. For instance, in 1916, British officials ignited a controversy by suggesting that the crew of a destroyed German zeppelin would receive a military funeral in England. "It is unfortunate the British official mind is so utterly out of touch with the public mind," wrote the *Evening Star* of London. "It is perhaps not too late to reconsider this egregious official blunder and to give these baby killers a plain, decent funeral." See "Plain Burial for Zep Crew," *Kansas City Star*, September 5, 1916, 10.

96. Fortescue, "Entire Fort."

97. "Germany Objects to Colored troops," *New York Times*, September 16, 1915, 2; and "Wild Night Ride of Verdun Wounded," *New York Times*, December 18, 1916, 2.

98. "Dead Canadian Officer Impaled; Soldiers Think He Was Crucified," *Washington Post*, May 16, 1915, 15; "French Officer Recites Atrocities," *New York Times*, November 21, 1915, 2; "Germans Say French Tortured Wounded," *New York Times*, October 3, 1914, 2; "Girls Mutilated, Children Beheaded, Wounded Foe Drowned by Germans," *Washington Post*, September 25, 1914, 5; and "'Missing' Men Return," *Washington Post*, September 27, 1914, R4. See also, "French Atrocity Charged," *Oregonian*, September 25, 1914, 4; "Germany Accuses France," *Wall Street Journal*, October 22, 1914, 4; and, "War News from Berlin," *New York Times*, March 20, 1915, 3.

99. "'Earless Peter,' Death Dealer," *Washington Post*, July 19, 1916, 4.

100. "Soldatik Interesting Views of the Fighting," *San Jose Mercury Herald*, March 14, 1915, 30.

101. "Unbelievable," *Idaho Daily Times*, October 6, 1914, 4.

102. See, for examples: "Zeppelin Bombs Fall in Antwerp," *New York Times*, August 26, 1914; "A Woman's War Time Diary; When the Zeppelin Bomb Fell in Paris," *Grand Forks Daily Herald*, October 7, 1914, 4.

103. "Berlin Denies Repulses," *New York Times*, October 16, 1914, 1.

104. "Tells of Austrian Savagery in Serbia," *New York Times*, May 18, 1915, 3.

105. "Millions Starving in War-Torn Poland," *New York Times*, July 2, 1915, 4.

106. "Burn Babies to Death," *Washington Post*, September 14, 1916, 2.

107. See "Torpedoes Sink 2 British Ships Life Loss Heavy," *Fort Worth Star-Telegram*, March 29, 1915, 1; "Murder on the High Seas," *New York Times*, November 12, 1915, 10; and, "Fifty Lives Lost in U-Boat Attack on the Sussex," *New York Times*, March 26, 1916.

108. "Died in Fleeing Kurds," *Washington Post*, April 26, 1915, 3.

109. "Armenian Atrocities," *Lexington Herald*, December 5, 1915, 1.

110. "Moslem Butchery Grows in Horror," *State*, November 27, 1915, 1.

111. "What Father Dakras Saw of Massacres in Turkey," *Washington Post*, November 28, 1915, M5.

112. Cate Haste, "The Machinery of Propaganda," in *Propaganda*, ed. Robert Jackall (New York: University Press, 1995), 105–36.

113. FirstWorldWar.com, http://www.firstworldwar.com/source/london1839.htm, "Primary Documents - Treaty of London, 1839," (accessed January 7, 2010).

114. "Frenchmen in Armored Motors Hunt Foe With All Guns Going," *Washington Post*, October 17, 1914, 2.

115. "Mother's Simple Story Proof of German Guilt, Says French Courrier," *Washington Post*, September 27, 1914, 4.

116. "Most Hideous Crimes in the History of Civilization Have Been Traced to Germans in Invasion of Belgium," *Macon Daily Telegraph*, May 13, 1915, 1.

117. "Women and Children as Shields While the Enemy Dig Trenches," *Washington Post*, November 29, 1914, W4.

118. "Hear Belgian Side Is Mercier's Plea," *New York Times*, February 2, 1916, 3.

119. "Tells of Slaughter Near Muelhausen," *New York Times*, August 23, 1914, 2.

120. "Teutons Kill Priests," *Washington Post*, January 24, 1915, R5.

121. "Unspeakable Atrocities Committed by Germans in Belgium Premeditated," *Idaho Daily Statesman*, May 13, 1915, 1.

122. "Cavell Execution Is Held to Be Butchery," *Duluth News-Tribune*, October 23, 1915, 9.

123. "Died Like a Heroine," *Washington Post*, October 23, 1915, 1.

124. "The Case of Edith Cavell," *New York Times*, October 31, 1915, SM1.

125. "Woman Spy's Death Epochal," *Oregonian*, November 28, 1915, 11.

126. "Warns the English of Atrocity Tales," September 27, 1914, 3.

127. "Letter to the Editor," October 25, 1915, 4.

128. Like most evidence of the "Rape of Belgium," these dairy entries were fed to American newspapers by the French War Office. "Use Soldiers' Diaries to Answer Denials," *New York Times*, January 22, 1915, 2.

129. "Tabulating Butchery," *State*, May 15, 1915, 4.

130. "The Crime Unpardonable," *Philadelphia Inquirer*, October 29, 1915, 10.

131. "France Unites to Honor Its Marne Dead," *Idaho Daily Statesman*, September 11, 1916, 1; Nixola Greeley-Smith, "Noble Women of France Give Loved Ones to Save Nation, but Do Not Weep, Says Countess DePerigny," *Washington Post*, June 11, 1916, MT3; and, "Women of France Changed by War," *New York Times*, May 30, 1915, SM18.

132. "London Puts on No Mourning Garb," *New York Times*, April 5, 1915, 2.

133. "Finds All England Alive to War Work," *New York Times*, September 18, 1915, 4.

134. "Sir James Barrie Looks for Long War," *New York Times*, September 18, 1914, 4.

135. "War Silence Crazes Women; Censorship Also Has Caused Many Thousands of Suicides," *Washington Post,* December 9, 1914, 4.

136. "Many Become War 'Widows,'" *Washington Post,* October 1, 1916, S4.

137. "War Levels All Classes," *Fort Worth Star-Telegram,* July 30, 1915, 5.

138. "Widowed by the War," *Washington Post,* April 25, 1915, E11.

139. "Conan Doyle Is Converted; Famous Writer Declares He Now Believes Spiritualism," *Miami Herald,* November 28, 1916, 11; and "Science and Spiritualism," *Oregonian,* January 15, 1917, 7.

140. See, for examples: "Alfred Ernst of St. Louis Is Dead," *Kansas City Star,* February 15, 1917, 2; "Norman Prince Dies From His Injuries," *New York Times,* October 16, 1916, 2; "Obituary 1—No Title," *New York Times,* July 12, 1915, 7; "Obituary 2—No Title," *New York Times,* June 24, 1915, C3; "Two Americans Killed," *New York Times,* June 26, 1915, 2; and, "U.S. Youth Killed in Egypt," *Washington Post,* September 29, 1915, 2.

141. "Alan Seeger, Soldier and Poet," *New York Times,* December 24, 1916, BR570. See also: "American Killed at Loos; W. M. Nicholls, Annapolis Football Player, Among British Dead," *New York Times,* October 1, 1915, 2.

142. "Tribute to American Dead," *New York Times,* May 31, 1916, 3.

143. I was able to find only one article from this period that discusses in any detail the feelings of Americans who lost someone in the fighting. On June 25, 1916, the *Washington Post* published an article about Mr. and Mrs. John Jay Chapman of New York City, whose son Victor died while fighting with the Franco-American flying corps. The *Post* described the couple's stoic response to their son's death report: "Chapman's parents [...] received the news of their son's death with great calmness. [...] When told that the aeroplane fell within the French lines, Mr. Chapman said, 'Good!' He added: 'My son's life was given to a good cause.'" See "American Flier Dead," June 25, 1916, 3.

144. See, as examples: "American Couple Under German Fire," *New York Times,* October 1, 1914, 4; "American Killed on the Mount Temple by Raider's Shot, Says Captain of Another Unlisted Victim of Moewe," *New York Times,* January 31, 1917, 1; "Americans on Sunken Ship," *Los Angeles Times,* December 20, 1916, 11; "Richard Hall Dies in War," *Los Angeles Times,* December 26, 1915, 13; and "Two Americans on Arabic Missing After Submarine Sinks Great Liner Without Warning, Ending 20 Lives," *Washington Post,* August 20, 1915, 1.

145. Edward Robb Ellis, *Echoes of a Distant Thunder: Life in the United States, 1914–1918* (New York: Kodansha International, 1975), 193–202.

146. As the former German Colonial Secretary Bernhard Dernburg said following the sinking of the *Lusitania:* "The American people cannot visualize the spectacle of a hundred thousand [...] German children starving by slow degrees as a result of the British blockade, but they can visualize the pitiful face of a little child drowning amidst the wreckage caused by a German torpedo." See Niall Ferguson, *The War of the World: Twentieth-Century Conflict and the Descent of the West* (New York: Penguin, 2006), 114.

147. The casualty list included writer and artist Elbert Hubbard; Alfred G. Vanderbilt, heir of the great Vanderbilt family fortune; and, Charles Frohman, a renowned

Jewish American theatrical producer. See "Elbert Hubbard, Alfred G. Vanderbilt and Charles Frohman, Prominent Americans Go Down with Lusitania," *Daily Herald* (Biloxi, MS), May 8, 1915, 1.

148. "Shocks the President," *New York Times*, May 8, 1915, 1; and "Dangerous Possibilities," *New York Times*, May 8, 1915, 6.

149. "'Damnable!' Says Sunday," *New York Times*, May 8, 1915, 3.

150. "Lusitania with 188 Americans on Board Sunk by German Submarine," *Lexington Herald*, May 8, 1915, 1.

151. "A Woman Demands War," *New York Times*, May 13, 1915, 14.

152. "Demands Vengeance," *New York Times*, May 10, 1915, 6.

153. "Canadian Press Asks United States to Act," *New York Times*, May 9, 1915, 3.

154. "Mr. Wickersham Appeals for Action," *New York Times*, May 9, 1915, C2.

155. "Nothing to be Gained by War," *Oregonian*, May 10, 1915, 6.

156. "Sinking of the Lusitania," *Lexington Herald*, May 12, 1915, 4.

157. "Upheld in German Pulpits," *New York Times*, May 10, 1915, 4. Also see "Sinking Justified, Says Dr. Dernburg," *New York Times*, May 9, 1915, 4.

158. Letter to the editor, *Wilkes Barre Times Leader*, May 12, 1915, 8.

159. "Germany Sends Regret, and 'Sympathy', But Says the Blame Rests With England," *New York Times*, May 11, 1915, 1.

160. Throughout his first term, Wilson attempted to foster and maintain an isolationist and non-interventionist national attitude toward the Great War. He did so for several reasons. First, Wilson hated the idea of state-sponsored warfare. He was not a pacifist, but he feared that American belligerence would breed unhealthy militarism throughout the United States and weaken recently implemented social and economic reforms. Second, Wilson worried that U.S. entry into the war would fracture the American population along ethnic and ideological lines—German Americans, Austro Americans, Hungarian Americans, and English-hating Irish Americans on one side; Anglo-Saxons, Russian Americans, and people of French descent on the other (to say nothing of African Americans, religious pacifists, humanistic pacifists, anarchists, Socialists, and Communists). Third, Wilson hoped that by keeping the nation out of the fight, the United States might be able to play an objective role during the mediation of peace between the belligerents. Finally, it made economic sense to remain neutral. American financiers like J. P. Morgan were making a killing by lending money to cash-strapped European nations. Likewise, U.S. corporations were taking in unprecedented profits by selling explosives, chemicals, steel, and other goods and raw materials to both the Allied Forces and Central Powers. By 1916, seventy percent of American exports were going directly to the war zone. And none of this profiteering came at the expense of American soldiers' lives. See Ellis, *Echoes*, 235–40, 250–1; Ferguson, *The War of the World*, 115–6; and, "No Need to Fight, If Right," *New York Times*, May 11, 1915, 1.

161. "No Need to Fight, If Right."

162. "Leading Points in President's Note to Germany Demanding Redress for Attacks on Americans," *New York Times*, May 13, 1915, 1.

163. "The Sinking of the Lusitania," *Lexington Herald*, May 16, 1915, 3.

164. Ellis, *Echoes*, 216.

165. "Stocks Go Soaring on Wilson Speech," *New York Times*, May 12, 1915, 4.

166. Communication scholar David A. Copeland writes: "Many Americans added the sinking of the *Lusitania* to the growing list of German 'atrocities,' real and fabricated. It became clear to all, no less so the German government itself, that if the United States chose to abandon its neutrality, it would not weigh in on the side of the Central Powers." See *American War Reporting*, 57.

167. Arthur S. Link and William M. Leary Jr., "Election of 1916," in *History of American Presidential Elections 1789–1968, Vol. III*, ed. Arthur M. Schlesinger Jr. (New York: Chelsea House, 1971), 2245–345.

168. David M. Kennedy, *Over Here: The First World War and American Society* (Oxford: Oxford University Press, 1980), 31–2; "Veterans Back Wilson," *New York Times*, August 19, 1915, 5.

169. "U.S. Army Right Size for Good Day's Butchery," *Duluth News-Tribune*, November 20, 1915, 1.

170. Republished in "Prospect of Asiatic Hordes Being Led by Germany Into War Should Arouse America," *Washington Post*, January 4, 1916, 5.

171. "America Is Invaded Again in the Films," *New York Times*, January 7, 1916, 11; Walter G. Fuller, "The Battle Cry of Peace," *The Masses*, December 1915, quoted in William L. O'Neill, ed., *Echoes of Revolt: The Masses 1911–1917* (Chicago: Quadrangle Books, 1966), 275–6.

172. "Gen. Wood Wants Army of 210,000," *New York Times*, January 20, 1916, 1.

173. "U.S. Couldn't Halt Foe," *Washington Post*, October 7, 1915, 5.

174. "Military Training in Our Schools," *New York Times*, September 18, 1915, 8.

175. "Roosevelt Firm Against Germany," *New York Times*, July 12, 1915, 1; "Roosevelt Hints at Hughes for 1916," *New York Times*, July 20, 1915, 20; "Roosevelt's New Word," *New York Times*, July 25, 1915, 11; and "Roosevelt Heaps Blame on America," *New York Times*, December 1, 1915, 4.

176. "The Kansas Spirit," *New York Times*, January 20, 1916, 8.

177. "Fists and Pacifists," *New York Times*, March 31, 1916, 10.

178. "La Follette in Effigy," *New York Times*, March 6, 1917, 1.

179. Kennedy, *Over Here*, 12.

180. "Lodge Ridicules Wilson," *New York Times*, August 20, 1916, 5.

181. "Declaration of Principles Adopted by the Progressive National Committee," *New York Times*, January 12, 1916, 8.

182. Ellis, *Echoes*, 297.

183. "Colonel Attacks Wilson's Courage," *New York Times*, October 29, 1916, 1.

184. "Hughes Praises Flag," *Washington Post*, July 5, 1916, 1.

185. "National Rights More Important Than Peace," *Washington Post*, July 28, 1915, 6.

186. "As Women Think of War," *New York Times*, August 23, 1915, 8.

187. Alfred E. Myers, *New York Times*, "The Courage Not to Fight," May 12, 1915, 12.

188. "Is Perfectly Neutral."

189. Kennedy, *Over Here*, 30.

190. "Ford Defies His Critics," *New York Times*, December 2, 1915, 2.

191. Irving Fisher, "Ten Reasons Why I Shall Vote for Wilson," *New York Times*, August 27, 1916, SM14.

192. Frederick C. Giffin, *Six Who Protested: Radical Opposition to the First World War* (Port Washington, NY: Kennikat Press, 1977), 21, 62–3, 80, 93, 104, 121; "Anarchy," *New York Times*, March 23, 1914, 10.

193. Chaz Bufe and Mitchell Cowen Verter, *Dreams of Freedom: A Ricardo Flores Magón Reader* (Oakland, CA: AK Press, 2005), 295–6.

194. "Pacifists in Protest," *Washington Post*, February 9, 1916, 5.

195. "Strike Against War," Helen Keller, http://gos.sbc.edu/k/keller.html (accessed February 5, 2017).

196. "Want Referendum on War," *New York Times*, February 5, 1917, 7.

197. "Dr. Jacobi Calls for a Secretary of Peace," *New York Times*, January 23, 1916, SM7.

198. "Who Pays?" *Washington Post*, November 25, 1914, 6.

199. Glenn Watkins, *Proof Through the Night* (Berkeley: University of California Press, 2003), 247–9; *History Matters*, "'I Didn't Raise My Boy to Be a Soldier': Singing Against the War," n.d., http://historymatters.gmu.edu/d/4942/ (accessed June 18, 2010).

200. "Suggests a Harem for Peace Women," *Duluth News-Tribune*, October 25, 1915, 10.

201. Kennedy, *Over Here*, 32–3.

202. "Wilson Dope Drawn from Poetic Lines," *Duluth News-Tribune*, October 27, 1916, 1.

203. Ellis, *Echoes*, 294–7. In June of 1916, the *New York Times* observed that Wilson had become "determined to meet the attempted abduction of the Stars and Stripes by outdoing the Republicans." See "Convention in a Blaze," *New York Times*, June 15, 1916, 1.

204. Kennedy, *Over Here*, 33–5.

205. "Colonel Attacks Wilson's Courage."

206. Hughes was so wedded to the "preparedness" and pro-war lobbies that most Americans assumed that a vote for Hughes was essentially a vote for war. As a result, many women publicly supported Wilson by default, for he, unlike Hughes, would not necessarily send their sons and husbands to fight and die. In Portland, Oregon, a train of Hughes campaigners was met by a riotous mob of women, who chased the visitors out of town with cries of "We want Wilson!" and "Where's the casket?" and "Fetch a coffin!" See "Jail Woman Heckler," *Washington Post*, October 15, 1916, A3.

207. Kennedy, *Over Here*, 12.

208. Ellis, *Echoes*, 307.

209. "Calls Hyphen a Failure," *New York Times*, February 1, 1916, 1.

Chapter 2

"Body and Soul and Spirit"

Mobilization, Conscription, and Mass Death, 1917–1918

In April of 1917, Woodrow Wilson committed one of the swiftest about-faces in U.S. presidential history. Abandoning the staunch anti-war platform of his 1916 presidential campaign, he went before Congress and asked for a declaration of war against Germany.[1] Members of the House and Senate overwhelmingly supported the president's idealistic call to make the world "safe for democracy" and plunged the United States into the Great War. The battle cries on Capitol Hill, however, did not necessarily express the sentiments of the American people. For three years, Americans had received a graphic if distant view of the war in all its apparent terror, violence, and death, and many had come to see the conflict as a senseless, apocalyptic, and strictly European affair that the United States could and should stay out of. Recognizing the anti-war and isolationist streaks that coursed through public discourse and consciousness, and comprehending the obvious incongruity between his pre and postelection stances, President Wilson spearheaded the development of a series of wartime laws, policies, and agencies that effectively made citizen (and noncitizen) support for the war effort a matter of compulsion, not choice. Establishing an unprecedented national draft,[2] a powerful propaganda and media censorship bureau, and a Justice Department bent on censuring and prosecuting dissenters, the Wilson Administration attempted to control the "body and soul and spirit" of every American "in the supreme effort of service and sacrifice."[3] Within months, the people of the United States were legally and rhetorically transformed (through language, law, and force) into either "seditious" subversives or loyal, subservient participants in the national war effort. By war's end in November of 1918, roughly 117,000 citizen-soldiers would die "over there," far from the shores of their homeland.

Utilizing rhetorical theorist Kenneth Burke's heuristic dichotomy of *motion* and *action* to analyze Wilson's address[4] and the nation's subsequent war effort, this chapter offers a rhetorical analysis of what I term the U.S. government and military's wartime "project of motion"—a program that sought to suppress dissent and symbolic action, and cast American intervention in the Great War as a matter of compulsion (motion), not choice (action). As the remaining chapters will show, this project created for the American public almost entirely false perceptions of the necessity, benefits, and human costs of U.S. participation in the war. In the postwar years, U.S. officials would face the monumental task of rhetorically accounting for the incongruity between false perceptions and the realities of U.S. belligerence "over there"—a task that would ultimately spawn the rhetorical invention of the U.S. soldier as a 'global force for good.'

A few words on the thoughts of Kenneth Burke are in order here. In *A Grammar of Motives*, Burke builds his analysis of human motives on his distinction between motion and action.[5] According to Burke, motions are events and behaviors that do not intentionally carry symbolic content. Exemplified by the realms of the natural world and "scientism" (which assumes that change is the result of purely physical, autonomous processes), motion is demonstrated by the rolling wave, the bee pollinating a flower, the billiard ball rolling across a table, or a twitching human eye. But if that same eye twitch were actually a wink, it would be considered an action, a purposive human behavior that intentionally carries symbolic content. In other words, action is "motion with intent," endemic to the realms of human affairs, ethics, and symbolism. Where motion implies inevitability and necessity, action implies agency, choice, and awareness of a behavior's potential consequences. As they pertain to rhetoric, motion and action are useful conceptual frameworks for understanding, describing, and debating pressing social issues.[6] And most importantly, people routinely characterize instances of motion as instances of action, and vice versa, in order to shift attitudes, blame, and responsibility.[7]

This chapter provides a comprehensive exploration of Wilson et al.'s "project of motion" (which, given Burke's theory, was itself a project of action). Beginning with the president's war address to Congress, I examine the wartime laws, policies, and agencies the Wilson Administration and the American Expeditionary Forces used to constrain and suppress U.S. citizens' and soldiers' abilities to act and express themselves freely.[8] Uncovering the motives behind this wartime project and the forms of thought and expression that were built around them, I show how prominent governmental, military, media, and cultural figures strategically cast instances of action as instances of motion (and instances of motion as action) to shape public attitudes, enforce draconian laws and policies, shift responsibility and blame to alleged evil enemies (both foreign and domestic), and construct and propagate national war aims. Inevitably, U.S. belligerence entailed the destruction of American life on a grand scale—a horrifying consequence and colossal material transformation that required appropriate and timely rhetorical compensations from the government. A controversy in late 1917 surrounding the treatment of the bodily remains of the nation's first casualties revealed the dormant anxieties and dilemmas that lurked just below the surface of the domestic war effort; for the first time, Americans realized that their fallen soldiers would not return to the homeland for some time (if ever). Ultimately, soldiers who were drafted and sent to fight, kill, and die in foreign nations on the other side of the world (as well as their families), had little say in the matter. During the period of American belligerence, families of the dead were encouraged to view their profound and devastating losses as necessary sacrifices for the national war effort and the fight to make the world "safe for democracy" (rather than for independence from tyranny, the preservation of the Union, or the natural resources of distant colonial territories in Asia). At the same time, public expressions of grief and anger were effectively forbidden by the government's wartime project of motion—thus, relatives of the dead were forced to keep their personal sentiments under wraps.

As we will see in the following chapters, this wartime suppression of emotion and expression that could be conceived of as undermining the war effort would give way to an explosion of symbolic action after the war, as Americans forcefully began demanding explanations and compensations for the premature deaths of their men. In time, the U.S. government would learn to appropriate the sentimental and domestic vernacular of angry and grieving families into its own official rhetoric so that it might satisfy the needs of the American people and justify the nation's participation in the war. In the years following World War I, the U.S. government would incorporate this sentimental vernacular into a series of commemoration projects (most notably, the establishment of a network of American military cemeteries throughout Western Europe) that, in combination, would reframe the national war effort as a *project of action* in which the American people—united around a shared set of principles and beliefs—had freely and willingly sacrificed their lives and their loved ones for the welfare of the world.

"THRUST" INTO WAR

On April 2, 1917, President Woodrow Wilson stood before Congress to ask for a declaration of war against Germany and its allies.[9] For two months, Germany had attempted to knock Britain out of the World War by sinking all foreign ships, including American vessels, entering blockaded zones of the Atlantic Ocean. Germany's unrestricted submarine campaign against ships capable of transporting resources to Britain and its allies resulted in the sinking of four unarmed American merchant boats and the deaths of 36 U.S. citizens. In light of these deaths and the controversy surrounding the Zimmerman Telegram, an alleged proposal from Germany to Mexico to make war on the United States, President Wilson had decided that the nation could no longer sit back and watch Germany's "cruel and unmanly business" continue.[10] The president who once had been "too proud to fight" and spoke of "peace at any cost" now urged those representing the people of the United States to support his call for war.

In his war message to Congress, Wilson claimed that he and his fellow countrymen and women, a "great peaceful people," had not wanted to fight, but that Germany's recent actions—uncommon "wrongs" that had "cut to the very roots of human life"—had left Americans with little choice. "We will not choose the path of submission and suffer the most sacred rights of our nation and our people to be ignored or violated," Wilson stated. "I advise that the Congress declare the recent course of the Imperial German Government to be in fact nothing less than war against the Government and people of the United States; *that it formally accept the status of belligerent which has thus been thrust upon it*" [emphasis added]. According to Wilson, Germany's actions had propelled the United States into war. "We enter this war only where we are clearly forced into it because there are no other means of defending our rights." Americans were blameless, as the decision for war had already been made for them by the nation by Germany. "We are now about to accept [the] gage of battle with this natural foe to liberty and shall, if necessary, spend the whole force of the nation to check and nullify its pretensions and its power."[11] Violently pushed into *motion* by Germany's intentional and antagonistic *actions*, the United States would now meet German force with an even greater force.

Casting American intervention as a just endeavor that would be conducted "without passion," Wilson rhetorically dissociated the German people from their supposedly evil rulers. "We have no quarrel with the German people," Wilson said. "We have no feeling towards them but one of sympathy and friendship. It was not upon their impulse that their Government acted in entering this war." Wilson argued that the German people were victims of a despotic regime—the kind of hated regime that generations of European immigrants had abandoned for a new life in America. Wilson stated that the German submarine campaign "was a war determined upon as wars used to be determined upon in the old, unhappy days [...] waged in the interest of dynasties or of little groups of ambitious men who were accustomed to use their fellow men as pawns and tools." Through these words, Wilson distinguished German autocracy, a system in which a select few could plunge millions of people into war, and American democracy, a system in which the president, at least theoretically, was constitutionally bound to consult Congress prior to military action. Of course, what Wilson did not say was that in order to defeat the German government, Americans would have to kill many German people.[12] (As everyone knows, government officials are never the first to die in a war.) But Wilson's statements and careful omissions preemptively exculpated Americans of the destruction of German people that belligerence and regime changes in Germany and Austria would entail. And just as importantly, the president's words helped construct an identifiable, tangible enemy—the Kaiser and his cohort—in the minds of Americans.[13]

Wilson laid out a series of lofty goals for the American war effort—goals that indicated his utopian vision of a world in which all nations were democratic and members of an organized "league of honor" where differences could be worked out peacefully. In an effort to tie his global dream to American interests and security, Wilson claimed that Germany's sinking of U.S. commerce ships had constituted "warfare against mankind [...] war against all nations." Wilson equated American belligerence to the preservation of "civilization itself," and insisted that Americans would gladly fight for ideals that "shall bring peace and safety to all nations and make the world itself at last free." These ideals included "the principles of right and of fair play"; "the right of those who submit to authority to have a voice in their own governments"; "the rights and liberties of small nations"; "the principles of peace and justice in the life of the world as against selfish autocratic power"; and, "the ultimate peace of the world and [...] the liberation of its peoples, the German peoples included." Americans, Wilson declared to Congress and countless mediated audiences around the world, would not fight for power, territory, wealth, or natural resources.[14] Instead, they would fight (and, by implication, if need be *die*) to make the world "safe for democracy":

> To such a task we can dedicate our lives and our fortunes, everything that we are and everything that we have, with the pride of those who know that the day has come when America is privileged to spend her blood and her might for the principles that gave her birth and happiness and the peace which she has treasured. God helping her, she can do no other.[15]

In a few short paragraphs, Wilson transitioned from the interests of the nation, to those of all of "civilization," to those of all the peoples of the world, to those of all of God's creation. By amplifying the United States' subject position to the point where it enveloped all of humanity's alleged hopes and aspirations for democracy and liberty, he effectively represented the nation as the potential savior of the world—something akin to a giant, globetrotting, modern-day Christian Crusader.

But until that moment, it had not been evident to the majority of Americans that countrymen of theirs would, in fact, willingly fight, spill blood, and die in Europe for anything, let alone ideals as seemingly unattainable as "the ultimate peace of the world." For two and a half years, Americans had witnessed from afar the horrors and unprecedented human destruction of the Great War. Just a few months prior, Wilson himself had mounted a successful reelection campaign on the slogan, "He Kept Us Out of War!" His victory had been considered by many to be a referendum against American belligerence. In October of 1916 (long after the sinking of the *Lusitania*), Wilson had justified American neutrality by publicly commenting that the Great War had been caused "by nothing in particular" and that the aims of the belligerents on both sides were "virtually the same."[16] In the months between his reelection and his war address to Congress, the president and his advisers had kept a close watch on public opinion and had found few expressions of desire to go to war. William C. Durant, the founder of General Motors, returned from a cross-country trip and reported to the White House that he had "met only one man between New York and California who wanted war." And in March 1917, British observers, keen on finding a way to draw the United States into the fight against Germany, had determined that there was a "remarkable lack of excitement or enthusiasm [for war]." Despite the many groups that had previously been in favor of preparedness and intervention, the British agents concluded: "There is no indication [...] of any pro-Ally enthusiasm except among that body of ardent pro-Allies intellectually important, but numerically far less important, which has shown its warm sympathy from the very beginning of the war."[17] Now, just weeks after this telling British report, President Wilson stood before the American people, drawing a line in the sand.

Likely recognizing the stark incongruity between his preelection and postelection attitudes, and anticipating the difficulties that such an incongruity would pose to corralling support from the already reluctant American polis, Wilson cast support for the war effort as a matter of *compulsion*, not *choice*. "What this will involve is clear," Wilson preached. It would involve Wall Street extending "the most liberal financial credits" to "governments now at war with Germany." It would involve "the organization and mobilization of all the material resources of the country to supply the materials of war." It would involve supplying the Navy "with the best means of dealing with the enemy's submarines"—a program that would be funded by a "well conceived taxation" of citizens' incomes (rather than borrowing from other nations). Perhaps most importantly, victory would require a national draft. "It will involve the immediate addition to the armed forces of the United States already provided for by law in case of war at least 500,000 men," Wilson contended, "who should, in my opinion, be chosen upon the principle of universal liability to service, and also the authorization of subsequent additional increments of equal force so soon as they may be needed and can be handled in training." Furthermore, Wilson warned that the government would not only commandeer citizens' bodies, money, and labor, but would demand their minds and "allegiance" too. Americans, whether of German descent or otherwise, would be compelled to back the national war effort no matter what. "If there should be disloyalty," Wilson ominously threatened, "it will be dealt with a firm hand of stern repression." Foreshadowing the draconian wartime laws and policies that, ironically, would contradict the supposed (and rarely, if ever, fulfilled) democratic ideals for which Americans were meant to fight and die in Europe, Wilson indicated his intention to compel loyalty (one could either wholeheartedly support the war effort or be a traitor), suppress opposition to the war effort, and replace every American's will with the will of the U.S. government.

When Wilson finished, all but a few Senators and Representatives jumped to their feet, applauded, waved flags, and shouted words of approval. Over the next few days, Republicans (who had wanted to go to war for some time) and Democrats (who wished to support their president) in both the House and Senate deliberated over the war measure. Only a relative handful of Congress members rejected Wilson's call for war. The most vocal opponent was Senator Robert La Follette of Wisconsin (a staunch opponent of intervention), who (unsurprisingly) claimed that he had received from citizens 15,000 letters and telegrams that opposed the war at a ratio of 9 to 1. Appealing to common knowledge of the deadly and ghastly conditions of the Great War, La Follete denounced Wilson's push for war, which he claimed was, itself, autocratic in nature: "The poor, sir, who are the ones called upon to rot in the trenches, have no organized power, have no press to voice their will upon this question of peace or war, but, oh, Mr. President, at some time they will be heard!" Furthermore, La Follette predicted that Wall Street would be the only true beneficiaries of the fighting. As for making the world "safe for democracy," he pointed out that of all the nations with which the United States was about to ally itself, only France and now the czarless Russia were democratic states. La Follette's call for a national referendum on the war question was ignored. In the House, Representative Jeannette Rankin of Montana—a social worker, suffragist, and the first female elected to Congress—took a similarly principled stance against the measure, and stated: "I want to stand by my country, but I cannot vote for war." In the end, La Follette, Rankin, and their cohort were greatly outnumbered; the Senate adopted the war resolution by a vote of 82 to 6; the House by a vote of 373 to 50. On April 6, 1917, President Wilson signed the joint Congressional declaration of war against Germany.[18] The nation was officially at war. By the end of the year, the lives of young Americans would be claimed on the battlefields of Europe.

MOTION, LEGISLATED

The government's wartime project began in earnest on April 5, 1917, the very day that Congress declared war on Germany. On that day, Secretary of War Newton D. Baker submitted to Congress a preliminary version of the Selective Service Act, legislation that called for a national military draft that would supply the needed personnel for the newly established American Expeditionary Forces (AEF). (It is worth noting that the word "expedition" has two main definitions: "a journey or voyage undertaken by a group of people with a particular purpose" and "promptness or speed in doing something.") On April 6, President Wilson issued an executive order limiting the rights of "enemy aliens" and subjecting them to summary arrest and internment.[19] Hours later, Justice Department officials, without reference to the courts or obtaining a warrant, detained "sixty alleged ringleaders in German plots, conspiracies, and machinations" in several major cities around the country. Representing just a handful of the thousands of "German operatives" that were supposedly under government surveillance, the group was sent to prison without possibility of bail for the duration of the war. Newspaper accounts of the arrests served as clear warnings to potential saboteurs and agitators.[20] On April 7, Wilson issued a confidential executive order permitting the dismissal of civil service employees merely on the *suspicion of disloyalty* during wartime, a measure that preemptively silenced any government worker who might express opposition to some aspect of the war effort.[21] On April 28, he authorized the Navy to censor transatlantic cables and radio stations while giving similar power over telephone and domestic telegraph lines to the army.[22] American newspapers stated that the purpose of this censorship was to "prevent the transmission [...] of information that might be of value to Germany."[23] Like other war-related orders, legislation, and policies enacted during the period of American belligerence, this executive order simultaneously indicated that subversives and enemies were, indeed, present in the United States (a notion that tends to increase public clamor for 'governmental protection' and justify governmental violations of civil liberties) and warned would-be subversives to watch their backs.

These initial activities and executive orders turned out to be only precursors of a series of broader, sweeping wartime laws that sought to transform autonomous American citizens into *objects of motion* for the war machine. The earliest, and perhaps most radical, of these laws was the Selective Service Act, which called for the United States' first *nationwide* draft. In its original form, the bill provided that the army be brought to full war strength, that the National Guard be federalized, and that a half million men should be drafted, with a second 500,000 to be called when President Wilson deemed necessary (this process would quickly raise over 1,727,000 soldiers for the war effort.)

All unmarried males between the ages of 21 and 30 were to be subject to the draft, and they would be drafted in proportion to the populations of the various states. (In actuality, as the war progressed and the need for soldierly bodies increased, the draft would expand to include men between the ages of 18 and 45, married and unmarried alike. By the end of the war, 23,456,021 men, or half the adult male population of the United States, would be compelled to register for the draft; of these, 4,800,000 would don a uniform in domestic training camps or in the battlefields of Europe.)[24] Registrants would be called to duty through the random determinations of a national lottery— an ingenious method that shifted responsibility and blame from government officials (the very people responsible and blameworthy for sending American men to fight, kill, and die in Europe) to the gods of fate and chance (the gods of *motion*).[25]

The idea of the national draft, however, was highly controversial. For many Americans, the word "conscription" was a dirty word that held autocratic connotations; after all, Germany and Austria-Hungary—the United States' newest enemies—had traditionally drafted men into their armies. Furthermore, since the American Revolution, the public had typically opposed (sometimes violently) the idea of federally mandated compulsory service.[26] During Congressional debates over the proposed draft, a handful of Senators and Representatives cited these cultural and historical phenomena in denouncements of the bill. These nervous legislators equated "conscript" with "convict" and "slave"; predicted that anti-draft rioting "all over the United States" would "add more joy to the German heart than any other news which could be conveyed"; and, claimed that a draft would "Prussianize America" and "produce a sulky, unwilling, indifferent army."[27]

Opponents of the draft, however, were soundly defeated, and the bill was passed by a wide margin and signed into law by the president on May 18, 1917. Recognizing that public acceptance of conscription and a swift and smooth enactment of the draft were far from givens, Wilson and the War Department attempted to cast conscription in terms of altruism and "service." This project began with the very naming of the legislation: the Selective *Service* Act (emphasis added). As historian David M. Kennedy keenly observes: "'Service' was a kind of rhetorical vessel into which were being poured the often contradictory emotional and political impulses of the day [...] a fittingly ambivalent term, at once connoting the autonomy of the individual will and the obligation of the individual to serve a sphere wider than his own." Insisting that the draft was something akin to a voluntary affair, Secretary of War Newton D. Baker and his Selective Service administrator, Provost Marshal General Enoch H. Crowder, established a series of "national registration days" during which draft-eligible men were encouraged (as well as required by law) to register with their local draft boards. Nationally, there were 5,000 draft boards, each made up of four or five appointed local citizens.[28] Newspapers across the country published Presidential proclamations (in Gothic font often associated with legal and religious documents) announcing national registration days under the headline, "Call to Arms." In unambiguous terms, American men were urged to 'answer the call' as if by choice and for love of country.[29] By putting the administration of the draft into the hands of friends and neighbors of the men to be affected (these draft boards were designed to serve as buffers between the individual citizen and the Federal Government), and by giving draft-eligible men the opportunity to bring themselves physically to designated spots, the national registration days diverted and grounded resentment and discontent at the local level and advanced the dubious notion that the draft represented both local self-government at its finest and the willing and non-coerced "service" of American men.[30] Here, it was useful and convenient for the Wilson Administration and the War Department to cast this program of *motion* (the draft) as a program of *action* (voluntary enlistment).

Of course, conscription had very little to do with voluntarism. While the original Selective Service Act of 1917 allowed draft exemptions for married men, workers in industries essential to the war effort, members of "well-recognized" pacifistic religions, and "those found to be physically or morally deficient," every other man between the age of 21 and 30 was compelled to register and, if selected by a national lottery, to "serve" in the military. Those who refused to register or serve—and those who helped draft-eligible men avoid registering or serving—were subject to cruel and sometimes unusual treatment. Although the Selective Service Act stated that avoiding conscription or aiding draft dodgers was punishable by a fine of $1,000 or imprisonment for up to one year, government officials and private vigilante groups feverishly pursued and disciplined "slackers" in ways that greatly exceeded the language of the bill. In Springfield, Illinois, for example, an older couple was jailed for ninety days simply for privately advising their son not to register.[31] In Pittsburgh, Chicago, Boston, New York, and other major cities, Justice Department officials, local police officers, vigilante groups, and armed soldiers and sailors descended upon streets and businesses to hunt delinquents. One such "slacker raid" in New York City led to the detainment of 50,000 draft-age men, many of whom were apprehended at bayonet-point in ball parks, restaurants, or on street corners and forced to show their Selective Service documents; of these, 13,000 turned out to be draft dodgers.[32] Pitched battles between draft resisters and armed state and county officials led to the deaths of at least twenty people across the country.[33] At prisons and military training camps throughout the nation, nonreligious conscientious objectors suffered all kinds of torture: many were beaten; forced to sleep on cement floors; forbidden to read or write or even talk; placed in extended solitary confinement; chained to the doors of their cells; hung upside down with their faces in human excrement; and, in one infamous case, jabbed with bayonets. At Fort Riley in Kansas, an unlucky conscientious objector who went on hunger strike was tortured, forcibly fed, court-martialed, and sentenced to life imprisonment.[34] Quite simply, able-bodied men of draft age had no choice but to register and, if summoned, report for active duty.[35]

The government's tenacious pursuit of draft dodgers and cruel treatment of conscientious objectors were justified in public comments issued from prominent American elites. The canon of the Episcopal Cathedral of St. John the Divine in Manhattan, for instance, preached to his congregation that conscientious objectors were "wolves in sheep's clothing."[36] Editors at the *New York Times* published the names and residences of draft dodgers,[37] and wrote that if a self-professed conscientious objector "puts his belief into practice, we should either put him to death or shut him up in an asylum as a madman." The perpetual warmonger Theodore Roosevelt traveled around the country snarling that most conscientious objectors were "slackers, pure and simple, or else traitorous pro-Germans" who should "permanently be sent out of the country as soon as possible." His cousin, Assistant Secretary of the Navy Franklin D. Roosevelt, issued similar statements that denounced "slackers."[38] Nicholas Murray Butler, the president of Columbia University, publicly claimed that conscientious objectors were "morally half-witted," while Secretary of War Newton D. Baker announced that any conscientious objector whose sincerity was questioned, or who engaged in propaganda, or who was "sullen and defiant," would be "promptly brought to trial by court martial."[39] The effects of such statements could be felt across the country, as many Americans came to view draft dodgers as something akin to enemies of the state. Across the United States, robed members of the Ku Klux Klan hunted down draft dodgers, while other extremist groups called for all conscientious objectors and delinquents to be shot on sight. In cities throughout the nation, "patriotic women" scornfully handed yellow feathers to young men in civilian clothing so as to shame them into voluntarily enlisting.[40] From church halls to schoolrooms to town squares, prominent figures and powerful groups from all walks of life vilified the very notions of dissent and pacifism as disloyalty to the homeland (and, if implicitly, assent and violence as virtuous).

Such sentiments even affected the attitudes and policies of local draft boards—many local draft board members viewed conscientious objectors with abject disdain. A November 1917 Selective Service survey asked each local draft board to describe its treatment of (1) religious objectors; (2) conscientious objectors; (3) the morally deficient; and (4) persons already under arrest or on bail on charges of crime. The draft board of Russell County, Alabama, responded:

Ans. 1. Send them to the front.
Ans. 2. Send them to the front.
Ans. 3. Send them to the front.
Ans. 4. Had none.

Similarly, a draft board from Oakland California, answered:

1. Should be Drafted.
2. Should be Drafted.
3. Had none. Should be Drafted—discipline might help him.
4. Had one. Was treated as others.[41]

Such comments reflected the pervasive attitude that the demands of the collective, national war effort trumped the personal desires and beliefs of individual citizens (and especially pacifists). Furthermore, these responses implied that religious and conscientious objectors were social parasites who, much like the "morally deficient" and criminal elements, needed to be eradicated. In many cases, certainly, they would be shipped off to war, only to return in flag-draped coffins.

Once drafted, recruits were sent to one of thirty-two hastily built military camps around the country to undergo "basic" training that would, in theory, quickly transform them into professional warriors. In reality, most of the nation's training camps were little more than glorified barracks with muddy fields where recruits received deficient and outdated martial instruction. For starters, the traditional-minded leader of the AEF, General John J. Pershing, considered trench warfare defeatist, and called for training in offensive, open warfare. Although machine guns and artillery were the main killing machines in Europe, Pershing demanded heavy instruction in the rifle and bayonet, which he considered "the supreme weapons of the infantry soldier."[42] To make matters worse, most camps lacked basic essentials: blankets, uniforms, machine guns, artillery guns, and worst of all, seasoned instructors. Lacking hand grenades, recruits practiced lobbing rocks. Lacking rifles, they marched with broomsticks. Many soldiers studied horseshoeing without horses. At Camp Colt near Gettysburg, Pennsylvania, a young officer named Dwight D. Eisenhower struggled to train thousands of men in tank warfare without having a single, actual tank at his disposal.[43] Many soldiers arrived in France without ever having fired a weapon—a reality that surely cost countless men their lives.[44]

The difficulties of this quixotic venture were compounded by the hetero-geneous makeup of the nation's draftees. Camp instructors had roughly four months[45] (in some cases, only four weeks)[46] to mold country boys who had never seen indoor plumbing or automobiles, city boys who were afraid of the forest, uneducated men who could not tell their left hand from their right, and immigrants and aliens who could not speak English, into an orderly and modern fighting force.[47] Official postwar reports on the makeup of the American fighting force indicate the challenges (both real and perceived) of training such a diverse population of men, and reveal the military's biased and racist opinions of immigrants (Germans in particular) and African Americans:

> The records show that country boys made a better physical record than city boys, white than colored, native-born better than foreign-born. The differ-ences were so considerable that 100,000 country boys would furnish for the military service 4,790 more soldiers than would an equal number of city boys. The average mental age of the United States soldier was between 13 and 14 years according to the mental tests given in the [Selective Draft] examinations. Alarming illiteracy conditions were found by means of the draft examination. Of men of military age there were 700,000 who could neither read nor write. [...] The total number of aliens registered [for conscription] was 3,877,083. [...] Enemy aliens [non-citizen German immigrants] registered in the draft numbered 158,809.[48]

Ironically, noncitizen German immigrants were officially classified as "enemy aliens" (clearly a pejorative term), yet were still swept up by the draft and sent to fight (and potentially die) in Europe on behalf of the United States.

Considering the fact that the Great War was defined by trench warfare and new technologies like heavy artillery, machine guns, field telephones, trucks, tanks, and airplanes, American troops were, by and large, poorly trained. Who knows how many U.S. casualties resulted from this lack of proper instruction? Yet, as President Wilson and others would claim after the war, by emphasizing General Pershing's offensively oriented tactics, the U.S. mili-tary succeeded in instilling an aggressive instinct and spirit of attack in most recruits; like well-functioning components of the war machine, American soldiers learned to charge when ordered, whatever dangers lied ahead.[49] After the war, President Wilson would explain that the American army was raised so rapidly because the men were trained to go only one way—"forward."[50] The speed with which American men were rounded up, trained, and shipped to Europe was captured in the lyrics of George M. Cohan's smash hit song, "Over There":

Johnnie, get your gun, get your gun, get your gun,
Take it on the run, on the run, on the run [...]
Every son of liberty. hurry right away, no delay, go today.[51]

Indeed, the U.S. military endeavored to turn draftees with such diverse names as Acullo, Benitto, Dooley, Hajek, Moskala, Ozbourn, Perez, Smith, and Truemper, into an army of "Johnnies"—*objects of motion* racing from here (the United States) to "over there" (Europe) and into battle without delay.

Now that the question of securing and sending soldierly bodies to Europe had been answered, the Wilson Administration and Congress turned their attention to controlling wartime public discourse and behavior at home. Over a twelve-month period, Congress passed three sweeping and infamous pieces of legislation that restricted free speech and buttressed Wilson's *project of motion*. The Espionage Act of June 1917 made it a crime, punishable by up to twenty years' imprisonment and a $10,000 fine, to "make or convey false reports or false statements with intent to interfere with the operation or success of the military or naval forces of the United States"; to "cause or attempt to cause insubordination, disloyalty, mutiny, or refusal of duty in the military or naval forces"; or to "willfully obstruct the recruiting or enlistment service of the United States." It also empowered the Postmaster General to declare "unmailable" all letters, circulars, newspapers, pamphlets, books, and other materials that urged "treason, insurrection, or forcible resistance to any law of the United States." Those who used the postal service to transmit such materials faced stiff fines and jail time. The Trading-with-the-Enemy Act of October 1917 legalized government censorship of *all* communications moving in or out of the United States, and allowed the Postmaster General to demand translations of newspaper or magazine articles published in foreign languages—a move designed to keep suspect German-language newspapers in check. And the Sedition Act of May 1918 amended and broadened the Espionage Act by making it a federal crime to write, publish, or even *utter*

> any disloyal, profane, scurrilous, or abusive language about the form of government of the United States, or the Constitution of the United States, or the military or naval forces of the United States, or the flag of the United States, or the uniform of the Army or Navy of the United States, or any language intended to bring [any of the above] into contempt, scorn, contumely, or disrepute.

Aimed chiefly at Socialists, pacifists, anarchists, and other prominent agitators, the Sedition Act also enhanced the Postmaster General's powers to ban publications deemed treasonable or seditious from circulation.[52] While the intent of these three laws and the punishments they entailed were clear enough, the looseness of the laws' language made it nearly impossible to determine the official boundaries of permissible discourse regarding the national war effort. What, exactly, constituted "disloyal, profane, scurrilous, or abusive language?" How were "treason," "insurrection," and "sedition" to be defined? And who would define them? Perhaps intentionally designed, these ambiguities essentially granted government officials sweeping powers to interpret and enforce the laws as they saw fit. They also incentivized self-repression of behavior and speech that might be construed as illegal; every person living in the United States was wise to keep personal thoughts not wholly in line with the national war effort to her or himself. Ironically, the very anti-war language President Wilson had used to get reelected could now land the average American behind bars. In any case, the mere existence of this legislation—let alone its strict enforcement—indicated the government's awareness of widespread, and potentially disruptive, anti-war sentiment.

Armed with the expansive powers granted by the Espionage, Trading-with-the-Enemy, and Sedition Acts, Postmaster General Albert S. Burleson and Attorney General Thomas W. Gregory set out to crush domestic dissent and anti-war speech of any kind. Serving as President Wilson's loyal henchmen, Burleson and Gregory stretched their newly acquired wartime powers to the greatest limits and, in doing so, helped usher in one of the most blatantly repressive periods of American history. At Wilson's bidding,[53] Burleson directed most of his attention toward monitoring and silencing the radical press and foreign-language circulations. By October 1917, Burleson had begun stripping second-class mailing privileges from periodicals that had the audacity to, in his words, "impugn the motives of the government and thus encourage insubordination," claim "that the government is controlled by Wall Street or munition manufacturers," or criticize "improperly our Allies." As a conservative, nativistic Southerner, Burleson was particularly interested in eliminating Socialist periodicals altogether. Publicly, Burleson declared that he would bar from circulation only those Socialist papers that contained treasonable or seditious language. But, he added, "the trouble is that most Socialist papers do contain such matter." The *American Socialist* was banned immediately and was soon followed by *Solidarity* (the journal of the Industrial Workers of the World), the *Rebel* (the publication of the Tenant Farmers Union), the *New York Call*, and the *Milwaukee Leader*. Most famously, Burleson banned from the mails the August 1917 issue of *The Masses* (a popular Socialist political and literary magazine) because it contained four anti-war cartoons and a poem defending anarchist anti-war activists Emma Goldman and Alexander Berkman. When editors at *The Masses* proposed to avoid such content in the future, Burleson still refused to restore the magazine's second-class mailing privileges on the ground that it had skipped an issue—the very issue that Burleson had pulled from circulation!—and was thus ineligible for such privileges as a regularly issued "periodical." This incident effectively brought *The Masses* to an end.[54]

Burleson was just as aggressive with foreign-language (particularly German) publications, and demanded translations of all articles or editorials referring to the government, to any of the belligerent powers, or to the conduct of the war. Faced with such a costly procedure, many foreign-language papers either prudently adopted a position of unqualified support for the government's war effort or simply shut down, many never to appear again. Within the first twelve months of American belligerence, forty-four major periodicals lost their mailing privileges and another thirty retained them only by agreeing to print *nothing more concerning the war*. Perhaps most disturbingly, Burleson gave local postmasters the authority to open citizens' private letters and read them. Whenever local postmasters discovered a remark they considered treasonous, they asked the government to prosecute. Conrad Kornmann of Sioux Falls, South Dakota, wrote to a friend that he opposed the idea of government war bonds; he was fined $1,000 and sent to jail for ten years. L. N. Legendre of Los Angeles was sent to prison for two years for expressing in a letter: "This is a war fostered by Morgan and the rich."[55] Such cases served as warnings to all Americans, and showed just how much power the U.S. government of the 20th century had to invade the most personal aspects of citizens' lives.

Burleson's zealous devotion to stamping out "disloyal utterances" was matched only by the efforts of his partner in crime fighting, Attorney General Thomas Gregory. Claiming that those who impeded the national war effort "sinned against the sovereignty of America and I know of no crime so serious as this," Gregory feverishly wielded his new powers to pursue and prosecute all instances of wartime dissent. Having only a few hundred Justice Department employees at his disposal (at the time, the Justice Department was quite small, and the Attorney General did not yet have the power to use the fledgling Bureau of Investigation as a resource), Gregory turned to the quasi-vigilante group the American Protective League (APL) for help. Securing $275,000 from President Wilson's emergency war fund, Gregory secretly bankrolled the APL and developed an "unofficial," nationwide network of informants, commandos, and provocateurs for his immediate assistance. While privately reassuring Wilson of the APL's propriety, Gregory encouraged his 250,000 legionnaires to spy on and report neighbors, fellow workers, office-mates, and anyone of suspect character.

Authorized by official-looking badges that read "American Protective League—Secret Service," many of these "agents" bugged, burglarized, slandered, and illegally arrested fellow American citizens. Others opened mail, intercepted telegrams, committed outright physical assault against suspected dissenters, and helped conduct dubious "slacker raids" (Gregory was publicly embarrassed when an officer of the Bureau of Investigation inadvertently admitted to the press that, on average, 99 out of 100 men were mistakenly arrested in "slacker raids"). Predictably, under the guise of patriotism, APL members used their largely unchecked powers to promote right-wing social and economic views and harass African Americans, German Americans, and other ethnic minorities. Despite these nefarious activities, Gregory boasted in a letter to a friend that "I have today several hundred thousand private citizens—some as individuals, most of them as members of patriotic bodies, engaged in [...] assisting the heavily over-worked Federal authorities in keeping an eye on disloyal individuals and making reports of disloyal utterances." Much like the civilian spy networks that would emerge in the USSR and, decades later, Communist Cuba, the APL served as the government's ears and eyes at the most local levels of society and generated an endless flow of "intelligence" for officials. Within the first two months of the national war effort, APL members were sending roughly 1,000 letters to the Justice Department each day. (Of these, however, an estimated 90 percent were of no value to Gregory's war-related efforts.) By the end of the war, the APL claimed to have found 3 million cases of disloyalty. In a 1918 report to Congress, Attorney General Gregory gleefully declared: "It is safe to say that never in its history has this country been so thoroughly policed."[56]

While his private army "thoroughly policed" the streets, Gregory oversaw and encouraged the prosecution of hundreds of alleged dissidents in court. Federal District Judges and U.S. Attorneys across the land eagerly supported the Attorney General's war on disloyalty, seeking and handing down dubious convictions with near-reckless abandon. Assistant Attorney General John Lord O'Brian wryly noted that every U.S. Attorney had become "an angel of life and death clothed with the power to walk up and down in his district, saying, 'This one will I spare, and that one will I smite.'"[57] The chief targets of this nationwide judicial movement were Socialists, members of the Industrial Workers of the World (or "Wobblies"), and anarchists (political activists whose worldviews were, generally speaking, antithetical to the spirit of the wartime laws). In Chicago, William D. Haywood and 100 other Wobblies were sent to jail—some for as long as 20 years—for encouraging "thousands to refuse to register or submit to the draft," printing and circulating "disloyal, seditious and unpatriotic literature and periodicals," and causing "insubordination and disloyalty by means of publications or speeches."[58] Haywood's colleague Eugene V. Debs was sent to prison for giving a seditious speech in Canton, Ohio. Denouncing war as a means of settling international disputes, condemning war profiteers, and declaring that "the purpose of the Allies is exactly the purpose of the Central Powers," Debs had stated:

And here let me emphasize the fact—and it cannot be repeated too often—that the working class who fight all the battles, the working class who make the supreme sacrifices, the working class who freely shed their blood and furnish the corpses, have never yet had a voice in either declaring war or making peace. It is the ruling class that invariably does both. They alone declare war and they alone make peace. "Yours not to reason why/Yours but to do and die." That is their motto and we object on the part of the awakening workers of this nation.[59]

Debs received a ten-year sentence for publicly elucidating who, exactly, would be shedding their blood and furnishing the corpses.[60] In North Dakota, Socialist Kate Richard O'Hare was given a five years' sentence for publicly comparing mothers who allowed their sons to become soldiers to "brood cows" (the implication being that they were breeding their sons like animals for slaughter).[61] Socialist Charles Schenck was sentenced to six months' hard time for printing and distributing a leaflet that recited the Thirteenth Amendment provision against "involuntary servitude" as an argument against the draft,[62] while Socialist Rose Pastor Stokes received a ten-year sentence for stating in a letter to the *Kansas City Star*: "No government which is *for* the profiteers can also be *for* the people, and I am for the people while the government is for the profiteers."[63] Anarchist Emma Goldman was handed a two-year prison term for publicly counseling "defiance of the Selective Draft law"; in her magazine *Mother Earth*, she had encouraged all conscientious objectors "to affirm their liberty of conscience, and to translate their objection to human slaughter by refusing to participate in the killing of their fellow men." Her comrade Alexander Berkman received a similar sentence for publishing in his newspaper, *The Blast*: "Conscription is the abdication of your rights as a citizen. Conscription is the cemetery where every vestige of your liberty is to be buried. Registration is its undertaker."[64] During the twenty months of U.S. belligerence, seemingly every prominent figure of American radicalism was swept up and effectively 'disappeared' for committing speech acts that challenged officially sanctioned meanings of the national war effort. The official parameters of appropriate speech and behavior had been set— those who strayed beyond did so at great risk.

In one of the strangest cases, Los Angeles film producer Robert Goldstein was fined $500 and sentenced to ten years of hard time because his movie *The Spirit of '76*—a historically accurate piece on the American Revolution— depicted British atrocities against colonialists; the judge in the case stated that the film tended "to question the good faith of our ally, Great Britain."[65] Sadly, Goldstein was just one of 2,000 people prosecuted under the Espionage and Sedition Acts during the years of American belligerence.[66] However justified or dubious in nature, such cases were highly publicized and had a 'chilling effect' on the general public. As Kennedy tells us, every American became keenly aware that to "speak up for immigrants or to defend the rights of labor was to risk being persecuted for disloyalty. And to criticize the course of the war, or to question American or Allied peace aims, was to risk outright prosecution for treason."[67] The government's program to silence the political Left and stamp out all real and perceived domestic opponents of the war effort was so thorough and successful that by the time of Armistice, hardly a liberal voice could be found in the American public sphere—a fact resplendent in tragic irony. Bemoaning the Democratic Party's Congressional losses in the November 1918 elections and anticipating Republican opposition to his idealistic vision for the postwar Versailles Treaty,[68] President Wilson—the very man who had dispatched Burleson and Gregory to lead the wartime fight against sedition—asked a personal adviser where he could turn to for political support. He received the following, brutally honest answer: "All the radical or liberal friends of your anti-imperialist war policy were either silenced or intimidated. The Department of Justice and the Post-Office were allowed to silence or intimidate them. There was no voice left to argue for your sort of peace. When we came to this election the reactionary Republicans had a clean record of anti-Hun imperialistic patriotism. Their opponents, your friends, were often either besmirched or obscured."[69] Thus, by crushing democratic ideals and practices in the United States during the war, President Wilson was unable to obtain the necessary domestic support for his postwar campaign to extend democracy to the rest of the world.

"BODY AND SOUL AND SPIRIT"

On April 5, 1917, Secretary of War Newton D. Baker submitted to Congress a preliminary version of the Selective Service Act, legislation that called for a national military draft. The next day, President Wilson established through executive order the Committee on Public Information (CPI), the nation's first propaganda ministry. While compulsory military service would seek citizens' bodies, the CPI would seek the "soul and spirit"[70] of every American. Operating without specific powers of enforcement, but against the backdrop of forceful and draconian wartime laws like the Espionage and Sedition Acts, the CPI set out to make sure that the United States was represented to the masses "as a strong man fully armed and believing in the cause for which he was fighting."[71] If the AEF carried the nation's sword during the Great War, the CPI wielded its pen.

President Wilson appointed George Creel as the CPI's chairman. A former muckraking journalist from Kansas City who had worked for Wilson's publicity team during the 1916 presidential campaign, Creel brought together, under one organizational umbrella, prominent journalists, advertisers, novelists, intellectuals, moral crusaders, and artists to create an all-pervasive system of communication that would touch nearly every aspect of Americans' private and civic lives. In early 1917, as the nation's entry into the Great War seemed increasingly likely, Creel had privately suggested to Wilson that a successful war effort would require an independent government agency to coordinate "not propaganda as the Germans defined it, but propaganda in the truest sense of the word, meaning the 'propagation of faith.'"[72] As Creel later remarked after the war, victory depended on fostering "a passionate belief in the justice of America's cause" and "weld[ing] the people of the United States into one white-hot mass instinct with fraternity, devotion, courage, and deathless determination."[73] With the creation of the CPI, Creel was able to enact his vision and oversee, as he put it, "the fight for the minds of men" in an ideological war that's "battle-line ran through every home in every country."[74] Thus, while the CPI's efforts would concentrate on America's splintered and contentious society,[75] the propaganda agency would, much like the U.S. armed forces, extend its work overseas and "Carry the Gospel of Americanism to Every Corner of the Globe."[76] Creel's three main goals for the CPI were:

1. To make America's own purposes and ideals clear both to ourselves and to the world, whether ally or enemy.
2. A thorough presentation of the aims, methods, and ideals of the dynastic and feudal government of Germany.
3. Giving information which would help in a constructive way in the daily tasks of a nation at war.[77]

Relatively benign, these stated goals masked, as historian David M. Kennedy puts it, Creel's "overbearing concern for 'correct' opinion, for expression, for language itself, and the creation of an enormous propaganda apparatus to nurture the desired state of mind and excoriate all dissenters."[78] Given practically unlimited resources and independence to fight for the "second lines"[79] (i.e., the hearts and minds of civilian populations), the CPI utilized every available means of (what scholars Robert Jackall and Janice M. Hirota term) "shaping opinion through symbol manipulation and management" both at home and abroad.[80] In so doing, the CPI advanced the government's project of motion and dictated the boundaries of permissible wartime symbolic action.

Creel's mission to shape public opinion began with the implementation of a system of strict media censorship. For three years, the media had provided a relatively uncensored and disturbing picture of the war in Europe to the American people. In Creel's mind, American victory in the war depended on redrawing this picture. The U.S. War Department had started planning for censorship in 1914, shortly after the eruption of the war in Europe. In 1916, War Department researchers released an internal memo entitled, "The Proper Relationship Between the Army and the Press in War," which described the military's needs as "paramount" when compared with those of the media and the American public and warned of the possibility for critical news accounts to damage the armed forces' wartime efficiency.[81]

In March of 1917, War Department officials got their hands on a copy of the "Censorship Book for the German Press," a top secret, official German pamphlet that detailed the media censorship regulations issued by the Prussian Ministry of War. In what may have become the blueprint for American censorship practices, this pamphlet laid out the rules "as to what publications should be suppressed in the interests of the fatherland." Among many things, the German pamphlet forbade the publication of: opinion-editorials that called for the extermination of foreign peoples and thus, besmirched Germany's good name; anything "which might awaken exaggerated hopes, unfounded fears or downheartedness in the interior"; "critical comments concerning the conduct of military operations"; "picture collections and illustrated magazines" that might have undesired effects on "educated people"; "letters of members of the army or Navy without the approval of the military authorities"; anything "which is calculated to disturb the unity of the German people and of the press" or that might harm "the maintenance of the spirit of sacrifice and resolution"; the word "Menschenmaterial" (man material) as an expression for "replacements"; "sensational descriptions of the horrors of war"; "reports concerning so called fraternization scenes between friends and enemies in the trenches"; and, strangely, anything "concerning the phonographic recording of sayings, legends and songs of prisoners of war of various races which are to serve scientific interests." Most importantly, unauthorized representations of soldierly dead were banned from circulation:

> Pictures of dead German soldiers are to be excluded from publication if the features of the dead person are too clear that recognition is possible. Pictures of wounded or mutilated German soldiers are allowed publication only if they carry out the aim of bringing into relief the care and careful nursing which they receive rather than the suffering of such men and if the names are given. [...] The publication of casualty lists before their official dissemination by military authorities is forbidden. [...] The statistics of our losses may not be published.

Though the pamphlet did not explicitly state *why* representations of the dead should be highly censored, the reason was patently clear: German officials believed that such representations would demoralize the German public, paint a negative image of the war and its human costs, and, thus, disrupt the national war effort. Furthermore, censorship of representations of the dead corresponded with the German government's desire to control news and information from the war zone in order to manipulate public discourse and the passions of the German people back home. German leaders believed that victory at the front lines depended on the cooperation of a loyal and subservient national press behind the lines. "Our newspapers should not write what the people like to hear and what would therefore increase the sale of the papers in the streets," the pamphlet stated. "Instead of guessing as to what our generals and troops will accomplish in the field, basing these hazards upon their imperfect knowledge of affairs, they should be much more concerned in calculating the effects of their publications at home and abroad." In other words, the Germans figured that victory would not be possible without heavy-handed, governmental control over wartime *symbolic action*. The *story of the war* had to be officially regulated and maintained.[82]

As director of the CPI, George Creel immediately initiated an American program of media censorship that mirrored Germany's. Throughout the period of U.S. belligerence, this program gave Creel and the powers he served more or less complete control over what Americans knew and understood about events overseas and in domestic military camps. On May 27, 1917, Creel issued a self-censorship card (edited by President Wilson himself) to journalists and editors at every American newspaper and magazine. Seeking to avoid a First Amendment showdown, Creel requested that the media show "self-restraint" in publishing war-related news that had not gone through the CPI first. The censorship card placed news in three categories: "dangerous" material that should not be published, such as information regarding current military operations "except that officially given out"; questionable war-related stories, such as rumors focused on the technology of warfare, which journalists were asked to clear with the CPI before publication; and, material that had no connection to the national war effort and therefore could be broadcast as the editor saw fit.[83] Creel's call for media self-censorship, however, was not a suggestion, but rather a direction. As a handful of journalists and editors discovered the hard way, if they ignored Creel's command they could be prosecuted under the three federal laws discussed earlier in this chapter. In the rare instances during the war when media outlets disobeyed Creel's self-censorship guidelines, or contradicted or challenged CPI-endorsed information, Creel was quick to accuse them of "having given aid and comfort to the enemy," the very Constitutional definition of treason. Observing Creel's modus operandi, U.S. Navy Secretary Josephus Daniels began calling the Espionage Act the "Big Stick behind voluntary censorship."[84] Indeed, it was in editors' and journalists' best interest to "self-censor."

On the other side of the Atlantic Ocean, the AEF imposed a complementary and effective system of combat-zone media censorship. War reporters were forced to sign a "Visiting Correspondent's Agreement" that forbade publishing or repeating *any* information acquired without censorship by the Intelligence Section of the General Staff. Before beginning a tour, reporters were forced to post a bond, subject to forfeit for any violation of accreditation rules, including censorship. While reporters were allowed to carry personal photographic cameras, field censorship virtually killed objective photojournalism, as few images of modern warfare and life in the battle-zone were consistent with the romantic view of war still lingering from the end of the 19th century. All journalistic photographs and reports eventually fell to the CPI's office in Paris. Anything deemed likely to injure national morale back home or "cause unnecessary and unwarranted anxiety to the families of men at the front," including images of death and other horrors, was suppressed. The Paris office even suppressed photographs of African-American and white soldiers relaxing together, which CPI officials feared would anger white Southerners. Similarly, images of American soldiers drinking were quashed so as not to offend teetotalers back home. Civilian combat reporters soon learned what would pass inspection and began censoring themselves; as a result, only bland upbeat and blatantly patriotic reporting made its way back to the United States. Remarkably, but unsurprisingly, not a single image of a dead American soldier's body appeared in print while the war was fought. Reports and photographs that passed muster in Paris were then sent on to CPI officials in the States. There, Creel and his underlings determined what was suitable for circulation and public consumption. This system of tight censorship made the CPI indispensable to the American media, for the CPI, alone, could release such materials as casualty lists and interviews with high-ranking government and military personnel. The CPI also operated the only clearinghouse for press questions about the war. In effect, every piece of war information that reached the average American was endorsed by Creel and the CPI.[85] The uncensored view of the war Americans had enjoyed before U.S. belligerence had been blocked; it no longer existed.

While overseeing this program of media censorship, Creel established a series of departments within the CPI, each charged with a different task, but all operating with one vision.[86] The News Division produced a daily journal, the *Official Bulletin*, with a circulation of 100,000 throughout the war, as well as regular dispatches, often complete with pre-prepared editorials, for distribution to U.S. newspapers. Delivered via wire, radio, and mail, these bulletins ensured that the CPI's messages were uniformly transmitted and received each day in every corner of the country.[87] The Publication Division enlisted academics at top universities to write pamphlets for the *Red, White and Blue Series*, the *War Information Series*, and the *Loyalty Leaflets*. Presented as works of rigorous scholarly thought, these essays—with titles like "How the War Came to America," "Conquest and Kultur," and "American

Loyalty"—were little more than didactic and coercive articulations of the nation's supposedly righteous role in the war. Millions of copies of these publications were distributed across the country and throughout the world, many translated into other languages.[88] The Division of Syndicated Features employed American authors and essayists to write persuasive feature stories and articles for the nation's press. Prominent writers like Samuel Hopkins Adams, Mary Roberts Rinehart, and Walter Lippmann were crucial to the CPI's relentless bid to frame the American war effort as a democratic crusade against German despotism.[89] Each day, these writers crafted news reports that depicted the average German soldier as a cold-blooded butcher and "undeveloped savage," and the Kaiser and his cohort as evil puppet masters—"expert liars trained in the school of Prussian kultur [who] furnish the German people with the news they read."[90] And each day, newspapers published letters from local readers that echoed the CPI's teachings.[91]

The CPI's Division of Advertising worked closely with New York City ad agencies to develop eye-catching newspaper and magazine advertisements for Liberty Loan drives, Red Cross fundraisers, the "Spies and Lies" campaign (which warned that German spies were operating in the States), and other CPI initiatives.[92] Illustrated CPI advertisements appeared in popular magazines like the *Saturday Evening Post*, ominously urging readers to report to the Justice Department any person "who spreads pessimistic stories […] cries for peace, or belittles our efforts to win the war."[93] Such ads brought the perverse nature of sanctioned wartime thought—which held the desire for peace as a vice rather than a virtue—further into the domestic sphere. The Division of Cartoons issued a weekly bulletin that synchronized the work of the nation's cartoonists, those lowbrow artists who tickled the minds and funny-bones of children and adults alike. Each week, the Division of Cartoons "suggested" a number of particular themes that cartoonists should address. Examples included: to encourage women to take the industrial places of men fighting in Europe; to show workers the disastrous results of striking during wartime; to warn against the folly of overconfidence "even though the boys over there seem to have the Huns on the run"; to encourage families and girlfriends to send AWOL soldiers back to duty with a smile; and, to discourage enthusiasm over premature "peace propaganda" "until the last vestige of Germany's crime is atoned for."[94] Thus, this section of the American newspaper, typically reserved for humorous escapism or farcical political commentary, became another site for the CPI to disseminate its direct messages. It also stood as one more example of just how inescapable CPI propaganda was on a day-to-day level.

The CPI's efforts were not just confined to the written word. Rather, they extended to nearly every conceivable venue where public attention could be accessed. For instance, the CPI brought a traveling war exposition—complete with huge guns, the remnants of German U-boats and planes, and a mock battle—to state fairs and major cities throughout the country.[95] The CPI created the "League of Oppressed Nations," an organization that coordinated the patriotic activities of 33 ethnic "loyalty groups" and staged parades and rallies where foreign-born citizens—viewed with suspicion by native-born Americans—could publicly demonstrate their allegiance to the United States.[96] Such efforts sought to fuse unassimilated immigrant communities into one continuous unit around a single, consensual set of "American" values (including freedom, equality, justice, and prosperity).[97] The CPI infiltrated public schools around the United States; students viewed war photographs issued by the CPI, recited war songs from a CPI brochure, studied CPI-sponsored war maps with teachers, and brought CPI literature home for their parents.[98] Creel created the CPI's Division of Industrial Relations, oversaw the establishment of a special propaganda arm within the Department of Labor, and bankrolled the American Alliance for Labor and Democracy (a flag-waving, anti-socialist workers' union). Determined to keep working classes "industrious, patriotic, and quiet" during the war, these three organizations inundated factories and shipyards with posters, speakers, and slogans designed to counter the radical charge (proffered by the International Workers of the World and other labor agitators) that the Great War was a capitalists' war in which workers had little to gain.[99] Again, the CPI left no rock unturned and attempted to infiltrate the hearts and minds of Americans from every angle and in every venue. Whether the average American wholeheartedly believed *everything* the CPI generated is unknowable. But there is little doubt that the CPI successfully conditioned the populous to recognize and accept the CPI's ideology, rhetoric, and lexicon, as those of the nation itself.

The CPI's Speaking Division sent thousands of voluntary orators, including members of the Four Minute Men, to movie houses, fraternal lodges, labor unions, garages, lumber camps, churches, colleges, and even Indian reservations across the United States to give highly orchestrated speeches on topics such as "Why We Are Fighting," "Unmasking German Propaganda," and "Where Did You Get Your Facts?" Each week, the CPI sent its 75,000 orators a bulletin that provided a fresh list of "important points," suggestions for outlines and opening remarks, and a couple of "typical illustrative speeches." In turn, the veritable army of speakers broadcast the CPI's messages through testimonial-like presentations, creating a nationwide echo chamber of pro-war talking points.[100] Meanwhile, the Division of Pictorial Publicity contracted talented painters of various styles to produce hundreds of gripping visual images that were mass-produced as public posters. Notable artists like James Montgomery Flagg, N. C. Wyeth, and Edmund Tarbell created memorable images of wounded Allied soldiers bravely going "over the top" of trench walls, innocent women and children drowning after German U-boat attacks, and the "Spirit of America" as a re-embodied Joan of Arc, all of them designed to foster allegiance to the war effort, sympathy for citizens of allied nations, or hatred of the enemy.[101] The most famous and perhaps most effective poster developed during this project was Flagg's portrait of Uncle Sam, dressed in his red, white, and blue costume, looking potential recruits in the eye with the command "I Want You."[102] Displayed in general stores and post offices, on telephone poles and alley walls,[103] these posters were designed to cut through processes of contemplation and elicit knee-jerk responses in favor of the national war effort.

The CPI also spread its messages through the new visual medium of cinema. During the period of American belligerence, the CPI's Division of Films produced, promoted, approved, or distributed for public consumption an endless stream of weekly newsreels, documentaries, and fictional films about American war technologies, the social dimensions of life in the military, and the accomplishments of the AEF in Europe. Propaganda films like *Pershing's Crusaders* offered exciting, but carefully selected, documentary footage of American operations in Europe,[104] and were billed to American audiences as showing "the grim earnestness of the United States Government in its war activities and its determination to stamp out Kaiserism":

> You see Americans taking over the fighting trenches. [...] You see the first German prisoners captured by our brave boys. [...] You also see what Uncle Sam's countless civilian army is doing "over here." Miles of cantonments grow over-night. You see the raw recruit become the hardened fighter. [...] Mighty guns and projectiles are made before your very eyes. [...] You realize that every American is doing his best to help win this war. [...] It is a picture that every soldier's mother, wife, or sweetheart will want to see. YOU MAY SEE YOUR BOY OVER THERE.

Sold in part on the ludicrous notion that desperate American women might see upon the silver screen images of their beloved men who were stationed overseas, these films were nothing short of works of political indoctrination. While such movies were supposed to mobilize support of the national war effort, other CPI films were designed to encourage contempt for Germany and its leaders; advertisements for *The Kaiser, the Beast of Berlin* claimed: "It makes Americans fighting mad."[105] Other CPI films, such as *Our Colored Fighters* and *Woman's Part in the War*, were produced with niche audiences in mind.[106]

Americans, however, were not the Division of Films' only targets, as the CPI hoped to manage foreign perceptions of American culture, policies, and military operations via the new and dazzling medium of cinema. Through an export licensing agreement, the Division of Films forced American producers of movies meant for international consumption to require their foreign exhibitors to show CPI propaganda films as well.[107] This licensing agreement also enabled the Division of Films to end the exportation of gangster movies, which key members of the CPI believed were tarnishing the United States' image abroad.[108] In addition, the Division of Films worked closely with the National Association of the Motion Picture Industry—Hollywood's most influential association of movie executives, actors, and theater owners—to produce short instructional films, arrange public speaking activities of movie stars, and create feature films in support of the war effort. Recognizing that there was much to be gained by helping the CPI achieve its goals, Hollywood studios released a series of films (such as *The Unbeliever*) that deified the common U.S. soldier, vilified German soldiers, offered sanitized portrayals of trench combat (to ease the fears of American families), and exaggerated the positive effects that the war was having on national unity and American manhood.[109] "In the whole undertaking the effort was to gain the greatest patriotic use of the camera and the drama and human interest it could convey, without endangering military secrets," write historians James R. Mock and Cedric Larson.[110]

Throughout 1917 and 1918, it was practically impossible for Americans to avoid CPI propaganda during their day-to-day routines. As Mock and Larson put it: "Through every known channel of communication the Committee carried straight to the people its message of Wilson's idealism, a war to end war, and America to the rescue of civilization. [The Committee] was able to address itself directly to the minds and hearts of Americans, however isolated they might appear to be from the main stream of martial activity"[111] (a strategy that Hitler and his cohort would later take to extremes in 1930s Germany).War-related information was categorized either as CPI-approved (and therefore "factual") or as "rumor" (and therefore potentially "seditious" and "pro-German"). A precursor to the propaganda machines of Nazi Germany and Stalinist Russia,[112] the CPI used its stranglehold on information to flood American consciousness with ideas, slogans, and arguments that effectively narrowed citizens' possible ways of being down to two: one could either wholeheartedly support every aspect of the nation's war effort, or one could be a traitor. According to the CPI, there was no room for anything in between.

The CPI's propaganda helped inflame tensions, fear, and intolerance across the country. Whether out of patriotic fervor or out of fear of being labeled traitorous, the American press and millions of private citizens imbibed, regurgitated, and acted upon the CPI's carefully crafted system of thought and language. Dissent of any form became equated with disloyalty; anything English or French was to be extolled, while everything German was to be hated and treated with suspicion. German Americans, once regarded as easily acculturated and upright citizens, became prime targets for those wishing to display their patriotism. Promotions in the business world, government, and military were denied to persons who had German names, while a German name was often sufficient evidence for the APL to launch an investigation into the private affairs of a person. City officials across the country altered the names of towns, villages, streets, parks, and schools that bore German names. Germantown, Nebraska, was renamed Garland after a local soldier who died in Europe; East Germantown, Indiana, was changed to Pershing; Berlin, Iowa, became Lincoln. Everyday words like "hamburger," "sauerkraut," and "German measles" were replaced by "liberty sandwich," "liberty cabbage," and (unbelievably) "liberty measles." Renowned symphonies and opera companies in Pittsburgh, Boston, Philadelphia, and New York banned the works of Beethoven and other "disloyal music." In the most infamous example of anti-German sentiment, a lynch mob in Maryville, Illinois, murdered Robert Prager, a German alien, under suspicion that he was a spy. A trial of the mob's leaders followed, during which the defense counsel called their deed "patriotic murder." When the judge read the jury's verdict of not guilty, one jury member shouted: "Well, I guess nobody can say we aren't loyal now!" The *Washington Post* remarked: "In spite of excesses such as lynching, it is a healthful and wholesome awakening in the interior of the country."[113] (It seemed that in war time the press was capable of being not just patriotic, but blindly so.)

German Americans were not the only victims of this vigilantism, hatred, and suspicion. In such a cultural atmosphere, every citizen was a potential target. The head of the Iowa Council of Defense declared that every person in the United States should join a patriotic society, denounce *all* those persons who dared even to discuss peace, and generally "find out what his neighbor thinks." To do anything less was anti-American.[114] Across the nation, chapters of the vigilante group the American Defense League compiled lists that classified every citizen as "loyal, disloyal, doubtful, [or] unknown."[115] And newspapers published so-called "slacker lists" that publicly shamed individuals who did not purchase the appropriate amount of government war bonds. On October 15, 1918, the *Olympia* (WA) *Daily Recorder* published a front-page exposé on W. L. Gregg, a local dentist who refused to purchase war bonds from the Thurston County Liberty Loan Adjustment Committee. Publishing Gregg's work address (presumably to invite hostile actions against Gregg and his clientele), the write-up stated:

> Last spring Dr. Gregg considered his financial condition sufficiently prosperous to trade his Buick for a new six-cylinder automobile, which we understand is entirely paid for, and yet he refuses to buy bonds.
>
> Many reports of Dr. Gregg's pro-German tendencies have gone the rounds, and so far as we can ascertain, he has bought no bonds of any Liberty Loan.

> Several days ago the Adjustment Committee notified Dr. Gregg that $500.00 was his share of the Fourth Liberty Loan. [...] On being advised to use his credit in buying bonds, whereby he could buy on the installment plan, he stated he was "Unwilling to do so," and was absolutely "Not in sympathy with this war or this country in its conduct of the war."
>
> Alien enemies are truly undesirable, but the American who is a leach on the community and does nothing to help his Government is still worse. Citizens of this class are entitled to the Kaiser's iron cross.[116]

Offering innuendo, ad hominem attacks, and not-so-veiled threats of violence, this chilling public statement reflected the unmistakably undemocratic tenor of CPI propaganda. In Olympia, just as in every corner of the nation, the private individual was subject to the supposed will of the collective. Americans who did not enthusiastically support the war effort—in this case, those who did not purchase government bonds to fund mass murder on the other side of the world—could be compelled to do so, either through public shaming or more forceful means.

"GRESHAM, ENRIGHT, AND HAY!"

On November 5, 1917, headlines across the country announced that the United States had suffered its first official combat casualties of the Great War.[117] The *Washington Post* declared: "Germans Raid Trench, Kill 3." The *Los Angeles Times* reported: "Three Are Slain by a German Raiding Party." And the *Pittsburgh Post* proclaimed: "Huns Raid Trenches; Three of Our Boys Are Dead." Though at first U.S. military censors withheld the names of the soldiers killed and the location where the skirmish took place, some crucial details emerged from the initial accounts. Readers learned that during the dark morning hours of November 3, a German "raiding party" stalked and attacked a much smaller group of U.S. soldiers who had been training with French forces somewhere in the trenches of the Western Front. Employing their "favorite trick" of targeting inexperienced opponents, the veteran "Teutons"[118] launched "a desperate effort [...] in the form of a heavy barrage fire, which isolated a salient of the American trench, and apparently left a small force of Americans at the mercy of their enemies." Killing three Americans, wounding five, and taking twelve more as prisoners, the "Huns" hastily "retreated to the protection of their own earthworks before American reinforcements could arrive" to exact revenge.

An account from a German prisoner who had witnessed the attack indicated that the three dead soldiers had "fought gamely" before they succumbed, thus the War Department was confident that the Americans "did well" in their first test of battle. However, this German prisoner's sentiments were not shared by his compatriots writ large; in a tone of nationalistic outrage, the *Los Angeles Times* described a Berlin newspaper opinion-editorial, entitled "Good Morning, Boys," which mocked the U.S. casualties: "Perhaps your boss, Wilson, will reconsider his newest line of business before we grab off more of his young people," the German newspaper purportedly stated. Encouraged to feel indignation over the nation's first combat deaths in Europe, Americans were also reassured that the sacrifice was not in vain: "Though first blood may thus have been scored by Germany," wrote the *Washington Post*, "officials see this advantage—Germany will know that the United States is actually on the firing line." Furthermore, opined the *Post*, the American public would have to get used to the grim reality that many U.S. soldiers would die in the war: "it is part of the game."[119]

For months, government and military officials had hoped that the nation's first combat deaths would invigorate the domestic war effort with a clear and productive sense of collective sacrifice and national purpose. Just before the AEFs arrival in Europe, British and French military leaders had conveyed to their American counterparts that U.S. citizens would not realize the urgency of the international crisis until American troops had been "well blooded."[120] Less privately, on July 27, 1917, the *New York Times* had published an essay entitled, "First Casualty List Will Arouse American War Spirit," in which British Captain John Hay Beith had argued that the first U.S. deaths would make "American enthusiasm kindled for the allied cause." Beith had asserted that the ethnically heterogeneous people of the United States, "miners from Pennsylvania [...] cowboys from Wyoming [...] a polyglot laboring class from everywhere"—"a far larger and less amenable population" than the respective poleis of the Revolutionary War and Civil War eras—would be transfigured into one, unified collective by the first official combat deaths of American doughboys. Equating America's tepid martial spirit with Britain's initial wartime experience, Beith had written:

> Heaven knows, it took us long enough, and we were only a hundred miles from the very heart of things! An ounce of experience—a Zeppelin here, a torpedoed liner there—can awake more national spirit in five minutes than a ton of imagination can achieve in five years.
>
> So it is only natural that America, removed from all risk of actual invasion, should require a little time to adjust herself to new conditions and to reawaken that martial and indomitable spirit which has made her such a formidable fighting power in the past. The landing of Gen. Pershing's troops has already done much. The first casualty list, alas! will do ten times more.[121]

Thus, Beith had attempted to charge preemptively that inevitable moment when the first American soldiers would fall in battle with intense, reverberating social power.

During the summer of 1917, the American media had thirsted for a tale of wartime sacrifice, and had made much of any injury or death suffered by U.S. soldiers who, though not yet engaged in direct combat with the enemy, were moving closer to the Western Front.[122] For instance, the *Washington Post* had reported on the "first field casualty among the armed forces" (an American soldier who was injured while mishandling a French bomb).[123] In August, the *New York Times* had announced "the first casualty in the Marine Corps expeditionary contingent" (a marine who was killed in a motorcycle accident).[124] The most substantial of these 'first' stories had emerged in September 1917, when German warplanes attacked a field hospital and killed four U.S. army medics. "America's first sacrifice to German frightfulness in Europe," the *Washington Post* had exclaimed. Citing official reports, the media had described how the "defenseless" hospital staff, surrounded by the bursts of "death-dealing missiles," tended to the casualties with "the utmost bravery." One nurse "was slightly wounded about the face and her clothing was torn to shreds, but bravely she went on with her duties." To add insult to injury, the German aviators had dropped coins over the demolished camp "as souvenirs that the Americans might not forget the raid and as tribute to America's supposed love of money." Reporters had been dispatched across the United States to the homes of the four medics killed, in some cases breaking the tragic story to the parents of the dead (it seems that while publicizing these deaths to the American newspapers, the CPI and the military had neglected to contact the families of the dead directly). "I regret that my son did not have a chance to die fighting," one mother had responded to the news. "He had no chance to fight back in an air raid." Another parent, Rudolph Rubino of New York City, had stood beside his weeping wife as he told the press: "I am an American. Therefore, I have given up my son. I left Germany when I was fifteen. There has never been a spark of love left for the vile nation that gave me birth... I am more of an American now than ever." M. D. Wood, a bricklayer from Streator, Illinois, who had been informed by his local newspaper that his son was dead, cried out loud: "Oh, God, how can I tell my wife; I've been half expecting this. He was our baby... But she is an American mother and she will understand."[125] Notably, each of these parents had been quick to cast their personal loss as a willing sacrifice for the nation—an indication that the government's crackdown on "disloyalty" had sunk in—at least per the rhetoric displayed in such news reports.

Though entailing the real and provocative wartime suffering of American soldiers and families, as well as addressing certain themes of patriotic death and loyalty that would remain relevant throughout the war, each of these 'first' stories had disappeared within a few days of their publishing. Like the helpless victims of the *Lusitania* attack, the casualties in these vignettes had not died in the glory of battle for the nation. Instead, the dead had been more like passive victims of chance and German "barbarity"—hardly any national redemption could be found in the loss of a soldier's hand, the slip of a motor-cycle, or the wanton slaughter of unarmed medics. In a sense, these 'first' sto-ries had emphasized the impotence of the casualties and their inability to fight back against the wartime forces of death. In the case of the hospital bombing, this figurative impotence had been brought into starker contrast by the heavy presence of women who, whether tending to the wounded while seminude or grieving for their "babies" who "did not have a chance to die fighting," had been the most central and active characters. The nation's casualties had not yet embodied the masculine ethos associated with dying on the battlefield—an ethos upon which productive narratives of courage, sacrifice, and patriotic death could be more easily built.

The reports of November 5, 1917, however, filled this conspicuous void. In accord with many of Beith's predictions, the news of the nation's first offi-cial combat deaths assumed a central and long-lasting place in the national discourse of the war. In the days, weeks, and months following the initial accounts, the media obsessively (and patriotically) reported on the three slain men, their families and hometowns, and the events surrounding their deaths. Like much of the war news before the period of U.S. belligerence, the stories of the nation's first slain soldiers were extremely graphic (something the CPI would come to censor for the sake of maintaining public morale). Americans learned that the dead soldiers—Thomas F. Enright of Pittsburgh, Merle Hay of Des Moines, and James Gresham of Evansville, Indiana—had "fought bravely against a numerically superior enemy force, a handful of men fighting until they were smothered." Inflicting an untold number of casualties upon the Germans (who supposedly had removed their dead before retreating), the Americans had met the kind of violent ends befitting modern-day gladiators: the three men were beaten and stomped to death in hand-to-hand combat, their throats slashed with blunt German knives for good measure. (One can only imagine how the soldiers' next of kin must have felt about these details.) "The whole American Expeditionary Forces are thrilled by the fight put up by their comrades," wrote the *Los Angeles Times*, "and all are anxious to get a chance to deal a blow [...] America has begun to pour out fighting blood on the battle grounds of Europe." The *Pueblo Chieftain* echoed these sentiments, reporting that the Second Colorado Infantry had "inaugurated a custom of drinking a toast to the memory of Hay, Gresham and Enright [...] a grim pledge to do their uttermost against the foe." The *Pittsburgh Post* compared their deaths to those of Davy Crockett and the "defenders of the Alamo," while *Life Magazine* published a poem by Christopher Morley that read: "Gresham and Enright and Hay!/There are no words to say/Our love, our noble pride/For these, our first who died." Practically overnight, the three soldiers were made into a kind of holy trinity around which political, economic, and cultural capi-tal could be mobilized. Leaping from the physical to the metaphysical—from the realm of worldly materiality to the realm of ideas—the three fallen soldiers represented the nation's baptism by fire. These young men became so familiar to the public that within months the U.S. government began placing melodramatic newspaper advertisements (underwritten by American banks and corporations) asking citizens to purchase war bonds "in memoriam" of Gresham, Enright, and Hay. The Red Cross, seeking private donations for its wartime efforts, did the same: "They gave till they died! What will you give?"[126] While not all Americans could go and fight in Europe, many could sacrifice some money for the cause.

Perhaps officials were surprised to discover that, just as swiftly as the deaths of Gresham, Enright, and Hay "kindled" America's war passions, the event also ushered in sobering and contentious questions regarding the proper treatment and burial of American war dead. It became apparent that the meaning of American soldiers' deaths might be bifurcated. On the one hand the war dead could be celebrated and venerated on a somewhat abstract national level for their patriotic sacrifice. On the other hand the war dead might also represent the grim suffering and loss of American families and local communities that, despite the heroic rhetoric attached to the deaths of their men, would be deeply concerned about the treatment of fallen soldiers' material remains. A troubling and, for relatives of drafted soldiers, *morbid* question started to percolate: What would happen to the average soldier's body if, God forbid, he were killed in this savage and brutal war? This was a question that the government, intent on rapidly mobilizing the national war spirit, had not yet explicitly addressed.

On November 5, the same day the initial story broke, Private Thomas Enright's sister, Mary Irwin, mailed a short letter[127] to Secretary of War Newton D. Baker requesting the return of her brother's remains. It read:

QMC Washington D. C.
November 5–1917
Mr. Newton Baker
　　You informed me that my brother Private Thomas F. Enright was killed in France.
　　I would like to know how his body is killed and if you would have the body sent to Pittsburgh for burrial.

> Sincerely Yours
> Mrs Frank Irwin
> 6641 Premo St.
> Pittsburgh Pa.

Signing in her husband's name and limiting her sparse message to two matter-of-fact sentences, Irwin cast herself not as a hysterical, grieving sister of the departed, but rather as a dutiful and somewhat stoic woman who simply wished to see that her brother's body was treated properly. Her tone was one of simple inquiry, not confrontation or profound mourning. And the brevity of her note limited the chances of expressing something that might be misinterpreted as "seditious" or "treasonous."

As Gresham, Enright, and Hay were mythologized from coast to coast, the treatment and commemoration of Enright's body became not only a private concern for Mary Irwin, but also a public matter for local groups that wished to stake a claim in the dead soldier's immense and growing symbolic power. Over the following weeks, Irwin's private appeal was expressed in loftier terms by a number of influential figures and groups from Pittsburgh.[128] Guy E. Campbell, U.S. Representative of the 32nd District, Pennsylvania, wrote a letter to Secretary of War Newton D. Baker in which he made patriotic appeals for the return of Enright's corpse:

At a recent meeting of the United Spanish War Veterans, of Pittsburgh, Pa., resolutions were adopted requesting the co-operation of Members of Congress, public officials and civic organizations in seeking the return to the United States of the body of Private Thomas Enright, the first Pittsburgher to fall in France in the service of his country.

While I appreciate that as the casualties increase, it will be impossible to forward the remains of stricken soldiers to the United States, it seems to me it would be a fitting and just tribute to the first of the fallen to return their bodies to their friends, for burial at home. Accordingly I respectfully ask that such action be taken in this case, and that the body of Private Enright be brought from France at the earliest opportunity.[129]

Channeling the spirit of the Pittsburgh community's growing demand for Enright's body, the Allegheny County Commissioners adopted a resolution on the matter and sent it to Secretary Baker. The resolution read, in part:

WHEREAS, Thomas Enright a native of the City of Pittsburgh, laid down his life at the call of his country on the battlefields of France, and

WHEREAS, we feel that the people of this city and county desire that this young man who has made the supreme sacrifice on the altar of patriotism should be laid at rest in his home city by the people who honor his name, and

WHEREAS, the said Thomas Enright is the first Pittsburgher to give up his life under the flag of his country in this war and the people of this city and county would like to honor and cherish his memory, now therefore be it

RESOLVED, that the County Commissioners do hereby request of Secretary of War Baker that the body of said Thomas Enright be transported by the War Department from France to Pittsburgh in order that he may be laid at rest in his home city.[130]

In short order, Mary Irwin's personal request for her brother's bodily remains was consumed by a civic project that sought to establish a permanent link between the city of Pittsburgh and the nation's first "supreme sacrifice" in the Great War.

These publicized,[131] official entreaties, however, failed to reflect the opinions of every citizen of Pittsburgh. In fact, they elicited a wave of negative reactions from many locals, who, like their counterparts, felt emboldened to share their thoughts directly with Secretary Baker. (Unlike today, Americans had not yet been conditioned to the automatic, knee-jerk reaction of 'honoring' U.S. troops no matter the circumstance.) In a letter dated November 20, 1917, one woman, identifying herself only as "a very patriotic Pittsburgh Mother,"[132] questioned the motives of Enright's relatives and warned against the potential effects of immediate repatriation. Citing her memory of Pittsburgh's commemoration of Francis P. DeLowry, one the first U.S. soldiers to die in the Battle of Veracruz (1914),[133] she wrote:

When that young DeLowry the first Pitts boy killed at the Mexican border was brought home, St. Mary's church to which he belonged made a gala day out of the funeral. Vice Pres. Marshall who happened to be passing through Pitts. attended there were street parade which were filmed and run in the movies and the family certainly found he was more valuable dead than alive as he was a regular scamp when living.

Now young Enrights people have about the same plan in view they are trying to arrange for a grand military funeral and have asked the Spanish War veterans to intercede are getting up a petition to have the name of the St. where his folks live changed to his name etc. so why bring his body home while other boys as dear to their people will be buried in France. I think this should be wisely considered + know it will be if you stop to think for in case he is brought home you will be besieged with like requests and we would be justified in making them.[134]

With the tone of a jealous, petty neighbor, this "very patriotic Pittsburgh mother" urged the government to contemplate the Pandora's Box that would be opened with the return of Enright's remains. In a letter of similar content, James B. Cramer of Pittsburgh wrote to Secretary Baker:

My dear sir:- It seems harsh to say so, but *do* you think it quite *fair* or *just* to have our government go to the expense of having the body of *one* soldier—even tho he were among the first to fall brought over to his home city + *not accord* that same thing to the bodies of the first dozen or first score or first hundred who fell fighting as bravely as he did? [...] Private Enright's friends have in Pittsburgh say they'll move heaven and earth but they'll get his body here but the parents of others have no "pull" no influence, no money to get their loved sons brought back. Hundreds of us right here in Pittsburg protest against such

discrimination, and ask you *not* to establish such a precedent at the expense of
the feelings of thousands of others.[135]

Evoking the democratic principle of equality and the expectation that *all*
U.S. citizens would be treated in an *identical* fashion, Cramer asked the government to consider the "feelings" of those whose sons might not die such
noteworthy deaths. In essence, Cramer wanted to know if the death of one
soldier (a cog in the machine) could be more meaningful that the deaths of all
others. Clearly, the question of what to do with Enright's body was one that
had many possible answers.

Predictably, government and military officials chose the answer that
entailed the least amount of visible complications for the national war effort:
the bodies of American soldierly dead would remain in Europe until the end
of the war. In private letters of response to the writers mentioned above, the
Quartermaster Corps stated that, on the recommendation of U.S. Commanding General John J. Pershing, and in "view of the difficulties in shipping
[soldiers'] remains home," Secretary Baker had requested that "bodies of
deceased officers and soldiers be not shipped from France to the United States
during the continuance of the war."[136] Publicly, the decision was also laid at
the feet of French authorities; on December 30, 1917, a *Washington Post*
headline announced: "France Wants U.S. Dead: Gen. Sibert Asks That First
Three Soldiers Killed Be Buried There."[137] The French, it seemed, were not
willing to part with these (potentially) rhetorically useful corpses. Skirting
the personal, domestic, and emotional implications of denying the return of
American war dead, the U.S. military settled, at least temporarily, the matter
of repatriation as efficiently as possible. Whether dead or alive, citizen or
soldier, not even one individual would be permitted to disrupt the national
war machine. Of course, the fact that an Allied victory was not guaranteed
meant that American war dead might be left in Europe forever—a notion that
surely terrified next of kin.

Indications of a simmering controversy, however, spurred the military to
conduct an elaborate funeral for Gresham, Enright, and Hay, which would
help reduce the anxieties of Americans back home, whose men—inching
ever closer to full out combat with the enemy—could meet similar ends. On
November 9, 1917, the *Washington Post* reported that the three soldiers had
received a beautiful and moving funeral. "The first three American soldiers
killed in the trenches in France tonight are sleeping in French soil," the *Post*
stated. "With a guard of French infantrymen in their picturesque uniforms
of red and horizon blue standing on one side and a detachment of American
soldiers on the other, the flag wrapped caskets were lowered in the grave as
a bugler blew taps and the batteries at the front fired minute guns." At the
ceremony, General Paul Bordeaux of the French Army delivered an emphatic

eulogy, proclaiming, "They have fallen facing the foe in a hard and desperate hand-to-hand fight. Honor to them. Their families, friends, and fellow citizens will be proud when they learn of their deaths. [...] We inscribe on their tombs: 'Here Lie the First Soldiers of the Republic of the United States to Fall on the Soil of France for Liberty and Justice.'" Something like Simonides's ancient epitaph to Spartans killed at Thermopylae, Gresham, Enright, and Hays' grave markers supposedly would mark and consecrate the spot where heroic soldiers had spilled their blood: "The passerby will stop and uncover his head," Bordeaux stated. "Travelers and men of heart will go out of their way to come here to pay their respective tributes."[138] Bordeaux insinuated that American sacrifices in Europe would be remembered for generations to come.

A week later, General Pershing paid a personal visit to the three graves. The *Washington Post* described Pershing's visit as a pilgrimage of sorts. Drawing attention to the material aspects of the men's resting places, which were "situated on a green hill, overlooking a small village," the *Post* described in a front-page article how Pershing had "showed especial interest in the simple markers upon the graves, recording the name, company and regiment of each of the Americans buried there, and in a wreath of native flowers hung within the inclosure [*sic*]."[139] This intimate portrait of Pershing's gravesite visit suggested that the man responsible for sending U.S. troops into battle would not take the deaths of his men lightly. For the first time since American entry into the war, government and military officials were fathoming the depths of emotion and grief that, as greater numbers of soldiers died, would engulf families and communities across the nation.

Back in Pittsburgh, a civic plan to change the name of the road that Thomas Enright had lived on from "Premo Street" to "Enright Street" was derailed; opponents to the plan discovered that Enright had, in fact, never resided on Premo Street; furthermore, he had only lived in Pittsburgh for short periods of his life.[140] In similar fashion, a proposal to construct a Pittsburgh playground in Enright's memory was never realized.[141] Instead of the return of her brother's remains or the establishment of a public memorial in his name, the only memento Mary Irwin received during the war was a French "Croix du Guerre" medal.[142] Sent by the French Army to the families of Privates Gresham and Hay as well, the medals were meant to stand as souvenirs of the dead soldiers' ultimate sacrifice. On February 15, 1918, the *Los Angeles Times* described the "Croix du Guerres" sent to the three families in terms that stretched religious, pro-war rhetoric to the point of absurdity:

In this case the cross of war is a cross of glory, just as truly as was the cross on which the Saviour died. The cross is an ancient symbol and has many meanings, but perhaps the greatest significance of the sign lies in the fact that it is an emblem of compromise, especially since the death of the Man of Galilee. The cross is an indication of an unsolved issue and signifies a compromise between matter and spirit, between God and man, between justice and mercy—a compromise that is necessary until the children of men shall come into a realization of the unity of life.[143]

As we will see, the "Croixe du Guerre" medals signified nothing this hyperbolic to the relatives of Gresham, Enright, and Hay. After the war, Gresham and Enright's families would reveal in letters to the government that their desires regarding the treatment of bodily remains had little in common with the national, pro-war discourse that had coalesced around their loved ones' deaths (a point I will return to in the following chapter).

The case of Gresham, Enright, and Hay, revealed the dormant anxieties and dilemmas that lurked just below the surface of the national war effort. Their deaths laid bare the tension between honoring the dead in a way that would satisfy the emotional needs of the living and treating each grieving family the same. Moreover, their deaths triggered public conversations about what it meant for U.S. soldiers to die on foreign soil and what would constitute the proper treatment and commemoration of dead soldiers. Although Gresham, Enright, and Hay, would fade from the public's imagination as U.S. belligerence ramped up and hundreds of American troops were killed in battle each

Figure 2.1 Thomas Enright's grave, Saint Mary Catholic Cemetery, Pittsburgh, PA, present-day. Author's own photograph.

day, the events in the immediate aftermath of their deaths foreshadowed the controversies and conflicts that would emerge during the postwar years.

OVER THERE

As late as August 1917, the AEF was grossly unprepared for the crucial and inevitable task of handling dead soldiers' remains properly. No clear system had yet been put into practice. This lack of preparedness became obvious on August 21, 1917, when U.S. Marine Frederick Wahlstrom of Brooklyn crashed his motorcycle, fractured his skull, and died of cerebral hemorrhage in Bazoilles, France. The first Marine to perish in Europe (albeit, not in battle), Wahlstrom was buried, along with his only identification tag, in a temporary grave next to a U.S. Army Hospital.[144] His personal effects, including a ring and gold watch, were handed over to Chaplain G. Livingston Bayard of the U.S. Army, who in turn gave them to Major Henry M. Butler of the 5th Regiment Marines. On August 23, just two days after his passing, Wahlstrom's possessions were, strangely enough, sold off in a public auction. Prior to 1917, U.S. Army regulations had authorized the auctioning of dead soldiers' possessions, but only under particular circumstances: "If there be no legal representatives present to receive the effects, a list of them will be sent to the nearest relative of the deceased. If not claimed within a reasonable time, they will be sold at auction and accounted for."[145] Thus, it seems that such a practice had been acceptable, if not common, in the years leading up to American belligerence. But the decision to sell Wahlstrom's effects to the highest bidder after such a short period of time, and before contacting his next of kin on the other side of the Atlantic, indicated an appalling lack of consideration for the dead soldier and his loved ones—a point that became all the starker when Wahlstrom's relatives inquired about his watch and ring. Here, we witness the military beginning to recognize and grapple with an inescapable truth: that every fallen U.S. soldier killed overseas would leave behind loved ones with needs, expectations, questions, and emotions. The letters from Wahlstrom's family sparked a joint investigation by the Quartermaster Corps and the Marines, who both sought (unsuccessfully) to trace the whereabouts of the objects. Those individuals who were directly involved in the Wahlstrom affair were ordered not to repeat their actions, and were told that the War Department would soon be issuing to all the military branches a standard procedure for handling the dead.[146]

In fact, two weeks prior to the Wahlstrom affair, military officials back home had settled on a universal system for dealing with American war dead. The War Department recognized the fact that the process of retrieving, identifying, burying, and keeping track of soldierly remains during the war was no easy task, and was one at which the belligerent nations had mostly failed. When the United States entered the Great War, the lifeless bodies of an estimated one million soldiers, friend and foe, remained unburied in the Western Front's No Man's Land exposed to all sorts of degradation. Troops in the trenches on both sides had learned to live and fight among the rotting corpses (a truly terrifying prospect famously recounted and portrayed in postwar disillusionment literature and art, respectively), but such unsanitary conditions had helped spread diseases that were just as deadly as bullets, bayonets, bombs, and poison gas.[147] On August 7, 1917, the War Department established the Graves Registration Services (a unit within the Quartermaster Corps) to mitigate this terrible reality of the Great War, provide some semblance of respectful treatment of American war dead, prevent U.S. bodies from falling into enemy hands, and avoid situations like the Wahlstrom affair (a controversy that occurred before the system could be universally applied in Europe).[148] Comprised mostly of men who had been deemed incapacitated for active field service,[149] the Graves Registration Service (GRS) tackled this sacred, pressing, ghastly, and dangerous duty.

Under the guidance of Major (formerly Chaplain) Charles C. Pierce,[150] the GRS attempted to fulfill six crucial tasks: to (1) position units along the battle lines to identify and mark graves during and immediately following combat activities; (2) establish and maintain all battlefield cemeteries and graves that contained dead American soldiers; (3) to keep strict records of the burials; (4) assist in identification when the remains of U.S. dead were relocated from temporary battlefield graves to more permanent burial grounds; (5) correspond with families and friends of the dead; and, (6) coordinate mortuary affairs with European governments.[151] The conditions of the war zone made these undertakings extremely precarious—identification and burial efforts often were performed under fire. But, if one official account is to be believed, GRS men consistently and bravely risked their own lives to secure the proper treatment of U.S. war dead:

> Service became imbued with the spirit of service for their fallen comrades, that fidelity of identification became almost a religion. No risk was too dangerous, no effort too great, if it promised identification of a "buddy's" remains. These units followed closely our victorious troops, searching for the un-buried, exhuming the hastily buried, and recording the burials. Many difficulties were encountered, but the work went on ceaselessly.[152]

The allusion to religion in this passage suggests several things about the attitude with which the GRS servicemen approached their job. First, religious faith calls for absolute devotion to one's beliefs at all times, in any situation, and in face of any threat. The acts of recovering, identifying, burying, and providing ecclesiastical rites to fallen soldiers amid mass artillery barrages and close-quarters fighting (a common scenario for GRS servicemen[153]) surely required a similar absolute devotion (specifically, a devotion to the belief that every dead American soldier deserved to be treated properly). Second, religions tend to view death as an occasion of major significance and beauty—the moment of transition from this life to the afterlife. As a result, many religions emphasize the proper handling of the human corpse, for proper handling of the human corpse facilitates a more peaceful transition from this world to the next. By placing monumental importance on mortuary affairs and setting out specific guidelines for handling the dead, many religions imbue the corpse with a sacred quality and give the faithful the conviction and psychological tools necessary to overcome the repulsive dimensions of rotting human flesh. Military training surely instilled in GRS servicemen the compulsion to obey orders upon command but a religious sensibility or perspective must have been essential for enduring this intimate and constant interaction with badly decomposed bodies.[154] As the block quote above indicates, many GRS servicemen must have viewed their work with the dead as something more than a contribution to the war machine—as something approaching the divine. Such a view would have made it easier to suppress all-too-human reactions to dead bodies (abhorrence, grief, and fear) and complete the difficult task at hand—to turn the grotesque (rotting human flesh and bone) into something beautiful (an American soldier lying in his grave).[155]

Often working in coordination with Red Cross volunteers,[156] the GRS recorded data concerning the identity, burial location, personal possessions, and cause of death for the respective fallen soldier. This data was useful for both the GRS' own mission and for passing along to next of kin back home (when deemed appropriate). In addition to dental records, dog tags, and descriptions of the state of the body (level of decomposition, missing limbs, etc.), GRS "Search Reports" contained eyewitness accounts from comrades of the deceased or those who worked to bury them. Providing a glimpse of the respective soldier's last living moments, the typical account read something like this:

Co C—58th Infantry—
4th Division.   CARTER, Lester G.—Priv. 2109410

Killed in action July 19/1918
Buried: Chevilion, France: Grave No 291.
    After the attack on Chezy and while the Company was digging in soldier was struck with shrapnel which tore off his leg, he died shortly after.

Informant: SCHMIDT, Lawrence, A.—Sgt. 2024853
              Co C—56th Infantry—

Signed: HOWES, Edward B.—1st Lieut.
              58th Infantry[157]

or this:

Hdqrs. Co. 7 Inf?   Emrich Chas. Louis. Cook.
Fell from train May 31st/18
    At Troyes as the whole Div. was going up to the front some of us sat on the
ration wagon, as it went under a bridge Cook Emrich was killed instantly, his
head was torn off. The train coming after picked up his dead body. I was an eye
witness. Buried in Troyes.
    Height 5', stout, light complexioned, red hair and blue eyes, knew him one
year, from Pittsburg; Christian name Charles; no other Emrich in the Company.
    Informant: Carney William Sgt. 540117.
                        Emb. Center.
                        Hdqrs. Co. 7. Inf.
    Home Address: Taunton, Mass. RFD. No. I.
                        Jan. 18th 1919.
                        Mary H. Carroll, Searcher[158]

Once this detailed (and often disturbing) information was gathered by the
GRS, the War Department would send (via telegram) a sanitized and succinct notice of death to next of kin. The parents of Clarence T. Sutcliffe, for
example, received from the War Department this telegram concerning their
son's death:

Washington, August 3, 1918
Mrs. Humphrey D. Sutcliffe,
Miami, Fla.
    Deeply regret to inform you that Corporal Clarence T. Sutcliffe, infantry, is
officially reported as killed in action July 19.
                                          McCain, the Adjutant General[159]

For many recipients, surely, the dissonance between the brevity of such a
telegram and the monumental tragedy of its meaning must have been at once
staggering and infuriating. Letters housed at the U.S. National Archives and
Records Administration indicate that the concise nature of the telegrams
spurred many next of kin to seek additional information. For example, after
receiving such a telegram, Mrs. O. S. Webb of Claremore, Oklahoma, sent a
handwritten letter to her son's commanding officer in which she pleaded for
further details:

Dear Sir:
    Of course you must know that I another American Mother, most frantic over
the saddest news I ever received in my life in the message from the Adjutant
General, announcing the death of my precious boy, with Bronchial Pneumonia,
Oct. 10, and that boy was, Priv. Sam J. Web. We wired for particulars but of

course received none. We have been terribly uneasy for weeks. [...] Please let us know—Did he have Influenza? Did he die on board ship—was he buried at sea? Did he reach France, to die there? Was he cared for well—did he realize he was to die? [...] He had a few little things he wanted to send home [...] among them was a Kodak. [...] As we have no picture of him we would love to have those things. [...] Please send us some word and his things C.O.D. if you can. Sam volunteered—and made the supreme sacrifice for his country. I am proud to give him up—but it hurts. I have another boy in the 306 # Motor Supply Train Quartermasters Corps Co 5. Sergt H. S. Webb. If I have to give him up too, my grief will be unspeakable. If you just could tell me it was all a terrible mistake! May I hear from you soon?

Yours Respectfully

Mrs. O. S. Webb
Claremore
Okla.
U.S.A

P.S. Is there some way young soldier or the nurse whom Sam might have known who would write me and tell me all about it? I enclose stamps for a reply.

Four months later, Mrs. Webb received a letter of response from Major Charles C. Pierce (head of the GRS). Pierce provided certain details regarding the location of her son's temporary grave, but stated: "I regret that I am unable to give you information relative to the death of your son. [...] However, I am today requesting the Chaplain of [your son's] company to communicate with you, giving, if possible, the particulars of his death." Whether Mrs. Webb ever received the information she so desperately sought remains unknown.[160] In any event, few Americans were able (for both financial reasons and the impossibility of traveling to Europe during the war) to go and search for their loved ones' graves as families had during the Civil War.[161] Yet the pain, longing, and desperation of those left behind might have to be acknowledged, if not fully assuaged, one way or another.

George H. Edwards, the Mayor of Kansas City, Missouri, received a telegram informing him that his son, George Jr., had died in Trieste, Italy. Ironically, when the United States had first entered the war, Edwards had been a vocal supporter of the national draft and had publicly argued to his constituents that "a man may be compelled by force against will without regard to personal interests, or even religious or political belief, to take his place in the army ranks."[162] Eighteen months later, Edwards experienced the pain shared by so many Americans whose loved ones had been drafted, sent abroad, and consumed by the war. Like Mrs. Webb of Claremore, Oklahoma, and countless other grief-stricken parents, Edwards sought further information regarding his son's death and body. "Please wire details death Lieut. George H Edwards Jr Qm Corps," he requested in a succinct telegram to the GRS. In a letter of reply, the War Department told the mayor that the "particulars relating to this soldier's death have not yet reached this office from overseas." In reality, the War Department must have known the truth of the matter, which had been previously recorded in his GRS report:

> First Lieut George H Edwards Jr QM Corps died midnight [...] from self inflicted pistol wounds in head. He was on duty with Colonel McIntosh, American Food Commission. Board of officers finds that deceased was insane and that death was in line of duty and not due to his own misconduct.[163]

Why the War Department withheld this distressing information at that time—and whether Mayor Edwards and his family ever learned the true circumstances of George Jr.'s demise—remains unclear. The only public statement issued by the mayor's office makes no reference to the fact of suicide: "A message was received yesterday by George H. Edwards [...] from the War Department, informing him of the death of his son. [...] The message was meager and gave no details other than death was from illness."[164] It seems likely that a person of Mayor Edwards's stature would, in time, get the full story if he so desired. Perhaps he did learn of his son's suicide, and in light of his previous patriotic posturing, felt ashamed of his son's suicide (a complex and taboo form of death, devoid of heroic glory); for just a few months after expressing his desire for repatriation, the mayor reversed his position and told the War Department that he did not want his son's body returned home. Today, George Jr.'s grave can be found in the Suresnes American Cemetery just outside Paris.[165] His headstone bares no sign of the exact nature of his death.

In many cases, it was simply impossible to provide grieving next of kin with any information beyond the fact of death. Given the intensity and relentlessness of the fighting along the Western Front, fallen soldiers were often hastily buried in shallow, haphazard graves with minimal attention to identification. Frequently there were mix-ups, such as when, in the heat of battle, identification markers were placed above the wrong graves. In countless instances, solders' bodies were decimated or decomposed in such a way as to make identification unfeasible; in time, these soldiers would be permanently classified as "unknown." Throughout the war, the bodies of living and dead soldiers alike were torched by flamethrowers, obliterated by high explosive shells, and crushed beneath tanks, their bodily remains incinerated, atomized, pulverized, and lost forever. This is to say nothing of the infamous, almost-alive mud of the war zone, which sucked fallen soldiers into the surface of the earth. Thus, despite the GRS' best efforts, it was not uncommon for the identity or whereabouts of a dead body to be lost forever.[166] Toward the end of the war, and in the months following Armistice, the GRS and the War

Figure 2.2 A temporary American Cemetery in France. U.S. National Archives and Records Administration, Record Group 165.

Department began receiving letters from families who sought information regarding the whereabouts of missing soldiers' (and their bodily remains). Some next of kin clung to the hope that a mix-up had been made, and that their loved one might still be alive somewhere in the war-torn expanses of Europe. For instance, Mary De Long of Chicago wrote:

> My son [Hez] was reported killed in action between August 3rd and 13th, 1918. [...] I feel that he might possibly be a prisoner and somebody else accidently identified as my son. There were so many boys over there, that mistakes might happen [...] I read in the paper how the Ex-Kaiser had been using a place called the "Kadinen Estate" as an experimental agriculture and cattle breeding farm. [...] Is there any way of investigating to find out if there could be any prisoners on that estate or any place else in the interior of Germany?

The War Department sent a letter of response saying that, although Hez's whereabouts were not known, the military would do everything in its power to find him. In 1921, nearly three years after the war's end, the GRS finally located Hez De Long's body in a shallow, isolated grave near the Vesle River in St. Thibaut, France. Unlike many grieving Americans whose sons, husbands, brothers, and boyfriends were never found, Mary De Long eventually was able to have her son's body returned home to Chicago.[167]

Despite the dedicated work of the GRS, infantrymen (who were usually untrained in funerary practices) were the ones initially responsible for, and capable of, burying comrades who fell in action—a fact that ultimately made proper treatment and identification of the dead a problematic affair. Though soldiers did their best to honor the fallen and meet the protocol of the War Department, the chaos of war frequently made the task difficult (or impossible). Often, necessity dictated the mass burial of fallen U.S. soldiers. As the GRS noted in a 1920 report:

> When there were a considerable number of dead, it was often found convenient to bury them in long trenches, partitioned off, to keep the bodies separate. Over each one, when possible, a cross was erected to which was attached one identification tag, the other being buried with the body. When a chaplain superintended the burials, brief prayers were said over the graves. Naturally, by the very character of the circumstances of warfare, many individual burials were made hastily by the comrades of the soldiers. They were often accomplished under shell-fire, sometimes at night, often in isolated and not easily accessible places; but orindarily the endeavor was made to observe as much care and system in the burials as the circumstances would permit.[168]

Such battlefield circumstances caused many soldiers to be misidentified, not only in name, but also in religious affiliation. Because the modern AEF was composed of conscripted citizen-soldiers from every ethnic and religious community in the nation, this lack of proper treatment resulted in unintended consequences that shook the spirits of soldiers at the Front and families back home alike. Describing the actualities of a temporary American battlefield cemetery, Lisa M. Budreau writes:

> Across the spacious fields of uniformly lined American crosses, intermittent Star of David headboards marked the dead of the Jewish faith. During the war, orders were issued that triangular headboards, instead of crosses, should be placed over known Jewish graves, but many people claimed it was nearly impossible to enforce those regulations. "Great difficulty is experienced in determining whether a dead soldier is Roman Catholic, Protestant, or a Jew," explained a chaplain in 1918. But the mistakes did not go unnoticed by other soldiers. "Yesterday, I visited the cemetery where our dead comrades were laid to rest, and there were our Jewish boys, the sons of Moses and Jacob with a cross at the head of their graves," wrote an AEF private to his rabbi. [...] So it was not surprising that in May 1919, when the Red Cross began sending grave photographs home to families, many of the dead had not been identified as Jewish and still bore the symbolic cross. The image proved shocking to recipients of both faiths.[169]

Thus, during and immediately following the war, it became clear that the initial battlefield treatment of American soldierly dead could emit emotional and spiritual reverberations that spread through the trenches of Europe, across the Atlantic, into the homes of grieving families. A wave of suffering and sorrow had begun to cascade over the homeland, and in time the waters would become too high and turbulent for the government to ignore.

DEATH: THE SOLDIER'S PERSPECTIVE

The bulk of the GRS's work did not begin until the second half of 1918. Though the United States declared war on April 6, 1917, it took more than a year for the nation to mobilize its vast potential and make an effective battle-field contribution to the Allied effort. This delay, which frustrated French and British political and military leaders, was due in large part to General John J. Pershing's refusal to amalgamate American troops with the Allied forces. If U.S. soldiers were going to die on the battlefields of Europe, the ever-nationalistic General reasoned, it would be under the direction of an American command and under the colors of an independent fighting force. Pershing also believed that this war of attrition might extend into 1919 or 1920 (an alarming notion that was tactfully kept secret from both the American public and U.S. troops). Taking this long view, Pershing determined that the nation's manpower should be trained, strengthened, and preserved for as long as possible. Thus, even as hundreds of thousands of American soldiers poured into France throughout late 1917 and early 1918—and while the Allied nations depleted their male populations at an unsustainable pace—Pershing successfully kept American troops out of the fighting long enough to create a separate, autonomous army that (in his mind) might deliver a final and decisive blow against the staggering enemy forces.[170]

When the AEF finally engaged in battle at Cantigny in May 1918, at Belleau Wood in June, along the Marne River in July, and near Chateau-Thierry in August, U.S. troops experienced firsthand the carnage and terror of the Great War—the very horrors that the CPI endeavored to hide from Americans back home. By the end of the summer, the AEF endured roughly 25,000 casualties.[171] Although seeing limited action as an independent army near St. Mihiel in September, the AEF nonetheless suffered 7,000 casualties in just four days. During the frightful Meuse-Argonne campaign of mid-October and November, the AEF sustained 100,000 casualties, including over 15,000 killed in action. Over the course of six brutal months (May-November, 1918), the United States suffered roughly 320,000 casualties, including more than 115,000 dead.[172]

As the numbers of killed, wounded, and missing soldiers increased exponentially throughout 1918, senior U.S. commanders attempted to maintain and project a positive attitude. Recognizing the correlation between their battle orders and the daily destruction of American men, most military brass maintained a safe distance from the frontlines so as to avoid physical contact with the realities of the slaughter. Those senior leaders who did experience the horrors of the war were (like every other witness) deeply shaken. General Robert Bullard, for example, Commander of the 1st Division at the Battle of Cantigny, was traumatized by the wretched sight of an American soldier lying on the ground with a "helmet crushed into his brain." During a visit to a battlefield hospital, General Pershing noticed a dent in the covers where a convalesced soldier's right arm should have been. The young man apologized and said to Pershing: "I cannot salute you, sir." Afterward, Pershing privately wept in his vehicle and told an aide that he found it difficult to see soldiers who had been maimed as a direct result of his orders. Such interactions became rare as American commanders decided that it was better not to let such terrible realities cloud their judgments. No, the thinking went, in this war of attrition it was far more practical to think of soldiers—whether dead or alive—as numbers and expendable, if valuable, pieces of the greater war machine (in other words, as objects of motion). Perhaps in an effort to ease their burdens, senior officers began to see the number of "acceptable" U.S. casualties as something that could be measured in proportion to risk. Some even went so far as to measure a unit's fighting spirit and effectiveness by the number of casualties it suffered—a simultaneously logical and illogical proposition that encouraged some younger field officers to gamble with their men's lives in the name of glory. For instance, during the Meuse-Argonne Offensive, General Charles Summerall visited Brigadier General Douglas MacArthur's 84th Brigade on the night before an assault. "Give me Chatillon or a list of five thousand casualties," Summerall told MacArthur, to which the young officer replied: "If this Brigade does not capture Chatillon you can publish a casualty list of the entire brigade with the Brigade Commander's name at the top." Such psychological approaches to (and rhetorical compensations for) the inevitability of mass death helped commanding officers suppress feelings of guilt (which were kept private in any case) and reinforced (through actions that wrought deathly outcomes) the burgeoning ideograph of the universal, sacrificial U.S. soldier.[173]

In contrast to their superiors, junior officers in the field became intimately familiar with the day-to-day mass murder upon which victory apparently depended. In the words of Captain John Thomas of the 1st Battalion, 5th Marines, officers in the field "lived obscenely in the cellars with the dead, and saw men die in the orange flash of *minenwerfer* shells, terribly and without consolation of glory." Younger officers and future army leaders like George Patton, George Marshall, Joseph Stilwell, Ernest Harmon, and Mark Clark could not help but bear witness to the terror that senior commanders wished to avoid at all costs. Stilwell, for example, was haunted by "heads lying around still in helmets, hunks of bodies, thigh bones, jaws, hands, pieces of old rags hanging to them and a leg sticking out of a dugout which a soldier had utilized on which to hang things." Even gung-ho figures like Patton and MacArthur were permanently shaken by the nature of the Great War; Patton would later remember that "men were being blown to bits" all around him, while MacArthur would recall that the dead were so thick during the Aisne-Marne Offensive that "we tumbled over them. There must have been at least 2,000 of those sprawled bodies. [...] The stench was suffocating. The moans and cries of wounded men sounded everywhere." Such terror—such depraved bloodletting and suffering—caused many field officers to measure the success of a given operation by the number of their men who survived intact (a far different standard than the one held by senior officers).[174]

As field officers struggled to keep casualty rates low, many came to believe that incompetence and indifference within the higher echelon of command was contributing to unnecessary deaths. Most historians agree that American commanding officers—and especially General Pershing—failed to comprehend the speed and complexity of modern tactics and operations. Battle plans were often based upon obsolete methods developed years before during U.S. military campaigns in Cuba, Manila, and Mexico. A large (if ultimately unquantifiable) portion of American deaths in the Great War has been attributed to Pershing's relentless bid to utilize outdated "open warfare" tactics—a process of "driving the enemy out into the open and engaging him in a war of movement"—instead of trench warfare methods. Pershing's beloved tactics proved to be ineffective against enemy machine guns, which mowed down exposed American troops with ease. During the war, the Germans soberly noted that the AEF's "close, deeply arranged" attack formations created "absolutely colossal [American] casualties." Following the war, one AEF lieutenant lamented: "We learned small unit tactics from the Germans. They were costly teachers." To make matters worse, incompetence, miscommunication, and bad planning at the senior level sparked incidents of friendly fire—perhaps the most tragic, senseless, and irredeemable kind of battle death.[175] What kind of meaning could possibly be found in such loss of life?

Because of this perceived mismanagement from above, seasoned field officers learned to ignore dubious orders or conduct them in ways that might diminish the loss of American life. For instance, after driving the Germans out of the French town of Sergy, MacArthur disregarded official orders to stay put, and pursued the withdrawing enemy; in that moment, he justified the decision by claiming it would "save us many thousands of precious lives" in the future. Unfortunately, on-the-ground leaders like MacArthur and Patton became rare commodities as young officers were killed in battle at disturbing and unanticipated rates. In response to a ceaseless hemorrhaging of battlefield leadership, the AEF developed an officer's training school that, by mid-1918, rapidly graduated a staggering 5,000 infantry officers each month. What should have been taught over a period of many months was taught in mere weeks as the AEF rushed to funnel officers into the field. Quickly thrust into battle, the vast majority of replacement officers lacked simple but necessary skills, like the ability to locate map coordinates accurately. These deficiencies could have deadly effects; as one U.S. officer quipped during the war, "[A] lot of men are buried in the Argonne because" of them.[176]

It should be noted that not every U.S. field officer attributed the nation's high casualty rates to incompetent commanders and inexperienced replacement officers. Second Lieutenant Leland C. Stevenson of the 3rd Division, AEF, for example, believed that U.S. losses—"much higher than those of our allies"—were "largely due to the spirit and temperament of the American soldier." In a memo to the Division's Chief of Staff concerning the lethal effects of the German machine gun, Stevenson opined:

> The American is always anxious to attack. Rather than slow up the attack and reduce the Machine Gun by the proper methods, the American will rush the gun with utter disregard for the danger, and usually capture it, with the result that many are killed and wounded. Many gallant deeds have been performed by our men in this manner and many brave soldiers have given their lives because of their utter disregard for enemy Machine Guns. I am convinced that this is due to the temperament and training of the American, not to tactical errors. Recklessness and willingness "to take a chance" are purely American characteristics and naturally, are going to manifest themselves in battle. Much experience will help to overcome losses from these cases, but they will always be high.[177]

Whether or not Stevenson's analysis was accurate, U.S. military brass certainly encouraged troops to attack upon command and without regard for personal safety. Immediately following successful (and, for the soldiers themselves, invariably terrifying and bloody) assaults, commanding officers (including General John J. Pershing himself) issued "General Orders" that praised infantrymen for their courage. "You rushed into the fight as though to a fete," soldiers of the 28th Division were told after conducting a harrowing counterattack in the Second Battle of the Marne. "Your magnificent courage completely routed a surprised enemy and your indomitable tenacity checked the counter-attacks of his fresh divisions. Furthermore, you have really felt your superiority over the barbarous enemy of the whole human race, against whom the children of Liberty are striving. To attack him is to vanish him."[178] Such commendations often eulogized specific fallen soldiers for moving forward at the cost of their own lives and thus, exhibiting "fearlessness," "bravery," and "extraordinary heroism in action."[179] Yet, while praising the departed, such commendations encouraged survivors not to dwell on their fallen comrades, but rather to keep moving forward. In August of 1918, an AEF General Order delivered to the 4th Division ended thusly: "We mourn our dead. For the living, there is the work of to-morrow."[180] That same month,

Major General Charles H. Muir issued a General Orders asking soldiers of the 28th Division to focus on the enemies' casualties rather than their own:

[We have] inflicted on the enemy far more loss than [we have] suffered from him. In a single gas application [we] inflicted more damage than the enemy inflicted on [us] by gas since [our] entry into the battle. [...] It is desired that these facts be brought to the attention of all, in order that the tendency of new troops to allow their minds to dwell on their own losses to the exclusion of what they had done to the enemy may be reduced to the minimum. [...] Let all be of good heart. We have inflicted more loss than we have suffered; we are better men individually than our enemies. A little more grit, a little more effort, a little more determination to keep our enemies down and the Division will have the right to look upon itself as an organization of veterans.[181]

To show that he was not indifferent to the emotional traumas of combat death, General Pershing himself sent a memo to the entire AEF, reminding them that their fallen compatriots would live on in glory after the war was over: "We have paid for our success in the lives of many of our brave comrades. We shall cherish their memory always, and claim for our history and literature their bravery, achievement and sacrifice."[182] Perhaps these official expressions of admiration brought some measure of comfort to tired (and certainly traumatized) soldiers; perhaps it helped steel them for whatever lied ahead. Whatever the case, it should be noted that the ceaseless enjoiners to keep moving forward were reinforced by a draconian policy that gave infantrymen little choice but to obey every order: in September of 1918, General Pershing authorized field officers to shoot on sight any American soldier who ran away or refused to attack. A memorandum from the Headquarters of the 28th Division AEF stated: "Officers and non-commissioned officers are authorized and directed to KILL any man so conducting himself it is necessary to bring an end to such conduct."[183] Ironically enough, Pershing—the source of this order—would eventually play a central and public role in the establishment and maintenance of overseas U.S. military cemeteries—sites meant to honor and display the heroism and sacrifice of American citizen-soldiers—during the postwar years.

Those who came closest to the terror of combat were, of course, the infantrymen who were called upon to do the killing, the dying, and the taking of enemy lines. Either drafted by the federal government or serving voluntarily out of patriotic devotion, hundreds of thousands of American citizen-soldiers—teachers, students, farmers, clerks, factory workers, the unemployed, immigrants recently arrived, and so on—found themselves on the muddy battlefields and ravaged forests of Europe, surrounded by the apocalyptic nightmare that was the Great War. It did not take long for the average combat soldier to realize that the ghastly "meat grinder" the press had described in great detail in the years before American belligerence—the senseless, state-sponsored holocaust that, in time, would be represented again and again in the postwar disillusionment literature of Ernest Hemingway, John Dos Passos, E. E. Cummings, William Faulkner, Harry Crosby, and others—was all too real. Within the war zone, the specter of death hung over every man at every moment, threatening to touch down (in the form of an artillery shell), emerge from the muddy ground (in the form of a disfigured corpse), or call out (in the form of a temporary grave marker) at any instant. Death was everywhere; it was relentless; and, in all likelihood, it consumed the thoughts of most American fighting men.

We can be sure of this last point thanks to the wartime diary of Fred Wertenbach, a draftee from Pittsburgh, Pennsylvania. Stationed at the Western Front in France as a member of Company G, 111th Infantry, 28th Division, AEF, Wertenbach secretly recorded his daily experiences in a personal journal. At that time, U.S. military regulations forbade soldiers from carrying diaries for fear that they could fall into enemy hands and reveal valuable intelligence.[184] With his German name, and with the knowledge that such a diary was contrary to orders, Wertenbach had to be careful so as not to be considered a spy. Thankfully, Wertenbach took the risk and created a permanent record of the Great War from the infantryman's perspective. Housed at the Soldiers and Sailors Memorial Hall and Museum in Pittsburgh, his diary provides an extremely rare, authentic, and uncensored look at the war—in all its banality and terror—and reveals the physical and psychological traumas suffered by American soldiers in Europe. Perhaps more than anything, Wertenbach's written words display his obsession with death—an obsession that intensified with each passing day.[185]

Much like Paul Bäumer, the young German soldier in Erich Maria Remarque's classic World War I novel, *All Quiet on the Western Front* (1929), Fred Wertenbach entered the war as an apple-cheeked youth brimming with naïve fantasies of battlefield glamour. His entries from January to mid-May 1918 exude enthusiasm for the macho aspects of military training,[186] anxiety as to whether the war will be over before he's shipped to Europe,[187] and an unwavering devotion to the nation. Although they occasionally address the challenges of homesickness, bad food, incompetent officers, and endless marches through the woods, Wertenbach's entries from this period remain wholeheartedly upbeat and gung-ho. Fancying himself to be a poet, Wertenbach jots down this original, star-spangled rhyme early in the diary:

"Our Life and Our Flag"

Here's to our life and our flag
God grant when comes the worst
We may give up the first to save the last
But never yield the last to save the first.[188]

The CPI could not have put it better.

The most startling aspect of reading Wertenbach's diary is to witness the speed with which the war's evil and deadly realities transform this young citizen-soldier into a jaded, grizzled, and traumatized combat vet. Similar (again) to *All Quiet*'s Paul Bäumer, Wertenbach quickly shed his innocent worldviews after he was deployed to the Western Front and experienced the incomprehensible physical pain, mental suffering, and mass murder entailed by the Great War. As days and weeks are marked in his diary, initial rosy observations regarding the thrills of traveling to France through submarine-infested waters and witnessing a German bombing raid ("a baptism of fire")[189] give way to somber, disenchanted reports teeming with disgust for the nature of state-sponsored warfare. For example, just days after arriving in France, Wertenbach bemoans the hatred and inhumanity that is instilled in soldiers (a bayonet instructor tells Wertenbach, "If a German pleads that he has a wife and eleven children you tell him, 'Your wife's a widow and your kiddies are orphans now' and let him have it!") and addresses the gaps between domestic perceptions of the war and the on-the-ground realities: "This life here is not what it is pictured in the U.S. I'd like to be back. [...] Believe me, I am going to let the next war take care of itself. [...] The U.S. double crossed us. [...] Bless the U.S. but God save the greatest country on earth from militarism."[190] Notably, in a description of a daylong training march somewhere near the Front, Wertenbach reflects upon the dehumanizing nature of military service: "We arose at 500 AM and left at 600 AM. From 600 AM until 700 PM is 13 hrs. Not bad, Uncle Sam. 13 hrs. gone for you. We are animals. Rise, eat, work, eat and go straight to bed in our billets, as it is called."[191] Here, Wertenbach compares himself to an animal—an object of motion that has no choice but to hand over every waking moment—his total self—to the war effort (an effort he no longer wholeheartedly believes in). His only reprieve from this routine—his only reminder that he is human after all—is his diary, which he has to keep secret from everyone around him. Ruing his condition, Wertenbach writes: "I keep thinking of home and mother and—and all the things that are good and true." Having received his earlier wish of getting to Europe in time to fight, he now confesses: "I wish the war would end soon."[192]

By mid-June, 1918, Wertenbach found himself directly in the war zone. In his journal, previous laments regarding military life seem downright rosy. In essence, his entries from June to December 1918 stand as one long disquisition on death. Consider the following progression of selected entries:

Sunday, June 23

We are marching to Chateau-Thierry as replacement American troops. Went past ripening fields of crops and grains. The grave fields make me think of soldiers. [...] One fellow said "There's a cemetery" another drummed in "Oh, don't bother pointing it out."

Friday, June 28
Rumor has it we are to leave tomorrow to 2nd line [...] I wonder if I will get killed, crippled, or pass through it all unscathed.

Monday, July 8
Heard the drone of planes overhead. Ominous sound, these Bosche bombers [...] heavy, portentous.

Tuesday, July 16
At 3:00 AM pulled into a woods having gone through a barrage of H.E. + gas shells. We were to remain there until daybreak. I saw an entrance to a dugout and crawled in. You can bet I got out of there promptly. There was a man lying dead inside, an American soldier. I slept in a trench because of the artillery fire. At about 800 I strolled around the woods, only to find dead Am. Soldiers everywhere.

July 18–20
Tonkowsly got killed and about 20 of our men wounded by shrapnel. [...] I can feel myself going to pieces because of the lack of sleep and the strain. [...] I heard Berbeich died and Red Gelman had an arm blown off. I do hate to look at these dead men. [...] Thompson + I took a dead German Lieut.'s field case and would have buried him but he lay in open ground and it was too dangerous.

July 23–26
I have been given a dead or wounded man's equipment. My specialty is dead men's equipage [...] German equipment and dead are about everywhere. [...] Damn Jerry; damn war + damn everything. [...] If I ever have children and I say war to them and they don't cry, I'll paddle them until they do. [...] Our death list is going up. Snipers. Damn.

Sunday, July 28
Am leaving out casualties because we are forbidden to tabulate them [...] GOT STRICT ORDERS—NO DIARIES SO I CAN'T MENTION ANY OF WHAT REALLY HAPPENS

July 31–August 1
There is a depressing feeling in the company because of our dead [...] We lost quite a bit up in Agremonte Woods—known as Dead Man's Woods—when we attacked from there. Only had two killed, but—

Monday, August 12
Summerfield, Hagstiohn, Signrolla and Carmali were killed and more injured. Our company captured 30 machine guns. German dead were lying everywhere unburied, because German snipers shoot, wait, fire at us when we tried to get our wounded. I went down with rations and saw an American foot with his shoe. It

had been blown off by a shell. I heard Mud and Lazer were killed by our own barrage.

Wednesday, August 21

Heat and flies here are terrible. The flies think we are dead and refuse to leave until touched.

Tuesday, September 3

Saw an aeroplane scrap today, nine Bosche against three Amer. One Amer. fell from a height of 10,000 ft to certain death. Things here are quiet but the scene will soon change. There we will pay for our quiet moments. Always some one dying. When I look back at our dead—whew! If only these maggoty bodies didn't haunt us so. Damn War! But above all, damn these slim meals—and no meals.

Thursday, September 5

Moved toward the front, up past 3 khaki clad bogs along the road, killed. Then, on the side of the hill an Amer doughboy, asleep in death, in a shallow trench. It gave me a chill in the stomach. I'm sick of this damn war. I want to go home. War is all right—when you dont have to kill or be killed. Hell with it all. In morn we go in the thick of it. We are on the side of a hill about 100 yds from the Germans. More to be killed. I'm sick, sick, deniably sick of it all. If I could, I'd chuck it.

September 6–8

Pool + Heiser are killed, quite a few wounded while I narrowly escaped death several times. I am hit on the knee, wrist, elbow, shoulder and twice on the head from shell fragments. [...] Bert, Lang, Atkinson, Atricna, Hailman killed [...]. Every bush had them Zam! And a few guys lie kicking. Andy Sehalt and I dragged in a shell shock man after his buddies wouldn't help me. Then Andy + Chalsey. Hast almost went shell shock in the barrage. Kerns showed white the white feather, pretending shell shock after got the ammo through. McNeily + I got three Bosche. [...] We were released at 4:00 A.M. this morning. Last night will live always with me. [...] Out of shellfire, out of hellfire our casualties are seven killed and about thirty or more in the hospital. The glory of war! Humor for the ammunition sellers.

Wednesday, September 11

We are about eight kilos back of the Marne. Saw several Iconic Allemande graves and many French ones.

Sunday, September 15

I went to church. Father Conmidy had the mass and I expected him to mention Chaplain Keith but he did not. Chaplain Keith was gassed when we were up the line and died from it. I am kept busy on requisitions.

September 25–26

I am writing this in a hospital at Vichy. I remember hiking into the Argonne, getting sicker and sicker. Then over the top. The machine guns stopped us but we went on. Our Capt Schlosser was sniped off. We made a second attack and then things went woozy. There was a dead German in a shell hole. I was so sick I made sure he was dead and then I lay down and everything went black. [...] I thought the sky was the ocean up side down and then it came to me stretcher bearers were carrying me back somewhere.

Tuesday, October 1

Vichy is a town whose welfare depends on tourists. Its water is famous. One hotel here the Rub is one of the biggest hotels in France. The doctors remodel men who have been deformed here and wonderful cures are made.

Tuesday, October 15

I wrote Ish sometime ago to hold my mail until I return to the company. If he has, it means "bakoo" mail when I get back. But I miss Edith and Ellen Kafer. But love is gone from the world only comradeship remains. And hate—hate of men, of my own Germanic blood, who would kill and destroy our soul.

Wednesday, October 16

I wonder if I am to die "up there." Twice have I been offered bomb proof jobs and each time I have refused. I could remain here as a strong up here.

   Tis all a checker board of nights and days
   Where Destiny with men for pieces plays
   Hither + Thither moves and mates and slays
   There one by one back in the cupboard lays (Omar Khayyam)

We cant stop Fate. My path is there; my feet must follow it. Whither it leads I know not. But Kismet, grant please grant, that I die bravely, if die I must.

Thursday, October 17

How strange life is—why should I have been born in 1895 and sentenced to this hell of slaughter? I dont want to take any one's life—what happened up there was not my fault. I had to do it. I am still seeing the kid holding on to his mother's hand and his German dad so stalwart beside her! Why should he have brought such a picture in his map case, anyway? Why why why?

Friday, October 18

Sometimes I wish I were a clod—and could not feel so acutely fear, hate, etc as I do. Some of my buddies here are like that. But these nights on patrol when I touched a lifeless body I shivered. And when we captured those three I almost murdered them in cold blood I was so taut.

Saturday, October 26

We had inspection today but I did not stand it. We have to sleep by our lonesome because of fear of influenza. One man has his head at the top next to man has his feet at the head so as not to inhale each others breath.

Tuesday, November 5

Rtd to company at noon today. Krews told me Isherwood was dead. I feel too bad to write home of it. Edith and his mother are in my thoughts constantly. He died a brave man's death. Only a boy—I always called him the Kid—he performed in a way creditable to many an older man. Enlisted in Freedom's defense at 15 years, died at age of seventeen. May God rest his soul and grant I die as bravely if die I must here in France. I believe I will see him sometime.

Thursday, November 7

Going to and from the place I kept thinking of the Kid. So near the end of the war and then to be killed. Perhaps I will join him if we go in. We are slated to leave here very soon, perhaps after I go asleep I will be awakened and ordered to roll my pack.

Friday, November 8

Ramello has been seriously wounded and may die. Damn war, the glory of war—if these war makers had eaten their meal near decaying human bodies; if they would see what the rats feast upon if they could stand beside wrecks of men, God knows their thoughts would be of peace too.

Saturday, November 9

We are to leave tonight, so the Loop says. Our packs are rolled and we are ready. Damn Rumor reports Germany and an armistice is soon to begin. I hope it comes after we take one final fling at Jerry. I will try not for revenge but square accounts for the kid. The Jerry bullet was explosive and was a dirty thing. If I shall die up there, I hope I die quickly and bravely.

Monday, November 11

We slept last night on the bare damp ground. There was ice on the water in shell holes. At 11:00 A.M. our barrage and the enemy's ceased. From Purgatory to Paradise in sixty seconds. We were half doubtful of an armistice for a while. Gruber + I went over to the enemy but got cold feet when we could hear them talking. We heard them shooting and singing when 11:00 came and also a German bugler blowing Taps. Thank God it is over. We had nine killed in our btn. Pvt Paul was killed in our company two minutes before 11:00 A.M.

Thursday, November 21

Why, oh why must I go to school to learn to throw bombs after a war is over. But the school goes on.

Thursday, November 28

Dreamed last night of Isherwood and our Captain. They are both dead but some how I cannot realize Ish is gone. I always think of him at night and sometimes I imagine he is to come near me sometime again.

Sunday, December 1

At last we had a day again in which there was no bloody rain. When I go back to God's own land I'll dream of France to beat the band and in these dreams most of all the time I'll see a land of mud and slime of towns by huge shell racked and torn, a fugitive, perhaps, forlorn upon a highway where the breeze sings songs of sorrow in the trees a land of broken hearts of men who passed through hell to peace again.

Wednesday, December 25

Christmas there comes a sadness tonight. So many dead—for what? How am I ever going to pick up the old existence again? A clerk! And dead men's faces leering at me from the row of figures. Peace on earth—shall I ever find it again?

December 29–31

"To 1918"

Oh! Nineteen eighteen! What is thou thoast bought
This taste of hell like Satan clutch to me
Ths disregard of lessons so long taught
Of Christian life that meant so much to me
Oh! Nineteen eighteen! Traitor art thou now
To take from life its sweetness are the youth
Has fled the blood—and then to teach me how
To sneer at Honor, Virtue, Freedom, Truth
Oh! Nineteen eighteen! My hast thou of me
Acquire made—and I just twenty-three
And Yet—who knows Perhaps I am to bless
This world some way of which I do not know
Perhaps to bring to some one happiness
Or else to ease the load of others' woe
God grant it may be so—and when I did
And seek a dwelling in that strange Somewhere
I may find comfort in the thought that I
Helped lighten oft some mortal's weight of care
That facing my Creator I may say
"I helped my brother in a by gone day"
        FSW
        Andilly Langres, France

Undated [presumably 1919]

"ALONE"
I SHARED HIS GRUB ON A MARINE HILLSIDE
WHEN WE FIRST HEARD THE BULLETS HUM
WHEN WE THOUGHT THAT THE BOSCHE WOULD COME
WITH HIM I DREAMED THE WORLD OLD DREAM
OF HOME—AND BRIGHT HEARTHSTONE
FATE RULED HE SHOULD DIE A SOLDIER'S DEATH

AND I   CAME BACK   ALONE
               FSW

"THE RAIN"
AND THEN, WHEN THE BUGLE SUMMONS
WE SOLDIERS TO MARCH AND DRILL
TO LEARN OF GRENADE AND TRENCHES
THE MOST MODERN WAYS TO KILL
IT ISN'T THE THOUGHT THAT PERHAPS WE'LL LIE
'NEATH A FOREIGN SOIL THAT MAKES US SIGH
IT'S THE RAIN, RAIN, RAIN
               FSW

The war Wertenbach describes is sickening and devoid of heroism, redemption, and meaning. It is a war in which planes are "ominous" and "portentious." It is a war in which a fighter pilot's fiery plunge to earth is not dazzling in its terror, but rather just another banal reminder of the "certain death" that lingers above each soldier's head. It is a war in which average men like Wertenbach—office clerks back home—are forced to see, smell, and touch dead men in trenches, dead men in scarred forests and shell holes— "maggoty," "lifeless" bodies everywhere—and abandoned appendages torn from men's bodies. It is a war in which the true enemy is, perhaps, less the German boy whose wallet contains a picture of his mother and father, and more the "ammunition sellers" and "war makers" of the world. It is a war in which haphazard battlefield cemeteries remind the living that they, too, might "lie 'neath a foreign soil'" forever. It is a war in which death threatens to strike at any moment—even in one's sleep—in the form of a bullet, bomb, bayonet, gas cloud, or comrade's infectious cough; no one can escape "Kismet" (or fate). It is a war in which one is unable to bury and remember the dead properly. It is a war that makes one "taut," capable of slaughtering helpless prisoners. It is a war that needlessly and brutally transforms young men into ghosts that will haunt survivors forever: "So many dead—for what? How am I ever going to pick up the old existence again? A clerk! And dead men's faces leering at me from the row of figures. Peace on earth—shall I ever find it again?" It is a war—a "Damn War!"—without beauty, reason, or the celebration of life.

As the famous works of postwar disillusionment writers and artists would later reveal, Wertenbach's attitudes about the war were not uncommon: for those who experienced its endless terrors, the Great War was nothing short of a living nightmare. Although the U.S. military banned diaries and personal journals during the war, information about the hideous realities of the war zone occasionally leaked and circulated to troops both near and far from the Western Front. In one notable instance, an officer disseminated grim casualty statistics from the Front to recruits at an Army training camp in Virginia; the conscripts became depressed upon learning that the average life span of an artillery officer in battle was an hour and thirty-five minutes, the average lifespan of a lieutenant just two to three hours.[193] For many American men, the experience of being drafted, plucked from home, and sent to fight on the other side of the ocean was traumatic enough; such glimpses of the doom that awaited them could be almost too much to handle. Thus, during the war, the U.S. military did everything it could to monitor the morale of American soldiers (especially those who had not yet witnessed the realities of the war) and censor distressing information from the Front.

These official efforts came in several forms. One tactic was to censor each piece of mail sent and received by soldiers in Europe. Upon arriving in France, every American soldier received a pamphlet that explained this censorship policy and the reasons behind it:

THERE ARE ONLY TWO WAYS TO MAIL LETTERS:
1—Hand them unsealed to your company officer. Remember that he reads many letters in his capacity of company censor and your letter is to him an entirely impersonal communication, of which he does not remember the details or the writer once it has been read.
2—Place your letters unsealed in a "blue envelope," seal the envelope, and mail it to the Base Censor, A.E.F., Paris. Each "blue envelope" may contain several letters, providing all are written by the same man and that each is enclosed within its.

DON'T TALK TOO MUCH:

Officers, enlisted men, and militarized civilians with the American Expeditionary Forces in France are forbidden to discuss or mention in public places, or to impart to anyone except in the official discharge of their duties, anything of military nature or anything whatever concerning information directly or indirectly obtained through connection with the A. E. F.

Do not express your opinion on military matters nor on the general situation. Be loyal to your Government and your superiors. Trust them to conduct the war while you attend to your own particular part in it.

Avoid in any way giving the impression of pessimism either in your conversation or you attitude. In all ways be confident in the success of our armies and of our cause.

All members of the American Expeditionary Forces are forbidden to take photographs, unless photography is a part of their official duties...

WHEN YOU WRITE A LETTER OR POST CARD:

DON'T put too much faith in the discretion of the people you write to. They may be very patriotic, yet quite unable to recognize an enemy agent or what information may be of value to the enemy.

REMEMBER that writing or receiving of letters in war time is a privilege, not a right. In many wars of the past soldiers were not allowed to write letters at all.[194]

This policy was the most straightforward and practical way of suppressing the dissemination of frank and honest information about the atrocious realities of the war zone. It also allowed military intelligence officers to identify soldiers who posed a threat to morale at the front lines. For instance, Private Mike Molata was targeted for investigation after censors intercepted the following letter:

> November 4th, 1918
> A letter from your brother Michel—
> Hellow dear Brother Andrew—
> I am in haste to inform you that thanks to the Lord I am enjoying good health. Wish you the same. I pray the Lord that we should meet again.
> I have not yet arrived to destination and I don't know when we will reach our place.
> They have already taken away from me all that I carried. Soon I'll go to the front line, perhaps in about a week I will go into the trenches.
> Good-bye, I remain your brother
> Michel
> Perhaps we will no more see one another. I thus request you to try to get the Insurance because I may be killed. Good-bye. Greetings to all, wish you the best of luck.
> It's bad brother.

Molata's gloomy tone and straightforward, honest assessment of the situation—"It's bad brother"—seems to have been enough to draw the attention of his superiors.[195]

The military recognized that it could not completely control the flow of information between soldiers and correspondents behind the lines and back home. However, military officials believed that they could identify, filter out, and perhaps reprogram fresh recruits who possessed low morale before they entered the trenches and tainted the spirits of their comrades. By August of 1918, the AEF had set up a covert spy system within the Le Mans Classification Camp, the facility where every new U.S. soldier was processed upon arrival in France. Each day, a team of undercover intelligence officers posed as fresh recruits and engaged suspicious characters in conversation with the hope of weeding out "defeatists" who lacked the fighting spirit or harbored anti-war sentiments. Daily reports of this covert operation (now housed at the National Archives) reveal the military's deep suspicion of ethnic and racial minorities, the pervasive anti-war streak that, despite official efforts, coursed through the U.S. ranks, and the insufficient training that many soldiers (who were about to face the test of battle) had received. Predictably, the undercover operatives directed much of their attention to first generation Americans, many of whom could not speak English or even provide papers proving their U.S. citizenship. A report dated August 19, 1918, stated:

An unusually high percentage of men of alien birth—mostly Italians, with a few Russians, Lithuanians and Russian poles—was contained in the morning group. Now and then men of Austrian or German birth make their appearance—but in every instance they said they had early emigrated to the United States and had no near relatives in enemy countries and were more than willing to go to the front. [...]

The morale of the replacements was invariably good. A number of men—with enemy alien blood in their veins—professed a disinclination to go to the front—but additional conversation with them showed that if they once reached the front there was little doubt but that they could be trusted. Several cases of near-malingering were also noted. [...]

Two defeatists—both of them of Russian birth—were discovered among the men and together with another Russian who is disinclined to go to the front to fight—but prefers to go into quartermaster work (he is a Jew)—are being held in the camp awaiting disposition from this office. The two men are:

Private Andy Stavisky, 2427338, born in Russia of Russian parents. [...] He is sullen and generally refused to answer questions put to him in English. [...]

Private Joseph N. Levitas [...]. His main contention is that he was forced to become a citizen of the United States against his will. It is believed that this man should be put in the guardhouse pending disposition of his case. Native-born

Americans have been jeering at him and goading him on—making him worse—if anything.[196]

On August 27, the agents reported that 317 soldiers had passed through the clearinghouse that day and that the "general morale of the men was high—most of them being southerners of native birth." They cautioned, however, that several individuals would "bear further watching":

> Private Joseph Francis, 3168467, a Turk. This man has brothers in the Turkish army and does not want to fight against the Germans for fear his brother may be with the Germans. He was in the United States for 15 years but has no naturalization papers. [...]
> A number of Italians who came through the camp on this date were not citizens of the United States. This situation appears frequently.[197]

Despite their skepticism of nonwhite Anglo-Saxon Protestant recruits, the agents believed that most replacement troops had been properly conditioned by government and military propaganda to accept their lot and trust in the supposed righteousness of the national war effort:

> Conversation with the average soldier at the camp shows that he gives but little thought to the American aims in the war, according to a report from one of the operatives. The latter states that the men believe we tried our utmost to keep out of the war by preserving our neutrality and that Germany persistently sunk our ships and killed our citizens until we had to go to war. They take the situation for granted without going into the detailed reasons for its existence.[198]

If the hearts and minds of most recruits were well prepared for combat, the physical conditioning of many soldiers—particularly African-American troops—was occasionally called into question. For instance, on October 2, 1918, the agents at Le Mans issued the following warning:

1. Most of the members of the 539th Engineers (colored), who are now undergoing training at the Forwarding Area, have been in the service less than two months and many of them have been in a little more than a month. Some of the men arrived at Camp Gordon on one day and were shipped out with the organization early the next morning for Hoboken. A little more than four weeks ago many of these Negroes were working on southern plantations in their bare feet.
2. The above resume accounts for the fact that there is so much sickness and death among them. They were sent to France without any training at all.

Since they were not hardened even to a slight degree makes them easy victims for pneumonia. Forty of them were taken to the hospital in one day. The sick calls, from all information the writer could obtain, run as high as from 25 to 40 percent. Of course some of this is imaginary but the biggest part is not.

3. The system of training at the Forwarding Area, especially the gas defense work, is very efficient. The noncommissioned officers there know their subject and are a hard-working lot. These specialists tell me that if these Negroes are ever subject to a gas attack they will probably all be killed because their minds cannot grasp the training.

4. It was a wanton waste of life and money to bring the 539th Engineers to France. By no means should they be kept in this area for the winter. What is left of them should be made into labor battalions and sent to a warmer part.[199]

Beyond revealing the AEF's racist assumptions about African Americans and the subordinate role black soldiers were meant to play in the national war effort, this report provides further evidence of just how inadequately trained and prepared many conscripted U.S. soldiers were. We can only imagine what members of the 539th Engineers felt and thought as they were plucked from their communities, transported to a different part of the country, and shipped to Europe to fight for a nation that considered African Americans second-class citizens—all within a matter of weeks; what they felt and thought as they witnessed scores of their comrades perish from pneumonia; what these untrained men felt and thought as they waited for their marching orders. We do know, however, that, like every other conscripted soldier in the AEF, members of the 539th Engineers had little power over their fate. Against their will, they had been turned into useful objects of motion for the war machine. That reality, though, would be scrubbed from the government's rhetoric and public memory projects during the postwar years.

During the period of U.S. belligerence, the Wilson Administration embarked upon a bold, yet dubious, project that sought nothing less than the complete transformation of every American into a compliant and useful object of motion for the nation's war machine. Entailing the heavy-handed repression of dissent, the censorship and manipulation of war information and death reports, the pursuit for control over the "body and soul and spirit" of each private citizen (and noncitizen), and the management of public imaginations concerning the emotional and politically charged issues of patriotic death, just killing, collective sacrifice, proper burial, and public commemoration, this governmental venture successfully and severely constrained

Americans' abilities to act and express themselves freely on these and other war-related matters.

While this suppression of *symbolic action* helped facilitate the rapid mobilization of resources, bodies, and collective will seemingly required for victory "over there," it fostered a giant yet (because of the stringent federal and military laws and policies) often concealed reserve of emotion and resentment in the hearts and minds of many Americans—particularly those whose loved ones were drafted and eventually lost in the fighting. As we will see clearly in the remaining chapters, this reserve of emotion and resentment would explode like a powder keg, as thousands of grieving American families would publicly express their feelings concerning the meaning of their loved ones' deaths in Europe and the government's duty to treat soldiers' bodily remains properly. In other words, the U.S. government's wartime *project of motion* would spark a postwar reaction of *symbolic action*. But in time, the government would learn to compensate for this backlash by appropriating the emotional and sentimental vernacular of grieving families into both its own official rhetoric *and* the final visual presentation of permanent American military cemeteries in Europe—sites where dead U.S. soldiers, once *objects of motion* for the war machine, would become useful *objects of symbolic action* for the nation-state. And ultimately, those responsible for the design and establishment of America's overseas military cemeteries would blend aspects of the lofty, nationalistic rhetoric found in Wilson's war address to Congress with the more personal, emotional, and domestic sensibilities found in citizens' expressions of sorrow.

NOTES

1. Scholars have debated the reasons Wilson abandoned his anti-war position after the 1916 presidential election. As leading American World War I historian David M. Kennedy shows, in 1917 Wilson publicly justified his request for war as a defense of the nation's neutral rights (seemingly violated by German submarine assaults) and an opportunity for the United States to vanquish autocracy in Europe and mold a lasting peace based on democratic principles and collective, global security. Left-leaning scholars, however, have taken Wilson's public claims to task. Richard Hofstadter, for example, argues: "This was rationalization of the flimsiest sort [... Wilson] was forced to find legal reasons for policies that were based not upon law but upon the balance of power and economic necessities." Hofstadter notes that in a 1919 speech in St. Louis, Wilson stated: "Why, my fellow citizens, is there any man here or any woman, let me say is there any child here, who does not know that the seed of war in the modern world is industrial and commercial rivalry? The real reason that the war that we have just finished took place was that Germany was afraid

her commercial rivals were going to get the better of her, and the reason why some nations went into the war against Germany was that they thought Germany would get the commercial advantage of them. [...] This war, in its inception was a commercial and industrial war. It was not a political war." Expanding upon Hofstadter's thoughts, Howard Zinn believes that Wilson, and the statesmen, bankers, and capitalists who supported Wilson's call for war, were motivated by purely financial considerations: "American capitalism needed international rivalry—and periodic war—to create an artificial community of interest between rich and poor, supplanting the genuine community of interest among the poor that showed itself in sporadic movements." See Richard Hofstadter, *The Age of Reform* (New York: Vintage, 1955), 276–9; David M. Kennedy, *Over Here: The First World War and American Society* (Oxford: Oxford University Press, 1980), 3–12; and, Howard Zinn, *A People's History of the United States: 1492–Present* (New York: HarperCollins, 1980), 359–64.

2. Throughout American history, compulsory military service has emerged periodically in various forms. During the Revolutionary War, state governments assumed the colonies' authority to raise short-term militia forces through conscription, if necessary. During the Civil War, the North adopted a Federal draft in 1863, but permitted men to hire a substitute or pay a commutation fee of $3000 to avoid service. Roughly eight percent of Union troops were draftees—the rest were volunteers. World War I was the first war in which the United States relied primarily upon conscription; there were no loopholes for men of age who wished not to fight (as there had been in the past). See John Whiteclay Chambers II, "Conscription," in *The Oxford Companion to American Military History*, ed. John Whiteclay Chambers II (Oxford: Oxford University Press, 1999), 180–2.

3. Creel, *How We Advertised America*, 5.

4. Considered one of the most important political speeches of American 20th-century history, Wilson's 1917 war address has received considerable attention from historians and presidential rhetoric scholars. Producing works too numerous to engage or list exhaustively here, scholars have analyzed the speech from various perspectives. Some have engaged it through the spectrum of "the presidency and the rhetoric of foreign crisis." Others have engaged it as an act of the presidential "selling of war." Others have examined its deployment of rhetorical devices. Still others have viewed the speech as an articulation of Wilsonian Progressivism. Admittedly, I do not adequately account for this scholarship in this book. My hope is that my analysis of Wilson's speech, and the subsequent national war effort, through Burke's heuristic concept of motion/action will supplement this already vast and excellent body of work. For examples of this scholarship, see Katherine H. Adams, *Progressive Politics and the Training of America's Persuaders* (Mahwah, NJ: L. Eribaum Associates, 1999); Denise M. Bostdorff, *The Presidency and the Rhetoric of Foreign Crisis* (Columbia: University of South Carolina Press, 1994); Karlyn Kohrs Campbell and Kathleen Hall Jamieson, *Presidents Creating the Presidency: Deeds Done in Words* (Chicago: University of Chicago Press, 2008); Richard Ellis, *Speaking to the People: The Rhetorical Presidency in Historical Perspective* (Amherst: University of Massachusetts Press, 1998); Wayne Fields, *Union of Words: A History of Presidential Eloquence* (New York: Free Press, 1996); Amos Kiewe, ed., *The Modern Presidency and Crisis Rhetoric* (Westport, CT: Praeger, 1994); Robert Alexander Kraig, *Woodrow*

Wilson and the Lost World of the Oratorical Statesman (College Station: Texas A&M University Press, 2006); Eugene Secunda and Terence P. Moran, *Selling War to America: From the Spanish American War to the Global War on Terror* (Westport, CT: Praeger Security International, 2007); and, David Zarefsky, "Presidential Rhetoric and the Power of Definition," *Presidential Studies Quarterly* 34.3 (2004): 607–19.

5. A canonical text for contemporary rhetorical scholars, this book explores human motives and the forms of thought and expression they take. As Burke puts it: "What is involved, when we say what people are doing and why they are doing it? An answer to that question is the subject of this book." Kenneth Burke, *A Grammar of Motives* (Berkeley: University of California Press, 1945), xv. Burke expands upon his discussion of motion/action in *Dramatism and Development* (Barre, MA: Clark University Press, 1972).

6. A familiar example of this application of the framework of motion and action is the long-standing Christian debate regarding individual free will under an omnipotent, providential deity. If God has predetermined all human behaviors and fates, then humans have been set in *motion* by powers beyond their control. If, on the other hand, God has given man free will to "respond to His grace," then humans could be viewed as agents of *action* who are aware of the potential consequences of their behaviors and choices.

7. An obvious contemporary example of the rhetorical alchemy that allows people to identify instances of action as instances of motion (and vice versa) is the 2010 BP oil spill in the Gulf of Mexico. Whereas environmental groups claimed that BP was ethically, legally, and financially responsible for the environmental disaster because the company had deliberatively chosen cheaper and riskier deepwater drilling procedures to save time and money (and thus cast the event in terms of *action*), BP denied that it had any knowledge of the potential hazards of its methods and argued that (in the words of BP-apologist Senator Rand Paul) "sometimes accidents happen" (and thus cast the event in terms of *motion*). See Kate Phillips, "After Explaining a Provocative Remark, Paul Makes Another," *New York Times*, May 22, 2010, A10.

8. I do not mean to suggest that the government's wartime project ended what had been a utopist period of democracy in which citizens had enjoyed and exercised the freedom to express themselves as autonomous members of society. Realities such as racial segregation and the persistence of women's disfranchisement belie such a notion. Nor do I mean to say that the censorship and the suppression of free expression were unique to the American experience in the Great War, as similar things occurred during previous American wars.

9. This section cites the contemporary newspaper article, "Full Text of the Address by the President to Congress," *Los Angeles Times*, April 3, 1917, I1.

10. In his speech to Congress, Wilson cited the Zimmermann Telegram as proof of German "criminal intrigues" against U.S. national security: "That [the German government] means to stir up enemies against us at our very doors the intercepted Zimmermann note to the German Minister at Mexico City is eloquent evidence." See ibid.

11. Wilson's argument that Americans were a peaceful people who had been provoked into war was not new to presidential rhetoric, as McKinley had used a similar claim in his Spanish-American War address. See Robert L. Ivie, "Presidential Motives for War," *Quarterly Journal of Speech* 60.3 (1974): 337–45.

12. Not that Wilson or too many of his appreciative listeners were necessarily worried about the deaths of Germans.

13. Throughout the period of U.S. belligerence, American propaganda and media texts (newspapers, films, books) cast Kaiser Wilhelm II as the nation's true enemy, the purest symbol of German savagery, and the one person most responsible for the war in Europe. The millions of German and Austro-Hungarian troops fighting on land and sea were consolidated into and anthropomorphized by caricatures of the Kaiser—his fate was his military's fate (and vice versa). On the flip side, the U.S. military became embodied in the fictional character Uncle Sam—his needs were the military's needs (and vice versa). Convenient and shorthand representations of good and evil, these icons appeared routinely, if subtly, in the everyday texts; consider the following title of a newspaper article that addressed Germany's weakening control over the Atlantic Ocean: "Uncle Sam Tightens His Grip on the Kaiser's Throat," *The Patriot* (Harrisburg, Pennsylvania), July 21, 1917, 18.

14. Wilson stated: "We desire no conquest, no dominion. We seek no indemnities for ourselves, no material compensation for the sacrifices we shall freely make. We are but one of the champions of the rights of mankind. We shall be satisfied when those rights have been made as secure as the faith and the freedom of nations can make them." "Full Text," *Los Angeles Times*.

15. Ibid.

16. H. C. F. Bell, *Woodrow Wilson and the People* (Garden City, New York: Country Life Press, 1945), 211.

17. H. C. Peterson, *Propaganda for War: The Campaign Against American Neutrality, 1914–1917* (Port Washington, NY: Kennikat Press, 1939), 309–10.

18. Edward Robb Ellis, *Echoes of a Distant Thunder: Life in the United States, 1914–1918* (New York: Kodansha International, 1975), 321, 324, 330–1.

19. Theodore Kornweibel Jr., *"Investigate Everything": Federal Efforts to Compel Black Loyalty During World War I* (Bloomington, IN: Indiana University Press, 2002), 18–19.

20. "Wholesale Plot Arrests," *New York Times*, April 7, 1917, 1.

21. This executive order was distributed to all government employees, who were warned to "support government policy; both in conduct and in sympathy." See Commission on Protecting and Reducing Government Secrecy, *Report of the Commission on Protecting and Reducing Government Secrecy* (Washington, DC: Government Printing Office, 1997), A-15, quoted in Timothy L. Ericson, "Building Our Own 'Iron Curtain': The Emergence of Secrecy in American Government," *American Archivist* 68.1 (Spring/Summer 2005): 18–52, 34.

22. Kornweibel, *"Investigate Everything,"* 19.

23. See, for instance, "To Censor Every Foreign Message," *Daily Herald* (Biloxi, Mississippi), April 26, 1917, 6.

24. Ellis, *Echoes*, 340, 354.

25. As one man stated in a war-related letter to the *New York Times*: "The conscription law was put over as democratic and giving every one as fair a chance as gambling devices and the law of chance can provide." "Answers a Draft Wail," *New York Times*, August 29, 1917, 7.

26. Up to that point, Americans had always resisted compulsory military service. Presidents Washington, Jefferson, and Madison had failed in their attempts

to persuade Congress to pass selective service legislation during the Revolutionary War, the War of 1812, and the Mexican War of 1846, respectively. During the Civil War, President Lincoln's call for conscription led to violent riots across the Northern states. Memories of such tempestuous events lingered as Congress debated Wilson's proposed legislation. See Ellis, *Echoes*, 340.

27. Ibid, 340–1.

28. Kennedy, *Over Here*, 152–4.

29. Ellis, *Echoes*, 342.

30. Kennedy, *Over Here*, 152–3.

31. Ellis, *Echoes*, 343, 346–7.

32. Kennedy, *Over Here*, 165–6.

33. Ellis, *Echoes*, 343.

34. During American belligerence, a total of 337,649 men attempted to dodge the draft, and the government brought legal action against 220,747 of them; of these, 163,738 were arrested and tried in court. Some were acquitted while many others were found guilty and jailed, some for as long as ten years. See Ellis, *Echoes*, 350–1, 354; Kennedy, *Over Here*, 165.

35. By May, 1918, the government even began targeting undrafted men who had dutifully registered but who were not visibly contributing to the domestic war effort. "Idlers, unemployed and those of draft age not engaged in essential or useful employment will be rounded up for military service unless they apply themselves at once to some sort of labor that will dovetail into the plans of the Administration for winning the war," the *New York Times* reported. The so-called "Work or Fight" order, handed down from Selective Service Director Maj. Gen. Enoch Crowder, was officially aimed at "idle men of draft age hanging around pool rooms and race tracks, against men of draft age affiliated with the I. W. W. movement, men serving food or drink in hotels, public places and social clubs, elevator operators, doormen, footmen, ushers and persons connected with games, sports, and amusements." At the same time, President Wilson urged state governors to establish local anti-loafing laws that would compel all men between the ages of 18 and 50 "to engage in some useful employment." See *New York Times*, "Work or Fight, Warning to All on Draft Rolls," May 24, 1918, 1.

36. Ellis, *Echoes*, 350.

37. See, for example, "Roundup Begins of Draft Dodgers," *New York Times*, September 29, 1917, 18.

38. Ellis, *Echoes*, 346, 350.

39. Ellis, *Echoes*, 350; Kennedy, *Over Here*, 165.

40. Ellis, *Echoes*, 346, 350.

41. U.S. National Archives and Records Administration II, College Park, Maryland in the Records of the Selective Service System, World War I (Record Group 163), under "Provost Marshal General's Office, Local Board Experience," File Number 163.470.78.16.00.

42. Byron Farwell, *Over There: The United States in the Great War, 1917–1918* (New York: W. W. Norton & Company, 1999), 64.

43. Ellis, *Echoes*, 359–60.

44. Farwell, *Over There*, 65.

45. Before American entry into the Great War, every U.S. soldier had received at least nine months of training. In order to raise a massive army quickly, this standard was reduced to four months. See Theodore Wilson, "Training and Indoctrination," in Chambers, *The Oxford Companion*, 728–31.

46. When the 90th Division shipped out for Europe in June of 1918, only 35 percent of its personnel had received more than four weeks of formal military instruction. See Farwell, *Over There*, 65.

47. Ibid, 61–5.

48. Frederick M. Kerby, "A Complete Condensed History of the Great World War," unknown newspaper, 1920, in the John Doran Jr. Papers, Archives of the Soldiers and Sailors Memorial Hall and Museum, Pittsburgh, Pennsylvania.

49. Wilson, "Training and Indoctrination."

50. Thomas A. Bailey, *Voices of America: The Nation's Story in Slogans, Sayings, and Songs* (New York: Free Press, 1976), 344.

51. Glenn Watkins, *Proof through the Night: Music and the Great War* (Berkeley: University of California Press, 2003), 257–9.

52. See Ellis, *Echoes*, 436; Michael Emery and Edwin Emery, *The Press and America: An Interpretive History of the Mass Media* (Boston: Allyn and Bacon, 1996), 259–60.

53. Shortly after the establishment of the Espionage Act, Wilson asked Burleson to stifle an obscure paper called *The Peoples' Counsellor*, declaring that "one conviction would probably scotch a great many snakes." See Ellis, *Echoes*, 441.

54. Kennedy, *Over Here*, 76–7, 84.

55. Ellis, *Echoes*, 437–9; Emery and Emery, *The Press and America*, 259–60.

56. Kennedy, *Over Here*, 78–82; Kornweibel, *Investigate Everything*, 15–16, 22; and, Zinn, *A People's History*, 369.

57. Kennedy, *Over Here*, 83.

58. Giffin, *Six Who Protested*, 126–7.

59. Eugene V. Debs, "The Canton, Ohio Speech," Marxists Internet Archive, http://www.marxists.org/archive/debs/works/1918/canton.htm, (accessed August 23, 2010).

60. Giffin, *Six Who Protested*, 43.

61. "Woman Freed by Wilson," *Oregonian*, May 30, 1920, 17.

62. Zinn, *A People's History*, 365.

63. Ellis, *Echoes,* 440.

64. See "Emma Goldman and A. Berkman Behind the Bars," *New York Times*, June 16, 1917, 1; Giffin, *Six Who Protested*, 106–15.

65. Zinn, *A People's History*, 371.

66. Paul L. Murphy, "Espionage and Sedition Acts of World War I," in Chambers, *The Oxford Companion*, 251–2.

67. Kennedy, *Over Here*, 89.

68. Following the war, President Wilson attempted to forge a progressive peace settlement (the Treaty of Versailles) that would, among many things, establish the League of Nations (an international forum where nations' differences could be worked out peacefully) and prevent the outright transfer of German overseas colonies to the victors (so that the Allied nations would not look like plunderers). Now in control of Congress, Republicans warned that they would not approve a treaty

containing a Covenant of the League of Nations as then drafted, which they argued compromised American sovereignty. The Republicans forced Wilson to secure Allied agreement that the League of Nations would have no power to interfere in "internal" matters like tariffs and immigration; that any country would have the right to withdraw from the League; and that American claims under the Monroe Doctrine would be beyond the League's purview. Wilson's demand for these concessions at the Paris Peace Conference emboldened the European representatives to fight harder for the realization of their own national ambitions; most notably, France and Britain sought to stick Germany with an astronomical reparations bill and officially saddle Germany with the moral responsibility for allegedly having started the war. Wilson's vision for the Versailles Treaty quickly disintegrated, and postwar peace became a peace of vengeance rather than compromise. See Kennedy, *Over Here*, 357–63; Thomas J. Knock, "Treaty of Versailles," in Chambers, *The Oxford Companion*, 748.

69. Kennedy, *Over Here*, 89.

70. This phrase is found in George Creel's *How We Advertised America*: "The war-will, the will-to-win, of a democracy depends upon the degree to which each one of all the people of that democracy can concentrate and consecrate body and soul and spirit in the supreme effort of service and sacrifice. What had to be driven home was that all business was the nation's business, and every task a common task for a single purpose" (5).

71. Ibid, xv.

72. George Creel, *Rebel at Large: Recollections of Fifty Crowded Years* (New York: G. P. Putnam's Sons, 1947), 158, quoted in Robert Jackall and Janice M. Hirota, "America's First Propaganda Ministry: The Committee on Public Information During the Great War," in *Propaganda*, ed. Robert Jackall (New York: New York University Press, 1995), 137–73, 138.

73. Creel, *How We Advertised America*, 5.

74. Ibid, 3.

75. Reflecting on the social divisiveness of the war years, Creel would write decades later: "During the three and a half years of our neutrality the United States had been torn by a thousand divisive prejudices, with public opinion stunned and muddled by the pull and haul of Allied and German propaganda. The sentiment of the West was still isolationist; the Northwest buzzed with talk of a 'rich man's war,' waged to salvage Wall Street loans; men and women of Irish stock were 'neutral,' not caring who whipped England and in every state demagogues raved against 'warmongers,' although the Du Ponts and other so-called 'merchants of death' did not have enough powder on hand to arm squirrel hunters." See Creel, *Rebel at Large*, 157.

76. This phrase is taken from the title of Creel's 1920 book, *How We Advertised America*. Creel writes: "Under the pressure of tremendous necessities an organization grew that not only reached deep into every American community, but that carried to every corner of the civilized globe the full message of America's idealism, unselfishness, and indomitable purpose" (4).

77. Ibid, 104–8.

78. Kennedy, *Over Here*, 62.

79. This term is borrowed from the first chapter of Creel's *How We Advertised America*, which is titled, "The 'Second Lines.'"

80. Jackall and Hirota, "America's First," 138.

81. Michael S. Sweeney, *The Military and the Press: An Uneasy Truce* (Evanston, IL: Northwestern University Press, 2006), 44.

82. This pamphlet can be found in the U.S. National Archives and Records Administration II, College Park, Maryland in the Records of the American Expeditionary Forces, World War I (Record Group 120), under "Press Censorship," File Number 120.290.80.35.01. By the late summer of 1918, the CPI would cease to publish casualty lists much as the Germans had done. See David A. Copeland, *The Greenwood Library of American War Reporting: World War I and World War II, the European Theater* (Westport, CT: 2005), 152.

83. See Sweeney, *The Military and the Press*, 49; "Censor Creel Gives Out Rules for Newspapers," *New York Times*, May 28, 1917, 1.

84. Sweeney, *The Military and the Press*, 48–50.

85. Ibid, 46–7, 52–4.

86. At its peak, the CPI employed 150,000 men and women in its various divisions. See Peter Buitenhuis, *The Great War of Words: British, American, and Canadian Propaganda and Fiction, 1914–1933* (Vancouver: University of British Columbia Press, 1987), 70–1.

87. Jackall and Hirota, "America's First," 138–9; Secunda and Moran, *Selling War*, 33.

88. Jackall and Hirota, "America's First," 139. Historian Michael S. Sweeney argues that these pamphlets generally "took information out of context, highlighted militaristic German statements while ignoring others, and presented some information as fact when it was open to doubt." See *The Military and the Press*, 47. One example of these pamphlets is *Why America Fights Germany*, written by English professor John S. P. Tatlock of Stanford University. This essay depicts an imaginary German invasion of America and subsequent occupation of a small New Jersey town. Needless to say, the German invaders commit the worst atrocities: pillage, rape, arson, and murder. Tatlock's chilling story ends with an emotional call for enlistment. See Buitenhuis, *The Great War of Words*, 73.

89. Jackall and Hirota, "America's First," 138–40. One of the initial architects of the CPI, Lippmann saw firsthand just how influential state-sponsored "psychological warfare" could be on public opinion. Disillusioned with the beast he had helped create, Lippmann came to believe that the only way to inform citizens of a mass society (many of whom "are mentally children or barbarians") properly would be to establish an "intelligence bureau," to pursue "the common interests [that] very largely elude public opinion [...] managed only by a specialized class whose personal interests reach beyond the locality." Lippmann articulated this argument, without a sense of irony, in his famous book, *Public Opinion* (New York: Harcourt, Brace & Company, 1922). See pages 75 and 310.

90. See, for instance, "Germans Balking at False War Reports," *Olympia Daily Recorder*, October 30, 1917, 2; "German Officers Joke as They Order Russians Butchered in Cold Blood," *Idaho Daily Statesman*, November 6, 1917, 1; and, "1871—History Repeating Itself—1918," *Wyoming State Tribune*, April 11, 1918, 4.

91. For instance, see "Opinions of Others Told by Letters," *Duluth News Tribune*, December 27, 1917, 6.

92. The Division of Advertising forged a special bond with the American Association of Advertising Agencies (AAAA), an organization representing 115 firms.

The AAAA endlessly purchased ad space in newspapers and journals and donated it to the CPI. The AAAA also helped the Division of Advertising in every aspect of creating effective ads. For instance, it showed the Division of Advertising how to offer multiple appeals in advertisements in order to reach out to different audiences at the same time. As one trade magazine noted in May of 1917, the CPI's first Liberty Loan drive simultaneously offered appeals to "the wealthy through patriotism and the fact that the bonds are nontaxable [...] to the middle classes [...] through patriotism and the fact that to purchase a bond will be the beginning of a beneficial habit of thrift [...] to the poorer classes the absolute safety of the investment [... and] to the foreign born [...] that here is an opportunity for them to prove [...] their loyalty." The AAAA's actions were not completely altruistic; by aiding the CPI, the organization developed goodwill with politicians and military brass that, in time, translated into lucrative government contracts for its members during the postwar years. Jackall and Hirota, "America's First," 145–8, 153.

93. James R. Mock and Cedric Larson, *Words That Won the War: The Story of the Committee on Public Information, 1917–1919* (Princeton: Princeton University Press, 1939), 122–3, quoted in Kennedy, *Over Here*, 61–2.

94. Some cartoonists enthusiastically embraced the CPI's mission and created cartoons that exceeded even the Division of Cartoons' expectations. Syndicated cartoonist C. R. Macauley, for example, became famous for his caricatures of "soap-box traitors" (anyone who opposed any aspect of the nation's war policies) and his portraits of the bestial "Hun," usually depicted as a bayoneted gorilla wearing a Prussian spiked helmet. See Mock and Larson, *Words*, 143.

95. Ibid, 141.

96. Ibid, 155–6.

97. The CPI translated propagandistic materials into a myriad of languages and distributed them to every major ethnic community in the United States. It hired bilingual university professors to monitor foreign-language publications in their areas to make sure CPI materials were being properly digested by the nation's "hyphenates." The CPI also encouraged ethnic groups to bring propaganda back to their European homelands, either through writing or in person. During the war, Creel personally urged General Pershing to let wounded Italian-American soldiers convalesce in Italy (rather than return to more concentrated medical centers in France and England), where they could spread CPI doctrine to locals. See Kennedy, *Over Here*, 65–6.

98. Mock and Larson, *Words*, 7.

99. Such efforts were wholeheartedly supported by employers, who were generally resolved that the war should not provide an opportunity for unions and radical labor groups to increase their power. See Jackall and Hirota, "America's First," 153–5; Kennedy, *Over Here*, 70–2.

100. Speech topics varied week to week to match the needs of the war effort. For example, the first topic (May 12–21, 1917) was "Universal Service by Selective Draft"; the next (May 22–June 15) was "First Liberty Loan"; the third (June 18–25) was "Red Cross." Though these topics may seem benign, orators often cited dubious and emotional accounts of German *Schrecklichkeit* (the deliberate policy of terrorism) to urge Americans to buy War Bonds or reduce consumption of wheat so that soldiers would have more. CPI orators spoke to an estimated 14.5 million listeners during the war. In New York City alone, 1,600 speakers addressed 500,000 each week, speaking

in English, Yiddish, or Italian. See Leslie Midkoff DeBauche, *Reel Patriotism: The Movies and World War I* (Madison: University of Wisconsin Press, 1997); Jackall and Hirota, "America's First," 140, 150, 152; Mock and Larson, *Words*, 120–5; and, Secunda and Moran, *Selling War*, 33.

101. Jackall and Hirota, "America's First," 141, 151.

102. Secunda and Moran, *Selling War*, 36.

103. Mock and Larson, *Words*, 7.

104. Because U.S. government and military leaders believed that victory depended not only on military might, but also on official management of representations and public perceptions of the war, nearly every aspect of America's initial foray into battle was documented by the Army Signal Corps, both in photography and cinematic film, so that the CPI might have a cache of visual materials to utilize back home. See Secunda and Moran, *Selling War*, 34. As the *Duluth News Tribune* remarked (without irony or criticism): "When General Pershing and his flotilla of American fighters first sighted the shores of France last year, they were greeted by the click of motion picture cameras, as well as by the joyous shouts of the French people. From that moment on, every important step that General Pershing and his men have taken in the movement against the gray-green hordes of kaiserdom has been recorded upon the film by United States camera men." See "Pershing and His Lads in Wonder Film 'Pershing's Crusaders,' at Strand Arouses Patriotic Tingle," August 22, 1918, 6.

105. This film portrayed Kaiser Wilhelm as a blood-drunk monster hell-bent on unleashing his German brand of terror upon the civilized world. Mock and Larson, *Words*, 151–2.

106. Ibid, 138–41.

107. Specifically, the licensing agreement had three simple, but effective, rules: (1) that every shipment for entertainment film from the United States should contain at least 20 percent "education material"; (2) that not a single foot of American entertainment film would be sold to any exhibitor who refused to show the Committee's war films; and, (3) that no American picture of any kind would be sold to houses where any sort of German film was being used. Not coincidentally, these rules helped Hollywood squeeze out German competition (which, due to the war, had come to a near standstill), dominate important foreign markets, and thus become a film capital of the world. See Secunda and Moran, *Selling War*, 34.

108. Jackall and Hirota, "America's First," 145.

109. By cooperating with the government, Hollywood was able to thrive during the war years and become the dominating cinematic force it is today. While the film industries in France, Germany, and other belligerent European nations came to a standstill during the war, Hollywood continued to produce films for entertainment-starved domestic and international audiences. The CPI's foreign licensing agreement only insured American dominance in theaters across Europe and the rest of the globe. Furthermore, by producing films like *The Unbeliever*—a fictional tale about an U.S. soldier who comes to appreciate religion, democracy, and his fellow man while fighting in Europe—Hollywood developed invaluable goodwill with the government and the public at large. After the war, Hollywood's wartime patriotism provided a buffer against governmental censorship and served as a selling point when major film

companies began to trade their stock on Wall Street. See Debauche, *Reel Patriotism*, especially pages 34, 40, 108, 109–10, 125–6, 176.

110. Mock and Larson, *Words*, 154.

111. Ibid, 5.

112. Ibid, 4.

113. Jennifer D. Keene, *The United States and the First World War* (Essex, England: Pearson, 2000), 34–6; Kennedy, *Over Here*, 67–8; and Frederick C. Luebke, *Bonds of Loyalty: German-Americans and World War I* (DeKalb, IL: Northern Illinois University Press, 1974), 5–10, 212–4, 244–9.

114. Kennedy, *Over Here*, 68.

115. "Vigilantes to be Organized in Every City," *Idaho Daily Statesman*, November 15, 1917, 2.

116. "Slacker List," Olympia Daily Recorder, October 15, 1918, 1.

117. Throughout the war, American newspapers used various terms interchangeably to describe the conflict, including, "the Great War," "the World War," "the European War," and "the War in Europe." See "Salient Points Emerging from Latest News of the Great War," *Columbus Enquirer-Sun* (Georgia), August 12, 1914, 1; "Where Great Britain's Ally Japan May Enter the World War," *Kansas City Star*, August 10, 1914, 8; "Nordons Trapped by Crisis Abroad, Local Choristers Believed Unable to Return Because of the European War," *Duluth News Tribune*, August 6, 1914, 4; and, "Highlights of the War in Europe Briefly Told," *Philadelphia Inquirer*, August 2, 1914, 1.

118. "Teuton" was the name of an ancient Germanic people. During World War I, Americans often employed the word to connote the supposed savagery and barbarity of their German and Austro-Hungarian enemies.

119. "All in the Day's Work," *Washington Post*, November 5, 1917, 6; "American Soldiers Killed and Wounded," *Pittsburgh Post*, November 5, 1917, 1; "Attack Before Daylight," *New York Times*, November 5, 1917, 1; "Germans Raid Trench, Kill 3, Wound 5, Take 12 U.S. Men Prisoner," *Washington Post*, November 5, 1917, 1; and, "Twelve Americans Captured, Three Are Slain by a German Raiding Party," *Los Angeles Times*, November 5, 1917, I1.

120. Tasker Bliss to Newton D. Baker, May 25, 1917, in Frederick Palmer, *Bliss, Peacemaker: The Life and Letters of General Tasker Bliss* (New York: Dodd, Mead, and Company, 1934), 153, quoted in Evan Andrew Huelfer, *The "Casualty Issue" in American Military Practice: The Impact of World War I* (Westport, CT: Praeger, 2003), 2.

121. John Hay Beith, "First Casualty List," *New York Times*, July 27, 1917, 5.

122. Touching upon this phenomenon, historian Byron Farwell writes: "Throughout the war much was made of 'firsts.'" See Farwell, *Over There*, 106–9.

123. "Mails Free to Sammy," *Washington Post*, July 27, 1917, 4.

124. "First Death in Marines," *New York Times*, August 29, 1917, 8.

125. "Father Curses Germany," *Washington Post*, September 9, 1917, 7; "Four Americans Killed by Raiders," *New York Times*, September 9, 1917, 3; "Hun Airmen Deride American Victims," *Washington Post*, September 9, 1917, 1; "Mother Clings to Hope," *Washington Post*, September 9, 1917, 7; "Two of U.S. Army Hurt,"

Washington Post, September 11, 1917, 2; and, "Victim Was Only 17," *Washington Post*, September 9, 1917, 7.

126. "Americans, Greatly Outnumbered, Fight to Death!" *Los Angeles Times*, November 6, 1917, 1; "As the Defenders of the Alamo," *Pittsburgh Gazette*, November 7, 1917, 6; Farwell, *Over There*, 108; "Resist Huns to Death" *Washington Post*, January 21, 1918, 9; "Second Colorado Infantry Was Encamped in Pueblo Few Months," *Pueblo Chieftain*, December 30, 1917, 12; "They Gave Till They Died! What Will You Give?" *Fort Worth Star-Telegram*, May 19, 1918, 53; and, "We Salute You!" *Miami Herald Record*, April 12, 1918, 5.

127. Mary Irwin to the Quartermaster Corps, November 5, 1917, "Burial Case File" (BCF) for Thomas F. Enright, Records of the Office of the Quartermaster General (RG 92), U.S. National Archives and Records Administration II, College Park, Maryland (NARA). Unless noted, such letters appear in their original form without editorial corrections.

128. A similar movement immediately took place in Evansville, Indiana, the hometown of Pvt. James Gresham. See "Memorial to Private Gresham," *New York Times*, November 7, 1917, 8.

129. Guy E. Campbell to Newton D. Baker, November 21, 1917, BCF for Thomas F. Enright, RG 92, NARA.

130. W. S. McClatchey to Newton D. Baker, BCF for Thomas F. Enright, RG 92, NARA.

131. See, for example: "Americans Killed Must Lie in France Until War Ends," *New York Times*, November 28, 1917, 1.

132. By identifying herself only as "a very patriotic Pittsburgh Mother," this letter writer simultaneously indicated her devotion to the country; established her credibility to speak about Pittsburgh affairs; implied that, as a mother, she might have a son in the war and thus, something at stake in the question of repatriation; and, maintained her anonymity so as to avoid persecution should her words have violated the Espionage Act or some other wartime rule.

133. "Bodies of Heroes Sent to Homes," *Columbus Ledger*, May 12, 1914, 1; "Dead Sailor's Mother Visited by Marshall," *Fort Worth Star-Telegram*, May 15, 1914, 2.

134. Anonymous to Newton D. Baker, received November 20, 1917, BCF for Thomas F. Enright, RG 92, NARA.

135. James B. Cramer to Newton D. Baker, November 26, 1917, BCF for Thomas F. Enright, RG 92, NARA.

136. These letters can be found in BCF for Thomas F. Enright, RG 92, NARA: Henry G. Sharpe to "Mrs. Frank Irwin," November 8, 1917; Thomas Cruse to Guy E. Campbell, November 26, 1917; Henry G. Sharpe to W. S. McClatchey, November 26, 1917; and, Henry G. Sharpe to James B. Cramer, December 3, 1917.

137. "France Wants U.S. Dead," *Washington Post*, December 30, 1917, 6.

138. "America's Dead Are Buried Near Front," *Washington Post*, November 9, 1917, 4.

139. "Gen. Pershing At Soldiers' Graves," *Washington Post*, November 19, 1917, 1.

140. "Enright Street Objected To," *Pittsburgh Post*, November 13, 1917, 2; and "Name Street for Private Enright," *New York Times*, November 10, 1917.

141. "Playground May Be Provided in Memory of Private Enright," *Pittsburgh Post*, November 13, 1917, 4; Michael Connors, "Finding Private Enright," *Pittsburgh Post-Gazette*, November 11, 2007, http://www.post-gazette.com/pg/07315/832688–109.stm (accessed August 25, 2009).

142. "War Cross for Enright," *New York Times*, February 4, 1918, 3.

143. "The Cross," *Los Angeles Times*, February 15, 1918, I14.

144. The military had not yet given each soldier two tags—one to be kept with his corpse and the other to be nailed to his temporary grave marker in the event of death.

145. United States of America War Office, *Regulations for the Army of the United States, 1913: Corrected to April 15, 1917 (Changes, Nos. 1 to 55)* (Washington, DC: Government Printing Office, 1917), 24.

146. BCF for Frederick Wahlstrom, RG 92, NARA.

147. J. M. Winter, *The Experience of World War I* (New York: Oxford University Press, 1995), 146, quoted in Michael Sledge, *Soldier Dead: How We Recover, Identify, Bury, & Honor Our Military Fallen* (New York: Columbia University Press, 2005), 14–15.

148. William G. Eckert, "History of the U.S. Army Graves Registration Service (1917–1950s)," *American Journal of Forensic Medicine and Pathology* 4.3 (September, 1983): 231–43.

149. William R. White, "Our Soldier Dead," *The Quartermaster Review* (May–June 1930), http://www.qmfound.com/soldier_dead.htm (accessed August 27, 2009).

150. Pierce was selected for this position because had completed similar work in the Philippine Islands during the Spanish-American War. The War Department chose him because he had been credited with fulfilling his charge in the Philippines "without a single case of unidentified dead." See *History of the American Graves Registration Service: QMC in Europe*, vol. 1 (Washington, DC: The Library Office of the Quartermaster General, 1920), 14.

151. John Ellis, *Eye-Deep in Hell: Trench Warfare in World War I* (Baltimore: The Johns Hopkins University Press, 1989), 59, quoted in Sledge, *Soldier Dead*, 36–7.

152. White, "Our Soldier Dead."

153. There is ample evidence that GRS personnel routinely risked their lives while completing their work. For instance, one military account from the time period commends the members of Advance Group #1, Graves Registration Service, for their bravery under fire: "On April 20 [1918], Lieut. McCormick and his group arrived at Mandres and began their work under heavy shell-fire and gas, and although troops were in dug-outs, these men immediately went to the cemetery and in order to preserve records and locations, repaired and erected new crosses as fast as the olds ones were blown down. They also completed the extension of the cemetery, this work occupying a period of one and a half hours, during which time shells were falling continually and they were subject to mustard gas. They gathered many bodies which had first been in the hands of the Germans, and were later retaken by American counter-attacks. Identification was especially difficult, all papers and tags having been removed and most of the bodies being in a terrible condition and past recognition. The Lieutenant in command particularly mentioned Sergeant Keating and Private Larue and Murphy as having been responsible for the most gruesome part of the work of identification,

regardless of the danger attendant upon their work. This group of men was in charge of everything at Mandres from the time the bodies were brought in, until they were interred and marked with crosses and proper name plates were attached." See *History of the American Graves Registration Service*, 14–15.

154. It is hard to imagine or put into words just how badly decomposed most of the corpses the GRS handled must have been. One witness, Charles J. Wynne, 2nd Lt. Inf. U.S.A., gives us an idea in his account of GRS activity in the Chateau-Thierry area. According to Wynne, the GRS men labored under shell-fire to recover, identify, and bury the bodies of American troops that had "been decaying for a period of two and three weeks, where the stench and rotten condition of the bodies made the works such that Burial parties feared and neglected to search these bodies even shortly after death for identification." The GRS personnel discovered it "necessary to gather various parts and limbs of bodies together before burial." See letter from Charles J. Wynne, 2nd Lt. Inf. USA, in J. Dell's Notes, *Graves Registration Service*, NARA, RG 92, 5–6, quoted in Sledge, *Soldier Dead*, 46.

155. Ultimately, the task of burying American fallen could have a demoralizing effect on the members of the GRS. A song that spread through several GRS African-American labor units reflected the impacts of this work: "I've got a grave diggin' feelin' in my heart/I've got a grave diggin' feelin' in my heart/Everybody died in the AEF/Only one burial squad wuz left/I've got a grave diggin' feelin' in my heart." See Mark Meigs, *Optimism at Armageddon: Voices of American Soldiers Participants in the First World War* (New York: New York University Press, 1997), 143.

156. Despite its crucial role during the war, the Graves Registration Service faced a shortage of resources. Thus, it relied heavily on the support of the Red Cross. See Sledge, *Soldier Dead*, 195.

157. BCF for Lester G. Carter, RG 92, NARA.

158. BCF for Charles L. Emrich, RG 92, NARA.

159. See "Clarence Sutcliffe First Miami Boy to Lose Life on Firing Line," *The Miami Herald*, August 4, 1918, 1.

160. BCF for Sam J. Webb, RG 92, NARA.

161. During the American Civil War, families routinely traveled to distant regions to search for missing kin or soldierly graves. See Drew Gilpin Faust, *This Republic of Suffering: Death and the American Civil War* (New York: Alfred A. Knopf, 2008), 127–30.

162. "Would Enjoin Governor in Enforcing Draft Registration," *Columbus Ledger*, May 31, 1917, 1.

163. BCF for George H. Edwards, Jr., RG 92, NARA.

164. "Lieut. G. H. Edwards Dead," *Kansas City Star*, March 2, 1919, 11.

165. BCF for George H. Edwards, Jr., RG 92, NARA.

166. White, "Our Soldier Dead."

167. BCF for Hez O. De Long, Mary De Long to John J. Pershing.

168. *History of the American Graves Registration Service*, 46.

169. As many as 200,000 American Jews may have served for the AEF; roughly fifty thousand were shipped overseas to the theater of war. Budreau, *Bodies of War*, 120–1.

170. Huelfer, *The "Casualty Issue,"* 3.

171. Here, the term "casualties" is defined as soldiers either killed in action, wounded in action, missing in action, or captured.

172. By the end of the war, 126,000 American soldiers would perish in the war (more than half from disease or other noncombat related deaths). See Huelfer, *The "Casualty Issue,"* vii–xv.

173. Historian Alistair Horne states that many commanders in the World War "tended to regard casualties as merely figures on a Quartermaster's return." Horne has dubbed such senior commanders as "Chateau" commanders—officers who remained far removed from the front lines and issued their orders from French chateaus. See Huelfer, *The "Casualty Issue,"* 5–8.

174. Huelfer, *The "Casualty Issue,"* 8–10.

175. Huelfer, *The "Casualty Issue,"* 12–16.

176. Ibid.

177. Leland C. Stevenson to Chief of Staff, October 18, 1918, "Reports Related to the Morale of American Troops, 1917–1918," RG 120, Record of the American Expeditionary Forces (WWI), NARA.

178. George W. Cooper, *Our Second Battalion: The Accurate and Authentic History of the Second Battalion 111th Infantry* (Pittsburgh: Second Battalion Book Company, 1920), 273.

179. See, for instance, the AEF's praise of the 80th Division following a fierce battle in the Ardennes region: *History of the 318th Infantry Regiment of the 80th Division, 1917–1919* (Richmond: William Byrd Press, 1920), 82.

180. Christian A. Bach and Henry Noble Hall, *The Fourth Division: Its Services and Achievements in the World War* (Garden City, New York: Country Life Press, 1920), 299.

181. *History of the 110th Infantry (10th Pa.) of the 28th Division, U.S.A., 1917–1919: A Compilation of Orders, Citations, Maps, Records and Illustrations Relating to the 3rd Pa. Inf., 10th Pa. Inf., and 110th U.S. Inf.* (Greensburg, PA: The Association, 1920), 147.

182. Ibid.

183. See *History of the 110th*, 147; Marshall Cavendish Corporation, *History of World War I: Victory and Defeat, 1917–1918* (Tarrytown, NY: Marshall Cavendish Corporation, 2002), 466. Soldiers on both sides of the conflict were discouraged from fleeing combat by the threat of military execution, a draconian deterrent that the British army even used against underage soldiers. See David Lister, *Die Hard, Aby! Abraham Bevistein—The Boy Soldier Shot to Encourage Others* (South Yorkshire: Pen and Sword, 2005); Gerard Christopher Oram, *Military Executions During World War I* (New York: Palgrave Macmillan, 2003).

184. It is reasonable to surmise that the military also wished to control soldiers' thoughts in every possible way. Keeping a diary usually entails reflecting upon the events of a day in a critical and honest manner and exploring previously held assumptions about one's place in the world. Such reflecting and exploring can lead one to challenge the assumptions and premises upon which one's reality has been constructed. If sanctioned, such critical thinking (as appeared in Wertenbach's diary) surely would have undermined the U.S. military's project of motion—a project that conditioned citizen-soldiers to "go over the top" without hesitation and attempt to kill the enemy. Furthermore, had they been permitted, diaries likely would have contained irrefutable evidence against domestic perceptions of the realities of the Great War;

thus, diaries would have belied potential official postwar efforts to whitewash domestic perceptions and public memories of the American war effort.

185. I express my deepest appreciation to Michael Kraus, Curator at Soldiers and Sailors Memorial Hall and Museum, for making Wertenbach's diary accessible to me. See Fred Wertenbach, "World War I Diary 1918 of F. Wertenbach Co. G 111th US Infantry R.E.F.," Archives of the Soldiers and Sailors Memorial Hall and Museum, Pittsburgh, Pennsylvania.

186. For instance, on January 16, Wertenbach describes the thrills of training for trench warfare: "As the weather was nice we went over the top. It was great. We went crouched in the trenches and at our commander's command 'Over!' we went over. We left from the raised trench down upon the prone dummies, then left a trench in the retreating Bosche; then into the double lines of dummies. It was great, I tell you."

187. Bemoaning the vast distance between Camp Hancock in Georgia and the battlefields of Europe, Wertenbach writes on January 13: "I should have joined the regs and been over. We will never go, as Pershing wants no boys scouts. [...] I wonder if we'll ever get over. Wish I was in the Marines."

188. Wertenbach, February 19, 1918, diary.

189. Wertenbach, May 10–12 and 15, 1918, diary.

190. Wertenbach, May 23–25, 27, and 30, 1918, diary.

191. Wertenbach, June 5, 1918, diary.

192. Wertenbach, June 4, 1918, diary.

193. Huelfer, *The "Casualty Issue,"* 3.

194. "Press/Censorship," Record Group 120, Records of the Expeditionary Forces (World War I), Box 6127, File: "Censorship Rules of Press," National Records and Archives Administration II, College Park, Maryland USA.

195. "Reports Related to the Morale of American Troops, 1917–18," Record Group 120, Box 1, Entry 195, National Archives and Records Administration II, College Park, Maryland USA.

196. Ibid, report dated August 19, 1918.

197. Ibid, August 27, 1918.

198. Ibid, August 28, 1918.

199. Ibid.

Chapter 3

A Crisis of Speech

Addressing Mass Death and the Trauma of War, 1918–1922

In November 1920, the U.S. War Department received a note from Emma Cuff, an African-American cook from Eckman, West Virginia, whose son William had died in the so-called Great War: "MY DEAR SIR MY SON HAS NO CHILDREN NOR WIFE I AM HIS MOTHER his father is dead an i have no place that i can call my own and i dont believe that i want my sons body destearbed, if he is in france let him remain untill the judgment in france YOURS as ever." Like tens of thousands of grieving citizens across the nation, Cuff had received inquiries from the War Department seeking consent to bury her son's remains in one of the nascent permanent American military cemeteries in Europe. In other words, the very source of trauma and sadness for people like Emma Cuff (the government/military that forced able-bodied men to fight and die overseas) now sought one last sacrifice from next of kin: to give up the bodily remains of their beloved for inclusion in an official, international memory project. Assuming the subject position of a widowed mother, Cuff spoke plainly, yet eloquently: Since she was homeless and William was wifeless, the government could assume responsibility for his dead body and bury it in France. In a few short lines Cuff gave up her son, her most precious treasure, once more to the American nation and invoked an unspoken ethical contract that would hold the government accountable for the proper treatment of his body until judgment day. Moreover, her note represented one more crucial 'vote' cast in favor of the government's controversial plan to construct monumental military cemeteries on foreign soil, where public memory of U.S. sacrifice in the war would be kept alive through the permanent display of soldiers' graves.[1]

Drawing primarily upon original research of thousands of "Burial Case Files" housed in the U.S. National Archives and Records Administration (NARA),[2] this chapter examines the explosive and illustrative national controversy regarding the plan for overseas cemeteries, and brings forth the voices of 'ordinary' U.S. citizens (and noncitizens) who, after the Armistice, responded to government inquiries regarding the final disposition of their loved ones' bodies. Although many relatives simply filled out and returned forms issued by the War Department, others crafted messages of varied, and often poetic, rhetorical appeals to express their opinions regarding the plan to bury American war dead in distant lands. These letters serve as what historian Robert S. McElvaine terms "immediate testimony"—personal statements that reveal the contemporary views of people who lived through a particular historical moment.[3] While historical letters have limitations as primary sources of evidence,[4] I have done my best to interpret each individual letter within all of its available contextual information.[5] The following pages recover the immediate testimonies of a range of American citizens: from those who relinquished the care of corpses to the government, to those who demanded, sometimes bitterly, the return of loved ones' remains to the United States, to members of the African-American community whose men had fought and died for a nation that treated blacks as inferior citizens. The correspondence discussed here offers views into the complexities of the feelings, ideologies, traditions, social strata, and rights of U.S. citizens who were prompted by the death of their kin to consider both their own relation to the nation and the human costs that U.S. intervention in global affairs entailed.

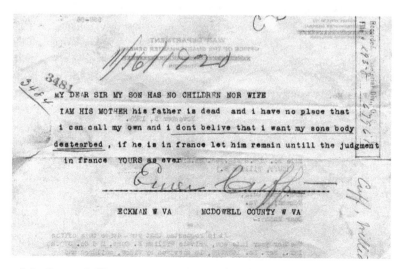

Figure 3.1   Emma Cuff's message. U.S. National Archives and Records Administration, Record Group 92.

Figure 3.2 Emma Cuff's Gold Star Mothers pilgrimage photograph. U.S. National Archives and Records Administration, Record Group 92.

Beyond capturing the sentiments of a past generation of Americans, this textual corpus would come to serve as an inventional resource for officials developing an administrative rhetoric that at once could satisfy the needs of U.S. citizens and advocate for the establishment of symbolic and monumental cemeteries in Europe. In this chapter I argue that through the process of communication in initiated with grieving families, the U.S. War Department learned to temper its highly bureaucratic and nationalistic speech with a softer, more personal and sentimental vernacular appropriated from the letters of next of kin. In doing so, the War Department was able to make a stronger public case for its controversial plan to bury soldiers in symbolic overseas cemeteries. And through this process, government and military officials came to recognize the opportunity (if not outright necessity) of manufacturing a new, generic, ideographical image of the U.S. soldier as a model of unassailable virtue, strength, sacrifice, and righteousness—that is, 'a global force for good'—that might have persuasive value for domestic and international populations in perpetuity. In sum, I argue that the ideograph of the 'modern U.S. soldier' can be traced directly back to the political vicissitudes of this historical *kairotic*[6] moment and the intimate, unnerving negotiations between the War Department and grieving American citizens and communities between 1918 and 1922.

AMERICA'S WAR DEAD

By war's end in November 1918, U.S. Army General John J. Pershing anticipated the postwar requisite of memorializing America's fallen and justifying
their deaths. Having found that many troop units throughout Western Europe
had already built sporadic battlefield monuments that "bore inexact relation
to the scope of the achievements they were commemorating" and "for the
most part were poorly designed," he believed that "the entire story of the
American Expeditionary Forces should properly be monumented from the
national viewpoint."[7] Arguably the most internationally famous military
figure at the time, Pershing became a main catalyst behind a federal plan to
consolidate 2,400 temporary battlefield cemeteries and isolated graves into a
few carefully designed, monumental cemeteries.[8] Constructed on or near the
fields and forests where "Doughboys" had fought and perished, these burial
grounds—sacralized as *American* sites—were meant to link the dead symbolically back to U.S. soil, and the national purpose rooted there. Objects of
motion for the war effort in life, the soldiers would be objects of symbolic
action in death. Helping to assuage public concerns over the war's massive
human tolls, these sites (not coincidentally) might also express the nation's
emerging prominent role on the world's stage to a transnational audience
across time.

However, unlike its Australian, British, and Canadian counterparts,
whose "losses in the Great War were so large as to make the choice of
removal impossible," the U.S. government was not in a position to force
families to leave their dead in continental Europe.[9] The precedent for repa-
triating soldiers killed abroad had been set twenty years earlier when, after
the Spanish-American War, the U.S. government returned all war dead to
the homeland; thus, most Americans assumed that Great War casualties
eventually would be brought back to the United States.[10] Furthermore, as
early as 1917, the War Department told families that it was "the intention
of the Department to have the remains [of the dead] disinterred and shipped
to [the legal next of kin] at the expense of the Government" as soon as
possible.[11] Officials' postwar ambitions had become incongruent with their
wartime assurances.

Yet despite these lingering promises of repatriation, the War Department
set out to pursue the burgeoning plan for permanent American military cemeteries in Europe. In early 1919, the Quartermaster Corps (QMC), a branch of
the War Department, began a campaign to register the sentiments of families
whose loved ones had been identified in improvised graves and cemeteries
across the continent. That year 75,000 families were mailed a letter and a
small card of inquiry regarding their kin's final resting place. Each card,

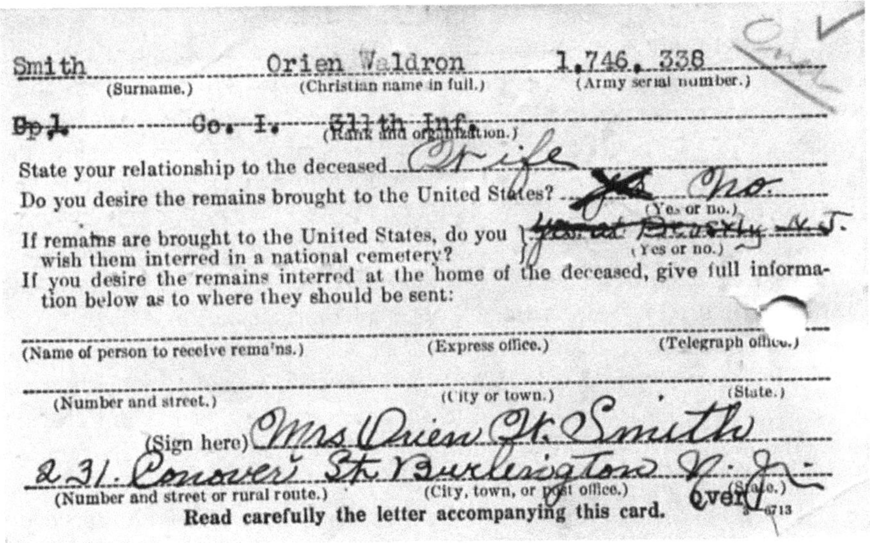

Smith (Surname.) Orien Waldron (Christian name in full.) 1,746,338 (Army serial number.)

Cpl. Co. I. 311th Inf. (Rank and organization.)

State your relationship to the deceased Wife

Do you desire the remains brought to the United States? ~~Yes~~ no. (Yes or no.)

If remains are brought to the United States, do you wish them interred in a national cemetery? ~~Yes at Brooklyn N.J.~~ (Yes or no.)

If you desire the remains interred at the home of the deceased, give full information below as to where they should be sent:

(Name of person to receive remains.) (Express office.) (Telegraph office.)

(Number and street.) (City or town.) (State.)

(Sign here) Mrs Orien W. Smith

231. Conover St. Burlington N.J.

(Number and street or rural route.) (City, town, or post office.) (State.)

Read carefully the letter accompanying this card. Over

Figure 3.3 An example of the inquiry card sent to next of kin. U.S. National Archives and Records Administration, Record Group 92.

inscribed with the respective soldier's name, Army serial number, and rank and organization, unsympathetically expressed the following:

State your relationship to the deceased ______________________
Do you desire the remains brought to the United States? __________ (yes or no)
If remains are brought to the United States, do you wish them interred in a national cemetery? __________ (yes or no)
If you desire the remains interred at the home of the deceased, give full information below as to where they should be sent: ______________________

Approximately 65,000 inquiry cards were returned to the War Department that year. Seventy-one percent of the respondents were in favor of bringing the dead home.[12] This percentage irked General John J. Pershing, Secretary of War Newton D. Baker, and other military leaders, who publicly campaigned to leave the dead in European soil, where "[t]he graves of our soldiers [would] constitute [...] a perpetual reminder to our allies of the liberty and ideals upon which the greatness of America rests."[13] In October 1919, Congressional leaders who feared that Pershing and other military figures might unduly use propaganda to influence public sentiment over the repatriation of soldier dead attempted to wrest control of the burial policies from the War Department, but to little avail.[14] In truth, such suspicions were not unfounded, as many kin indicated through their own words that reports of the plan for overseas cemeteries had persuaded them to leave the dead in Europe. For instance, Mrs. Georgia V. Reager of Shreveport, Louisiana, wrote to the QMC: "Some months ago I filled out the card sent of my husband [...] be returned to the United States as soon as possible. However, after further consideration and learning the views of General Pershing and others concerning this matter, I have concluded that it is best to let the body rest where it has been placed."[15]

In 1920, the Graves Registration Service (GRS), a division within the QMC (and the corps responsible for military mortuary affairs), began issuing GRS Form 120 to relatives of the dead. This form asked next of kin to indicate (again) whether they desired the respective soldier's body returned to their address, buried in a domestic national cemetery, or left in Europe.[16] Over the next two years those who requested the return of bodily remains through GRS Form 120 were required to jump through one more hoop and send a telegram to the GRS (paid for by the government) to confirm this decision. On March 31, 1922, the War Department stopped accepting requests for the return of bodies except in cases of families whose loved ones had not yet been identified; thereafter, all unclaimed bodies would rest in perpetuity in an overseas cemetery.[17] In the following pages, I will bring forth and analyze the responses that were elicited by this process of consultation between government officials and a truly heterogeneous community of grieving Americans that occurred from 1919 and 1922. In doing so, we can begin to imagine what next of kin were feeling and understand the emotional and spiritual turmoil with which the U.S. government had to contend in the immediate postwar years.

ANXIETY AND ANGER

For many families the process of extracting accurate information and conveying their wishes to the proper authorities was one of anxiety and uncertainty. A common problem was that newspaper reports of governmental burial policies often countered the information next of kin received from the War Department. In August 1921, Charles Hubert, a salesman from Yonkers, New York, wrote to the War Department: "I read in several papers lately that *all* the American soldiers that died in Europe are to be sent home! My son Harold W. Hubert was killed and buried over there, and *we do not want* his body sent here." The QMC responded in what can only be described as a 'telegraphic' voice: "Newspaper reports to the effect that the remains of all soldier dead are being returned to this country are in error. The remains are being returned only in those cases where the legal next of kin definitely

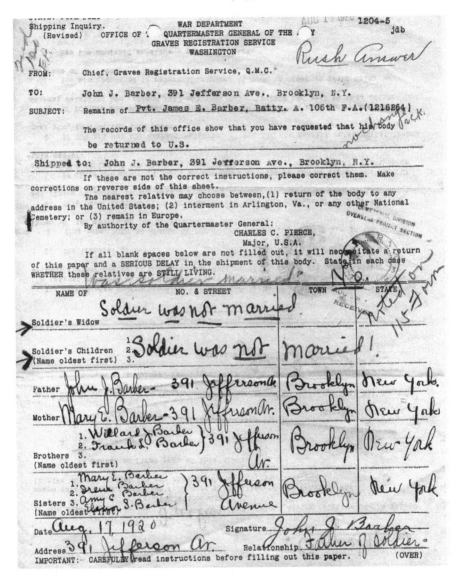

Figure 3.4 An example of GRS Form 120. U.S. National Archives and Records Administration, Record Group 92.

request such action."[18] Other next of kin were anxious to make sure that their wishes were properly expressed and received. For some this meant writing not only in spaces designated on cards and forms, but in the margins and on the back of government-issued documents as well. For instance, Nora Dooley of New York City indicated on the front of her GRS Form 120 that she wished to leave her son's remains in Europe. On the back of the form she emphasized this request: "Yes. Leave him rest in peace."[19] Jennie Peters, a Native American from the Menominee Indian Reservation in Keshena, Wisconsin, indicated on the margins of her War Department inquiry card that she would properly handle her son's corpse herself: "I will take care of the body when it gets to [me]."[20] Some next of kin betrayed a near paranoia in their attempts to make sure that the authorities had the information necessary to carry out their wishes. In a series of letters, Josie Kneale of Oakland California, who requested the return of her brother's body, continually mentioned that she no longer lived at 2412 11th Avenue, but now resided at 2117 11th Avenue—even after the QMC stated that the change had been recorded.[21]

Anxiety often spilled over into anger for families who felt that their wishes were not being fulfilled in a timely and proper fashion. Addressing complications concerning the return of his son's body, Patrick Ayres, a farmer from Heflin, Alabama, shared his frustrations with the War Department:

> [I]n Reply to your letter [of recent date], I never have signed for him to Stay in france I signed for his boddy to be braught back home I will send you A letter I received from the War Department that shows that I have ask for him I waunt him returned home [...] read careful mark your record I dont waunt no more mistakes please write me by return mail dont forget to return his boddy.[22]

Marie Jewell of Mix, Louisiana, expressed similar frustrations. Throughout 1919 and 1920, Jewell sent seven letters to the QMC, each asking for her son's corpse. On August 8, 1919, she claimed, "There seems to be a growing sentiment in favor of leaving their bodies in France, among those who have never loved and lost like Gen. Pershing; but they can never feel, nor ever know the great yearning desire we mothers, who have given our all, have to get back all that is mortal of our precious sons." When Jewell received a *second* GRS Form 120 in June 1920, she pasted a scathing note to the back of the form. Perhaps sensing that her previous, and thoughtfully crafted, correspondence had been ignored, she stated, "My wish *has been expressed many* times as to the return of my son's body. Records must *not* be accurate. Hewitt Charles Jewell's father, Ben Jewell, is deceased, and I am next nearest living relative, his mother. Ship body to [me]."[23] Likewise, Jacob Hablitzel Sr., a farmer from Eustis, Nebraska, was aggravated by the War Department's apparently shoddy recordkeeping. On the back of an inquiry card returned to the QMC, he angrily scrawled: "You must have your records in a hell of a shape. Just received word from the Capt. Francis G. Coates, Battery E, 8th F. A. that my Son J. Hablitzel jr. was never a member of his organization. What garantee have I got that his identical bones and not somebody else's are shipped back to me [...] I think it is rotten."[24] Some next of kin expressed indignation over seeing other families receive remains before they did. Frances Schmidt of Urbana, Ohio, grumbled, "Twice I have requested the return of the body of [Cpl.] Ivan F. Schmidt [...] Why do I not get some word? The rest of the boys are being returned. Why not my son?"[25] These letters reveal that the process of communication initiated by the War Department gave voice to grieving families who might otherwise have remained silent on the matter of repatriation. But this process of consultation also raised the expectations of next of kin, who were often disappointed when their expressed wishes were not fulfilled in a flawless manner. Compelled to remain quiet during the period of American belligerence, next of kin were now making their voices heard.

LEGAL NEXT OF KIN

As much as the War Department may have wished to ameliorate any anger felt by relatives of the dead, it enacted and enforced a peculiar policy that unnecessarily antagonized mourning families and reinforced contemporary notions that American women were fundamentally second-class citizens who had limited authority (even in matters concerning the dead). The final resting place of a soldier's remains was governed solely by the desires of the "legal next of kin," which the War Department defined as the soldier's widow or children. If a dead soldier had been unmarried (as was common), or if his widow had remarried since his death, then the right to dictate disposition was given to the soldier's father. If a dead soldier left no widow, child, or father, the right to dictate final disposition went to the mother, then to the nearest male relative.[26] The patriarchal bias of this policy embittered many women whose justifiable claims to bodily remains were denied. Nellie McDonald of Binghamton, New York, for example, requested the mortal remains of her nephew whom she had raised as her own child:

> Dear sir I am the Soldurs Aunt and one Who have looked after him for years and one Who he has given as his nearest relative and it is my desire and Wish to have his Body sent home to me. he Was as dear to me as any son could be to a mother he has a father Who never cared for him in years. he gave me as his nearest relative all through the time he served his country you Will find it in the War Department red cross and Every place he Went I will close hopin to hear from you about sending the body to me.

In reply to this heartfelt letter, the QMC dryly stated: "[I]t is requested that you furnish documentary evidence of your appointment as legal guardian [...] or submit affidavits of two responsible citizens who have knowledge of the fact that you were responsible for the care of the late soldier until just prior to his enlistment in the Army." Regrettably, as McDonald was unable to produce such evidence, the QMC sent the body to the soldier's father per his request.[27] Sarah Jane Jaires of Quinlan, Texas, whose husband Elmer J. McCann had been killed by bomb shrapnel, wrote: "I see by the paper that all those who lost [their] lives in France were to be brought home. I have re married and living out west and will you please notify me if my [husband's] body comes back." In response, the QMC flatly stated that as a result of her remarriage, Jaires had lost the preferential right to direct final disposition. Because the QMC did not receive any requests from McCann's "legal next of kin," his remains were ultimately left in Europe.[28]

Sometimes the patriarchal bias of the War Department's policy led to out-right conflict between estranged family members, who involved the government in their feuds. For instance, Victor Christensen, a factory worker from Mohawk, New York, mailed this scathing letter to the War Department:

> You [sent] me sometimes ago a card to fill out concerning bringing the dead soldier back from Europe. I should consider it an outrage to ever do any such thing if you couldn't bring them back alive it is of no use (there is more dead ones in this country now than there ought to be) but the soil here is good enough for them, but I should think The Government would be satisfied they had done a good job to get rid of these young men, that they could let them alone now and let them rest in peace in the sacred soil where they lie now and not bring them back to this condemned country. If any body have filled out the card to the contrary and signed it with my name it is false.

A few months later, the QMC received a letter from Victor's estranged wife, Amelia Christensen: "The Father wrote and requested you not to return the body just to be mean to the Boy's Mother. I am his mother and think I have just as much right to have him returned to this Country." The QMC responded to Amelia with a less than encouraging reply: "[Y]ou are advised that the action of this office in the disposition of the remains of soldier dead in Europe is governed solely by the desires of the legal next of kin [...]. If the father will advise this office concurring with your request that the body of your son be returned to this country for private interment, same can be made a matter of record." To its credit, the QMC sent a series of letters to Victor asking if he would relinquish the right of determining the disposition of his son's body to Amelia. Receiving no response, the QMC then wrote to the Postmaster of Mohawk: "Please endeavor to locate Mr. Victor Christensen [...] Will you kindly secure a signed statement from him as to whether he concurs in the request of Mrs. Amelia Christensen [...] to have the remains returned to the United States and shipped to her." A few weeks later, the

QMC received the very same letter they had sent to the Postmaster. Scrawled at the bottom of the page was the following: "Mr. Christensen refused to answer any question and said that you must take the matter up direct with him. You will find him a hard man to deal with."[29] Here we see how the War Department's policies could sow further division at the most basic domestic level of American life.

Moreover, the case of the Christensens illustrates the breakdown of communication between the government and private citizens that could (and did) occur now that the military had relinquished some physical control over the bodies of soldiers back to relatives (who often disagreed on the question of burial).[30] But more importantly, it highlights the patriarchal bias of the War Department's policies—a bias that pushed many grieving women to reconsider the wartime rhetoric of the 'silent, supportive heroine' female subject position. Before and during U.S. entry into the war, the bulk of government and pro-war propaganda had tied 'patriotic womanhood' directly to the success of America's fighting forces. In light of the crisis of a foreign conflict and the reality of a national draft, women had been called upon to offer up their husbands and sons to service and to fulfill quietly any roles in the domestic front asked of them.[31] Surely many women were stunned to discover that after all of their wartime sacrifices (including the offering up of their men to the fates of war) and the political gains they had made through war work, they were being bypassed in the process of determining their son's or husband's final resting place. The War Department's miscalculated assumption that women would passively maintain the accommodating role prescribed to them during war raised bitter feelings among those whose claims to the dead were disregarded.

ECONOMIC CLASS

Although the Selective Service Act of 1917 had effectively 'democratized' the process of wartime conscription in the United States by drawing upon able-bodied males of all economic classes and prohibiting the hiring of substitutes, following the war many next of kin believed that their wealth, or lack thereof, might play a crucial role in the final disposition of the dead.[32] For example, despite public statements by the War Department that American bodies would not begin to return to the United States until late 1920, some next of kin attempted to use their wealth to expedite the process. In a March 1919 telegram to the GRS, Fred Keithan of Shenandoah, Pennsylvania, stated: "My son Frederick H Keithan died in Coblentz Germany [...] can I have his body will send a representative to Washington and post with you any amount of money to defray all expenses of the return please do not deny this request I want my boys remains."[33] Others referenced their working class status or poverty in emotional handwritten appeals. In November 1918, Eugene Head, a dairy farmer from Mahopac Falls, New York, wrote to the War Department: "I want very much to have my boys body returned, but as I am simply a laboring man working by the day, I feel unable to bear the expense myself. Will you kindly advise me on this subject."[34] In a January 1919 letter to Secretary of War Newton D. Baker, William Buente, a machinist from Pittsburgh, whose son Howard was killed in action, argued against the construction of overseas cemeteries that, in his view, could only be visited by the rich:

> As we are patiently waiting for our dear son's body to be returned to us, we ask of you as a sec of war, if you will do your utmost in bringing his body back to the good old 'U' 'S' 'A' where he was born and raised [...] I think as every mother father brother wife or sweetheart whose a member of the "Bring home the soldier dead" league thinks that as he was a brave American with American blood running through his veins. Why should he be deserted by us and our government and left sleeping on the other side. As the old saying of these fellows (NOT MEN) who did not lose anybody in the war 'Let them sleep where they fall.' This saying is not the truth as the majority of the bodies have been removed several times and finally to this large plot where hotels are now being built to accommodate the rich (those who lost NO ONE) but coming for curiosity and also for the French to make a little coin, and the poor (yes the poor) can stay at home look at the picture and never have an opportunity to lay flowers on his grave.[35]

In this letter, Buente makes the powerful suggestion that his son's bodily remains might become part of a larger spectacle that would make money for the French. We see in Buente's letter his keen awareness of the characteristics of twentieth century commercial culture—a culture in which even cemeteries could be marketed for mass consumption—and his consciousness of the dissonance between the personal pain of his family and the notion that the overseas cemeteries might become a curiosity for the wealthy.

In the end, William had the body of his son, Howard, buried in the Buente family plot at the Allegheny Cemetery in Pittsburgh. Nestled in the side of a secluded, unkempt grassy hill, Howard's inconspicuous headstone reads:

CORP. HOWARD A. BUENTE
Co.M., 320th Inf. 80th Div.
BORN SEPT. 6, 1895
KILLED IN ARRAS FRANCE
AUG. 14, 1918

It is uncertain how many people still visit Howard's grave. When I found his grave on Memorial Day of 2009, no one had yet planted an American flag in honor of his military service. But standing among the headstones of other Buente family members in this tiny corner of Allegheny Cemetery, Howard's headstone bears a quiet dignity befitting William's intentions. And in the descriptor "killed" (not "died" or "fell" or some other term with softer connotations), we can sense, even a century later, the anger and resentment of a grieving father.

BRING THEM HOME

As one might easily imagine, two distinct collective voices emerged from the correspondence sent to the War Department: one demanded the repatriation of war dead and the other requested foreign burial.[36] Generally, those in favor of returning the bodies of their sons, brothers, and husbands perceived a threat that the government, in its desire to construct symbolic cemeteries abroad, would somehow prevent the removal of American war dead from Europe. Such concerns were not baseless; at the time, newspaper headlines trumpeted Pershing's desire to leave the bodies in foreign soil, Congressional leaders called for the establishment of overseas cemeteries, and French health policies barred the immediate evacuation of war dead from France. Furthermore, despite the documents sent by the War Department to next of kin, as well as public assurances from Secretary Baker in late 1919 "that no body will remain abroad which is desired in this country,"[37] actual legislation guaranteeing families' rights to the bodies of soldier dead was not passed until March 4, 1921—nearly two and a half years after Armistice. Even after the enactment of Public Law No. 389, many next of kin, still waiting for their beloved's remains, seemed unable to take the government at its word. Thus, between 1919 and 1922, the War Department received countless emotional correspondence from citizens calling for the return of America's fallen.

Those who sought the return of bodily remains offered a range of arguments and pleas. Some relatives, such as Lydia Campbell of Mankato, Minnesota, employed patriotic rhetoric: "Any parents who gave their loved son to the great cause, *should* have the right to the body of that boy, who was given to his country, returned for interment in the country that he fought for & loved."[38] Lewis Brown, a teamster from Staten Island argued for the return of his son's body by evoking the inherent 'American-ness' of the dead:

[O]ur boys were good Enough to be taken away over there they should be good enough to Be Brought Back Again though they are Dead he was an american Bred & Born & his Forefathers Befor Dont you think this country of ours should

Keep its word—American First Please Record my Application for the Return of my Boy and you will Oblige his Father who wants it.[39]

For Campbell and Brown, then, the only proper place for the interment of American soldiers would be the United States—the country for which they fought and died; the land where they were "Bred & Born." To them, the notion that the government might not honor the minimal commitment of returning America's sacrificed war dead to the soil of their homeland was too outrageous to believe.

Other next of kin eschewed patriotic language and crafted letters that expressed more familial, tender sentiments instead. Such letters often focused on specific funerary practices. Henry Beyer, a coal truck driver from Chicago, wrote of his son's corpse: "We would like to have his body returned to [...] Chicago [...] where his body will be taken care of and placed in a vault for a few days."[40] Martha Swain, a family nurse from Norfolk, Virginia, wrote of her dead son David: "I truly want his body [sent] home so I can look after it as long as I live and to Know that I can be near it."[41] Addie Blosser of Bryon, Ohio, echoed this sentiment: "Sir i want my Dear boy body if can have it i Be sure it him and Burried it in our home grave yard it will pleas me so for he was so close to me then i Can go to his grave when i want to it seem so hard to have our boys die over there i wil be so thankful to get his body."[42] Such expressions indicated that many Americans adhered to traditions in which bodily death is not the final moment of life. Indeed, many next of kin believed in the resurrection of an individual's spirit in the afterlife; this resurrection depended on the proper treatment and burial of the dead. For many grieving relatives, this meant burying loved ones nearby, where they could constantly renew their contact with the spirit of the dead by being within the presence of their beloved's bodily remains.[43]

Sometimes next of kin insisted that they were fulfilling the wishes of the dead. For instance, Leta Matsler of Centralia, Illinois, claimed: "I am writing this as a request for the body of my dear son [...] to be returned to me, that his body may rest in his homeland which he loved and to which he longed to return."[44] Rosie Hajek of Chicago eloquently stated that her son had always been adamant about his final resting place: "His only wish was to be buried next to his father, he begged his Friends when he was in Rockford in Camp that if anything should happen to him in the battle they should tell his mother to fill out his dying wish [...]. All I want is to fulfill his dying wish and you could do it with gladness for laying down his young life."[45] Through romantic depictions of their sons' longings for the homeland these women argued for the privileged position of the next of kin as the best representatives and interpreters of the desires of the dead.

Other relatives made no such pretenses about fulfilling the wishes of the dead, but rather sought the return of bodily remains through emotional references to their own broken hearts. Carrie Bruce of Lawrence, Massachusetts, confessed: "[O]ur human hearts cry out in grief and loneliness, for the pitiful bit of comfort that can come in feeling sure that their dead bodies are being cared for."[46] Anna Sullivan of Scranton, Pennsylvania, whose son Richard had been killed during the Meuse-Argonne offensive, sadly stated: "The news of my son being killed in action was indeed a terrible shock to me, but the delay [...] in returning his remains to me has affected my heart almost to the breaking point."[47] And Charles Joyce, a fireman from Pittsburgh, whose sister Katherine had died while serving as a volunteer nurse in France, channeled his physical grief into prose:

> I send this letter [...] to see if My Dear Sister will be sent over her bodie I have so I can lay her where I can see her last resting place How Happy I would feel to have her near me so far she is I am hear Hartbroken as she was all I Had [...] but what it would mean to see my Dear Sister once again that sleeps in a lonely Grave among other Mothers Dear loved ones I am chocking must quit writing but please ansir this and I thank the War Dept for all there kindness I got her efects from france and not her O how I felt when they came with out her Dear Deasent Face for she was loved and and is Sadly mised by all whom Knew her Kindly ansir.[48]

For Joyce, just writing about the final disposition of his sister's remains was nearly too much to bear. He had been separated from his sister twice: once when she left for Europe, and again when she died. A third separation—this time her burial in foreign soil—would be just as wrenching, if not more so, than the previous two.

LET THEM REST

While the large majority of next of kin asked for repatriation, others were content to leave the dead in Europe. Many in this latter group crafted correspondence explaining why, even though simple responses to government-issued inquiry cards and forms would have guaranteed their wishes. It seems that the initial reaction for many next of kin—including those who supported the plan to build overseas cemeteries—to the bureaucratic inquiries was to respond as openly, fully, and personally as possible. John W. Graham, author of *The Gold Star Mother Pilgrimages of the 1930s*, writes, "The decision [...] to leave [a soldier's body] forever overseas must have been one of the most difficult choices a parent could have faced."[49] Many families attempted to make this point clear to the government.

It might seem ironic, but in correspondence from kin who wished to leave the dead in Europe, we can find references to the same feelings expressed by kin who advocated repatriation. For example, Eggert and Martha Martens of St. Louis used the power of patriotic rhetoric to express themselves: "In regards to the Remains of our Son Charles Martens (Deceased) [we] will say that he Died Like a true American Soldier and done his Duty for his Country and the ones he left behind him and Let him rest in peace with all his Comrades over there who fought Side by Side with him."[50] Others portrayed themselves as representatives for the dead. Clara Gagnon of Worcester, Massachusetts wrote of her son's body: "I think that it is better to leave his body there and I also think that were he able to speak it would be his wish."[51] Still others alluded to their broken hearts. Josephine and William Dugan of Brookline, Massachusetts, pasted a simple, yet touching, message on the back of their GRS Form 120: "[We wish Frank's] body to lay in the land where it fell though our hearts grieve for our Darling."[52] Thus, it seems that those in favor of foreign burial and those in favor of repatriation drew upon a familiar, universal discourse about war and sacrifice to mount opposing arguments.

Despite these similarities, testimonies from those in favor of foreign burial contained an assortment of separate arguments that supported the War Department's predisposition to leave the dead in Europe. Of these arguments, the most common centered upon a fear of "disturbing the dead." James Anderson of Phoenix, Mississippi, wrote of his son William's body: "I prefer that the body be not disturbed [...]. That troubles me more than any thing else about it remaining over there."[53] Ada Garner of Philadelphia, whose son lied in a temporary cemetery in St. Mihiel, France, stated: "I do not like the idea of him being disturbed and would like to have him remain in a permanent American Cemetery [in France]."[54] And Emily Dixon of Haverford, Pennsylvania, returned her War Department inquiry card with the following message: "I feel very strongly that the body of my husband should not be disturbed at all."[55] Perhaps by expressing this tender concern for letting the departed rest in peace, these kin were also attempting to reclaim the dead from their service to a government that, at least in these women's minds, may have been unconcerned with such matters. Others made religious allusions to an afterlife in which they might one day reunite with the dead. For example, Naomi Meily of Kansas City, Missouri, wrote: "[T]his is a hard problem to solve, that of leaving all that remains of the only one that is so near and dear to a Mother so far away from home and friends. But I have the blessed assurance of meeting him in that upper and better land where there will be no parting."[56] Some expressed gratitude for the government's promise to tend to the graves of American dead in perpetuity. Anna Fatout of Cumberland, Indiana, stated:

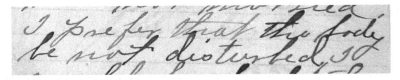

Figure 3.5 James Anderson expresses his wishes. U.S. National Archives and Records Administration, Record Group 92.

"I wish to let [my son's body] remain in France. It will always be cared for there. Were I to bring it to my home the grave when I am gone will perhaps be neglected. If I send it to Arlington Nat. Cem. I will feel it is almost as far away as it now is. *So let his body rest in France.*"[57] Charles Pancoast of Woodstown, New Jersey, revealed: "[I]t surely is a comfort and satisfaction to know that the government is taking good care of the bodies of soldiers who have given their lives in the cause civilization over in France."[58]

And some next of kin, still reeling from the initial shock of losing their beloved in the war, stated that the return of bodily remains would reopen wounds that had only started to heal. Mary Markle of Lore City, Ohio wrote: "i once advised the Government that i did not wont my Sons Body Brought to the States he will rest Just as Easy over ther as here and Please dont Bother me any more as it was hard anought to give him up with out having him Bring ofer here for me to See."[59] Mary Sanders of Indianapolis told the War Department: "I just can not think of bringing him back across that offul water again and while he died and was buried in France we will let him remain there for we could not see him any way."[60] Sanders, like many in her cohort, projected herself as a mother who simply wished no further suffering for her son or herself. We might question the notion that one more trip across the Atlantic—"that offul water"—could actually bother a corpse. But we can empathize with those who wished to forgo the pain that would come with the return of the dead. In a very real way, the government's offer to bury American fallen overseas saved many grieving families from experiencing the sorrow that a domestic burial might bring. Instead of seeking closure through familial rituals of death, people like Sanders clung to a hope that the dead could now rest in heavenly peace.

SECOND CLASS SOLDIERS, FIRST CLASS CORPSES

At the outbreak of U.S. participation in the Great War, leaders within the African-American community issued general support for the national war effort. Despite some undercurrents of resistance within the community, many blacks accepted W. E. B. Du Bois's prewar contentions that the conflict in

Europe represented an opportunity to show one's devotion to country and that the black community's grievances could be put on hold until war's end.[61] Unfortunately, any enthusiasm blacks felt for the war effort was coldly met with widespread discrimination from the U.S. military. For example, just before the U.S. declared war, Lt. Col. Charles Young, the highest-ranking black officer in the Army, was found physically unfit for duty and put on the retired list. Many African Americans believed that Young's forced retirement was meant to prevent the possibility of a black officer commanding drafted white soldiers in battle.[62] Additionally, the Army's violent reaction to the Houston Riot of 1917[63] led some prominent leaders, such as Rev. Dr. George F. Miller, to declare that the military would only serve as an extension of the racist U.S. society in which African Americans were forced to live.[64]

In most respects it was. During the war, the U.S. military utilized the majority of African-American recruits as laborers far from the battlefronts, labeling 89 percent of the 370,000 black draftees as too "moronic" to serve under fire. However, two "colored" divisions, the 92nd and 93rd, were formed and fought admirably on the front lines, often under the command of the French. Despite the fact that these divisions earned praise and respect from French soldiers and citizens, black soldiers faced increased segregation and racial violence from white Americans both abroad and upon return to the United States, at home.[65] For stark evidence of the U.S. military's racist views toward black soldiers, one can turn to the memo, "Secret Information Concerning Black American Troops." Written in August 1918 by Colonel Linard, a French liaison officer to General Pershing's staff, this document was distributed to French troops as a reminder of American color lines:

> Although a citizen of the United States, the black man is regarded by the white American as an inferior being with whom relations of business or service only are possible. The black is constantly being censured for his want of intelligence and discretion, his lack of civic and professional conscience, and for his tendency toward undue familiarity. The vices of the Negro are a constant menace to the American who has to repress them sternly... We may be courteous and amiable... but we cannot deal with them on the same plane with white American officers without deeply offending the latter. We must not eat with them, must not shake hands or seek to talk or meet with them outside the requirements of military service.[66]

This memo, linked directly to General Pershing's office, explicitly enunciates the U.S. military's bigoted, if unofficial, attitude toward African-American servicemen. This racist attitude was manifested and reinforced, often quite subtly, in the everyday life of the American soldier serving in Europe. Consider the article titled "Huns Starve and Ridicule U.S. Captives," which appeared on the front page of the first edition of 'the soldiers' paper,' *The*

Stars and Stripes. Through the words of a Frenchman who had escaped a German prisoner camp, the article details the abuse and humiliation of three white American prisoners of war at the hands of their captors. Starving and downtrodden, the Americans "were obliged to clean the streets and the latrines of the Crown Prince [...] in order to make them appear ridiculous." But worse than that, the soldiers were publicly photographed "standing between six negroes from Martinique; and when the photograph was taken the negroes were ordered to wear tall hats." That this staged photograph would count (in the words of *The Stars and Stripes*) as "ridicule" and "inhumane treatment"— and that the description of the event was designed to foster soldiers' hatred for the "Hun" enemy—shows just how engrained the anti-black attitude was in American military culture.[67]

Following war's end, African-American troops returned to a largely ungrateful nation steeped in the Jim Crow mentality. Limited opportunities to fight in the war had given black soldiers few opportunities to prove themselves to white America. Historian Jennifer Keene writes: "Instead of receiving acclaim, the achievements and contributions of black soldiers went underappreciated by mainstream society." For example, American Legion headquarters in the Southern states rejected applications from black posts; across the nation, only 1,862 black veterans of the war were admitted to the Legion. The U.S. Army itself advised black soldiers returning to the South, where 80% of the African-American population lived, not to wear their uniforms so as to avoid antagonizing whites. And ten of the seventy-seven African Americans lynched by mobs in 1919 were veterans of the war. It was apparent that little had changed for black veterans and their families, who probably agreed with W. E. B. Du Bois' somber postwar statement: "We return, we return from fighting, we return fighting."[68]

Incongruously, although the U.S. military treated African-American troops as second-class soldiers throughout the war, the bodies of fallen black soldiers became just as symbolically valuable as their white counterparts after Armistice. The War Department had every intention of burying dead African-American soldiers with white soldiers in Europe, for every dead black soldier left overseas represented one more headstone to be seen in a symbolic U.S. cemetery. Relatives of black soldiers received the same inquiry cards, letters, and forms as white families, and were encouraged to express their desires regarding the final disposition of loved ones' remains. Given the socioeconomic conditions of a large percentage of the African-American population at the time (nearly a quarter of the community was completely illiterate), it is likely that many black families were unable to effectively express their personal wishes and feelings.[69] Furthermore, we should consider how the patriarchal bias of the policies regarding the final disposition of war dead affected African-American widows. Given the explicit racist and sexist nature of American society at the time, we can safely assume that for many African-American widows, economic survival meant quickly remarrying another man; in getting remarried, widows forfeited their right of determining the final resting place of their dead husbands. But despite these social circumstances, the Record Group of the Office of the Quartermaster General does hold the correspondence of many African-American next of kin. While most African Americans requested the return of their loved one's body, the percentage that did so is on par with the percentage of whites that asked for the return of bodily remains.

Most African Americans who wrote back to the government were succinct. For example, Albert Dubose, a farmer from Bolivar, Tennessee, whose son had been killed in action during the Meuse-Argonne offensive, sent a telegram to the GRS stating: "Forward Private Will Dubose body here for burial."[70] Caesar Bradford, Principal of the Alto Colored Public School in Alto, Texas, wrote to the GRS: "It is my desire that you have the remains of my son Henry Etheridge Bradford returned to the United States and shipped to me, Caesar Bradford Alto, Texas, Cherokee County. Hope this is plainly understood."[71] But some African Americans crafted messages of longer and deeper expression. For instance, Stella Mitchell of Beaumont, Texas, whose son Leon Gilder had died of heart disease in France, wrote on the back of her GRS Form 120: "I have been thinking the matter over I would rather not to destirve the dead My belove son died over there that is the lords will not mine. Many thanks to you for your kindness and at the last day we will be brought togathere yet I Love him over there."[72] Other African Americans, perhaps doubting their ability to secure their beloved's remains from the government, hired lawyers to express their desires forcefully and effectively. In August 1919, the War Department received a letter from the law offices of Gilmer & Graves, who represented Etta Bouling of Charlottesville, Virginia. The letter read:

> Charles Bouling (1968130) Co. I, 365th Inf. was killed about the 28th of Oct. 1918, while his company was located in the Marbach sector near Metz. Mrs. Etta Bouling, an old colored woman of this city, the mother of Charles Bouling, is very anxious to have his body returned to this country. Request information as to what steps should be taken and the prospects of having the body returned.[73]

Some African Americans who requested burials at national cemeteries in the United States indicated that they could not afford to come to the funeral, as if they felt obligated to acknowledge some unspoken guardian role that they could not fulfill. Henry Creed, a laborer at a meat packing company in Chicago, whose son was to be buried in the Arlington National Cemetery, sent a telegram to the GRS, simply stating: "Have Corporal Abraham Creed buried cannot attend funeral."[74] Mattie Lou Fuston of Topeka, Kansas, sent a similar telegram message: "Bury Elmer Fuston in National Grave Yard I am unable to attend funeral."[75] A small percentage of African-American next of kin explicitly asked for the dead to remain in Europe. For some members of this group, the return of loved ones' bodies would take too much of a toll on their health. Willie Mae Bedford of Memphis wrote to the GRS: "I [received] your letter in regards to my husband remains Oscar Bedford Cook, serial no 1401628, Co A 370th Infantry. I do wish for the remains to [...] stay in france on the account of my illness."[76] Others simply refused to play the game of memorialization that returning the dead entailed. Elizabeth Somerville of Hackensack, New Jersey, whose foster son had died of pneumonia in Europe, responded to the burial inquiry card's question, "Do you desire the remains brought to the United States?" with the statement: "No. Since it is impossible to see him would rather his remains rest in France."[77]

Correspondence from African Americans regarding the final disposition of war dead was, generally speaking, succinct and void of the rhetorical flair often found in letters from whites. Though some grieving African Americans, like Emma Cuff, made references to both their familial relationships with the dead and the social contract they expected the government to fulfill, most correspondence from black families contained simple, straightforward requests unadorned with sentimentality. Perhaps African Americans felt less comfortable expressing private emotions to a government that had never treated them as full citizens. Maybe they did not feel entitled to, or properly equipped for, the same discursive space so many whites eagerly claimed. In light of the fact that African Americans had had little say in the events that led to the deaths of their beloved, as well as the reality that blacks faced increased disenfranchisement and racial violence in the United States during the postwar years, it seems probable that many grieving African Americans simply felt defeated. Instead of engaging the government in a personal process of negotiation, most grieving black families simply chose the most straightforward route to securing a peaceful resting place for their fallen men.

OFFICIAL APPROPRIATION OF A
SENTIMENTAL VERNACULAR

Ultimately, the correspondence between the War Department and grieving families centered on the fundamental and sacred obligation of the government to care properly for citizen-soldiers who had willingly died for the nation. Those in favor of repatriation and those in support of foreign burial alike invoked this social contract, sometimes in concrete terms. For instance,

John Lingle of Paoli Indiana, whose son had died of pneumonia in England, claimed that the plan to keep American dead in foreign soil constituted "a direct violation of the implied contract to those who went over never here to return as before."[78] William Roth, a grocer from New York City, wrote:

> As the father of one of those boys who paid the Supreme Sacrifice in France [...] allow me to protest against the cowardly newspaper propaganda which has for its object the influencing of our Government to change its policy in regards to the returning of the bodies of our soldier dead [...]. Now that he gave his life for that cause, can I (who gave him wholeheartedly to our government for that cause) [...] not have all that remains of him, his earthly clay, to revere and cherish while I live [?][79]

And Mollie Roycroft of Coker, Alabama, expressed her expectations to the government: "[Our] request is that Special care be taken of [our son's] Grave. [H]e was our only dear Son. So we gave all we had, and trust that you will take Special care of his Grave for his dear parents."[80] Families like the Roycrofts counted on the government to hold up its end of this tragic bargain.

The War Department was slow to account for the prominent place this social contract held in the hearts and minds of soldiers' relatives.[81] Instead of immediately addressing the pain and expectations of grieving families,

Figure 3.6 Mollie Roycroft's Gold Star Mothers pilgrimage photograph. U.S. National Archives and Records Administration, Record Group 92.

the War Department maintained the distant, highly bureaucratic voice it had used in its wartime communication with the bereaved.[82] Throughout 1919, all grieving families received an official form letter from the War Department that explained in further detail their options for burial of the dead. It read in part:

> The original plan [...] was to deliver the body in every case at the home address of the deceased to the person legally entitled to dispose of the remains. A desire has been expressed, however, in numerous instances to have the body remain abroad, and General Pershing is likely soon to enter into negotiations with the French and Allied Governments with the view of establishing permanent cemeteries for members of the American Expeditionary Forces [...]. A bill is now before Congress for the establishment of 'Fields of Honor' abroad, which will insure future care by the United States Government as national cemeteries are now cared for [...]. The Department is unable to state when it will be possible to begin the removal of the remains of the soldiers, but the information requested is being collected at this time in order that there may be no delay when the times comes for such removal.[83]

While addressing certain questions of burial, this official form letter, like others sent by the War Department after Armistice, lacked the personal touch needed to show appreciation for the wartime sacrifices of citizens, let alone persuade next of kin to bury their beloved in distant lands. The few attempts War Department officials made to speak directly to the suffering of bereaved families[84] were further undermined by highly publicized comments from leaders like Secretary of War Baker, who implored relatives of the dead to "sympathize with the feeling of the department that it is the wiser and better course to leave those bodies in France."[85] George Huddleston, U.S. Representative from Alabama, caused a mini-controversy when he intimated that next of kin who wanted the return of soldierly remains "were indulging in the luxury of sorrow."[86] Even when political and military figures seemingly regurgitated certain arguments put forth by relatives in favor of foreign burial, they seemed unable to convince the public at large of their concern for the average American family's suffering.[87]

By the early 1920s, Pershing and his cohort recognized the necessity of a new rhetorical approach. In April 1923, Pershing issued an order, published on the front page of the *New York Times*, urging the military to adopt a new literary style that contained "the personal touch so often lacking in correspondence with the public."[88] He knew that in order to secure the political will and economic resources necessary for the establishment of U.S. cemeteries in Europe, military and political figures needed to express fully, and continually, their deepest appreciation for the losses families had sustained in the war. In light of the growing opposition to the plan for overseas cemeteries,[89] the War

Department adopted a discursive style clearly tempered by the sentimental vernacular found in the correspondence of grieving families.

As early as November 1919, the War Department began closing its letters to all next of kin with the statement: "It is desired to express to you the deep and sincere sympathy of the Department on account of the loss you have sustained in the death of your" husband, brother, or son.[90] Over the next few years, War Department officials honed their literary skills, crafting messages that accounted for a range of emotions grieving families might have felt: "The Department is gratified that you have confided the mortal remains of this soldier to his country's care. He will rest, forever, in [...] France, with his many comrades, under the flag in defense of which he gave his young life and where his grave will be reverently cared for by a grateful nation."[91] In June 1920, Secretary Baker announced a rather progressive policy that would allow a friend or relative to accompany the body of a dead soldier from its port of arrival to the home of the deceased. "This arrangement is made in order that relatives who wish to do so may secure early control of the bodies of their loved ones and bestow upon them that sympathetic care which they so naturally desire to give."[92] In May 1921 President Warren G. Harding issued a proclamation that established Memorial Day, an annual holiday of commemoration for American war dead: "I invite my fellow citizens fittingly to pay homage on this day to a noble dead who sleep in homeland beneath the sea or on foreign fields, so that we who survive might enjoy the blessings of peace and happiness and to the end that liberty and justice, without which no nation can exist, shall live forever."[93] At the third "Armistice Day pilgrimage" in Washington, D.C., former President Woodrow Wilson delivered an address to thousands of World War veterans—some disabled—on the accomplishments of the "most ideal army that was ever thrown together." Though the speech was highly impersonal and jingoistic, Wilson broke down into tears three times at the sight of the men before him—a performance the veterans found deeply moving.[94] And in the late 1920s, the War Department sent a form letter and card to each of the 30,000 families that had left their beloved in Europe. The card, which stated the final resting place of the respective dead soldier, was marked with a gold star—a nod to the powerful Gold Star Mother movement that had spread throughout the United States.[95] The form letter read: "The Quartermaster General desires to invite your attention to the [enclosed] card which gives the permanent cemetery location of the soldier's grave in which you are interested [...]. Please be assured that in effecting removal of the dead, the utmost reverential care was exercised by those who performed this sacred duty. For the future, these graves will be perpetually maintained by the Government in a manner befitting the last resting place of our heroes."[96] Thus, appropriating the sentimental vernacular of grieving families, the War Department and politicians increasingly learned how to articulate and acknowledge the government's social contract with the families of soldierly dead.

In June 1923, President Harding appointed Pershing to head the American Battle Monuments Commission (ABMC).[97] Created by act of Congress, this seven-member board of politicians, military figures, and citizens, was given total authority over the planning, constructing, and maintaining of America's military cemeteries in Europe.[98] Over the following decade, Pershing played a dominant role in designing the sites and securing the appropriations necessary for the board's monumental visions.[99] Although the Commission would eventually tend to favor, in American culture scholar Ron Robin's words, "either pseudo-medieval styles or ponderous variations of classical designs" that evoked abstract democratic ideals and romantic notions of the Medieval Crusades,[100] the ABMC also incorporated the sentimental vernacular of grieving families into the final visual presentation of the cemeteries. For example, eschewing the "tablet grave marker model" found in Arlington National Cemetery, the ABMC opted for white marble headstones in the shape of the Latin cross, which connote familiar religious allusions of sacrifice, redemption, and rebirth.[101] At each site, the Commission constructed a 'non-sectarian' (though clearly Christian) chapel, where visitors (including, presumably, relatives of the dead) could contemplate the sacrifices of U.S. soldiers and offer prayers in their memory. On the walls of the chapels, the ABMC inscribed statements of a tender and spiritual nature. For instance, an engraving in the Meuse-Argonne American Cemetery chapel states, "This chapel is erected by the United States of America as a sacred rendezvous of a grateful people with its immortal dead," while the inscription across the face of the altar of the Somme American Cemetery chapel reads, "Thou O Lord has granted them eternal rest." And in one exceptional case, the ABMC would allow the mother of Lt. Walker Blaine Beale to erect a statue of her son in the St. Mihiel American Cemetery.[102] An accompanying engraving, written in French above the soldier's head, states: "He sleeps far from his family in the gentle land of France." This stirring stone figure—standing before a larger marble Christian Cross—still occupies a prominent place in the site's landscape (and, as a side note, is represented via stencil drawing on this book's cover).

There is little doubt that the process of consultation between the War Department and grieving families had deeply impacted Pershing. As one of the most instrumental figures in the creation of America's overseas cemeteries, as well as the catalyst behind the Army's adoption of a new affective style of communication, Pershing evolved from a warrior who ordered his men to battle (and death) into a symbol for the government's efforts to address the suffering of private citizens. The *New York Times* portrayed the general as a keeper of the dead who tenderly watched over Doughboys buried in Europe.[103] Over time, he became an outspoken advocate for the "Gold

Star Mother Pilgrimages" of the 1930s, a federally funded program that enabled mothers and widows of the dead to visit their loved ones' graves in Europe.[104] And in 1931, he told a party of Gold Star pilgrims visiting France that "mothers would realize [...] when they look out over the white crosses of the cemeteries where their sons and husbands lie, that the sacrifice was not in vain, and that their memories would be tenderly cherished down through the years."[105] Influenced by the unprecedented dialogue between the U.S. government and relatives of war dead, Pershing helped usher a new, sentimental discourse on soldierly sacrifice into both American public life and the still ongoing project of transnational memory that the U.S. overseas military cemeteries have entailed.[106]

"AMERICA SHOULD KEEP HER PROMISE"

Between January of 1920 and March of 1921, the sisters of Thomas F. Enright (one of the first three Americans combat casualties of the Great War) sent a series of heartbreaking (and progressively angrier) letters to the War Department in which they pleaded for the return of their famous brother's body:

West Etna Pa

Jan 11th—20
Dear Mr Baker.
I am the Sister of Thos F Enright Co. F 16th Infintry first Division killed in France Nov. 3rd 1917. i would like to have my brother body brought home as soon as possible and all the dead Soldier to. America should keep her promise and bring our dead soldier back home. Our boys should never sleep in France it is terrible the French dont want to send them back. Mr Baker i wish you would do all you can to get our dead boys back home my brother was one of the first three soldier killed in the great worlds war.

Your Truly
Mrs Johanna Trunzer
80 Dewey St
W. E. Pittsburg Pa

Agust 7–1920
Dear Mr Sharpe
A few words concerning the remains of my brother who died in France Nov 3-1917 Thomas F. Enright who body ye promised me to be brought bak after the war was over now the war is over almous 2 years and ye have not done it yet ye have brought other bodys home I think thoes 3 first boy

should be brought first it seems terrible it almost 3 yers since they have being killed my brother had served the Goverment 8 yeares I think they owne it to him just last week ther was a young man brough home from oure neighborhood it makes me feel afull to hink he is dead 3 years and this young man died last yeare I have moved from Pittsburgh I would like to heare from you soon

Very Truly Yours
Mrs Mary Irwin
1212 Mohanning Ave
Alliance Ohio

March 17–1921
Dear Sir I recived your letter concerning the remains of my brother Thomas F. Enright Co F 16 Inf I am sorry to say his Mother has being dead fore 20 years and also his Father fore 7 yeares I am his oldest Sister he Maid his home with me since Mother died he was a boy 14 years when oure Mother died I have told the War Dept fore 3 years that Mother and Father was dead I think it about time they should do something and brg him back to the land where he was born and raised the War Dept told us soon as the War was over they would bring him back now it over 2 years and not back yet he dont belong to France he belong to this Country we should have the Credit Thomas Mothe and Father is dead he 2 brother and 2 sister a sister dont seem able alike a Mother but I was a Mother to Thomas I have 4 sons my self and I bored that brother as much as my sones I do hope ye have his remain back soon Mrs Mary Irwin

1212 Mahoning Ave
Alliance Ohio

In July of 1921, Thomas Enright's body was finally returned to his family in Pittsburgh.[107] In fact, the bodies of Private Merle Hay and Corporal James Gresham were returned by family request as well.[108] Thus, nearly four long years after the infamous murders of America's wartime 'holy trinity,' these men's families ultimately chose not to leave their loved ones' bodily remains in Europe. The decision upset some portions of the country, as an op-ed in the *Davenport Democrat and Leader* indicated: "Sleeping together in the soil of France, the graves of Enright, Gresham and Hay would have been a shrine not only for Americans but for lovers of liberty from all parts of the world. Scattered in their home land, they cannot speak the message for freedom that they spoke from that resting place where France so frankly hoped that they might remain."[109] On July 24, 1921, ten thousand people gathered in Omaha, Nebraska, to witness the burial of Private Merle D. Hay and, thus, proved the *Davenport Democrat and Leader* editors wrong.[110]

Amidst the postwar crisis of speech, two contradictory and powerful social forces collided within the American public sphere. The first was the more personal and local suffering of families and communities from across the country who mourned the deaths of 116,516 soldiers, nurses, and personnel still lying in haphazard battlefield graves and muddy fields throughout Western Europe. Grieving for neighbors and relatives who had perished in defense of territory that was not the nation's own, a conglomeration of families of the fallen, civic groups, and local politicians demanded the proper treatment of American war dead.

The second, and quite opposite, force was the U.S. government and military's public, highly impersonal, and overtly political ambition to guide memories of American participation in the Great War through the establishment of permanent and officially sanctioned military cemeteries throughout Belgium, England, and France. By constructing an unprecedented series of blatantly pro-military gravesites that elided the thorny issue of domestic suffering on the same foreign lands where American soldiers had been cut down, U.S. officials intended to display to transnational audiences long-lasting visual and material arguments for the young nation's supposedly righteous and crucial role in the Great War.

As shown above, the U.S. government and military eventually learned that, in order to see the cemetery project come to fruition, officials needed to employ a new, softer brand of rhetoric that acknowledged the deep suffering, personal losses, and anger and angst of citizens-soldiers and their families. In time, the relevant institutions, General Pershing, President Wilson, and other leaders successfully appropriated and repurposed the sentimental, domestic vernacular found in the correspondence of grieving next of kin and secured the bodies of enough fallen soldiers to construct the proposed burial sites in Europe. Ironically, part of this transformation in official postwar rhetoric entailed the government/military—the very source of trauma for widows and others left behind—casting itself as some kind of source of therapeutic relief for grieving families, veterans, and other individuals and groups intimately wounded by the effects of World War I. To what degree this blatant paradox struck average contemporary Americans as *unseemly* is hard to know. But, as the following chapter will show, the planners and architects of the overseas cemeteries would creatively sidestep this paradox (and other thorny pressing issues) by discovering, developing, and emphasizing a novel and potent, if ultimately vague, ideograph: 'the universal, sacrificial U.S. soldier.'

NOTES

1. Emma Cuff to Charles C. Pierce, November 16, 1920, BCF for William Cuff, RG 92, NARA.

2. Within RG 92 there are 5,400 boxes, organized alphabetically, containing burial case files of soldiers killed in World War I. Each box holds roughly twenty individual files. To collect correspondence related to the final disposition of 400 soldiers, I requested every fourteenth box from the 5,400 available. From each of these boxes I collected data from the first file that contained what I call 'extra communication'—letters, notes, telegrams that went beyond the filling out of forms.

3. Robert S. McElvaine, *Down and Out in the Great Depression: Letters from the Forgotten Man* (Chapel Hill: University of North Carolina Press, 1983), 5.

4. Such letters often provide only fragments or snapshots of an ongoing correspondence, and they can tempt one to take the letter writer's words at face value. See Mary Jo Maynes, Jennifer L. Pierce, and Barbara Laslett, *Telling Stories: The Use of Personal Narratives in the Social Sciences and History* (Ithaca: Cornell University Press, 2008), 82–90.

5. I consider the subject position of each letter writer; the desires expressed by the writer in all accessible letters; the most likely motives of the writer; and, how each letter fits within the larger chain of correspondence between the writer and the government.

6. Again, for more on *kairos*, see, Jane Sutton, "Kairos," in *Encyclopedia of Rhetoric*, ed. Thomas O. Sloane (Oxford: Oxford University Press, 2001), 413–17.

7. Thomas North, General North's Manuscript (unpublished manuscript, courtesy of Oise-Aisne American Cemetery and Memorial Superintendent David Bedford, 2006), 1.

8. On February 28, 1919, as the American Expeditionary Forces prepared to start transporting U.S. soldiers home, General Pershing issued a General Orders to the entire A.E.F. that thanked the men for their service and indicated that many fallen comrades would be left behind. "Now that your service with the American Expeditionary Forces is about to terminate, I can not let you go without a personal word [...] In leaving the scenes of your victories, may I ask that you carry home your high ideals and continue to live as you have served—an honor to the principles for which you have fought and to the fallen comrades you leave behind [...] It is with pride in our success that I extend to you my sincere thanks for your splendid service to the army and to the nation." See Association of the 110th Infantry, *History of the 110th Infantry (10th Pa.) of the 28th Division, U.S.A., 1917–1919: A Compilation of Orders, Citations, Maps, Records and Illustrations Relating to the 3rd Pa. Inf., 10th Pa. Inf., and 110th U.S. Inf.* (Greensburg, PA: The Association, 1920), 151.

9. John W. Graham, *The Gold Star Pilgrimages of the 1930s* (Jefferson, NC: McFarland, 2004), 35.

10. G. Kurt Piehler, *Remembering War the American Way* (Washington: Smithsonian Institution Press, 1995), 94.

11. Henry G. Sharpe to Mattie Hicks, July 24, 1917, BCF for Clifton R. Hicks, RG 92, NARA.

12. House Committee on Foreign Affairs, *Hearings on Authorizing the Appointment of a Commission to Remove the Bodies of Deceased Soldiers, Sailors, and Marines, from Foreign Countries to the United States, and Defining Its Duties and Powers*, 66th Cong., 1st sess., 1919, 6.

13. "Pershing Against Removal of Dead," *New York Times*, August 24, 1919.

14. House Committee, *Hearings*.

15. Georgia V. Reager to QMC, September 20, 1919, BCF for Wallace C. Reager, RG 92, NARA.

16. The government claimed that this form allowed families who had changed their minds regarding final burial to issue new instructions ("'Village's'").

17. "30,496 A. E. F. Dead to Be Undisturbed in European Graves," *Washington Post*, April 9, 1922.

18. Charles Hubert, correspondence with War Department, August 4–12, 1921, BCF for Harold W. Hubert, RG 92, NARA.

19. Nora Dooley to War Department, September 2, 1920, BCF for Frank W. Dooley, RG 92, NARA.

20. Jennie Peters to War Department, n.d., BCF for John J. Peters, RG 92, NARA.

21. Josie Kneale, correspondence with War Department, BCF for Richard H. Dashwood, RG 92, NARA.

22. Patrick Ayres to War Department, April 25, 1920, BCF for Joseph I. Ayres, RG 92, NARA.

23. Marie Jewell, correspondence with QMC, 1919–1920, BCF for Hewitt C. Jewell, RG 92, NARA.

24. Jacob Hablitzel Sr. to QMC, April 16, 1919, BCF for Jacob Hablitzel Jr., RG 92, NARA.

25. Frances Schmidt to Charles C. Pierce, n.d., BCF for Ivan F. Schmidt, RG 92, NARA.

26. War Department, "Cemeterial Division Bulletin No. 10-F-W," BCF for John A. James, RG 92, NARA.

27. Nellie McDonald, correspondence with QMC, May 1920, BCF for Charles J. McGraw, RG 92, NARA.

28. Sarah Jane Jaires, correspondence with QMC, April 4, 1920–July 19, 1925, BCF for Elmer J. McCann, RG 92, NARA.

29. See BCF for Archibald P. Christensen, RG 92, NARA.

30. Lt. Col. Charles C. Pierce, Chief of the GRS, eventually recommended that in such a case the parent "designated by the deceased soldier in his emergency address" would be "held entitled to direct disposition of his remains." Quoted in Sledge, *Soldier Dead*, 41.

31. See Susan R. Grayzel, *Women and the First World War* (London: Pearson Education, 2002); Joanne Karetzky, *The Mustering of Support for World War I By The Ladies' Home Journal* (New York: Edwin Mellen, 1997); and, Kathleen Kennedy, *Disloyal Mothers and Scurrilous Citizens: Women and Subversion During World War I* (Bloomington: Indiana University Press, 1999).

32. This belief was wrong, as the financial condition of legal next of kin had no official bearing on the final disposition of soldierly remains. The government returned all bodily remains to any legal next of kin who desired them free of charge. Furthermore, the government gave families up to 100 U.S. dollars to hold private funerals. The government also covered costs for burials at domestic national cemeteries. See War Department, "Cemeterial."

33. Fred Keithan, telegram to GRS, March 2, 1919, BCF for Frederick H. Keithan, RG 92, NARA.

34. Eugene Head to War Department, November 23, 1918, BCF for Randolph Head, RG 92, NARA.

35. William Buente to Newton D. Baker, January 10, 1919, BCF for Howard A. Buente, RG 92, NARA.

36. This is not to say that all next of kin wholeheartedly supported either repatriation or foreign burial. Some were quite unsure of what they wanted. Carrie Andrews of Cleveland Ohio, for instance, wrote to the War Department: "Would like to know what the majority of the people are going to do—if they have there I would like my boy there if not will have him brought back." See Carrie Andrews to Adjutant General's Office, April 25, 1919, BCF for Clarence St. John, RG 92, NARA.

37. Quoted in Sledge, *Soldier Dead*, 136.

38. Lydia Campbell to P. C. Harris, December 12, 1919, BCF for Glenn H. Campbell, RG 92, NARA.

39. Lewis Brown to P. C. Harris, January 20, 1920, BCF for Martin O. Brown, RG 92, NARA.

40. Henry Beyer to GRS, June 1, 1920, BCF for Henry C. F. Beyer, RG 92, NARA.

41. Martha Swain to War Department, March 26 1920, BCF for David S. J. Swain, RG 92, NARA.

42. Addie Blosser to GRS, March 25, 1919, BCF for Carl F. Blosser, RG 92, NARA.

43. For information on late-nineteenth century religious interpretations of the corpse in the U.S., see Laderman, *The Sacred Remains*, 173–4.

44. Leta Matsler to GRS, February 14, 1919, BCF for Seymour A. Prestwood, RG 92, NARA.

45. Rosie Hajek to P. C. Harris, May 3, 1920, BCF for Joseph Hajek, RG 92, NARA.

46. Carrie W. Bruce to Charles C. Pierce, September 11, 1919, BCF for Alexander B. Bruce, RG 92, NARA.

47. Anna Sullivan to QMC, March 14, 1922, BCF for Richard A. Sullivan, RG 92, NARA.

48. Charles H. Joyce to GRS, June 4, 1920, BCF for Katherine M. Joyce, RG 92, NARA.

49. Graham, *The Gold Star Pilgrimages*, 35.

50. Eggert and Martha Martens to War Department, March 31, 1919, BCF for Charles Martens, RG 92, NARA.

51. Clara Gagnon to War Department, n.d., BCF for Robert E. Garner, RG 92, NARA.

52. Josephine and William Dugan to GRS, June 16, 1920, BCF for John F. Dugan, RG 92, NARA.

53. James Anderson to GRS, November 11, 1920, BCF for William M. Anderson, RG 92, NARA.

54. Ada Garner to QMC, n.d., BCF for Robert E. Garner, RG 92, NARA.

55. Emily Dixon, note to GRS, May 1919, BCF for William B. Dixon, RG 92, NARA.

56. Naomi Meily to War Department, November 1, 1920, BCF for Guy O. Meily, RG 92, NARA.

57. Anna Fatout, note to GRS, May 8, 1920, BCF for Ansel Fatout, RG 92, NARA.

58. Charles F. Pancoast to Charles C. Pierce, April 18, 1919, BCF for Charles Pancoast, RG 92, NARA.

59. Mary Markle, note to GRS, July 24, 1920, BCF for Oliver Markle, RG 92, NARA.

60. Mary Sanders to P. C. Harris, March 27, 1919, BCF for Eric F. Sanders, RG 92, NARA.

61. Richard Slotkin, *Lost Battalions: The Great War and the Crisis of American Nationality* (New York: Henry Holt, 2005), 47–51.

62. Marvin E. Fletcher, "World War I," in *Encyclopedia of African-American Culture and History*, eds. Jack Salzman, David Lionel Salzman, and Cornel West (New York: Simon, 1996), 2881–3: 2881.

63. The Houston Riot of 1917 stands as a shameful moment in the history of race relations in the U.S. In July 1917, members of the 24th Infantry Regiment—a colored regiment—were sent to Houston, Texas, to secure the construction site of Camp Logan, a National Guard training camp. For weeks, the black troops suffered racist taunts and behavior from local whites. Confronted with statements like "those niggers would look good with coils around their necks" and "in Texas it costs $25 to kill a buzzard and $5 to kill a nigger," black soldiers responded with verbal assaults and threats of their own. Within weeks racial tensions in Houston mounted to combustible levels. On August 23, 1917, word spread that a black soldier had been severely beaten and detained for trying to stop a Houston policeman from abusing a black woman. Seething with anger, one hundred black troops armed themselves and marched into downtown Houston, where they began a two-hour killing spree. By the end of the melee, the troops had killed fifteen whites, wounded twelve others, and suffered four casualties. The military swiftly court-martialed all 156 men who had missed roll call that day. Eventually, 54 troops were found guilty of premeditated murder and mutiny in time of war; thirteen were sentenced to death, while the rest received lifetime sentences of hard labor. Two subsequent courts-martial led to the death sentences of another sixteen men. The executions brought satisfaction to white southerners, who had been stunned by the sight of black soldiers fighting back against segregation and abuse. But for black communities across the nation, the episode stood as a crystallized example of racial injustice in America. See Stephen L. Harris, *Harlem's Hell Fighters: The African American 369th Infantry in World War I* (Washington: Brassey's, 2003), 108; Robert V. Haynes, *A Night of Violence: The Houston Riot of 1917* (Baton Rouge: Louisiana State University Press, 1976); and, Jennifer D. Keene, *World War I* (Westport, CT: Greenwood Press, 2006), 95–7.

64. Philip S. Foner, ed., *The Voice of Black America: Major Speeches by Negroes in the United States, 1797–1971* (New York: Simon and Schuster, 1972), 719–21.

65. Robert B. Edgerton, *Hidden Heroism: Black Soldiers in America's Wars* (Boulder: Westview, 2002), 69–99.

66. Slotkin, *Lost Battalions*, 253–4.

67. "Huns Starve and Ridicule U.S. Captives," *Stars and Stripes*, February 8, 1918. The military's attitude toward African-American soldiers stationed in Europe mirrored bigoted wartime domestic policies targeting black citizens back home. During the war, the Bureau of Investigation, the Justice and Post Office Departments, and military intelligence officers monitored and spied on African Americans in an effort to root out, suppress, and punish pro-German sympathizers and activists bent on leveraging racial change through the nation's war effort. In effect the government terrorized African-American communities throughout the country, yet it produced virtually no evidence of criminal anti-war behavior. See Theodore Kornweibel, Jr., *"Investigate Everything": Federal Efforts to Compel Black Loyalty During World War I* (Bloomington: Indiana University Press, 2002).

68. Keene, *World War I*, 187–90.

69. Thomas D. Snyder, ed., *120 Years of American Education: A Statistical Portrait* (Washington: U.S. Department of Education, 1993), 31.

70. Albert Dubose, telegram to GRS, August 31, 1921, BCF for Will Dubose, RG 92, NARA.

71. Caesar Bradford to GRS, January 4, 1921, BCF for Henry E. Bradford, RG 92, NARA.

72. Stella Mitchell, note to GRS, April 26, 1920, BCF for Leon Gilder, RG 92, NARA.

73. John S. Graves to War Department, August 12, 1919, BCF for Charles A. Bouling, RG 92, NARA.

74. Henry Creed, telegram to GRS, May 17, 1921, BCF for Abraham Creed, RG 92, NARA.

75. Mattie Lou Fuston, telegram to GRS, December 24, 1921, BCF for Elmer Fuston, RG 92, NARA.

76. Willie Mae Bedford to J. F. Butler, March 15, 1921, BCF for Oscar Bedford, RG 92, NARA.

77. Elizabeth Somerville to GRS, n.d., BCF for James Jackson, RG 92, NARA.

78. John Lingle to War Department, October 21, 1919, BCF for John A. Lingle Jr., RG 92 NARA.

79. William Roth to Senator Nicholas J. Wadsworth, April 28, 1921, BCF for Benjamin W. Roth, RG 92, NARA.

80. Mollie Roycroft to GRS, January 21, 1919, BCF for William T. Roycroft, RG 92, NARA.

81. Besides the fact that military personnel tend to communicate in a stoic, rather than emotional or sentimental, fashion, another cultural phenomenon may have contributed to the War Department and government's tone-deafness. As communication scholar Brenton Malin reveals, throughout the early decades of the twentieth century, American speech teachers championed a style of persuasion that privileged force and clarity over emotion. "Good vocal performance," Malin writes, "was to be controlled, controlling, and efficient." Brenton Malin, "Electrifying Speeches: Emotional Control and the Technological Aesthetic of the Voice in the Early 20th Century," *U.S. Journal of Social History* 45.1 (2011): 1–19.

82. In 1917, Mattie Hicks of Caryville, Florida, inquired about the return of her son's corpse: "Just rec'd a letter from the Adjutant Gen'l telling me the Sad news of my Sons death Clifton R. Hicks Company I, 28 Infantry at St. Nazaire France July 9. And I want the body Sent back home to me as he was only a boy not yet 17 years of age [...] Let me know at once." Hicks received a letter from the QMC that coldly stated: "In reply you are informed that it will not be practicable at this time to transport the remains of your son to the United States but as soon as it can be done it is the intention of the Department to have the remains disinterred and shipped to your address at the expense of the Government." See Mattie Hicks, correspondence with QMC, July 21–24, 1917, BCF for Clifton R. Hicks, RG 92, NARA.

83. P. C. Harris to Anastaceo Rodriguez, May 1919, BCF for Juan M. Rodriguez, RG 92, NARA.

84. During the postwar years, Lt. Col. Charles C. Pierce, Chief of the GRS, stood out for his efforts to comfort next of kin. A strong advocate for the rights of citizens to claim their beloved's remains, Pierce wrote many letters to families in an attempt to put a human face on the military. In a letter to Robert E. Buglune of Hubberston, Massachusetts, Pierce wrote of the Graves Registration Service's efforts to care for the temporary graves of soldiers in Europe: "It is a matter of grief to me that word must go from my office that is sure to cause sorrow to people at home, whose brave men have made war's supreme sacrifice for the sake of civilization. You have probably already received some notice of the regrettable casualty that causes me to write you; and if so, it may be that you will derive some measure of comfort and satisfaction from the fact that the body you cherish has been buried as noted above. ... May I count myself as your friend and be permitted to hope that you may have Divine comfort in your grief!" Although his letters made no guarantee of the return of the dead, they surely brought consolation to countless families. See House Committee, *Hearings*, 45; and, Charles C. Pierce to Robert Buglune, February 1919, BCF for Arthur R. Sargent, RG 92, NARA.

85. House Committee, *Hearings*, 9.

86. Ibid, 17–18.

87. As early as 1919, Pershing candidly lifted arguments from the letters of next of kin in his efforts to secure the establishment of overseas American cemeteries. For instance, Pershing claimed that by leaving bodies in Europe, the War Department was fulfilling the wishes of the dead: "Believe that could these soldiers speak for themselves they would wish to be left undisturbed in the place where, with their comrades, they fought the last fight." Borrowing from the sentimental vernacular of family letters, Representative George Huddleston of Alabama argued that repatriation would lead to "the reopening of heartbreaks, a reopening of grief and sorrow in every community when one of these bodies is carried back." Many next of kin were deeply offended by such statements. As one father said: "Shall anybody criticize me if I care to have my feelings stirred by the bringing back of my boy's body?" See "Pershing Against Removal of Dead," *Washington Post*, August 24, 1919; and, House Committee, *Hearings*, 18–21.

88. "Pershing Criticises Army Literary Style; Urges Clarity and the Personal Touch," *New York Times*, April 13, 1923.

89. Representative Oscar E. Bland of Indiana opined that "France is and has been throughout all the centuries the great battle ground of the world, and we do not know but what the cannon of future inventors may dig up those very graves in years to come." See House Committee, *Hearings*, 6. Some opponents claimed that if "American dead are left in France, the necessity for preserving the inviolability of our burial places will be more likely to involve the United States in future European wars"; quoted on page 56 of Ron Robin, "'A Foothold in Europe': The Aesthetics and Politics of American War Cemeteries in Western Europe," *Journal of American Studies* 29.1 (1995): 55–72. The plan faced intense opposition from the U.S. funeral industry as well, which stood to gain much from the return of war dead. See Graham, *The Gold Star Pilgrimages*, 40–41; Piehler, *Remembering War,* 96–97.

90. War Department to Argyle Pitman, November 21, 1919, BCF for Henry S. Pitman, RG 92, NARA.

91. QMC to J. E. Lowery, May 17, 1924, BCF for Robert W. Lowery, RG 92, NARA.

92. "To Accompany War Dead," *New York Times*, June 9, 1920.

93. "Harding, in Memorial Day Proclamation, Asks General Homage to War Dead on May 30," *New York Times*, May 4, 1921.

94. "Wilson Overcome Greeting Pilgrims; Predicts Triumph," *New York Times*, November 12, 1923.

95. Founded in 1918, the Gold Star Mothers was a grassroots organization of mothers and widows of U.S. soldiers killed in the Great War. Dedicated to honoring the sacrifice of American soldiers, the group was a powerful advocate for the rights of veterans and their families. See Graham, *The Gold Star Pilgrimages*, 12–17; Lotte Larsen Meyer, "Mourning in a Distant Land: Gold Star Pilgrimages to American Military Cemeteries in Europe, 1930–33," *Markers: Annual Journal of the Association for Gravestone Studies* 20 (2003): 31–75. We will return to the subject of these pilgrimages in the final chapter.

96. F. H. Pope to John MacIntyre, May 16, 1926, BCF for Harold V. MacIntyre, RG 92, NARA.

97. The following comments about the ABMC's intentions and the final visual presentation of America's overseas World War I cemeteries are introductory. We will examine these issues much more closely in the final chapter.

98. Elizabeth Nishiura, ed., *American Battle Monuments: A Guide to Military Cemeteries and Monuments Maintained by the American Battle Monuments Commission* (Detroit: Omnigraphics, 1989), 3.

99. Robin, "A Foothold in Europe," 58; "Pershing Arranges for War Memorials," *New York Times*, June 26, 1927; X. H. Price to John J. Pershing, February 12, 1925, in "Correspondence of the ABMC Chairman, Gen. John J. Pershing, 1923–45," Records of the American Battle Monuments Commission, Record Group 117, NARA.

100. Robin, "A Foothold in Europe," 60.

101. A small percentage of the headstones are in the shape of the Star of David to mark the graves of Jewish soldiers, as will be discussed in the following chapter.

102. Nadia Ezz-Eddine, "Re: St. Mihiel Cemetery statue," email to the author, December 11, 2008.

103. "Pershing Seeks a Plan to Preserve Memorials," *New York Times*, September 6, 1931.

104. Meyer, "Mourning," 48.

105. Graham, *The Gold Star Pilgrimages*, 142.

106. Sam Edwards, *Allies in Memory: World War II and the Politics of Transatlantic Commemoration, c. 1941–2001* (Cambridge: Cambridge University Press, 2015).

107. BCF for Thomas F. Enright, RG 92, NARA.

108. In the weeks following the death of her son James Bethel Gresham, Alice Dodd became something of a model for appropriate—that is, patriotic and stoic—wartime mourning practices. At a hastily arranged but much publicized memorial service in Evansville, Indiana, she declared: "Surely it is not for us to mourn! [...] My boy didn't like for me to wear somber clothing [...] He didn't like for me to look sad. And every mother's soldier feels the same. Women whose hearts are aching, cling to mourning. But in this case it isn't fitting. We must be no less brave than our sons, or brothers or husbands. Our chins must be as firm as theirs. For the sake of the boys who fall in France and the women left behind in America, I am taking off the crepe!" But by May of 1919, Dodd actively presented herself to the public as a mother distraught and overcome with loss. During an interview with journalist E. C. Rodgers, in which she appealed for the return of her son's bodily remains, Dodd stated: "Yes, I would like to have them bring back my boy. I cannot go over to where they have lain him. And even if I could, just coming once to his grave and then going away forever, would break my heart. I want to go near his final resting place often, every few days during the few years I have to live. It has been hard for me to see the boys come marching home so happy and smiling to their mothers' arms, and think that I cannot even go to my boy's grave! Only a mother knows how hard it is not to be able to see the spot where a son is sleeping the last long sleep; never to be able to kneel in prayer at his grave; never to be able to lay one flower with one's own hand upon the earth which covers him." The difference in tone between Dodd's wartime and postwar public appeals perfectly reflects the emotional fallout with which the U.S. government had to contend after World War I. See Marie Barnett, "'Women of America, Let Us Wear No Mourning!' Cries Mother of First Sammy Slain in Action in France," *Miami District Daily News*, November 25, 1917, 2; E. C. Rodgers, "First Gold Star War Mother Hopes and Prays for Return of Body of Her Son," *Salt Lake Telegram*, May 30, 1919, 13.

109. "The World Loses a Shrine of Freedom," *Davenport Democrat and Leader*, July 6, 1921, 6.

110. "10,000 Honor War Victim," *Oregonian*, July 25, 1921, 5.

Chapter 4

Why They Died

Public Memory and the Birth of the Modern U.S. Soldier, 1922–1933

The immediate postwar years can be understood as a *kairotic* moment[1]—a period of contestation and contingency in which prevailing meanings, understandings, and memories of the United States' participation in the Great War had not yet been settled, but were highly desired. It was an opportune moment for individuals and collectives—official, vernacular, or otherwise—to express publicly competing (and often directly opposing) moral statements about the perceived and real human, material, and ideological costs and benefits of the national war effort. The signing of the Armistice on November 11, 1918, essentially ushered in the last few (if extended) moments of the final act, so to speak, of the war's saga—the moments in which the meaning of the war seemingly would be determined. Discussing the rhetorical power of endings, rhetorician Kenneth Burke reminds us: "a history's *end* is a formal way of proclaiming its *essence* or *nature*, as with those who distinguish between a tragedy and a comedy by the outcome alone and who would transform 'tragedy' into 'comedy' merely by changing the last few moments of the last act."[2] Despite the armistice (a word that, it should be noted, means "an agreement made by opposing sides in a war to stop fighting for a certain time" or "a truce," rather than something more conclusive), the end of the history of America's participation in the war had yet to be written. The torrent of letters sent from grieving American families to the War Department regarding the final disposition of dead soldiers had revealed a postwar crisis of official language, an exhaustion of state-sanctioned vocabularies that could no longer (if they had ever been able to) account adequately for the feelings and suffering of private citizens (and non-citizens) whose loved ones had been sent to fight and die in Europe. In essence, Americans were experiencing and grappling with rhetorical and ideological "shell shock." Although the government had learned to appropriate the sentimental vernacular of grieving families into its own public rhetoric and had successfully secured its plan to bury dead Americans in permanent overseas military cemeteries, the symbolic action of ordinary mothers, fathers, wives, sisters, and brothers (who were no longer bound by draconian wartime laws to remain silent) revealed just how difficult it might be for the government to shape, determine, and control public memory of the Great War—a conflict of unprecedented scope and devastation that marked a new, frightening, and seemingly irrevocable turn in human warfare.

While it was clear that the nature and results of the World War I had shattered previous common-held notions of state-sponsored warfare and appropriate (or effective) war rhetoric, the universal and time immemorial human impulse to commemorate and revere the dead steadfastly remained, as countless unofficial commemoration projects were instigated just as soon as the war ended. For instance, when the guns stopped firing, American soldiers still stationed in Europe immediately began erecting unsanctioned, haphazard battlefield monuments in memory of their fallen comrades and the wartime accomplishments of their divisions and companies.[3] Across the United States, communities commissioned and erected public memorials—usually a generic bronze statue of a "Doughboy" or a tablet listing specific soldiers' names—in honor of local men who had fought and died overseas. Such memorials were, by any measure, meant to honor the wartime sacrifice, courage, and deeds of average U.S. soldiers and citizens. Often placed next to the booty of war (German artillery pieces that were distributed by the federal government across the nation) and alongside older Civil War monuments, these publicly visible memorials helped connect local communities to the events that had taken place in Europe and, as historian G. Kurt Piehler puts it, remind citizens how the national war effort between 1917 and 1918 "had continued the long process of reconciliation between North and South."[4] In Evansville, Indiana, the American Legion (a patriotic veterans organization established in 1919) began work on a memorial to local hero James Bethel Gresham (one of the first three U.S. casualties of the war) with the hope that it might become "an international shrine" to Americans who died in the war.[5] In South Carolina, Governor Robert A. Cooper appointed a commission to erect a memorial chapel in honor of local "white soldiers, sailors, marines and others who served in the world war" on the grounds of the University of South Carolina, and a separate commission to establish a "negro memorial" on the campus of the State Agricultural and Mechanical College ("a negro school").[6]

Perhaps due to both the disorienting nature of the Great War and nineteenth-century Romantic sensibilities still lingering within American popular imagination, other postwar commemoration projects entailed less militaristic, more humanistic, forms of memorialization. For instance, the New York Athletic Club in Manhattan unveiled a "memorial window commemorative of the twenty members of the [club] who lost their lives in the world war"; today the window still appears as it did years ago above the main entrance between the first and second floors of the club.[7] In Washington, D.C., Georgetown University planted 54 trees in memory of its 54 students who perished in Europe (a shockingly high casualty statistic) with the hope of representing the "intimate connection" between the school and the national war effort.[8] And politically progressive groups across the nation publicly campaigned for the establishment of alternative "living memorials"—public auditoriums, pools,

Figure 4.1   A typical "Doughboy" statue, Bolton Landing, NY. Courtesy of Susan Seitz.

gymnasiums, classrooms for adult education, office spaces for community organizations, bridges, and buildings erected in honor of the war dead— which would reflect the egalitarian and democratic spirit of the American war effort.[9] A supporter of the new "living memorial" movement wrote the *New York Times*:

> Have we no better way to keep alive the memory of the gallant men who died in the World War than by erecting memorials in cold, dead stone, such as arches, shafts or buildings for religious or communal use?
>
> If they could speak, which would they choose, these formal and lifeless memorials, or would they long to live in the memory of coming generations through new opportunities given to the growing soul of man, new and ever new life?
>
> Why not use the money planned for these votive offerings to endow scholarships in our public high schools, freely to be contended for by boys and girls who are eager for new opportunities of deepening life? Scholarship for college or university, scholarships for the arts, for research, for travel, all these possibilities firing the young soul with new endeavor, enriching each generation.[10]

These words reflected *both* a common belief that traditional memorials made of stone or metal alloy were somewhat gloomy, depressing, and archaic *and* a liberal assumption that every American memorial to the Great War held the possibility of being a vehicle for political action, social change, and a return to advancing civilization. Struggling to comprehend and adapt to 'the new way of the world' (i.e., twentieth-century global warfare), individuals and civic groups began to develop and embrace novel commemorative practices in the immediate postwar years.

Some of these memory projects eschewed nationalistic and life affirming sentiments in order to express (whether implicitly or explicitly) critical or disenchanted evaluations of the American war experience, in particular, or modern state-sponsored warfare, in general. Take, for example, the *History of the 110th Infantry of the 28th Division, U.S.A., 1917–1919*, one of the many "official" eyewitness accounts published by veterans groups during the 1920s. While chockfull of lofty and dramatic tales of individual and collective battlefield bravery, the book also provided extensive uncensored details regarding the final moments and resting places of regiment members who had been killed, "not for the purpose of glorifying those who [had died]," but rather "as a convenience for those seeking information," especially "relatives or friends" of the fallen.[11] A subtle, yet subversive, dig at the military and the federal government's joint inability to provide *all* grieving American families with sufficient information concerning their loved ones' demise, these unflinchingly graphic death reports revealed the disturbing fact that many

Doughboys had suffered nothing close to the "good death" which had been so important to American next of kin during the Civil War. As Drew Gilpin Faust demonstrates throughout her monumental book, *This Republic of Suffering: Death and the American Civil War*, families of Union and Confederate soldiers killed in the Civil War were fundamentally concerned about the question of whether their loved ones had died "the Good Death"—that dying men had been conscious in the final moments of life and had properly declared their devotion to Christianity. During the Civil War, soldiers of the North and South were expected to send letters to the families of their fallen comrades conveying detailed accounts of the dead soldiers' last words, or "dying declarations," as proof of "the Good Death" (whether the respective soldier had in fact died *appropriately* or not).[12] By contrast, the 110th Infantry's self-funded publication revealed in sober, matter-of-fact terms just how "bad" comrades' deaths had been "over there." Consider this entry for Samuel Crouse of Somerset, Pennsylvania, whose bodily remains were still missing in France:

Statement given by Pvt. Raymond I. Davis, Co. C, 110th Inf. "Lt. Crouse was killed on the morning of July 15, 1918, in the woods north of St. Agnan. I saw Lt. Crouse and W. Zimmerman run up a road and heard a volley of shots fired a few minutes later. Some time later, I saw him lying dead on the road. He had been hit in the forehead and died instantly."

Statement given by Pvt. Daniel McGuire, Co. C, 110th Inf. "Lt. Crouse and Pvt. Zimmerman were in a small trench together, when word was received that the Germans were behind them. Lt. Crouse jumped up and with Zimmerman came along the bushes about ten yards to the road along the hill. He then turned and ran up the road with the rifle. I was a prisoner and standing with six or eight Germans to the left of the road on a bank in the brush. Neither Lt. Crouse or Zimmerman saw us standing there. I called to them but they did not hear. Had the Germans not fired when they did, Lt. Crouse and Zimmerman would have continued on past us.

The Germans fired when they were within fifteen feet and hit Lt. Crouse in the head, tearing off one side of the skull."[13]

Taking matters into their own hands, veterans of the 110th Infantry gathered and published *all* and *any* available information regarding missing and killed comrades, however disturbing or traumatizing the news might be for next of kin and others. Antithetical to the wartime propaganda of the Committee on Public Information and the sparse death notification telegrams that the War Department had initially sent families of the fallen, these published death reports exposed the terrible things that had actually occurred in Europe and, in pragmatic terms, provided citizens valuable details that the government and military seemed unable or reluctant to give during and after the war.

Other memory projects were simply melancholic, and sought to attend to the profound and intimate suffering of grieving American women. For instance, Annie Kilburn Kilmer, mother of famed poet-soldier Joyce Kilmer, dedicated her 1920 book, *Memories of My Son Sergeant Joyce Kilmer*, to "the mothers who mourn with a proud heart for their sons who gave their lives for honour's sake." (Tellingly, Annie Kilmer uses the phrase "for honour's sake" rather than "the nation" or "the world.") The book's first page displayed a touching photograph of Annie sitting next to her apple-cheeked son, captioned: "Joyce Kilmer (Columbia, 1908), in graduation gown, with his mother."[14] Amid this swirling sea of commemoration movements and practices, the bodily remains of roughly 80,000 soldiers were shipped back to the United States (by families' requests) during the early 1920s.[15] Metaphorically speaking, a web of death was placed upon the nation's map. Delivered to next of kin in every state, to rural hamlets and giant urban centers alike, to every corner of the country, these repatriated bodily remains presented 80,000 opportunities for individuals and communities to remember the dead—and perhaps more important, America's participation in World War I—as *they* best saw fit.

Whatever political affiliations or feelings about the national war effort next of kin might have held, each dead soldier—lying silently and concealed in his coffin—represented a tangible and powerful reminder of the tragic (if apparently noble) human costs and sacrifices of America's participation in World War I. Each dead citizen-soldier, his life taken prematurely overseas, essentially 'bore witness' to the vast destruction of the distant war and, implicitly, the profound heartbreak of those left behind back home. In his insightful analysis of "witnessing," rhetorical scholar John Durham Peters tells us: "Aristotle noted that witnesses in a court of law testify at risk of punishment if they do not tell the truth; he considers dead witnesses more trustworthy than living ones—since they cannot be bribed." In other words, the undeniable absence of the dead 'speaks volumes'—their absence is the surest truth.[16] Still, in practical terms, it is (as always) the obligation (and sometimes burden) of the living to speak for, defend, honor, and/or seek justice for the departed. After the Great War, each dead U.S. soldier—each absent "witness"—required a proper burial ceremony of some kind. In turn, each burial ceremony afforded grieving next of kin and communities the chance to deliver eulogies and conduct rituals that might cast the alleged local, national, and international benefits of such profound, domestic, *personal* loss in doubt. And, to be sure, local newspapers were not shy to report the *melancholy* details of funeral services held for fallen soldiers during the postwar years. For example, in 1921, the *Philadelphia Inquirer* reported on a "solemn" burial ceremony that had been held for several men whose families lived in the same Philadelphia neighborhood: "Yesterday's solemn ceremonies closed the public mourning for our heroes who fell in France during the late combat [...] There was no pride, pomp and circumstance of glorious war evident; there was no intention of magnifying military operations. The silence for a few seconds when the city's pulse seemed to stop while prayers ascended to make war impossible was a finer tribute than all the fanfares which might have been made."[17] In sum, as the 116,516 Americans lost to World War I—the dead—could not speak for nor memorialize themselves in the postwar years, the living took up the mantle in multitudinous, conflicting, and sometimes purposefully raw, gloomy, and transgressive ways.[18]

While the U.S. government/military could not possibly have expected to contain, dictate, or suppress this explosion of diverse postwar commemoration projects, it *had* successfully retained legal control over the bodily remains of 35,000 dead American soldiers—the decaying remnants of men's bones, tissue, and organs—that would, in short order, become the focus and symbolic capital of an unprecedented network of monumental U.S. cemeteries in Western Europe. Political and military officials hoped that the graves and tombstones of these 35,000 soldiers, displayed to international audiences in aesthetically pleasing, emotionally moving, and most vitally, *American* cemeteries, would constitute permanent visual and material arguments for the United States' righteous role in the Great War, and buttress the emerging and useful (if somewhat antagonistic) claim that the young nation had "rescued" Europe from itself. In essence, the nascent overseas cemeteries constituted an opportunity for U.S. officials to claim and secure enduring moral high ground before the world's eyes by 'speaking for the dead.' As G. Kurt Piehler indicates, those in charge of planning and creating these burial grounds originally approached the project with an overarching belief that each "individual soldier's grave would serve as an enduring monument to the cause of freedom for which they bled and died."[19] In communicating such sustained and loaded messages to the peoples of Europe (and elsewhere), and by emphasizing the burgeoning image of the modern U.S. soldier as 'a global force for good' in particular, these overseas cemeteries—if constructed properly—might also impact or perhaps even trump—the meanings and rhetorical work of the countless, heterogeneous domestic commemoration practices simultaneously taking place throughout America. In other words, the unprecedented network of U.S. World War I cemeteries throughout Europe offered the nation's leaders and elites a grand opportunity to articulate the meaning of twentieth-century U.S. state-sponsored war (and its product: mass death) to Americans and the world at large. And much like the U.S. flag that Neil Armstrong and Buzz Aldrin planted on the moon fifty years later, the overseas cemeteries would serve as permanent extraterritorial (if not in this case extraterrestrial) signifiers of American might, triumph, and ascendancy.

The remainder of this chapter offers a rhetorical history of the establishment of America's World War I cemeteries and a visual rhetorical analysis of the sites' final physical presentation. Since I have already discussed the field of rhetorical history (in the introduction), here I will offer a brief description of visual rhetoric so as to orient the reader properly. Although visual rhetoric has become a popular subfield of communication and rhetoric studies—and despite the fact that countless rhetoric scholars have used the term "visual rhetoric" in their scholarship—visual rhetoric remains a rather ambiguous, broadly defined concept that is casually invoked in discussions of anything having to do with both the visual and the rhetorical. Rhetoric scholars Olson, Finnegan, and Hope have offered what stands as the most authoritative definition of visual rhetoric: "[V]isual rhetoric name[s] those symbolic actions enacted primarily through visual means, made meaningful through culturally derived ways of looking and seeing and endeavoring to influence diverse publics."[20] Building on this definition, we might think of visual rhetoric as the art, practice, and study of persuasive communication through visual (whether material or ephemeral, i.e., a roadside billboard versus a television advertisement) means. Any given visual object—including a cemetery, say—is something more than a manifestation or expression of a particular culture or historical moment. Rather, the visual rhetorical perspective encourages us to examine the motives, decisions, and constraints that led to a given object's final visual presentation; the original or intended audiences that the object's maker had in mind; the ways in which audiences have, in practice, interacted with and made meaning of the object; and, the ways that the object's meanings have lasted or changed over time.

In order to understand the significance, ideology, effects, and legacy of America's World War I cemeteries in Europe, it is crucial to trace the rich yet complicated series of events that ultimately led to the burial grounds' final presentation. Thus, the first half of this chapter uncovers the fundamental (yet, to date, *unappreciated*) role that the Commission of Fine Arts (CFA) played in the initial planning and designing of the sites. The nation's preeminent voice on cultural and artistic matters—comprised of leading artists, architects, civic planners, including individuals who had been responsible for the design of the Lincoln Memorial on the National Mall and other noteworthy modern projects—the CFA was authorized to develop the national burial grounds during the immediate postwar years. As we will see, this elite group of civic reformers enjoyed and exercised sweeping authority over the nation's overseas cemeteries. Yet, while the CFA set upon its mission from a highly enabled position, its efforts and plans were quite hampered and shaped by significant political forces, public expectations, and material realities (i.e., *constraints*) beyond their control. Hoping to extend its sensibilities to the visual presentation of the European sites while negotiating outside constraints, the CFA eventually set out to create cemeteries that would simultaneously: (1) reflect the order, regularity, and symmetry of the National Mall, rather than the meandering, sylvan, and somewhat disordered nature of nineteenth-century civic spaces like Arlington National Cemetery in Virginia; (2) meet the expectations of military leaders, who would want the cemeteries to serve as decidedly pro-war celebrations of American military prowess, and government officials, who would want the burial grounds to suture critical social divides and display the fallen, sacrificial U.S. soldier as an ideal model of the American citizen; and, (3) match the monumentality of other nation's World War cemeteries while conveying unique, discernible, and effective messages to heterogeneous international audiences—no small order. Though the CFA was highly constrained and, in time, would officially cede control over the establishment of the sites to the newly formed American Battle Monuments Commission (headed by none other than General John J. Pershing himself), ultimately its work on the project largely determined the final design, layout, and rhetorical effects of each permanent burial ground (a point that the limited scholarship on American World War I cemeteries has erroneously neglected).[21]

The second half of the chapter describes, analyzes, and interprets the physical presentation and rhetorical effects of the eight permanent overseas U.S. military cemeteries that were constructed in England, France, and Belgium during the 1920s. Here, I engage the work of cultural historian Ron Robin, who criticizes these burial grounds for their display of "a confusing mixture of various cultural trends" that neither addressed the contemporary suffering of next of kin nor effectively commemorated those who were buried. While perhaps Robin's negative assessment seems somewhat reasonable from a modern day visitor's point of view, I contend that it fails to contextualize the cemeteries within the turbulent period of their making, mistakes the sites' complex nature (and novel manipulation of the human senses) for architectural/artistic incompetency, and does not recognize the burial grounds' complex contemporary rhetorical effects and long-lasting cultural impact. In rebuttal, I endeavor to show that with the proper understanding of certain rhetorical constraints placed on the original planners, we can appreciate the cemeteries' ability to attend to the sorrow of grieving next of kin, satisfy the American public's desires for proper treatment of the nation's war dead, display to international audiences sustained visual and material arguments for the country's purported virtuous role in the war, and develop and advance the long-lasting and now common ideograph of the U.S. soldier as a sacrificial, universal, 'global force for good.'

Toward the end of the chapter, I argue that the unappreciated brilliance and potent symbolic action of these cemeteries can be found in their use of (what I term) "the third element"—the unspoken, often invisible, but always implied relationship between any two (or more) readily perceived elements (e.g., an American flag, medieval and religious iconography, the scent of a rosebush, the sound of tree branches gently swaying in the wind, the word "sacrifice") that exist (or appear, or are sensible, or are communicated) within close proximity of each other. By composing physical and visual ensembles out of an expansive set of *both* preexisting iconologies *and* emergent twentieth-century rhetorics, the cemetery planners created an infinite number of "third elements" that could at once help assuage the suffering of American citizens, reflect the alleged virtues of the nation, and establish the enduring mythology of the modern U.S. soldier. Rather than heavy-handedly dictating the meaning of the cemeteries and the deaths of the interred (as CPI posters might have done during the war), the planners seemingly left it up to visitors and mediated audiences (national and international) to decide which combinations of "third elements" would heal their spiritual wounds, speak most effectively to their own needs, and inspire. Breathing life into carefully arranged inanimate objects (including the mortal remains of fallen U.S. soldiers) for the sake of politics, memory, ideology, and rhetoric, the American overseas cemeteries—much like the nascent ideograph of the modern U.S. soldier itself—became vessels into which any individual or group's unique, idiosyncratic thoughts and feelings concerning the meaning of twentieth-century American soldierly death could be satisfactorily poured. The remaining pages of this chapter unpack and explain all of the ideas and claims above in careful detail.

THE CFA AND ITS CONSTRAINED
RHETORICAL POSITION

The task of designing America's overseas military cemeteries was initially assigned to the purview of the CFA, though not without some controversy. On June 2, 1919, U.S. Representative Simeon D. Hess of Ohio introduced a bill to Congress that called for the incorporation of the American Field of Honor Association, a citizens' group that would work closely with the National Commission of Fine Arts to design the nascent overseas burial grounds. Containing one of the first postwar articulations and rhetorical deployments of the ideograph of the 'modern, universal, sacrificial U.S. soldier,' Hess's bill declared that regular American citizens had earned (by virtue of their wartime efforts and sacrifices) the right to play a major role in the establishment of the cemeteries—permanent burial grounds that would honor "those who have made the supreme sacrifice in the cause of freedom and humanity" and the "perpetual bond of union between America and the nations with whom we have been associated in the World's War." Fess's populist bill, however, did not pass. In all likelihood, it was defeated behind closed doors by the War Department, which surely would not have wanted to relinquish control over the symbolic sites (nor the soldierly remains it had worked so hard to obtain). Sidestepping Congress and the American people, the Quartermaster General of the Army approached the CFA directly in 1919, and brought the commission into the military's fold. Ultimately, by early 1921, the power of determining the visual presentation of America's overseas cemeteries was securely in the hands of the CFA and Secretary of War John Weeks.[22]

Established by Congress in 1910, the CFA was the nation's preeminent voice on cultural and artistic matters during the early twentieth century:

Be it enacted by the Senate and House of Representatives of the United States of America in Congress assembled, That a permanent CFA is hereby created to be composed of seven well-qualified judges of the fine arts, who shall be appointed by the President [...] The President shall have authority to fill all vacancies. It shall be the duty of such commission to advise upon the location of statues, fountains, and monuments in the public squares, streets, and parks in the District of Columbia, and upon the selection of models for statues, fountains, and monuments erected under the authority of the United States and upon the selection of artists for the execution of the same [...] The commission shall also advise generally upon questions of art when required to do so by the President, or by any committee of either House of Congress.[23]

The CFA of the 1910s and early 1920s was comprised of titans of American art, architecture, and civic planning. Its first Chairman was Daniel Burnham, who famously designed the Flatiron Building in Manhattan, Union Station in Washington, D.C., and the fairgrounds of the 1893 World's Columbian Exposition in Chicago. Its original members included sculptor Daniel Chester French (who in 1920 would design the marble statue of a seated Abraham Lincoln in the Lincoln Memorial), landscape architect Frederick Law Olmsted, Jr. (whose father had planned New York City's Central Park), architect Thomas Hastings (designer of the landmark New York Public Library in Manhattan), and architect Cass Gilbert (former president of the American Institute Architects).[24] Committed to the ideologies of the "City Beautiful" movement[25] and the McMillan Plan,[26] and given a direct line to the power that coursed through the White House and Capitol Hill, this elite group of civic reformers enjoyed and exercised sweeping authority to shape early twentieth-century American public culture. When it assumed total creative control over America's permanent, overseas military cemeteries in 1921, the CFA was already managing the redesign of Washington, D.C.—a grand plan "to make the city of Washington conspicuous among national capitals in respect of dignity, orderliness, convenience, and beauty"[27]–and virtually rewriting the nation's patriotic visual lexicon.[28] The postwar plan for a network of monumental military cemeteries in Europe became a unique opportunity for the CFA to extend its symbolic action beyond national borders. In effect, the CFA wanted each cemetery to be a conceptual extension of the National Mall—a composed, extraterritorial (yet decidedly *American*) civic religious site where the interrelationship between ideology, physical space, human behavior, and the landscape of America's public imagination would manifest once more.

However, while the CFA was the authoritative (and often determining) voice on matters related to public art, architecture, and culture in the United States, the commission had to approach its plans for the visual presentation of the overseas military cemeteries with great care and tact. Although the CFA certainly desired to extend its preferred aesthetic style (a neoclassical, Beaux-Arts style that mimicked and venerated Greco-Roman traditions) and its ideologies regarding public space to the European sites without interference from outside parties, the network of cemeteries was a beast altogether different from the landscape of Washington, D.C., government coins, or the American flag (see footnote 28). To begin, the nascent sites were *cemeteries*—inherently sacred and emotionally charged spaces of profound social significance that would have to incorporate and display the remains of dead human beings appropriately.[29] Thus, the CFA would have to take contemporary sensibilities regarding the function and appearance of the American gravescape into account. The sites would not just be cemeteries, however—they would be *military cemeteries*. Therefore, the CFA would have to meet the expectations of leaders in the armed forces who would want the cemeteries to serve as decidedly pro-war celebrations of American military prowess and soldierly sacrifice, and governmental officials who would want the burial grounds to do the same rhetorical work that federally controlled Civil War cemeteries (like Gettysburg National Cemetery and Arlington National Cemetery) had attempted to do over the preceding decades (namely, suture critical social divides and display the dead soldier as an ideal model of the American citizen). Of course, the planned sites were not only military cemeteries—they were *overseas military cemeteries*. The CFA was compelled, therefore, to design sites that would simultaneously match the monumentality of other nations' WWI cemeteries, convey discernible and effective messages to heterogeneous international audiences, and symbolically re-link the interred soldiers to their homeland thousands of miles away—again, no small task.[30] On top of this, the CFA would have to weigh every aesthetic decision against economic considerations (the cost of obtaining suitable construction workers and masons in Europe, for example) and material realities (such as the relatively small number of dead bodies that had been left overseas). Finally, and most important, the CFA—an organization that held the emotional sensibilities of nineteenth-century Victorian culture in contempt[31]—would have to account for *both* the sentimental vernacular that the government had appropriated into its own postwar public rhetoric *and* the feelings of grieving (and often dejected or disenchanted) Americans whose sons, brothers, and fathers—destroyed in the prime of their lives supposedly for the good of the nation—required a proper and meaningful burial. In short, the CFA found itself in a highly constrained rhetorical position.

The CFA's aesthetic sensibilities and ideologies regarding public space were exhibited in its dramatic renovation of the National Mall in Washington, D.C. Pursuing and expanding upon the ideals of the McMillan Plan, the CFA spent the first half of the twentieth century attempting to transform the Mall into, as art historian Kirk Savage puts it, "a monumental center that was both concentrated and coherent, a well-regulated ensemble of memorials, museums, and other public buildings."[32] From its inception in 1910, the CFA set out to convert the Mall into a "flow of space"—a systematized, ordered, and "clean" expanse where carefully designed, harmonious, and awe-inspiring monuments displayed abstract, yet powerful, national ideals to visitors walking or driving on a predetermined grid of pathways and avenues.[33] As Savage explains, the project represented (and helped usher in) a radical "shift from the nineteenth-century concept of *public grounds* to the twentieth-century concept of *public space*."[34] No longer would pedestrians meander along winding paths and linger in the shade of beautiful (but, in the eyes of the CFA, *haphazardly situated*) tree gardens; no longer would visitors direct their attention to small monuments of various and incongruent meanings and distracting flower beds on the *ground*; no longer would tourists cut across grassy lawns, choosing to stop and go when and where they pleased, experiencing the natural beauty and exploring the eclectic diversions of the Mall as they best saw fit. Instead, pedestrians would be guided along newly constructed paths and roads (lined with freshly planted, uniformly spaced, gigantic elm trees[35]) that met at right angles, their eyes transfixed on the Washington Monument (that abstract, phallic white obelisk that obliterated human scale, dominated the Mall's vista, and served as a point of physical orientation), the dome of the Capitol, or the Lincoln Memorial.[36] The transfiguration of the Mall from *public grounds* into *public space* completely altered the visitor's agency and role. No longer the addresser—the person who stopped to consider natural or man-made objects tucked away into the Earth's surface, the agent whose attention breathed life into otherwise ignored and ignorable objects—the visitor became little more than the addressee, the receiver of the unavoidable, abstract messages of this ordered, dominating, regulating, and symbolic *space*. In essence, the visitor of the National Mall became little more than a prop in a grand panorama (a phenomenon the CFA intended to reproduce in the overseas military cemeteries).

Backed by the force of federal law, the CFA pursued its vision by evacuating alley dwellings (a "'cancer' in the life of Washington"[37]) and "cleaning up Pennsylvania Avenue"—tearing down "rooming houses, laundries, the cheapest class of hotels, and junk shops [that lined] the chief thoroughfare"[38] (in other words, forcibly displacing large portions the city's ethnic, minority, and underprivileged communities)—and erecting beautiful museums and federal agency buildings made of finest stone along the Mall's borders (the museums and buildings we see today). The CFA cut down ancient trees, uprooted gardens, and removed old memorials that violated the uniformity and symmetry of the envisioned space.[39] As Kirk Savage reveals, many D.C. residents viewed the CFA's aggressive attack on the established topography—and most important, the razing of the Mall's natural beauty—as something akin to a masculine "rape of the Mall." Savage writes: "[For them,] trees represented shade, comfort, companionship—all elements of the therapeutic sympathy"—a decidedly feminine set of concerns.[40] Advocates of the CFA's plan, however, dismissed these charges and publicly branded the CFA's critics as "ground-huggers."[41] The CFA was so committed to applying its aesthetic system to the National Mall and diminishing the previously multivocal nature of the space that, following World War I, it denied many veterans groups and divisions from erecting their own permanent memorials on the Mall.[42] In a similar vein, the commission adamantly opposed a 1920 Congressional plan to establish on the Mall "a memorial to Negro soldiers and sailors" of the Great War. The CFA claimed: "While recognizing the services of the Negro soldiers and sailors and that of other divisions of the population, the Commission thought that no action with regard to designating a site for a memorial proposed should be taken until such time as in the judgment of Congress it shall be decided to signalize in some appropriate way the participation of the United States in the World War." Punting the matter to the future, the CFA effectively halted the proposal (which, if enacted, would have complicated and disrupted the CFA's carefully composed visual ensemble).[43]

The CFA, however, constructed two elaborate Civil War monuments at the opposite ends of the Mall—the Lincoln Memorial and the Grant Memorial—with the intention of displaying a condensed and discernible timeline of the nation's history. Savage writes: "With the Washington Monument in the center, representing in abstract form the birth of the nation, the outer poles of their composition could be devoted to the solemn story of the nation's rebirth: what Lincoln at Gettysburg called 'a new birth of freedom.'"[44] At first glance triumphant in nature, the Lincoln and Grant memorials were—artistically speaking—revolutionary for their emotional and psychological complexity. As Savage argues, at the Lincoln Memorial—where "the colossal effigy" of an intense and pensive Lincoln simultaneously beckons visitors to approach him *and* gazes *past them* into the distance—"we are asked not to celebrate Lincoln's triumph but to experience in our own way the tragic load he had to carry."[45] And the Grant Memorial—"animated by the anonymous figures of soldiers engaged in desperate action"—lacks any kind of "redemptive narrative"; instead, Savage claims, it offers "an intense focus on the individual experience of combat" that threatens "to turn the monument's soldiers from heroes into victims, and the monument's viewers from reassured citizens intro traumatized witnesses."[46] Furthermore, the Lincoln and Grant memorials revealed the CFA's preference for a new type of memorial: the "spatial monument" (as Savage terms it)—a monument elevated above a broad flight of steps that, much like the Washington Monument, *always* transcends the subject position of the viewer below.[47] Thus, the CFA transformed the Mall into a tightly organized "flow of space" that amplified visions of American white male heroism through the careful placement of innovative and dominating, if somewhat abstract and cerebral, permanent memorials.[48]

The CFA's work on the National Mall also extended across the Potomac River, to Arlington National Cemetery. Possessing "the cooperation and support of Maj. Gen. Harry L. Rogers, Quartermaster General, United States Army," the CFA attempted to connect (both physically and symbolically) the cemetery to the National Mall, and apply an ordered aesthetic system to that sprawling and under-planned burial ground. Established in 1864, Arlington National Cemetery reflected nineteenth century principles of landscape composition: the headstones swept across rolling and irregular hills; random trees claimed prominent space to break up the order of the headstones; undulating (and poorly paved) roadways adapted to the land's contours, cutting back and forth throughout the cemetery; and grave markers came in different shapes and sizes, and often expressed personal, sentimental, and unique messages. In short, the eclecticism, disorder, and dissymmetry of the cemetery's physical presentation violated the fundamental sensibilities of the CFA. Furthermore, Arlington was a place of exploration, where the visitor was always the addresser and rarely the addressee.

In 1920, the CFA publicly announced its design plans for Arlington in a *Washington Post* op-ed. Recognizing the perceived sacredness of the site and the complexities of reworking a space where human bodies were buried, the CFA introduced its objectives by expressing a profound appreciation for the cemetery's purposes and meanings: "Arlington is a national shrine, sacred to the memory of the thousands of soldier dead, named and unnamed, who lie buried under the shade of its trees. This sacred character should be protected and fostered." Following these opening lines, the CFA laid out its plans. First, the commission proposed renovating and preserving Robert E. Lee's "Arlington House" on Mount Vernon, a domestic structure of "historical importance" (these words indicated that the cemetery, much like the Mall, could be a space for displaying the nation's historical timeline). Because "Arlington prospectively is a portion of the great central composition of Washington, extending from the Capitol through the Mall to the Monument and on to the Lincoln Memorial," the CFA advocated the construction of a grand and artistically beautiful bridge that would link "Arlington to the park system of Washington" (what we now know as the Arlington National Bridge).[49] The CFA recommended that a newly constructed amphitheater at Arlington "serve the double purpose of an auditorium [and] place for [burial services]"—in other words, a *designated venue* for certain kinds of sanctioned, patriotic rhetorical activity. It argued for "the improvement and development of roadways" that would accommodate cars and link neglected burial areas "now cut off from the main cemetery and rarely visited excepting by people searching for an individual grave." The CFA also hoped to instigate a new "planting scheme" (i.e., a human taming of wildlife) that would accentuate the burial ground's natural beauty, instill the site with a more masculine character,[50] and address particular deficiencies in the cemetery's visual presentation:

> This means the immediate selection and planting of thousands of trees in the now vacant spaces of Arlington. Today these treeless portions, so out of harmony with the general appearance of the cemetery, give on the idea that the graves of our latest heroes are being placed rather in a potter's field than in an honored location.
>
> Elaborate flower beds of gaudy flowers are a disturbance in Arlington. Until trees have been planted and roads and buildings repaired the money spent on the maintenance of flower beds should be minimized.

Finally, the CFA wanted to instill a greater sense of uniformity by eliminating the eclectic nature of the site's grave markers and spacing all soldiers' headstones evenly. Highlighting the fact that many officers' plots were elaborate and overweening (presumably because most Civil War officers had come from well-to-do families who could afford expensive, artistically beautiful headstones), the CFA stated: "The regulations against mausoleums, portraits, and unusual designs, should be enforced for the protection of the many against the self-assertion of the few. The officers whose careers need eulogy on a tombstone should not be accorded in Arlington the credit that history denies." Thus, the cemetery would begin to express forcefully the democratic ideal of equality. In conclusion, the CFA defended its plan with a somewhat overwrought appeal to the memory of the dead and the feelings of grieving families: "So much the Nation owes to the last resting place of those who have fought its battles, and to the relatives and friends who pay tribute to the memory of the heroes." Advancing the same principles that guided its work on the National Mall, the CFA effectively argued for the overhaul of Arlington (its plans would, in time, come to fruition).[51]

The CFA's project in Arlington not only represented the aesthetic philosophy of the commission, but also coincided with emerging contemporary American gravescape practices. In his essay, "Death on Display," rhetoric scholar Richard Morris historicizes, describes, and compares the aesthetic attributes and cultural receptions of (what he identifies as) the three major epochs of American "gravescape" design: "memento mori" (practiced until the early nineteenth century), "garden romance" (practiced throughout most of the nineteenth century), and "epic heroism" (practiced since the late nineteenth century). Memento mori gravescapes refer to early American church graveyards that were often situated in the heart of bustling urban life. Typified by cemeteries like the Granary Burial Ground in Boston, Massachusetts, memento mori gravescapes (as Morris puts it) "presented visitors with a singular rhetorical and cultural imperative: remember death, for the time of judgment is at hand." Asking passers-by to "remember death" (hence, "memento mori"), the cemetery's gravestones (often haphazard, chaotic, and unkempt in appearance) usually displayed gloomy inscriptions and (to the modern eye) *startling* death-related icons (such as skulls, crossed bones, coffins, shovels, picks, funeral shrouds, crashing waves, and hourglasses) that spoke to the literate and illiterate alike. Eschewing celebration of the heroic deeds and accomplishments of the deceased, and exhibiting messages regarding the presumably vast separation between the here and now and the afterlife, the memento mori gravescape offered a constant reminder of the traditional Christian worldview that life is little more than one long preparation for death (thus, one must live according the morals and standards of religious faith).[52]

With the rise of Romantic and Victorian sensibilities regarding life, death, and aesthetics, a very different kind of American gravescape was popularized throughout the mid-nineteenth century: the garden romance gravescape. A countryside (or "rural") cemetery that united the charm of nature and art, the garden romance gravescape sought to represent a more "humanistic" worldview that held death not as an otherworldly experience, but rather as a natural process. Epitomized by the Mount Auburn Cemetery in Cambridge, Massachusetts, the garden romance gravescape effectively cast death as a natural process, the deceased individual as a source of emotions (e.g., loss, grief, inspiration, serenity), and the cemetery as a social attraction—a place of congregation (with others and with nature) and recreation (day-tripping, picnicking, and hiking). As Morris tells us, visitors of the garden romance gravescape usually found rolling hills, meandering pathways, and "an extraordinary garden luxuriously adorned with nature and appointed with the most remarkable works of art money could supply." Often displaying inspirational nature and/or art icons (as opposed to somber religious and death-related symbols), grave markers were eclectic material and visual celebrations of the respective deceased individual's life and accomplishments. Typically bourgeois and exclusive (the poor usually could not afford to bury, nor visit, their dead there, while African Americans and people of color were often barred altogether from interring their departed), the garden romance graves-cape advanced an elite, enlightened, and *white* belief that "death is far less a struggle against chaos than an opportunity to understand and become" one with thyself, fellow human beings, nature, and the supernatural.[53]

The third epoch Morris identifies is the epic heroism[54] gravescape (estab-lished in cities, suburbs, and rural communities alike). Reflecting certain aspects of capitalist democracy and the industrial revolution,[55] and counter-acting the exclusivity, eclecticism, and sentimentality of the garden romance gravescape, the epic heroism gravescape was personified by the lawn ceme-tery, "an open vista, unobstructed by fences, memorials, aesthetic renderings, and flora" (as Morris puts it), where the dead were identified by seemingly identical, evenly spaced, flat markers that were level or nearly level with the ground. Developed during the mid- and late nineteenth century and ubiquitous by the early twentieth century, the epic heroism gravescape did not "invite viewers to contemplate nature or art or one's 'finer sentiments.'" Instead, much like the Washington Monument on the National Mall, the lawn cemetery displayed "an accomplishment of labor rather than of artistic skill," equated "size with significance," asserted "dominance over its environment, over nature," and privileged reason, reality, and the ideals of meritocracy over emotion, speculations on the afterlife, and liberal individualism. Eliminating all things that suggested death, sorrow, or pain, and instilling an undeniable sense of homogeneity, this "deathless" space made efficient use of valuable land, offered ordinary citizens an inexpensive and accessible place to bury their dead, and shifted aesthetic decision-making power from plot owners to a newly created professional position, the cemetery superintendent—who, much like the CFA, was authorized to dictate and manage the visual composi-tion of crucial civic space.[56]

Although the underlying principles and cultural meanings of the lawn cemetery dovetailed with many of the sensibilities and ideologies of the CFA, certain aspects of the epic heroism gravescape posed complications for the CFA's project in Europe. First, the epic heroism gravescape practi-cally *hid* its headstones in the grass; from a distance, the typical lawn cem-etery looked like a golf fairway or empty yet well-groomed pasture. Given the CFA's orientation toward *public space* rather than *public grounds*, as well as its general aspiration to dominate vistas with transcendent, vertical structures, the flat headstones—affixed in the soil and drawing each visitor's attention to the *ground*—were inherently *antithetical* to the CFA's protocol. Second, and perhaps more important, the epic heroism gravescape's erasure of emotion and sentimentality could not (and certainly would not) be an attribute of the European sites. On the one hand the CFA hoped to establish a network of overseas cemeteries that would honor the nation's war dead who had "fought bravely and successfully," become "objects of pilgrimages by our people," and make "American valor" "conspicuous" to "our own succeeding generation" and "our associates in the war."[57] That is to say, the overseas burial grounds would be overtly *rhetorical* in nature—not just "deathless" spaces like lawn cemeteries, devoid of emotion.[58] On the other hand the physical composition of the overseas cemeteries would have to acknowledge, in some noticeable way, the sentiments and feelings of next of kin who had relinquished the care of their loved ones' remains to the government.

Of course, the cemeteries the CFA hoped to build in Europe would be *military cemeteries*—therefore, they would have to function in the same ways that domestic military cemeteries had during the decades preceding the Great War. Throughout the nineteenth century, Americans had turned to the natural splendor and majestic wilderness of the United States as a primary source of national identity. Encompassing the Adirondacks, the Florida Everglades, the Gulf Coast, the Colorado Rockies, the Sierra Nevada, the Mississippi River, the Grand Canyon, and the Great Lakes, the young nation boasted a diverse and majestic set of natural splendors and environmental climates that could be matched by few nations (if any). According to History and Environmental Studies scholar Roderick Frazier Nash, during the late eighteenth and early nineteenth centuries it was "widely assumed that America's primary task was the justification of its newly won freedom":

> The nation's short history, weak traditions, and minor literary and artistic achievements seemed negligible compared to those of Europe. But in at least one respect Americans sensed that their country was different: wilderness had no counterpart in the Old World [...] nationalists argued that far from being a liability, wilderness was actually an American asset [...] by the middle decades of the nineteenth century wilderness was recognized as a cultural and moral resource and a basis for national self-esteem.[59]

The paintings of Thomas Cole and the other members of the Hudson River School, and the writings of Thoreau, Emerson, and Whitman, celebrated the American wilderness as the nation's most defining and virtuous characteristic.[60] By the 1890s, however, the United States had sufficiently developed its own literary, artistic, and musical canons; had conquered and domesticated most of its frontier (thus fulfilling the mandates of Manifest Destiny); and, had become an industrial and economic power in the international arena. Therefore, the U.S. had little time or incentive to worship its natural resources in the ways it had over the previous hundred years.[61] Moreover, given the traumatic social ruptures still troubling the nation in the wakes of the Civil

War and Reconstruction, the American wilderness must have seemed like a particular deficient, or at least peripheral, rhetorical resource for articulating the 're-birthed' country's identity—not least because the respective natural wonders of the North and the South shared so little in common.

In light of these cultural complications, during the 1890s, Civil War military cemeteries emerged as viable and effective political and rhetorical devices for expressing American identity and suturing critical national divides. Usually situated on or near the battlefields where Confederate and Union soldiers had killed each other and spilled their blood, these cemeteries were capable of simultaneously fostering therapeutic reconciliation between the North and the South (through relatively evenhanded commemoration of fallen soldiers from *both* sides) and displaying the dead citizen-soldier (whether Confederate or Union) as a paradigmatic symbol of supposedly American democratic virtues: fidelity, bravery, strength, sacrifice, and duty.[62]

Established by the Northern and Southern armies, private individuals, and grassroots veterans groups during the war itself, the 1860s, and the 1870s, the major burial grounds at Chickamauga and Chattanooga, Antietam, Shiloh, Gettysburg, and Vicksburg, had initially served as gathering places for next of kin and regiments from various states and regions to hold reunions and practice (often antagonistic) commemoration rituals in honor of the fallen. In keeping with the aesthetic sensibilities of the contemporary garden romance gravescape, these bucolic and sylvan cemeteries tended to feature grassy hills, giant boulders, shady paths, wildflowers, gently rolling creeks and springs, rustic stone walls, small forests, and haphazardly situated trees, for, as historian Timothy B. Smith tells us, each of these cemeteries was originally intended to be "a revered land rather than a landscaped and beautified commercial attraction."[63] As historian Edward T. Linenthal points out, the natural beauty of these "picturesque pastoral" cemeteries—constructed on or close to the fields of battle—made it difficult to think of the "great violence" and "horror" of combat.[64] Still, the violence of the Civil War was always present, for, as one of the founders of the Gettysburg Cemetery put it, the burial grounds were sacred in character because of their close proximity to the battlefields—the "contested and hallowed soil, already stained with the blood of the fallen."[65]

Much like the headstones and mausoleums erected in Mt. Auburn Cemetery and other "rural" burial grounds, the monuments that first appeared in these Civil War cemeteries were eclectic in nature, varying in size, design, material, and meaning.[66] And reflecting the mid-nineteenth-century American cultural emphasis on liberal individualism, these sites displayed an unprecedented pattern in American military funerary practices: that of memorializing each individual soldier with his own grave marker.[67] As Smith writes:

Before the Civil War, military dead were generally memorialized as a group, often with a single monument or marker. The [...] cemeteries of the 1860s, however, utilized individual plots with individual headboards or grave identifications. Perhaps Thomas B. Van Horne, a chaplain in the United States Army [in charge of the cemetery at Chattanooga] best summed up this developing attitude [when he] noted that extreme care would be taken to "secure a short military history of every officer and soldier interred in the cemetery whose remains have been identified [...] It seems eminently fitting that this should be done [as it] accords with our intense individualism as a people, and with the value we attach to individual life."[68]

But while the individual grave markers were meant to "secure a short military history of every officer and soldier interred," the cemeteries, in general, were not intended to preserve history in a completely factual manner, for each of them elided a thorny, inconvenient, but crucial aspect of the Civil War's narrative: black slavery. From their inceptions onwards, none of these major cemeteries incorporated the graves of black soldiers, celebrated the accomplishments of African Americans in the war, nor mentioned the institution of slavery as a central point of stasis between the Union and the Confederacy.[69] Even Arlington National Cemetery—established by the federal government on Robert E. Lee's estate (a decidedly provocative act intended to signal Northern supremacy)—failed to honor fallen African Americans in any discernible way. At Arlington, the graves of white Union soldiers were situated on the prominent and visible heights of Mt. Vernon, while the graves of African-American Union soldiers were placed at an inconspicuous section in the northeast corner of the estate; thus, at Arlington, African-American soldiers were racially segregated and marked in death just as they had been in life.[70]

By the 1890s, it was evident to veterans and politicians alike that Civil War cemeteries—and American war memorials in general—could be powerful symbolic resources for articulating national identity and healing festering social wounds. Between 1875 and 1877, Congress had funded the erection of monuments on eight Revolutionary War battlefields, where official celebrations of the centennial of the nation's independence could be held. One of the first documented gatherings of both Northern and Southern veterans came in 1875 at a centennial celebration for the Battle of Bunker Hill. According to Timothy B. Smith, "One hundred years after the birth of the nation, Americans of both sections celebrated their common heritage and their shared fight for independence. Both Northern and Southern whites could agree on the dedication and dominance of the American military and thus celebrated together their quest for independence and a republican government."[71] The lessons of the centennial festivities were not lost on the federal government.

As Smith tell us, it became clear that Civil War sites of historical importance could serve a similar function:

> Rather than fight over race, [white] Americans sought common bonds that would tie them together. What could be more honorable and reconciling than to concentrate on the passing veterans of the Civil War and their courage, bravery, and manliness on Civil War battlefields? [...] The primary celebration of the Civil War generation's bravery and courage [came] to be extolled on the original battlefields [and cemeteries], preserved as military parks.[72]

During the 1890s, veterans groups, veteran-lawmakers in Congress, and the War Department worked in unison to pass legislation that would make Civil War cemeteries and their surrounding battlefields federally funded, protected, and controlled military parks where memories of soldiers from *both* sides would be preserved for all time.[73] Their joint plan called for honoring aging white Southern and Northern veterans before they died, protecting the cemeteries and historic fields from the intrusions of the second industrial revolution (railroads, transportation routes, and urban sprawl),[74] purchasing private land on which some cemeteries and memorials had been constructed, and instilling rules of decorum and standards for the design of monuments and other objects placed in the parks (so as to prevent divisive rhetorical acts and combat visual eclecticism).[75]

In time, the legislation passed, and by the early 1900s, the federal government had established the country's first official military parks—sites that, as advocates put it, would "be of great interest and importance [...] to the country at large and to future generations,"[76] serve as "object lesson[s] of patriotism [of] absolute verity,"[77] celebrate the North and the South's "joint and precious heritage,"[78] and radiate with the "golden mist of American valor."[79] Designed to ignore the accomplishments, sacrifices, hardships, and status of African Americans, these sites were used to foster and promote the ideology of reconciliation between the North and the South as the young nation transitioned from a turbulent inaugural century to its next, and more promising, hundred years of existence. On July 4, 1913, President Woodrow Wilson highlighted this whitewashed spirit of reconciliation in his keynote address at the fiftieth anniversary of the battle at Gettysburg. Speaking before a group of Union and Confederate veterans on the Gettysburg battlefield, Wilson stated:

> How wholesome and healing the peace has been! We have found one another again as brothers and comrades, in arms, enemies no longer, generous friends rather, our battles long past, the quarrel forgotten—except we shall not forget the splendid valor, the manly devotion of the men then arrayed against one another, now grasping hands and smiling into each other's eyes.[80]

By the late 1910s and early 1920s, the Civil War cemeteries had evolved from unofficial, vernacular burial grounds into pilgrimage destinations, official national memorials, and beautiful tourist attractions[81]—sacred places that fostered reconciliation between politically and culturally divided white citizens, offered visitors a powerful imaginative entry into the past,[82] and served as holy sites where Americans could perform the emerging rituals of a new and powerful form of civic religion.[83]

Thus, by the time the CFA began formulating its design plans for the burial grounds in Europe, military cemeteries situated on or near the killing fields where interred soldiers had died had become effective vehicles for sustained articulations of national identity and the common heritage of all (or, at least *white*) Americans. Honoring each individual as a citizen-soldier (rather than, say, as a taxpayer, husband or participant in democratic processes), amplifying the American democratic virtue of sacrifice by displaying seemingly countless numbers of head stones,[84] obfuscating *and* alluding to the violence that had caused the dead soldiers' demise, and smoothing over unsavory and still unresolved contradictions of national history (e.g., slavery, Southern secession), the Civil War cemeteries (and surrounding government-sanctioned military parks) had become sites where the living could associate themselves with the causes, meanings, and democratic virtues supposedly embodied by the temporally distant, but somehow still physically palpable, mass bloodletting that had occurred in those very same spaces.[85] Re-mediated as war memorials, these burial grounds also revealed that public memory could be a dominant rhetorical resource for expressing national identity, that individual grave markers could effectively stand in place of dead U.S. soldiers as virtual replicas of human life (which simultaneously made the dead seem more alive *and* softened the profound loss of the nation's men),[86] and that military cemeteries could enlarge temporal horizons by situating particular crises within the nation's broader historical narrative.[87] While the CFA must have been troubled by the nineteenth-century aesthetic sensibilities exhibited by the visual presentation of the Civil War Cemeteries, it surely apprehended the fact that natural beauty still held rhetorical appeal for many Americans. And given the fact that the overseas military cemeteries would have to exhibit American democratic ideals like *equality*, the CFA would be compelled to incorporate the bodies of African Americans in a manner that the Civil War cemeteries had not (for to do otherwise would, in all likelihood, seem absurd, hypocritical, and confusing to international audiences). Still, the Civil War cemeteries—considered sacred by virtue of their proximity to tracts of land where American blood had been shed—were useful and instructive templates and references for the CFA as it undertook its project in Europe.

Of course, unlike soldiers of the Revolutionary War and the Civil War, American soldiers of the Great War had not shed their blood on *American* soil. Rather, their blood had been spilled on distant foreign territories. The reality that the nation's World War cemeteries would be constructed thousands of miles away from the homeland raised several daunting challenges for the CFA. First, the commission would have to discover ways of symbolically re-linking the cemeteries and the bloodstained killing fields of Europe (once the *old world*, and now, in a sense, the *new world*) with American soil. As Drew Gilpin Faust reveals in *This Republic of Suffering*, during the Civil War, American families had been shocked by the fact that their men (most of whom had never left their local counties) would be fighting and dying many miles away from home. As one South Carolina woman remarked in 1863, it was "much more painful" to give up a "loved one [who] is a stranger in a strange land." With respect to the World War I, one can only imagine the trauma families experienced when their loved ones were drafted and shipped overseas to fight and die.[88] Second, if the overseas burial grounds were going to serve as pilgrimage destinations for U.S. citizens (as the CFA hoped), the sites would have to feature particular aesthetic attributes and ideological meanings that Americans had been conditioned to expect and recognize in their national military cemeteries (and the National Mall). Third, given the cemeteries' location and the rhetorical work that U.S. political and military officials hoped to conduct through the sites,[89] the burial grounds would also have to speak to the hearts and minds of Europeans (and presumably, peoples from around the world)—an enormously difficult task that struck at the heart of *epideictic* rhetoric (ceremonial speech, i.e., speech intended to praise the virtues or condemn the vices of some person or group). As historian Seth G. Benardete writes: "To praise the Athenians at Athens, Socrates remarks, or the Spartans at Sparta is not very difficult; but to praise the Athenians at Sparta or the Spartans at Athens demands great rhetorical skill."[90] Finally, since the cemeteries were intended to be symbols of both the young *modern* nation's decisive role in the Great War and its newfound place on the world's stage, the sites would have to match, and perhaps even exceed, the monumentality and beauty of the cemeteries that France, England, and other European states (nations that already possessed older, famous, and respected aesthetic traditions) had constructed in honor of their respective fallen soldiers during the immediate postwar years (a point that will be addressed later in the chapter).

The CFA was further constrained by material realities. For instance, whereas the Commonwealth War Graves Commission of the United Kingdom had more than 400,000 dead bodies to work with (to put it bluntly) as it designed and established over 500 permanent cemeteries throughout Continental Europe, the CFA had just over 30,000 American bodies at its disposal.

Thus, it was evident that the CFA would not be able to construct hundreds of cemeteries as the United Kingdom and France had done, for each of these burial grounds would display a comparatively small number of headstones— a visual characteristic that might diminish each site's grandeur and make the task of exhibiting American sacrifice in the Great War all the more difficult. Furthermore, the CFA was compelled to squeeze as much symbolic power as possible out of each dead American; this meant that even the bodies of African-American soldiers (typically ignored in previous American war commemoration projects) and U.S. troops who had died less than manly and glorious deaths (disease, suicide) were invaluable to the CFA's project, and would have to be seamlessly incorporated into the visual presentation of the overseas cemeteries (and, by virtue of their inclusion, honored).[91]

Of course, the bodily remains of U.S. soldiers were not pieces of stone, metal, or soil that could be roughly handled, manipulated, and used like construction materials. No, they were pieces of human flesh and bone belonging to American war dead that demanded careful and downright reverent treatment.[92] This point became patently clear in 1925, when, while visiting one of the nascent permanent U.S. burial grounds in France, Senator David A. Reed was horrified to discover that soldiers' coffins were routinely removed from the soil and rearranged to suit the aesthetic presentation of the cemetery. "From this I heartily dissent," Reed proclaimed. "These graves 'not yet re-arranged' are graves made in war time, many of them made immediately after battle, and their irregularity is readily pardoned by everyone who understands this fact [...] It is possible to have cemeteries altogether beautiful without re-arranging the graves [...] Surely after seven years the bodies of the men are entitled to be left in peace."[93] Senator Reed was shocked that such an action would take place, even without the pressure of public scrutiny.

Several other material realities presented complex, if not overtly apparent, challenges to the CFA's project. For instance, the CFA faced the difficult task of properly marking the graves of the 1,600 dead U.S. soldiers whose identities were still unknown. What, exactly, would be the appropriate inscription for these men's headstones? Additionally, if constructed near battlefields of the Great War, the American cemeteries necessarily would be situated in rural areas that lacked functioning roads (either because they had never been built or because they had been destroyed by four years of fierce fighting). How would visitors make their way to these pilgrimage destinations if there were no roads or accessible accommodations for food and rest? These scarred, decimated, and still muddy territories, however, were not only isolated; they were also extremely *hazardous*. Besides containing thousands of yet-to-be-discovered human corpses, the killing fields and forests were still riddled with active landmines, bombs that had not detonated, and unexploded chemical shells—objects that posed great danger to anyone traveling to the American cemeteries or exploring the former war zone.[94] On top of being unsafe, the battlefields did not connote meanings that would be easily recognizable to American visitors. In comparison to names like "Valley Forge," "Gettysburg," "Antietam," and "Shiloh," which were immediately familiar to U.S. citizens, "Saint Mihiel" and "Bony" were certainly less than household terms. Moreover, whereas famous battles like Gettysburg had lasted just a few days, had been contained to a relatively small area of land, had entailed discernible (and thus easily glorifiable) acts of individual and collective military bravery, and had ended with clear winners and losers, American operations in Europe had been drawn out, massive battles of attrition involving tens of thousands of men, had taken place in unfamiliar and distant regions along the Western Front, had generally not entailed discernible acts of individual and collective military bravery (because of the technologies and tactics of modern warfare), and had rarely ended with clear victors and vanquished. Consequently, the battlefields on which American overseas military cemeteries would be constructed—ravaged terrain devoid of natural beauty—would not easily, nor inherently, indicate the glory of the U.S. military's accomplishments in the war.

The CFA was also confronted with the quandary of procuring construction materials (such as stone, concrete, and steel) in Europe that would meet its needs and lofty standards. While the United States certainly had ample resources for the CFA's overseas project, shipping blocks of Vermont marble (for example) across the Atlantic would be a costly affair. Furthermore, such an action held the potential of being construed as a kind of American invasion of Europe (a *symbolic*, rather than *military*, invasion, but an *invasion* nonetheless)—something the Wilson Administration certainly would not appreciate as it delicately negotiated postwar treaties with European allies and enemies alike. Therefore, the CFA would have to make due with the materials it could afford to purchase in Europe. Of course, the CFA would be unable to obtain materials from Germany or Austria (just as it would be unable to erect cemeteries in those nations), and the CFA would have to anticipate the possible connotations of any material it used (Italian marble, for instance, might communicate to American visitors something entirely different than American marble). In fact, when the cemetery planners selected Italian Carrara marble for soldiers' headstones, the Gold Star Mothers and Gold Star Fathers Associations (organizations for men and women who had lost their sons in the war) protested, and demanded the use of a more 'patriotic' stone, such as American granite (ultimately, the planners went with the Italian marble).[95] Finally, the CFA would have to consider the feelings, psychologies, and political goals of European military and governmental officials as it formulated and pitched its design plans (which would inevitably trumpet American greatness) and secured appropriate tracts of foreign land in perpetuity, for the permanent sites. Whereas the CFA wielded immense power in Washington, D.C., to do whatever it pleased, the commission would have to take into account, and satisfy, the sensibilities of foreign dignitaries so as to accomplish its goals and not offend. Ultimately, all of these material realities made it patently clear that few (if any) aspects of the CFA's overseas project would be devoid of signification—that no material or object could ever simply be a symbolically neutral or inert piece of matter.

The final, and perhaps most critical, constraint on the CFA was the implied mandate to recognize and represent through the cemeteries' physical presentation the feelings, deep personal sacrifice, and expectations of grieving American families who had left their loved ones in Europe.[96] The postwar correspondence between the government/military and relatives of dead soldiers during the immediate postwar years had exposed a complex and turbulent reserve of emotions—anxiety, anger, confusion, sadness, heartbreak, fear, and concern for the state of loved ones' souls—that, in time, the government had learned to attend to and appropriate into its own official public rhetoric. Thus, while the nascent overseas cemeteries were going to be *permanent* sites that spoke to audiences across time, they would certainly have to speak to relatives of the dead who would be alive for some time. Given the fact that the CFA generally rejected overt sentimentality as a source for artistic expression, this imperative must have been frustrating and inconvenient. But as it began devising its plans for overseas burial grounds, the CFA was careful to express publicly a profound appreciation of the suffering of next of kin. Editors at the *Washington Post* were key advocates for the CFA's project, and during the immediate postwar years the newspaper helped the CFA articulate its commitment to the needs and beliefs of next of kin. For instance, in 1921, the *Post* assured readers that the "many relatives of the glorious dead who elected to allow the mortal remains of their loved ones to lie in the soil for which they fought and fell will assuredly derive comfort and consolation" from the CFA's plans, which would undoubtedly design "tender and reverent" sites "where the American heroes sleep their last sleep and await the trump of the great accounting day."[97]

In summary, the CFA was in a constrained rhetorical position. Yet, at the same time, these aforementioned ideological, rhetorical, and material constraints necessarily pushed the CFA to consider aesthetic options and choices that it might not have otherwise contemplated. In other words, these limitations allowed the CFA to explore unforeseen possibilities that had not been evident, plausible, or fitting during its previous work on the National Mall and Arlington National Cemetery. Forced to take a seemingly countless number of undesired, external variables into account, the CFA was, in a way, simultaneously free to develop through the European sites a new, and potentially just as powerful, way of expressing its aesthetic ideals and political commitments (to an even larger audience, no less). In short, the CFA had the opportunity to invent an original form of American war commemoration that might announce to the world long-lasting and effective messages concerning the young nation's supposed ideals, political superiority, military prowess, newfound starring role on the international stage, and willingness to sacrifice its youth on behalf of the world and democratic ideals.

THE CFA'S PLANS

In March 1921, three members of the Commission of Fine Arts—Chairman Charles Moore, architect William Mitchell Kendall, and landscape architect James L. Greenleaf—traveled to Europe with officials from the War Department and the Graves Registration Service "with a view to preparing plans for the permanent American cemeteries in France and England." Visiting four potential cemetery sites in France (Suresnes, Romagne, Belleau Wood, and Bony) and one near London (Brookwood), these CFA members assessed the on-the-ground realities that would inevitably influence and shape their design plans for the overseas military cemeteries. Gathering information and ideas from temporary American burial grounds and permanent British and French cemeteries already established, Moore and his cohorts came face-to-face with distant lands that, until then, had been understood by most Americans as "over there." Upon returning to the United States, Moore and the CFA submitted to the President and Congress an official and carefully crafted report that described the European tour and laid out the CFA's visions for the overseas burial grounds. The CFA's 1921 report was the commission's first public expression[98] of its ideas for America's permanent World War cemeteries—ideas that, in time, would become material realities.[99] Containing photographs of the sites the CFA had visited in Europe and blueprints for the future permanent cemeteries (drafted by Major George Gibbs, Jr., formerly an engineer in Frederick Law Olmsted's landscape architecture firm),[100] the report was, just as important, a carefully crafted pitch for Congressional funding.

The 1921 report began with a statement about the general condition of America's 1,700 temporary cemeteries in Europe. Preemptively assuaging any public concerns regarding the treatment of the nation's war dead, the CFA claimed that "the existing cemeteries were excellently cared for, being neat, orderly, and well kept [...] even in the case of small cemeteries of isolated graves there was evidence of respectful and reverent care. There was no instance of neglect." Furthermore, Graves Registrations Service members "had done and were doing their work with painstaking care and with a close attention to the many and exacting details involved in identifications, the transshipment of bodies to the United States, and the reinterment of those which were to remain." While on their tour, the CFA representatives had encountered next of kin who had been searching for and visiting their loved ones' graves. The CFA was happy to report that the "provisions for relatives visiting the cemeteries were excellent, considering the changing conditions and the uncertainty of visits," and that "France has sufficiently recovered from the shocks of war to provide good food and shelter to visitors and at normal prices." In other words, it was perfectly reasonable to expect that Americans would be able to visit the overseas cemeteries without any apprehension or difficulty throughout the future (given the state of the land in these regions, this was a dubious assertion).[101] The CFA also addressed next of kin directly. Echoing the sentimental postwar rhetoric of the government and military, the CFA wrote:

> The first problem involved in the treatment of the American cemeteries in Europe is the adequate, reverent care of the remains of our soldiers—such care as shall justify the action of the relatives who elected to allow the bodies of their dead to remain in the soil for which they fought and died. In a majority of cases this action on the part of relatives in itself was an act of patriotism and sacrifice. They felt that by foregoing their right to have the bodies brought to the United States they were setting their mark and seal on the sacrifice made by sons and husbands and brothers. They had confidence that the Government would see to it that these graves would not be neglected, but would be held in respect and honor.

Speaking to relatives of the dead (as well as any American who might take interest in the matter), the CFA professed its fundamental concern with the proper handling of soldierly remains.[102]

Because U.S. casualty statistics were "small when compared with the losses of France and England" ("due to our entry late in the war"), the CFA advised concentrating "American dead in a comparatively few cemeteries" (as opposed to hundreds of little ones) so as to save on maintenance costs and magnify the visual effect of U.S. graves. The CFA recommended the establishment of six or seven cemeteries (eventually eight would be constructed). Though some of these consolidated burial grounds might contain fewer headstones than those displayed in other nations' cemeteries, each would effectively serve as a "permanent visible symbol in France of the entire strength and soul of America, devoted without reserve to the decision of a great cause." The CFA stated:

> Whether there are 1,000 or 10,000 graves in a given cemetery has no relation to the condition in which that cemetery should be maintained. The treatment of each burial place retained should be just as adequate as if all the American dead had found permanent rest in the land in which they perished [...] The fact that the graves of our soldiers in France are few as compared with those of the

French and the English, few even as compared with the Americans who fell, does not signify.[103]

The nation's smaller casualty statistics would not "signify," it seemed, as long as enough fallen soldiers were interred at each overseas cemetery—and more important, as long as the United States invested properly in the establishment and maintenance of each site. Referencing Arlington National Cemetery—the iconic military cemetery that was immediately familiar to most Americans—the CFA argued: "The treatment of our cemeteries [...] should be adequate [...] The lands occupied should be ample to secure an appropriate amount of space for each grave. By an appropriate amount is meant the same amount as is now allotted in the most adequately developed portions of the Arlington Military Cemetery." For the CFA, the rhetorical success of each cemetery depended on the acquisition of "an appropriate amount of space" (a claim that makes perfect sense when we consider the CFA's general philosophy of communicating through vast expanses of land, or *space*): "Unless the area of land included within them shall be increased appreciably and that land treated according to a well-considered plan, our participation in the war, in so far as it is visible to the eye, will be negligible." The CFA was happy to report that the United States' European allies were happy to offer land for the cemeteries in perpetuity, "as a free gift," but asserted, "Either the cemeteries should be well developed and well maintained or they should be abandoned":

> If this Government shall provide as suitably and as adequately for the World War cemeteries in Europe as it has provided for the military cemeteries in the United States, then the field of battle will also be the field of honor. Otherwise, the sooner all the bodies shall be withdrawn from France the better. Money will be saved and a more suitable treatment will be accorded to our dead. The time to decide the question is at the beginning. The cost should be counted now.[104]

Equating the nascent World War burial grounds with the popular Civil War cemeteries in the United States, the CFA effectively drew a line in the sand: the government should either fund the CFA's project without concern for expenses, or it should jettison the idea of permanent overseas cemeteries altogether.

So what did the CFA want the American overseas cemeteries to look like? The CFA began its exposition of its design plans by discussing the aesthetic attributes of the nation's temporary military cemeteries and British cemeteries that it admired. (Perhaps betraying a bias toward Anglophone culture, the CFA did not offer an analysis of France's or any other country's military burial grounds.) With regards to American temporary cemeteries, the CFA was impressed by their proximity to the battlegrounds "where our troops were engaged" and had fallen:

> They occupy sections of the battle fields over which our men fought bravely and successfully. They mark historic spots dear to the American heart. [The permanent cemeteries] will be the objects of pilgrimages by our people. Therefore they should be maintained permanently in all those places where American valor was conspicuous. Otherwise our participation in those historic battles is in danger of being lost sight of.[105]

Like the cemetery at Gettysburg, the overseas burial grounds would be situated on or near the fields where the interred had met their fate. The CFA was also taken with the white uniformly spaced wooden headstones in the temporary sites, which were "smaller and simpler than either the French or British." This comparative smallness enabled them "to be set farther apart [...] so that the green grass counts and the sense of quiet is greater." This was an effect that the CFA hoped to reproduce in the permanent cemeteries. Whatever the final design of the permanent headstones (ultimately made of durable stone) would be, the CFA believed that "the stones used should be uniform in size and design [...] All display of an individual character is as much out of place as civilian clothing worn by individual soldiers in a regiment drawn up on parade [...] the uniform size of the stone should be the rule"—something the CFA had so adamantly tried to implement in its redesign of Arlington.[106]

As for the U.K. cemeteries, the CFA praised their artistic beauty and utilization of symbolically significant natural elements. The CFA noted that Canadian maple trees had been planted in cemeteries where Canadian soldiers lied, Tasmanian eucalyptus trees where Australian soldiers were buried, the daisy bush in sites that held New Zealanders, and the scarlet poppy in predominantly English graveyards; and that "the best art of the empire" had been employed for the design of the cemeteries' landscape, headstones, and monuments. Each British cemetery was contained by "a wall, within or without which is a hedge of thorn, beech, hornbeam, yew, or holly, or a screen of pleached and trained limes or hornbeams"; thus, each site was explicitly demarcated from the surrounding land—a quality that subtly compelled visitors to feel as if they had entered *British* territory (even if they happened to be in rural France). The CFA also highlighted the fact that each U.K. cemetery displayed a large "Cross of Sacrifice and an altar-like Stone of Remembrance bearing the inscription 'Their name liveth forevermore'"—objects that, through name and appearance, immediately conveyed the pseudo-religious notion that British soldiers had willingly offered up their lives in defense of a greater good. There were also more explicit nods to religious devotion: each headstone bore a cross or other religious symbol to indicate the interred soldier's faith. Although relatives of the dead were permitted to "plant dwarf polyantha, rose bushes, or bulbs on a particular grave"—eclectic and sentimental rhetorical activity that the CFA would likely frown upon in its own sites—the commission praised the work of the Imperial War Graves Commission (IWGC), which had approached its mission "with the view of 'so designing and planting their cemeteries that they shall serve for all time as worthy and permanent memorials to those who have so gallantly laid down their lives for their countries and empire.'"[107] Again and again the CFA insisted that the American cemeteries, like the British sites, should be "permanent" cemeteries that would ensure that the sacrifices and accomplishments of U.S. soldiers in the Great War would never be "forgotten or neglected."[108]

After praising these aspects of the temporary American and permanent British cemeteries, the CFA formally proposed its plans for the future U.S. sites. The CFA began by pointing out a fundamental problem that would require immediate correction: regrettably (in the eyes of the CFA), the temporary American cemeteries were, much like the military cemeteries of other nations, situated on flat—and thus, *lackluster*—terrain. "The impression an American now gets on approaching one of our cemeteries is of a handkerchief spread out on the grass to dry," the CFA reported. "The white spot has no vital relation to the great expanse of rolling country; it is a speck, and incident."[109] Offering a delicate jab at the romance garden gravescape (which encouraged visitors to lounge on picnic blankets) and the epic heroism gravescape (distinct for its level and unimposing surface), the CFA argued that the permanent overseas cemeteries should be established on sites that were not only historically important, but that also featured steep slopes or hillsides that could serve as natural pedestals for soldiers' headstones. Places like Suresnes (a hilltop town overlooking Paris), Belleau Wood (the site of the U.S. Marines' first ever combat engagement), and Romagne-sous-Montfaucon (situated in the heart of the Meuse-Argonne war zone) were symbolically significant locales that *also* were endowed with naturally beautiful inclines, elevated plateaus, or gentle slopes. The grassy and forest-covered hills of towns and regions like these would be ideal for amplifying the splendor and *presence* of the (in relation to other nation's cemeteries, comparatively fewer) American headstones. And by situating the U.S. cemeteries on elevated land the CFA would be able to extend its ideology of *verticality* and *space* (as exhibited in its work on the National Mall) to Europe.

Wherever they were ultimately located, the U.S. cemeteries would require "[b]uildings for service, gateways, and fences" that would contain and clearly designate the sites as *American*. The CFA believed that each site should feature a furnished rest house (something absent in the cemeteries of other nations) that would meet "the necessity of providing for American visitors." Seemingly conceptualizing the journey to a distant U.S. cemetery as a pilgrimage (a journey that would require effort, time, and energy), the CFA keenly anticipated the needs of future 'pilgrims.' But while the buildings, gateways, and fences would be designed to signify a sense of *Americaness* (a concept so important to nativists like Theodore Roosevelt during the years of World War I), the CFA promised that all of these structures would "be of such design and construction that they will appear to be at home in the country. This means simplicity, good proportions, and absence of ornament for the sake of ornament [...] and the eschewing of anything approaching boastfulness. We should remember that we are building in countries with fine architectural traditions and long histories."[110] Thus, the CFA indicated its awareness of both the needs of future American visitors and the potential danger of offending the sites' permanent European hosts.

Within the cemeteries themselves, the CFA intended to plant carefully situated trees and shrubs. "Almost any tree that will grow in America will grow in France," the CFA wrote. "Trees are enduring and require less care and attention than any other forms of planting." *Trees* would be the most prominent natural feature of the sites, as the CFA perished the thought of incorporating flowerbeds and the like (which carried so many outdated and non-militaristic nineteenth-century sentimental meanings). "Shrubs should be used sparingly, and flowers not all. Invariably attention given to flower beds is exercised at the expense of trees and grass, which are of first consideration." However, so as not to completely dismiss the possibility of the visual display of flowers, the CFA stated that on "Decoration Day and like occasions the use of flowers to express remembrance and honor is to be encouraged, but the existing rule requiring the removal of flowers before they are withered should be adhered to."[111] In it possible that these words were meant to soothe the minds of grieving American women who expected that their departed loved ones would rest in peaceful *cemeteries*, not just colossal and somewhat sterile national war memorials.

The 1921 report also revealed the commission's desire to organize and manage (within reason) the immediate territories surrounding the nascent permanent burial grounds. "All care should be taken to relate each cemetery to the town near which it is situated," the CFA argued. "There should be no parched and uncared-for area through which one must pass to go from town to cemetery." To secure this result, the CFA would attempt to line the roads between the towns and the cemeteries with newly planted, evenly spaced trees (something akin to the elm-lined pathways on the National Mall). "No one feature will count more than the adequate treatment of those short stretches of roadway into which one turns from main highways to reach the American cemeteries."[112] As for the battlefields and inevitable war monuments that would surround the burial grounds, the CFA advised Congress to pass legislation that would allow the commission to impose a system of order, uniformity, and artistic beauty. "If the history of our national dealings with battlefields where Americans have fought and died may serve as a guide," the commission wrote, "the people of this country will not be satisfied merely with providing a God's acre for the bodies of the dead." Casting the war, not as the destructive, apocalyptic event that Americans had viewed from afar between 1914 and 1917, but rather as the nation's noble participation in the fight for the defense of civilization beyond its borders, the CFA claimed:

> The places where our men lie are historic places. They are parts of that far-stretching line along which civilization itself, as we believe, set barriers against the onslaughts of brute force. They represent our part in that struggle, and in that part justly we take pride and satisfaction [...] It has not been possible, even were it desirable, to control the design and location of monuments that have been erected in France by divisions, regiments, or organizations [...] The American monuments to be placed in the park spaces connected with our cemeteries, however, should be controlled first as to historical accuracy of the inscriptions by the historical branch of the War Department and as to design and location by the Commission of Fine Arts.[113]

To give a concrete example of this problem, the CFA described the visual chaos of the region surrounding Belleau Wood (one of the locales the CFA had selected):

> Near by are squares of French white crosses and German black crosses. The approach to the [future] American cemetery is like a labyrinth. The improvised landscape effects [of haphazard, unofficial monuments] bear eloquent testimony to the feelings of the men who paused in their grewsome [*sic*] tasks to pay tribute to the heroism of the brave boys [who died]. These designs, crude and amateurish, were the foretaste of what thought and training may provide when the time comes to make permanent improvements.[114]

Here we see that the CFA wanted to establish the cemeteries in physical spaces that would be, at least to some degree, harmonious with the visual composition of the burial grounds themselves. While the CFA knew that it could not completely dictate the transformation of these foreign territories in the same way it had been able to oversee the razing, sculpting, and transfiguration of Washington, D.C., the CFA desperately wanted to minimize and ameliorate the visual bedlam of the unruly war torn areas that, in time (and for *all time*), would serve as the entryways and backdrops to the permanent American cemeteries.

The CFA's report concluded with brief descriptions of the sites deemed suitable for the cemeteries. The first was Suresnes, a small commune in the western suburbs of Paris. Mostly containing the remains of soldiers who had died of illness in Parisian hospitals, the Suresnes cemetery would be "reached from the Arc de Triomphe in Paris by a drive down the Avenue du Bois de Boulogne, through the wooded park and across the Seine, and a climb up the steep slopes to the Boulevard George Washington [...] a direct and short approach from the railway station is provided for those visitors who [would] not motor thither." Because of its nearness to Paris, its potential to provide a beautiful view of the city skyline and the Eiffel Tower, and its (presumed) enticing capacity to connect symbolically (via geographical immediacy) modern American sacrifice with French sacrifice (Arc de Triomphe) and U.S. history (Boulevard George Washington), the Suresnes cemetery would surely be "the most visited of all the American cemeteries in France." Thus, the CFA reasoned, the cemetery "shall represent adequately the deepest sentiment, expressed in terms of good taste. Suresnes should be the gem." Other French locations included Belleau Wood in the Chateau-Thierry region, the site of a famous and bloody battle between U.S. Marines and German forces; Bony, a rural town in the infamous Somme sector; Romagne-sous-Montfaucon, where the remains of tens of thousands of U.S. soldiers who had perished in the Argonne Forest were interred; Thiaucourt, "a shadeless plain near St. Miehel" (it would not be "shadeless" once the CFA dealt with it); and Fere en Tardenois, a quiet, isolated village nestled between the Oise and Aisne Rivers. The CFA also suggested the establishment of a cemetery near Flanders Field in Belgium (where hundreds of American soldiers still rested in temporary graves), and a burial ground in Brookwood Cemetery, a famous rural gravescape thirty miles southwest of London (English land was at a premium, but the CFA had been able to secure from the British government a small, but "no less fitting and significant," space within this necropolis for the graves of U.S. sailors and soldiers who had died in England or the surrounding waters during the Great War).[115] The CFA claimed that each of these sites would be an ideal venue for the establishment of a permanent American cemetery that would "be as sacred as a temple or a church."[116] In closing, the CFA urged the President, Congress, and the American people to support its work in Europe, whatever the financial costs might be. "If our cemeteries are not to fall behind those of Great Britain and France, we must adopt some comprehensive plans and carry them out thoroughly, as those nations are doing." Evoking the memory and spirits of distant fallen U.S. soldiers, the commission stated: "No question of expense should stand in the way of carrying out each and everyone of these requirements. So much our self-respect and the duty we owe to our dead require."[117] With that, the CFA rested its case.

The CFA's 1921 report was sufficiently persuasive. Editors at the *Washington Post* publicly supported the commission's official proposal, and opined that the appropriation the CFA sought "for this highly decorative and comprehensive, yet simple, scheme is modest in amount, something like $3,000,000."[118] In December of 1921, the federal government formally approved the CFA's plans and gave Chairman Charles Moore the funds required "for the beautification of American military cemeteries in France, England and Belgium" and "the purchase of adjacent lands to protect" the burial grounds.[119] By late 1922, the CFA had secured (and in some cases, purchased) appropriate tracts of land for eight permanent cemeteries.[120] In October of 1922, the Graves Registration Service began transferring soldierly remains from temporary cemeteries to the designated burial grounds, "except in cases where grading of permanent cemeteries held up re-interments." And by early 1923, the reburials were completed, contracts with local construction workers and craftsmen were finalized, and the erection and maintenance of the sites commenced.[121] The CFA's visions for these gravescapes started coming to life.

On November 11, 1921 (the third anniversary of the Armistice), the federal government performed a carefully choreographed burial of an "Unknown Soldier" at Arlington National Cemetery. Mimicking similar postwar ceremonies conducted by France and Britain, this unprecedented civic ritual was meant to forge national unity around the remains of an unidentified soldier (a powerful and self-evident token of individual [by virtue of the corpse's singular nature] and collective [by virtue of the the corpse's anonymous and, therefore, synecdochical nature] American wartime sacrifice),[122] situate the Great War within the country's greater history,[123] and signify the government's appreciation of its women who had sacrificed their men for the good of the nation and the world.[124] As the *Kansas City Times* stated earlier in the year:

> The proposal to bring back from France the body of an unidentified American soldier for burial with military honors in the Arlington National Cemetery has the approval of General Pershing and should have that of the nation. In no better way could the republic pay tribute to its mighty dead than at the bier of one who lost not life alone but name and identity. This is the seal of our democracy [...] The spectacle of these things strikes deep into human hearts and minds. Every mother's loss is also the nation's loss, let the nation bow its head with mothers and mingle with hers its tears. They will turn from that bier with strengthened hearts, renewed faith and fresh courage for the future.[125]

While symbolizing both the strength of American democracy *and* the government's concern for grieving next of kin, the burial of the Unknown Soldier *also* helped link the CFA's project in Europe back to the homeland. A few months prior to the memorial service in Arlington, the Unknown Soldier had been selected during a solemn ceremony at the City Hall of Châlons-sur-Marne, France. There, General John J. Pershing had ushered Sergeant

Edward Younger, a wounded veteran of the war, into the building, where four caskets—each containing the remains of an unidentified soldier—had awaited him. These four caskets had been exhumed from the CFA's military cemeteries at Aisne-Marne, Meuse-Argonne, Somme, and Saint Mihiel—each contained a dead soldier that, in effect, stood in place of *all* dead American soldiers left overseas. With a bouquet of white roses in his hands, Sergeant Younger had circled the coffins three times, laid the flowers on a casket of his choosing, and thus selected the body of the nation's Unknown Soldier. Escorted across the Atlantic by General Pershing, the body of this unknown American symbolically shortened the distance between the overseas military cemeteries and American soil.[126] And like the citizen-soldiers who had been conscripted during the war, the Unknown Soldier had been randomly selected (this time in death, not in life).

THE AMERICAN BATTLE MONUMENTS COMMISSION

As the CFA began its work in Europe, two related, but antithetical, problems arose. In the United States, a substantial coalition of veterans, next of kin, and politicians expressed anger over what they perceived to be the CFA's *unchecked* authority to develop the visual presentation of the permanent overseas military cemeteries as it best saw fit. Major General John S. O'Ryan, of New York, articulated this criticism best in a public letter to the War Department. Demanding the creation of a commission composed of veterans of the American Expeditionary Forces that would assume control of the cemeteries abroad, O'Ryan asserted that the CFA (in essence, a group of elite intellectuals) had conducted "its activities in France without due regard to the wishes of the families of the dead," and that the partially constructed permanent cemeteries "furnished another example justifying the criticism that when official America undertakes to express sentiment it measures its sentiment by the number of dollars to be expended."[127] Meanwhile, on the other side of the ocean, the CFA felt that it did not possess *enough* authority to impose its aesthetic system on the European sites and their surrounding regions. Despite its best efforts, the CFA had been unable to stop private individuals and veterans groups from erecting their own unsanctioned memorials on the battlefields that were to serve as the cemeteries' backdrops.[128] Additionally, it seemed the CFA—composed of artists and architects, not politicians and generals—was having trouble securing foreign officials' approval for a plan to erect giant, permanent "relief map monuments, outline sketch map monuments, special monuments and bronze tablets" on battlefields where Americans had fought and died.[129] Whereas the CFA dominated discussions of culture in the United

States, it held minimal sway with foreign dignitaries (whose own countries had older, and perhaps, more impressive, "fine arts" traditions).

In the eyes of CFA Chairman Charles Moore, the solution appeared to lie in the establishment of a formal "battle monuments commission" composed of civilians, cultural experts, and political and military figures alike.[130] Officially approved by Congress and the President, such a body, it seemed, would be capable of deflecting domestic criticisms of the European project *and* executing the CFA's ambitious and ever-evolving plans for the overseas memorial landscape. In March of 1922, Senator Henry Cabot Lodge introduced (at President Harding's bidding) a bill providing for the creation and funding of an "American battle monument commission" that would develop and supervise the cemeteries and memorials abroad.[131] The *Washington Post* supported the legislation, asserting:

> Monuments commemorating the deeds and achievements of Americans in Europe are due those who served and those to whom heritage of their glory will descend. The bill provides for the raising of markers to the American forces as an organization. They would be commemorative of all who participated in the great conflict. And this is as it should be. The expenditure in money that would be required for the construction of the proposed monuments would be as nothing to the expenditure in sacrifice by those who made the raising of them in order.[132]

In March of 1923, Congress, *at the urging of the Commission of Fine Arts,*[133] passed Lodge's bill and formally established the American Battle Monuments Commission (ABMC). Composed of seven commissioners, each appointed by the President at his discretion, the ABMC became responsible for

> establishing or taking over from the Armed Forces permanent burial grounds in foreign countries and designing, constructing and maintaining permanent cemetery memorials at these burial sites; controlling as to design and materials, providing regulations for and supervising erection of all monuments, memorials, buildings and other structures in permanent United States cemetery memorials on foreign soil; and cooperating with American citizens, states, municipalities, or associations desiring to erect war memorials outside the continental limits of the United States.[134]

A few months later, President Harding named the first members of the board: General John J. Pershing (who would serve as its first Chairman); Robert G. Woodside, of Pennsylvania, a wounded veteran of the 3rd Division and twice National Commander-in-Chief of the Veterans of Foreign Wars; Senator David A. Reed of Pennsylvania, and former Representative Thomas W. Miller of Delaware, both 79th Division veterans; Representative John Philip Hill and Colonel D. John Markey, of Maryland veterans of the 29th Division;

and, Mrs. Fred W. Bentley of Illinois, a representative of the Gold Star Mothers who had lost her son in the war. (Major Xenophon H. Price, a career army engineer, was named Secretary.)[135] Although the ABMC was, much like the CFA, entirely white and dominated by men, this new commission signaled (to grieving families and foreign dignitaries alike) a radical shift in the way the United States would handle its overseas commemoration projects. Filled with political movers and shakers, heroes who had seen the blood and terror of the war firsthand and a mother who had sacrificed her son for the betterment of America and all of Europe, the ABMC looked nothing like a board of stuffy cultural know-it-alls who had never gotten their hands dirty. Rather, each member of the ABMC knew what it meant to fight and die in battle (or send others to fight and die in battle). More important—from General Pershing (arguably the most famous military figure in the world at that moment[136]) to Mrs. Bentley (a grieving mother)—each commissioner possessed symbolic capital that was easily identifiable to the American people and their European counterparts.

By all appearances, the newly formed ABMC had usurped the CFA's authority over the design and development of the overseas cemeteries. In reality, this was hardly the case (a crucial point that scholars have neglected).[137] Section 124 of the American Battle Monuments Act—a small provision quietly slipped into the lengthy legislation—stipulated: "Before any design for any memorial is accepted by the [ABMC], it shall be approved by the National Commission of Fine Arts."[138] The bill also prohibited any U.S. governmental figure or agency from helping private citizens or groups erect memorials in Europe without the prior consent of the CFA.[139] Thus, as progress on the sites continued throughout the 1920s, the ABMC was compelled to send every design plan and aesthetic decision to Washington, D.C., where it was scrutinized and rubber-stamped (or not) by the CFA, then sent back to Europe for the approval of foreign dignitaries. Inheriting sites already near completion, desperate for the professional guidance of Charles Moore and his cohort,[140] and compelled to submit every aesthetic decision to the CFA, the ABMC actually had *very little control* over the physical presentation of American battle monuments in Europe. In effect, the ABMC was a kind of Trojan Horse—an impressive and symbolically potent, but ultimately *empty*, vessel that could clandestinely smuggle the CFA's plans across the Atlantic and European borders. With international superstar "Black Jack" Pershing at the helm, the ABMC effectively publicized the overseas cemeteries to domestic audiences, enforced the moratorium on unsanctioned battlefield monuments,[141] negotiated land deals with governments and private citizens in France and Belgium,[142] and attended to daily oversight tasks at the eight American burial grounds. Meanwhile, the CFA was free to concentrate on, and dictate, the creative aspects of the project.

Further evidence of the CFA's ongoing and somewhat shadowy influence can be found in the fact that the ABMC hired Paul Cret as its supervising architect. One of the most influential Beaux-Arts style architects, neoclassical activists, and proponents of the City Beautiful and McMillan Plans in the United States, Cret had previously served as a member of the CFA (in fact, Charles Moore and the CFA had nominated Cret for the ABMC position).[143] Famous among elite circles for his conservative yet innovative and inspiring designs for the Organization of American States Building in Washington, D.C., the National Memorial Arch at Valley Forge National Historical Park, the Indianapolis Central Library in Indiana, and the Benjamin Franklin Bridge that connected Philadelphia and Camden, New Jersey, Cret opposed the self-aggrandizing excesses of the previous Gilded Age, yet sought to create civic architecture that transcended the everyday and utilitarian.[144] Criticizing the progressive push to establish "living memorials" after the Great War, Cret publicly stated: "Does our belief in 'utility,'—however temporary that utility may be,—denote a spirit superior to that which inspired the [...] Egyptian and Roman builders, who, intent upon conquering time, were willing to pay the price required, or does it bear witness only to a mean and short-sighted parsimony? [...] Suffice it to say that a work of commemorative architecture which has little chance of enduring is hardly worthy of the name."[145] In short, Cret was a CFA man through and through; his visions of a timeless, tasteful, awe-inspiring, yet *modernist*, brand of American civic architecture mirrored those of the CFA. Overseeing the day-to-day work of the ABMC's other architects (each of whom had strong ties to the CFA),[146] and designing the final visual presentation of the Flanders Field American Cemetery and Memorial in Belgium himself, Cret made sure the overseas project never strayed from the CFA's chosen path.

This is not to say that the ABMC's role in the design process was completely negligible. Chairman Pershing, in particular, took great interest in the day-to-day progress of the sites. Having always fancied himself a renaissance man of sorts,[147] Pershing did not hesitate to share his opinions with ABMC architects as they made important on-the-spot decisions.[148] Because "Black Jack" was, more or less, the face of the ABMC,[149] architects (including Cret) and other ABMC workers must have found it difficult to take his words lightly. Known for his blunt speaking style and willingness to express his beliefs (no matter how controversial),[150] Pershing surely cast a dominating presence during his visits to the burial grounds. And while Pershing and the other members of the ABMC could not speak authoritatively on matters of architecture and landscape design, they felt empowered to weigh in on smaller, but ultimately *pivotal*, aspects of the cemeteries' visual presentation. Most notably, at its third official meeting on November 8, 1923, the ABMC announced that, "it was the sense of the commission that the form

of the headstone used in the cemeteries abroad should be that of a cross."
Until that moment, the CFA had planned to erect standardized flat markers
like those seen at Arlington. Senator Reed, a religious conservative, was
particularly adamant about imbibing the overseas cemeteries with a Christian
character since, as he put it, "the United States is a Christian nation." (Following a series of heated negotiations with the Jewish Welfare Board, the
ABMC would also advocate the inclusion of headstones in the shape of the
Star of David for fallen Jewish soldiers.)[151] The ABMC's decision to erect
headstones in the shape of iconic religious symbols was an inspired and radical modification of the CFA's plans—but one that ultimately coincided with
the CFA's ideological emphasis on "space." As cultural historian Ron Robin
states, the "Latin crosses or Star of David perched on thin supports [...] created an optical illusion of even greater spaciousness and increased the 'private territory' of each individual plot."[152] In time, this grave marker design
would become the most prominent feature of America's cemeteries abroad,
and would help distinguish the sites from domestic military burial grounds
and the World War cemeteries of other nations. Still, every aesthetic decision—including the question of headstone design—had to meet the standards
and approval of the CFA. Thus, the CFA retained immense control over the
final visual presentation of the overseas cemeteries.

In June of 1924, the ABMC commissioners embarked on a six-week
tour through Western Europe to examine the progress of each permanent
American cemetery and acquire information and inspiration from the cemeteries of other nations. Two years later, it submitted a report of this tour
to President Calvin Coolidge and Congress. Conventionally titled, *Annual
Report of the American Battle Monuments Commission to the President
of the United States for the Fiscal Year 1925*, the report systematically,
yet eloquently, recounted the expedition's findings: "Each of the eight
American military cemeteries was visited for the purpose of obtaining
accurate first-hand knowledge of its condition and determining what further works of architecture and art were needed to make it a fitting resting
place for our heroic dead." Although pleased to announce that the general
condition of the U.S. cemeteries was satisfactory, the commission offered
a caveat: "There is [...] much still to be done."[153] Composed of seventy-
five pages of text and photographs depicting the physical attributes of the
evolving American cemeteries abroad and the World War cemeteries of
other European countries, the ABMC's 1926 report served as an appraisal
of the overseas project, a visual and verbal exposition of the monumental
cemeteries' splendor and beauty, a declaration of the work still yet to be
done, and a request for continued and adequate funding from Congress (as
the CFA and the ABMC's ambitions had expanded, the project's costs had
ballooned).

From a present-day perspective, the 1926 report stands as the most concise and transparent statement about the motives and decisions that led to the final visual presentation of American World War I cemeteries in Europe. Most notably, analysis of the document reveals the cemetery planners' fundamental concern for meeting the physical needs and influencing the emotions of itinerant visitors. Throughout the report, the commission articulated how the cemeteries' physical characteristics—geographical location, careful presentation of natural foliage, appearance of upkeep and investment, artistic and architectural aesthetics, prominently displayed lists of information, and general sense of uniformity and order—could frame audience reception of the visual/material expressions of U.S. participation in the Great War.

Consideration of the aesthetic value of each cemetery began with a description of its geographical location and surroundings. The ABMC revealed a distinct affinity for the burial grounds that were situated on hills and provided panoramic views for visitors (such as Suresnes Cemetery), or utilized peaceful, wooded inclines as scenic backdrops (Brookwood Cemetery). Whereas the IWGC cemeteries and most of the French cemeteries were situated on flat lawns, the ABMC cemeteries would be elevated on grass slopes whenever possible. The burial grounds that were positioned directly on battlefields still pock-marked with shell craters and blemished by corroding trenches and fossilized trees were, instead, praised for their proximity to historically significant (rather than naturally beautiful) surroundings; for instance, Meuse-Argonne Cemetery, the largest of the U.S. cemeteries (where 14,045 soldiers were interred), was credited for containing the remains of men who had given "their lives in the Meuse-Argonne operation, the greatest battle in American history and one of the most decisive offensives of the war." The ABMC suggested that the publication of an American guidebook to the devastated battlefields might amplify the significance of the cemeteries that were unfortunately situated and, just as vitally, combat the dissemination of "a large amount of inaccurate and misleading information concerning the work of the American forces." The most popular battlefield guidebooks, the ABMC stated, "have been prepared by Europeans and present everything from their own rather than the American point of view."[154] Because the U.S. cemeteries were surrounded by battlegrounds, these "inaccurate and misleading" histories would (in the ABMC's view) likely alter visitors' understandings and perceptions of the American burial grounds.

The report continued with a description of the cemeteries' presentation of natural foliage. "It has been stated by the National Commission of Fine Arts that in preparing the plans for these cemeteries the older parts of the Arlington National Cemetery, near Washington, were used as a model," the ABMC wrote. "In these parts, the headstones are small, of a uniform type and spaced rather far apart. The entire area is covered by large trees, and the combination of the headstones and trees, with the attendant light and shade, produces a very beautiful and restful effect." The report included a photograph of an old section of Arlington to reinforce the ABMC's point.[155] Natural foliage, consisting of carefully managed trees and shrubbery, was an inherent aspect of the CFA and the ABMC's plans. "The cemeteries have been designed with the idea that trees and shrubs will furnish the main element of beauty," the commission reported. "These of course are still in their early stages of growth, and the ultimate appearance of the cemeteries can only be visualized in imagination." Emphasizing the importance of natural beauty, the ABMC argued for the immediate funding of the planting process: "The growth of trees and shrubs should be encouraged by all possible means, and ample appropriations should be made for this purpose. The first step in this direction is to insure that the water supply at each cemetery is made adequate and certain." The future foliage, however, was not to detract from the permanent nature of the individual headstones themselves: "Growing flowers are not placed on each grave. In our cemeteries this was thought undesirable, because flowers bloom only at certain seasons of the year and the expense of growing them is very great." Thus, the cemetery planners were acutely aware of the status of the cemeteries as a work of art in which the landscape played almost as great a role as the visual organization of the dead themselves. In light of the plan to expand the use of trees and shrubs, the commission stated that the natural elements of the cemeteries were to remain well tended and kept up, as the ABMC members had been "impressed by the fact that the cemeteries have been well cared for, and in general are well arranged. The combined effect is altogether pleasing, especially when it is considered that the trees and shrubs have had such a short time to grow."[156] In time, the proper maintenance of landscape would become a permanent custom at each ABMC cemetery. In his memoir, William P. Jones, Jr., Director of Engineering and Maintenance for the ABMC from 1967 to 1974, recounts how he and other ABMC officers "literally became concerned if we found any weeds at all in the graves areas, lawns, or plantings." According to Jones, in comparison with the meticulously tended ABMC cemeteries, the Arlington Cemetery in Virginia "was a weed patch."[157]

The ABMC made it clear that Mother Nature, however well tended, could not alone provide the visual splendor required for cemetery visitors; additional architectural and artistic structures were still greatly needed at each site. The commission lamented the lack of decoration and artistic splendor visible at the undeveloped cemeteries: "Nothing has been done in these cemeteries in the way of works of architecture and art, except necessities, and these, as a general rule, are of the plain type. The caretakers' and rest houses are the only buildings. These are prominently located and are conspicuous for their lack of ornamentation."[158] The commission determined that each cemetery was to contain carefully planned architectural and artistic works that would complement the beauty and harmony inherent in its natural settings and foliage. For the most part, the expressiveness of these works would appeal to a religious sensibility. Nothing was to be of "the plain type." One of the commission's most forthright aesthetic decisions was to remove the wooden crosses that had marked the graves since the war and replace them with headstones made of white marble—a Star of David for those of Jewish faith, a Latin cross for all others:

> *Dr. Paul P. Cret, architect, of Philadelphia, was then asked to design suitable headstones of the same general dimensions as the wooden ones. As a result of this request Doctor Cret submitted to the commission a complete study of the question and four different designs for each headstone. Full-sized models were made of these and other designs by the Engineer reproduction plant of the Army and erected on the lawn at Washington Barracks. They were then inspected by the commission, which after much deliberation adopted unanimously the headstones shown in the accompanying photograph, these to be constructed of white stone or marble.*[159]

The ABMC supplemented this description with a photograph of Cret's final designs for the Latin cross headstone, with its artistic curves at the angles and slight flares to the arms, and the Star of David headstone.[160] The calculated decision to use marble headstones was in keeping with traditional western sensibilities (white marble was a favorite medium of the Ancient Greeks and Romans), and promoted the notion that the cemeteries were meant to be permanent sites of remembrance (wood rots, marble does not). The rows of white marble headstones were to glow radiantly against the green and flowery natural backdrop, reminding visitors who, exactly, served as the centerpiece of each cemetery. Furthermore, the headstones, manifestations of religious symbolism, would no doubt connote certain familiar meanings (sacrifice, salvation, and others) to most cemetery visitors.[161]

The planners' conception of the cemeteries entailed more than the organization and upkeep of the gravesites. Putting themselves in the place of future visitors, the ABMC expressed concern for the state of the cemeteries' approaches. Specifically, the entranceway and flagpole of each cemetery lacked the decorative quality needed to create a liminal zone, that crucial threshold where "the visitor is initiated into the meanings inscribed" within a given space.[162] The ABMC wrote: "One or more ornamental gateways of a type appropriate to a military cemetery have been placed at each cemetery [...] An ornamental flagpole has been placed in each cemetery, and an American flag flies from it during the day. This serves as a means of identification and is the first object seen when the cemetery is approached from a distance.

Figure 4.2   Paul Cret's headstone designs, as displayed in the 1926 report. U.S. National Archives and Records Administration, Record Group 117.

It is very appropriate that our soldiers rest under the flag for which they fought and gave their lives [...] The gateways and flagpoles are passable, but have not gone beyond that point."[163] From the quality of the gates and flagpoles, approaching visitors were to realize they were entering a distinct, and *American*, site that demanded some type of proper behavior and reaction. The condition of each gateway and flagpole called for further financial investment and artistic attention. The decision to place U.S. flags in prominent locations throughout the cemeteries reflected the iconic role that Old Glory had come to play in American life. In 1916, President Wilson had instigated the first observance of Flag Day—a national celebration of the American flag and a day for patriotic exercises and giving expression "to our thoughtful love of America." By the 1920s, the flag (redesigned by the CFA itself) had become a national totem—a sacred object of the nation's civil religion that demanded reverence and could mark a space as *American*.[164]

The report continued with a startling revelation: the planners believed that the cemeteries' architectural and artistic beauty would be enhanced by means of a chapel and a memorial to the missing. Years before, the CFA had toyed with the idea of building an enclosed prayer space at the Meuse-Argonne Cemetery—something that no other country had done.[165] Now, the ABMC was forcefully arguing that a "chapel of nonsectarian character should be erected in each of the cemeteries." Amplifying the sacred, religious ethos of each burial ground, these designated sites of prayer would serve many useful purposes. "If properly constructed," the commission wrote, the chapels would "give a sheltered place" for "meditation and prayer," offer visitors a "focus to the cemetery and thus attract attention away from the houses which are now the outstanding architectural features," and serve as a "testimonial of the Nation's debt to the men who are buried."[166] A unique, but inevitably costly, proposition, this idea reflected a mortuary trend that emerged during the 1920s: in an effort to become "one-stop, all-purpose establishment[s]," funeral homes had begun constructing on-site chapels where guests could sit, think, pray, and grieve.[167] The chapels also signified the ambitious nature of the CFA and the ABMC's plans. Finally, they represented the CFA's long-standing desire to control the movement and behaviors in crucial civic spaces; if funded and constructed, the chapels would serve as *designated* spaces where visitors would be encouraged and allowed to behave as they might in a church, temple, or mosque.

Artistically designed memorials to the missing, the ABMC determined, would augment the purposes of the chapels and the headstones: "Each battle-field cemetery should contain some sort of memorial upon which should be inscribed the names of those now carried as missing in action in the vicinity. This memorial will be the earthly record of these men in the same manner as the headstone is the earthly record of a man whose body has been located. This memorial can take the form of a separate monument or else of a memorial worked into the design of the chapels."[168] The memorials, like the headstones, were to serve as the "earthly record" of the dead (in this case, the missing dead). The commission's use of the term "earthly record" implied that the interred soldiers had been, or would be, accounted for in some other transcendent way (a notion that must have appealed to religious Americans).

Serving as architectural enhancements to the cemeteries, the memorials to the missing also represented the planners' broader, fundamental desire to construct 'lists' that reorganized the dead for public viewing. In its thoroughness, toward the end of the report, the ABMC recommended that each cemetery should have a "complete alphabetical list showing the location of all American graves in Europe regardless of whether they are in American cemeteries or not [...] a list of known dead whose bodies have not been recovered or identified [...] a list showing the graves in Europe according to organizations [and] an alphabetical list of women in our cemeteries."[169] These and other textual lists,[170] it seems, were meant to accomplish a series of tasks. First, they would reflect militaristic values of order and classification—American soldiers in death, as in life, were to be categorized and identified by function, position, gender, and other classifications. Second, the lists would verbally memorialize the individual and collective sacrifice of the dead. Third, they would remind visitors of the ABMC itself and its role in Europe (by displaying the names of the seven other cemeteries the ABMC had constructed elsewhere). Fourth, in keeping with the very nature of the cemeteries themselves, the lists would further account for, and put on display, soldiers whose bodies had never been found or identified. And perhaps most important of all, the lists would aid visitors who wished to identify particular interred soldiers. It is clear that the planners were fundamentally concerned with making the presentations of the dead accessible and understandable to visitors. Their concern was reflected not only in their discussion of these lists, but also in their discussion of the headstones: "As a result of the commission's investigation in Europe, it was informally suggested to the Secretary of War that before the permanent headstones were installed a study should be made concerning the abbreviations to be used on them. The reason for this is that many of the present abbreviations are so complicated that they can not be interpreted even by a person thoroughly familiar with Army organizations."[171] In these words, we can identify the planners' ambition to make the sites communicate clearly and effectively to itinerant visitors.

In order to communicate clearly and effectively, the ABMC argued, each cemetery would have to exude a sense of order and uniformity. As it unfolded, the report made it plain that the theme of *regularity* was a key component of the planners' designs. "All of the cemeteries [...] should be enclosed by masonry walls," the commission opined. "The present situation of having a wall on the road sides only is decidedly unattractive."[172] The ABMC asserted that visitor reactions would be greatly determined by the consistent nature of each cemetery's appearance. The arrangement of the wooden grave markers illustrated the commission's point:

> The graves in all cemeteries, with the exception of certain sections in the Oise-Aisne and Somme, have been arranged so that the markers are equidistant apart and in rows spaced at regular intervals. This regularity is very effective and adds greatly to the appearance of the cemetery. Where not regularly arranged, the effect is disturbing, as the graves are close together, and many spaces exist due to the removal of bodies for return to the United States and other places. This irregularity is very marked because in all cases these sections are immediately alongside of regularly arranged sections.[173]

For the planners, irregularity or inconsistency in the arrangement of the headstones produced an undesired and disturbing effect for the beholder. The ABMC believed that the grave markers of each cemetery were to be aligned equidistant apart from one another. Furthermore, the shapes of yet-to-be-made marble headstones were not to deviate from Dr. Cret's models: "The Commission considers it very important that no variations be made from the standard types of headstones adopted. The cemeteries were planned with this point in view, and a large part of their impressiveness and beauty will depend upon its being strictly carried out."[174] Thus, the planners had produced a plan that, much like an Army manual, say, was to be followed down to the last detail.

The ABMC expressed its acute awareness that the cemeteries were not only symbolic constructions, but also physical spaces upon which visitors would tread. Because each cemetery's design emulated a natural landscape, visitors were expected to spend a considerable amount of time walking around outdoors. Therefore, the commission was pleased with some of the steps that had been taken to accommodate the physical needs of itinerant visitors. For instance, the commission reported that rest rooms had been built at each cemetery. And the commission commended the extraordinary facilities at Meuse-Argonne Cemetery, stating that, "a rest house has been provided where meals may be obtained and a limited number of people can spend the night." However, more widespread consideration for the well-being of visitors, who would be far from home and exploring the cemeteries by foot, was required. For instance, the cemetery roads and paths needed repair so as to be easier on visitors' feet. "Most of the roads and paths [of the cemeteries] should be resurfaced, using very fine crushed stone," the ABMC wrote. "In some places this is very badly needed." Feet, as well as other body parts, would also benefit from sitting surfaces. Perhaps envisioning physically and emotionally exhausted elderly mothers who would require respites from all the walking, the ABMC contended that "[s]tone seats should be provided at each of the cemeteries. These can be of such a nature as to add to the beauty of a cemetery as well as to supply a real need. They should be carefully located so as to be useful and to take full advantage of the existing views."[175] While tending to feet and derrieres, "carefully located" stone seats would also allow visitors to maintain a connection with the cemetery via the beauty of the "existing views," even as visitors took breaks and rested.

Ultimately, the ABMC argued, the American military cemeteries abroad were to look as though the United States had invested proper amounts of money into them. The commission reported that the total cost of the memorials and chapels of the project would be $1,500,000. "This amount," the commission wrote, "is about 75 cents for each American soldier who served in Europe. It is believed that a more suitable, complete, and economical project can not be made." Furthermore, the ABMC declared, "[i]n the future the commission will require, besides the ordinary expenses of its office, a further appropriation of about $2,400,000 to complete the entire project as outlined in this report. When this project is completed, the entire operations of the American Expeditionary Forces in Europe during the World War will be properly commemorated." A suitable memorialization of America's dead, it seemed, depended on an increase of financial investment. After all, "the impression gained in almost every cemetery is that the work has been done with a minimum expenditure of funds. This is in direct contrast to the impression gained from a British cemetery, where everything is of the best."[176] The ABMC made it clear that the planners intended to produce sites of remembrance that not only honored the nation's war dead, but also rivaled the standards of commemoration held by Britain and other European nations.

The 1924 tour had taken the ABMC not only to the eight permanent American burial grounds, but also to British, French, Belgian, Italian, and German military cemeteries throughout Western Europe. The ABMC made it clear that the other nations' cemeteries had served as valuable sources of inspiration and models of what and what not to do inside the walls of the American cemeteries. In the 1926 report, the commission recounted its findings at these foreign cemeteries so as to reveal the origins of some of its ideas and amplify the necessity of matching the monumentality of other nations' burial grounds. For instance, the ABMC recounted how it had had met with members of Britain's Imperial War Graves Commission in the French town of Ypres to inspect various British cemeteries and memorials in the vicinity. Their tour leader, Colonel Sir Herbert Ellisen of the IWGC, had imparted some sobering information that revealed the magnitude of the British burial operations. "The British Empire had approximately 1,019,882 death casualties during the war," the ABMC reported. "There are about 1,000 British war cemeteries in France and Belgium, and British soldiers are buried in more than 1,500 communal cemeteries in these countries." Comparatively speaking, the magnitude of the British need to bury a million casualties overshadowed the American task of burying 116,000 dead.[177] The ABMC emphasized the impressive fact that, despite their postwar financial plight, the British had been able to maintain high standards of art and architecture for their expansive network of cemeteries.

With little doubt, the ABMC had attained more inspiration in the cemeteries of Britain than in the cemeteries of any other nation—it devoted ten pages of the report to British sites of remembrance. To begin, the ABMC was impressed with the consistency of design and theme they found in each British cemetery. "The British cemeteries have all been designed in accordance with certain general principles," the commission wrote. "The first of these is to secure, in so far as possible, the permanence of the graves... all engineering work is planned and executed with this idea of permanence in mind." The ABMC argued that the American cemeteries, like their British counterparts, should be built to last forever. "Another principle followed," the commission wrote, "is to make the graves themselves the most striking feature in the cemetery and the one to which the attention is irresistibly attracted." Above all else, the British cemeteries came across as *cemeteries,* where the markers of the dead, rather than edifices directly symbolic of the state, remained the main focus of each site. "To carry this out, the headstones are made of an attractive design, flowers are placed upon the graves, and the surroundings are planned so that the headstones will not be overshadowed by buildings or monuments." To support this description, the commission included a photograph of a British headstone. A medium shot, the photograph revealed the aesthetic play between the "attractive" glowing, white, marble marker and the site's ubiquitous natural foliage: the flowers on the graves, the green grass between the rows of headstones, and the hedges and trees in the background. The ABMC wished to reproduce such pleasing effects in its own sites.

The commission also paid notice to the general uniformity of the British headstones, stating, "The headstones are all of the same shape and general design. On each headstone to a known soldier the following appears: The name, age, military rank and unit; a cross or other appropriate religious emblem; a reproduction of the badge worn on the cap; and if the relatives desire, a text or other personal tribute chosen by them."[178] The vast numbers of British dead surely necessitated the mass production of a single model of headstone. But apart from meeting the demands of logistics, the standardized headstones worked to diminish the distinctions between individual British soldiers. Although militaristic hierarchy had kept the soldiers separated in life, the uniformity of the shape and design of the headstones made them virtually inseparable in death.

It should be noted, however, that the IWGC had sacrificed some of the uniformity of its cemeteries by allowing families of the dead to place personal inscriptions on the headstones. This policy had resulted in the appearance of thousands of texts that adhered to varied styles of remembrance. "In addition to the still hopeful ones about dawn and fleeing shadows," cultural historian Paul Fussell states in his famous book, *The Great War and Modern Memory,* "we find some which are more 'modern,' that is, more personal, particular, and hopeless." Some examples include: "Our dear Ted. He died for us": "Our Dick": "If love could have saved him he would not have died"; and "A sorrow too deep for words." According to Fussell, some of the personal inscriptions "read as if refusing to play the game of memorial language at all."[179] The fact that the 1926 report did not address this aspect of the British headstones fully indicates that the CFA and the ABMC were not interested in giving American families such an opportunity to disrupt the "memorial language" of the U.S. cemeteries.[180]

The ABMC closed its discussion of the British cemeteries by focusing on the religious symbolism, art, and accommodations for itinerant visitors present at each British site:

Each cemetery contains a large ornamental cross of white stone called the Cross of Sacrifice, which varies in dimensions with the size of the cemetery. This cross is the distinguishing feature of a British cemetery [...] The large cemeteries contain a Stone of Remembrance. This is a white monolith weighing about 10 tons and with the words "Their name liveth forevermore," carved on it [...] The larger cemeteries contain buildings and other works of art to relieve the bareness which would otherwise result and to afford shelter and seclusion for visitors.[181]

The overt Christian symbolism apparent in British headstones and each Cross of Sacrifice clearly struck the ABMC as something appropriate and necessary for its own sites. The commission was also duly impressed with the artistic qualities of the cemeteries. As Paul Fussell notes, the IWGC had contracted famed writer Rudyard Kipling "to devise almost all the verbal formulas employed by the Imperial War Graves Commission, from 'Their Name Liveth For Evermore,' carved on the large 'Stone of Remembrance' in each cemetery, to the words incised on headstones over the bodies of the unidentified: 'A Soldier of the Great War/Known unto God.'"[182] The fact that a public figure as influential as Kipling had been hired to enhance the rhetorical power of the IWGC cemeteries revealed the British commitment to maintaining a high-culture, artistic sensibility within their burial grounds. It is little wonder that the ABMC lamented that in the American cemeteries, "Nothing has been done [...] in the way of works of architecture and art." Finally, the ABMC lauded the buildings that provided shelter and seclusion to itinerant visitors of the British cemeteries—a feature it hoped to reproduce in the American burial grounds.[183]

In conclusion, the ABMC emphasized the staggering amount of money the British had invested in their military cemeteries and the speed in which the cemeteries were being constructed. "It is estimated that the work of the Imperial War Graves Commission will finally involve an expenditure of about $50,000,000," the ABMC stated, "and that the work will be entirely completed by the end of 1927."[184] Surely, the ABMC implicitly argued, the eight American cemeteries, in comparison with the 1,000 British cemeteries, deserved corresponding amounts of financial and physical devotion. "The commission is making all plans to complete the memorials of its project so that they can be dedicated on November 11, 1928, just 10 years after the signing of the armistice. This can be done, provided appropriations for the work are available."[185] In essence, the ABMC felt that if the British could afford to construct such places of memory and beauty, the Americans could do no less. Therefore, the necessary funds had to be appropriated for the commission to do its job.

In its report, the ABMC devoted much less discussion to the cemeteries of France, Belgium, Italy, and Germany. But of this group, French cemeteries received the most consideration. The ABMC noted that roughly half of the 237 French cemeteries were still undergoing completion. As in the British cemeteries, each identified French soldier would have an individual grave. The French, however, treated their unknown soldiers differently: "The remains of unidentified soldiers are to be placed in ossuaries located at various places along the front." Departing from the French, the Americans would bury the remains of unknown soldiers under individual headstones within the confines of the U.S. cemeteries. While the French cemeteries utilized the attractive qualities of flowers, trees, and shrubs, the cemeteries were "surrounded by live hedges" and "reinforced by barb wire," boundary markers that connoted feelings of exclusion rather than invitation. Of the French grave markers, the commission wrote: "The headstones will be of uniform design and will show the name, rank, unit, place and date of death, the words 'Mort pour la France,' and an emblem of religious faith (a cross for Christians, a Hebrew inscription for Jews, and a crescent for Mohammedans) [...] These headstones are made of artificial stone, cast in three pieces."[186] Though made of artificial stone, a material inferior to the white marble of the American headstones, the French headstones articulated the usual religious symbolism and identity markers of name, rank, and unit. The phrase "Mort pour la France" ("Died for France") clearly signified the alleged purpose of each French soldier's sacrifice.

Although the ABMC had traveled to Belgium and Italy, it offered little discussion of those nations' cemeteries. Of the Belgian sites, it wrote: "The Belgian procedure in regard to [military cemeteries and memorials] follows so closely that of the French that it will not be repeated here." As for the Italian cemeteries, the commission reported that, "The Italian cemeteries follow no general rules in their design, each one being developed individually to conform to local conditions and the ideas of the architect." While most of the Italian cemeteries were enclosed by masonry walls and most of the headstones were arranged in regular rows, the commission was not impressed with the fact that "a great deal of latitude is allowed in the decoration of individual graves." The ABMC reported that although each Italian cemetery adopted its own standard grave marker, "the use of a standard marker is optional, and the relatives may place any marker they desire over the grave. Most of the tombs of the higher ranking officers are very elaborate and ornate. Many of them have worked into their design fieldpieces and other relics of the war."[187] The ABMC surely rejected the independent nature of each Italian cemetery, which clearly violated the CFA's aesthetic and ideological sensibilities. Although they were dispersed throughout England France, and Belgium, the American cemeteries were to be regulated by identical principles to the extent possible.

Unsurprisingly, the ABMC devoted only five short lines to the German cemeteries:

> A number of German cemeteries and monuments were seen in France and Belgium. Pictures of some of these accompany this report. The headstones and monuments were all erected by the Germans during the war in the territory they occupied.
> German graves in France and Belgium are being cared for by these countries in the same manner as their own graves. This is in accordance with a provision in the Versailles treaty of peace.

The ABMC accompanied this brief passage with a stark photograph of four, irregular German headstones of dark color. Clearly the ABMC was not interested in glamorizing or emulating the sites that Germans had constructed "during the war in the territory they occupied."[188] While the American planners might borrow ideas from the cemeteries of the nation's wartime allies, they would never turn to the German cemeteries for inspiration.

The *Annual Report of the American Battle Monuments Commission to the President of the United States for the Fiscal Year 1925* achieved its intended effect. By June of 1927, President Coolidge and the governments of Britain, France, and Belgium had approved and publicly endorsed the plans outlined in the report, and the ABMC had secured all of the appropriations it had requested.[189] In essence, the CFA and the ABMC were untethered and free to turn their grand ideas into material realities. In late 1927, large quantities of white marble crosses and Stars of David started arriving from Italy; by 1929, their erection in the cemeteries was completed.[190] In 1932, the cemetery chapels (designed by Paul Cret and his team of architects) were finished. When construction of the ABMC's massive battlefield monuments (also designed by Cret and his cohort) ended in 1937, the commission held impressive dedication ceremonies at the eight American cemeteries (keynote speakers included General Pershing, Marshal Philippe Pétain, and President Franklin D. Roosevelt).[191] Twenty years after the United States' entry into the war, the nation's overseas military cemeteries were finally established.

THE CEMETERIES' FINAL VISUAL PRESENTATIONS

Still visited by tens of thousands of people each year, the eight U.S. World War I cemeteries in Europe appear today as they did when they were first opened to the public. Reflecting the planners' determination to impose a sense of regularity, all eight cemeteries share marked aesthetic qualities and ideological messages. For instance, each site contains neatly ordered and evenly spaced white marble headstones that cast their silhouettes on smooth green lawns, linear walking paths that meet at important axial intersections and intensify the feeling of geometric order, and an architecturally and artistically impressive stone chapel that is situated at a crucial (and often climactic) focal point. But at the same, each cemetery possesses unique visual characteristics that make it markedly distinct from the other sites; in other words, you have not seen all eight cemeteries if you have only seen one (or even several). This section offers brief descriptions of each American World War I cemetery so that we might begin to see the important similarities and differences between them.[192]

Flanders Field American Cemetery and Memorial is the smallest of the eight cemeteries. Displaying only 368 headstones, this quaint burial ground exudes a sense of peace that matches the spirit of John McCrae's famous poem, "In Flanders Field":

In Flanders fields the poppies blow
Between the crosses, row on row,
That mark our place; and in the sky
The larks, still bravely singing, fly
Scarce heard amid the guns below.[193]

Situated in the quiet suburban town of Waregem, Belgium, Flanders Field Cemetery is spectacular, yet gentle and low key. A graveled, tree-lined lane leads visitors from a bustling Waregem thoroughfare to the interior of this bucolic and awe-inspiring site. Closely cropped and manicured currant hedge, rhododendron, lilac, azalea, birch, ash, oak, elm, holly, maple, hydrangea, magnolia, spirea, and Japanese prune effectively transport visitors from the reality of modern life to an almost otherworldly and impossibly beautiful sanctuary. At the center of the cemetery stands a fifty-foot flagpole, atop which an American flag sways in the breeze. The flagpole's bronze-cast base features carved images of acanthus leaves, butterflies, seashells, oak leaves, acorns, and a circle of poppies—symbols meant draw one's mind to the natural splendors of everyday life and enhance one's sense of communion with nature.

The cemetery's interdenominational chapel[194] is relatively small, in keeping with the modest size of the burial ground. Designed by Paul Cret, it is set in a sunken garden, an attribute that provides greater depth to the small area and attracts attention to the Greco-Roman structure itself. Carved into the white Pouillenay stone above the chapel's bronze doors are the words: "GREET THEM EVER WITH GRATEFUL HEARTS." On the chapel's three outer walls appear inscriptions in English, Flemish, and French (but *not* German, one of Belgium's three official languages) that remind visitors of the alleged *universal, self-sacrificial nature of modern American soldiers*:

> THIS CHAPEL HAS BEEN ERECTED BY THE UNITED STATES OF AMERICA IN MEMORY OF HER SOLDIERS WHO FOUGHT AND DIED IN BELGIUM DURING THE WORLD WAR. THESE GRAVES ARE THE PERMANENT AND VISIBLE SYMBOL OF THE HEROIC DEVOTION WITH WHICH THEY GAVE THEIR LIVES TO THE COMMON CAUSE OF HUMANITY

Beneath these inscriptions visitors see bas-relief figures, classical in nature, signifying Grief (a nod to domestic suffering), Remembrance (a nod to America's post-World War I memorialization of fallen soldiers), and History (a nod to U.S. military accomplishments and might). Within the chapel, visitors discover an altar made of Grand Antique (black and white) marble, above which a rose-tinted marble panel displays a "crusader's sword" outlined in gold (all of which connotes religious sacrifice). Carved into the altar itself are the words: "I WILL RANSOM THEM FROM THE POWER OF THE GRAVE, I WILL REDEEM THEM FROM DEATH"—a quote from the biblical book of Hosea centered on the resurrection and eternal life of the righteous. Impressive candelabra and the flags of the United States, Belgium, France, Great Britain, and Italy flank the altar. The interior walls are made of rose-tinted marble and display the names of 43 American soldiers who died in Belgium, but whose bodies were never recovered. Above these names appear the Great Seal of the United States and the phrase, "IN MEMORY OF THOSE AMERICAN SOLDIERS WHO FOUGHT IN THIS REGION AND WHO SLEEP IN UNKNOWN GRAVES"—words meant to account for and revere Doughboys whose physical remains were never recovered or identified.

The chapel is the nexus of the cemetery, from which radial gravel pathways originate. Dividing and delineating the cemetery's four grave plots, these paths terminate at four shaded and secluded recesses. Designated as sites of contemplation, each of these nooks contains an ornamental urn on a pedestal, upon which are carved the insignia of the four American divisions that fought in Belgium (the 27th, 30th, 37th, and 91st). The graves themselves are evenly clustered so that ninety-two appear in each plot. Twenty-one unknown soldiers are buried at Flanders; each of their white marble headstones bears the statement:

HERE RESTS IN HONORED GLORY
A COMRADE IN ARMS
KNOWN BUT TO GOD

This inscription is similar to the one that appears on the Tomb of the Unknowns at Arlington National Cemetery ("HERE LIES IN HONORED GLORY AN AMERICAN SOLDIER KNOWN BUT TO GOD")—thus linking the overseas cemeteries once more to the homeland.

The grave markers of the other interred soldiers (some of which are shaped in the Star of David) display the respective soldier's name, rank, regiment, division, home state, and date of death. For instance, the headstone of Private Harry Volz—who died on the last day of the Great War—presents the following inscription:

HARRY VOLZ
PVT. 148 INF. 37 DIV.
WISCONSIN NOV. 10, 1918

Springing from the earth, yet still modest in height and close to the ground, the uniform and evenly spaced headstones radiate against the tidy green lawn and the English yew hedge, trees, and shrubs that frame each plot. Collectively, the white marble headstones address visitors from every angle and vantage point (near or distant). Individually, however, each marker—displaying unique information about the respective soldier buried below—respectfully invites visitors to approach and offer their undivided attention and careful consideration.

In contrast to the cemetery at Flanders Field, the Meuse-Argonne American Cemetery and Memorial in Romagne-Sous-Montfaucon, France, is impressive for its massive size. The largest of the eight cemeteries, Meuse-Argonne contains the graves of 14,246 fallen soldiers and spans 130 acres. The cemetery's land itself was captured by the 32nd Infantry Division during the Great War—thus many of the men buried there died on that very soil. Visitors are subtly reminded of this fact by the presence of the infamous Argonne Forest, which serves as the cemetery's backdrop. Visitors may enter the site through two portals, flanked by marble gatehouses; two eagle statues surmount each gatehouse. Generally rectangular in shape, the cemetery contains eight square plots of graves, each separated from the others by linear, tree-lined pathways; these linden trees provide a natural hallway of shade as visitors walk the paths. It should be noted that ABMC landscapers, to this day, vigilantly prune the tops and sides of these trees so as to make the trees appear uniformed, unchanging, and square-shaped; because each tree's growth is kept in check, it is possible to see the white rows of headstones from a distance. Situated on a relatively steep incline, the eight symmetrical grave plots induce visitors to walk uphill toward a memorial chapel that crests the slope.

In my experience, by the time one walks through the sea of seemingly countless headstones and reaches the stone chapel, one is physically tired and emotionally overwhelmed. The chapel is flanked by two loggias, open hallways that evoke thoughts of a monastery. The loggias contain an ornamental map of the Meuse-Argonne offensive and the incised names of 954 men whose remains were never recovered or identified. The floors of the pavilions at the ends of the loggias display directional arrows that direct visitors' attention toward the significant terrain where American soldiers fought and died. From one of the loggias, visitors can see the ABMC's Montfaucon Monument, a stone spire rising two hundred feet above the once devastated land. The chapel itself is Romanesque in style. In keeping with the "spatial monument" design that had become so prominent on the National Mall in Washington, a broad set of set of steps guide the visitor up to the chapel (in a similar manner as the steps of the Lincoln Memorial). In contrast to the gleaming bright stone of the chapel's exterior, the chapel entrance and the space inside look completely black and void of light—a visual effect that makes it seem as though one is about to pass from this world to some other. Reminding visitors of who should be in their thoughts (fallen U.S. servicemen), an inscription above the entrance reads: "IN SACRED SLEEP THEY REST." Inside, visitors walk past columns (on which are carved the heads of American soldiers), through a bronze filigree screen, and into an apse. In the center of the apse stands a flag-banked altar. As is common in various strictly religious venues (churches, Jewish temples, etc.), delicate sunlight passes through several stained glass windows to illuminate this silent space. Though instead of displaying images of saints or biblical figures (as examples), the colorful stained glass windows depict U.S. military insignia so as to commemorate and venerate the American regiments and divisions that fought in the region. Inscribed above the arches of the door, apse, and windows are the phrases:

GOD HATH TAKEN THEM UNTO HIMSELF
THEIR NAMES WILL LIVE FOR EVERMORE

PEACEFUL IS THERE SLEEP IN GOD
PERPETUAL LIGHT UPON THEM SHINES

Upon exiting the tranquil confines of the chapel and returning to the
outside world, one is greeted with a breathtaking, expansive vista of
the entire cemetery—and most conspicuously, the graves of fallen U.S.
soldiers—below.

Whereas the Meuse-Argonne Cemetery is impressive for its scale, the
Suresnes American Cemetery and Memorial stands out for its delicate
nature and meticulous, and perhaps unmatched, artistic and architectural
beauty. Situated on top of the wooded hill of Mont Valerien, the cemetery is elevated high above the city of Paris. Because of its proximity
to the City of Light, Suresnes has always been the most visited U.S.
World War I burial ground. Designed to be the "gem" in the crown of
America's cemeteries abroad, Suresnes features a gilded and gleaming
wrought-iron gate at its entrance. Upon entering, visitors are met with a
steep, linden-lined avenue that divides the two major grave plots. These
plots contain 1,541 graves, including the graves of a pair of brothers, a
pair of sisters (who had conducted volunteer work during the war), and
seven nurses. Carefully placed beech, weeping willow,[195] mountain ash,
horse chestnut, and paulownia trees appear intermittently throughout the
plots. The central pathway, and the grave plots themselves, guide visitors
upward toward a loggia-flanked chapel. Neatly manicured red polyantha
rose bushes create a border of color at the chapel's base, while tall pines,
yews, acacia, and hornbeam rise up behind the chapel to provide a naturally majestic frame.

One of the loggias at Suresnes features a sculpture in bas-relief of the
ghostlike figures of eleven weary U.S. soldiers. A memorial to unknown
soldiers, this frieze stands above the inscription: SOME THERE BE
WHICH HAVE NO SEPULCHRE. THEIR NAME LIVETH FOR EVER-
MORE. The other loggia leads to a "memorial room"—something no
other American cemetery features. Upon entering this subdued space,
one encounters a pure white statue of a grieving woman (an explicit and
moving representation of the domestic grief that gripped the nation after
the Great War). At the base of this elegant, yet melancholy, figure, visitors read the word: REMEMBRANCE. Walking across the Italian marble
floor to the back wall, one discovers a much longer statement that, once
again, advances *the ideograph of the universal, sacrificial modern U.S.
soldier*:

THE MEMORIAL HAS BEEN ERECTED BY THE UNITED STATES OF
AMERICA IN PROUD AND GRATEFUL MEMORY OF HER SOLDIERS,
SAILORS, AND MARINES WHO FAR FROM THEIR HOMES LAID
DOWN THEIR LIVES THAT THE WORLD MIGHT LIVE IN FREEDOM
AND INHERIT PEACE FROM THESE HONORED DEAD MAY WE TAKE
INCREASED DEVOTION TO THAT CAUSE FOR WHICH THEY GAVE
THE LAST FULL MEASURE

The chapel at Suresnes is made of a creamy French limestone. Four Romanesque columns support the chapel's peristyle; each of these columns presents
in large letters the inscription: PEACEFUL IS THEIR SLEEP IN GLORY.
Inside, the chapel's ceiling is paneled in French oak. A mosaic mural con-
stitutes the main aesthetic feature of this space. Situated behind the altar, it
depicts the Angel of Victory laying a palm branch on the graves of fallen
American soldiers. Four large bronze plaques are mounted on the walls, each
bearing the names of men who were buried or lost at sea during the Great
War. When leaving the chapel, visitors are greeted with a panoramic view of
Paris. The perspective makes it seem as though one is elevated high above the
Eiffel Tower (the tallest man-made structure in the world until 1930), which
can be easily seen in the distance.

If we conceptualize the Suresnes Cemetery as a "gem," then we might
think of the Aisne-Marne American Cemetery and Memorial in Belleau,
France, as a solid hunk of granite. Although it features objects of natural
beauty—red roses and multicolored shrubs like forsythia, laurel, boxwood,
Japanese plum, deutzia, mock orange, and Oregon grape—Aisne-Marne
exudes a decidedly stoic, militaristic, and masculine ethos unmatched by the
other sites. It maintains this character by virtue of its pro-war symbolism and
proximity to Belleau Wood, the forest where U.S. Marines engaged in battle
for the first time in American history. A pseudo-Mecca for the Marine Corps,
this cemetery mostly contains the graves of Marines who died in the Battle of
Belleau Wood or subsequent conflicts in the region. Aisne-Marne boasts the
tallest memorial chapel; standing eighty feet high, this phallic-like structure
(reminiscent of the Washington Monument on the National Mall) dominates
the visual plane. Set against the green of Belleau Wood's trees, the chapel
promotes unmistakable connotations of virility and strength. Carved into the
columns that flank the chapel's entrance are images of trench warfare: soldiers readying for a bayonet charge; automatic riflemen; artillery observers;
a machine gun crew; and, soldiers tossing grenades. The chapel's pediment
displays a prominent bas-relief carving of a medieval crusader in armor. This

Figure 4.3   Somme American Cemetery and Memorial, present-day. Author's own photograph.

barrage of pro-war, masculine symbolism continues inside. There, visitors discover a frieze that depicts a crusader whose shield bears a lion device for fortitude; scales for justice; a Gallic cock symbolic of France; a pommée cross on an apple blossom with a snake representing the Garden of Eden; and, a passion flower, a symbol of Christ's Crucifixion and Resurrection. Stained glass windows reinforce the message, depicting Saint Louis (one of the 'great crusaders'), Saint Michael triumphing over the dragon, and the Christian martyr Saint Denis (a patron saint of France). Featuring only one textual statement—the chapel altar is inscribed with the words, PEACEFUL THEY REST IN GLORY EVERLASTING—Aisne-Marne Cemetery makes the Flanders Field and Suresnes cemeteries seem downright verbose. A stoic celebration of masculine sacrifice and the violence of war, this site essentially lets the dead and the surrounding forests speak for themselves.[196]

Since we have begun to get a sense of the similarities and differences between America's World War I cemeteries, I will limit my description of the four remaining cemeteries to brief discussions of their unique features. The

Figure 4.4 Somme American Cemetery and Memorial, present-day. Author's own photograph.

Brookwood American Cemetery and Memorial in Surrey, England, is particularly small; covering just four acres, it holds the graves of 468 soldiers. This burial ground is unique in that it is located in the heart of a large, sprawling, labyrinthine civilian cemetery. Surrounded by a seemingly endless network of secular, Protestant, Catholic, Jewish, Islamic, Hindu, and Zoroastrian burial grounds, Brookwood is the most inconspicuous of all the American World War I cemeteries—one must truly work to find it. Upon reaching this secluded, shady spot, visitors must feel as though they have stumbled upon some fabled, undiscovered secret garden. The Oise-Aisne American Cemetery and Memorial in Seringes-Sur-Nesles, France, is famous for containing the grave of beloved poet Sergeant Joyce Kilmer, who was killed in battle just a short distance away. This site is also noteworthy for the fact that much of its symbolism emphasizes Christian themes of peace and rebirth. For instance, inside the chapel, an altar displays carvings of an olive tree for peace; a pelican feeding its young (a symbol of the atonement of Christ's redemptive sacrifice); the oak tree for strength, faith, and virtue; the eagle flying (Christ's Resurrection); and, the palm wreath and cross (the cross for Christian faith, the palm signifying the Christian's reward for his faith). The Saint-Mihiel American Cemetery and Memorial in Thiaucourt, France, is distinctive for its overtly sentimental rhetoric. In order to express its sympathy for grieving American women, the ABMC had allowed the mother of Lieutenant Walker Blaine Beale to commission and erect a statue of her son within the cemetery grounds. Dressed in his uniform, holding his helmet, and standing at ease, the effigy looks over the grave plot where the actual Walker Beale is interred. Below the statue appear the words:

> BLESSED ARE THEY THAT
> HAVE THE HOME LONGING
> FOR THEY SHALL GO HOME

A variation of the iconic hero statue, the Beale statue is a psychologically complex representation of a brave, but tragic, hero of the nation (not dissimilar to the effigy of Lincoln on the National Mall). An inscription on the exterior of the Saint-Miehel chapel also addresses (if somewhat subtly) the imagined sacred bond between fallen soldiers and their mothers back home:

> THIS CHAPEL HAS BEEN
> ERECTED BY THE UNITED
> STATES OF AMERICA IN
> GRATEFUL REMEMBRANCE OF
> HER SONS WHO DIED IN
> THE WORLD WAR

Finally, the Somme American Cemetery and Memorial in Bony, France, is remarkable for its spartan but effective design. Its squat, box-shaped chapel (the site's only prominent architectural feature) is located at the bottom of the cemetery's hill. Visitors enter the burial ground near the top of the slope, and work their way through the rows of headstones to reach the chapel. The chapel's interior is dark and subdued, as the only source of light is a cross-shaped window made of crystal glass; it feels as though one has entered a stone womb of sorts. Outside, the endless fields of grain that surround Somme Cemetery make it hard to imagine that this very land was once the site of mass murder, bloodshed, and psychic trauma. Of course, the 1,844 white marble headstones on display at this quiet, isolated burial ground serve as sober reminders of the Great War's ruthless tax on human life.

Figure 4.5 Chapel window, Aisne-Marne American Cemetery and Memorial, present-day. Author's own photograph.

A VISUAL RHETORICAL ANALYSIS

Despite the recent "boom" in public memory and visual/material culture studies across the humanities,[197] America's overseas World War I cemeteries have received scant attention from scholars. Whereas the military cemeteries of Britain, France, Germany, and Russia have been the foci of many scholarly works,[198] the American sites have been virtually ignored. The limited work that has been done rarely goes beyond thin descriptions of the American cemeteries' visual presentation[199] or all-too-brief accounts of scholars' contemporary, on-site, phenomenological interactions with the sites.[200] Cultural historian Ron Robin has offered the most thorough history and analytical critique of the American cemeteries abroad, but (I contend) his interpretations and judgments of the sites' political meanings and overall effectiveness fall victim to a lack of contextual understanding (a point I address below). Recently, Lisa M. Budreau, a research historian at the Office of The Surgeon General of the United States, engaged the sites in her book, *Bodies of War: World War I and the Politics of Commemoration in America, 1919–1933*. Although Budreau devotes an entire chapter to the American overseas burial grounds, Budreau does little more than echo Ron Robin's previous assertions. And like Robin, G. Kurt Piehler, et al, Budreau ignores the rhetorical foundations that emerged *during* the war (as her book's title explicitly reveals) and fails to appreciate the CFA's dominant role in the postwar project (again, a point I address below). In short, America's overseas World War I cemeteries have not received the careful scholarly consideration they deserve.

What explains this dearth of scholarship? Surely it is not a lack of interest in the intersections of American war rhetoric, public memory, and visual/ material culture, for these intersections have become popular subjects of study in recent years. Perhaps the biggest factor is the Atlantic Ocean; while American scholars have relatively easy access to pertinent historical documents held at the U.S. National Archives and other repositories, conducting on-site research at the eight cemeteries abroad (in order to bring the documents to life) is a costly and time-consuming proposition; at the same time, while European scholars enjoy immediate physical access to the U.S. burial grounds, crucial information (written in *English*) concerning the sites' genealogy and meanings can only be found thousands of miles away in American archives and libraries; in other words, a truly thorough analysis of the sites requires much hard work, dedication, and investment of resources.[201] The lack of scholarship may also be explained by the fact that the historical, ideological, rhetorical, and physical complexities of these idiosyncratic burial grounds (which are, themselves, dispersed across Western Europe) are overwhelming to the individual scholar; thus, it is far easier to pay mere lip service to the cemeteries' appearance and supposed political meanings.

Whatever the case, the standing research has been relatively simplistic and deficient. Working without the foundational knowledge I have sought to provide in this book, scholars have not had at their disposal the analytical tools necessary for an appropriate understanding of the sites and their significance. As a result, the cemeteries have received a rather misguided and negative appraisal. Without doubt, their harshest critic has been Ron Robin, who generally considers the sites to be coercive, yet failed, articulations of American political and military might. Neglecting the CFA's central role in the establishment of the cemeteries, lumping the World War I sites with the U.S. World War II overseas cemeteries built twenty years later, and claiming that the burial grounds' visual presentation reflects General Pershing's alleged personal agenda (a personal agenda for which he provides little evidence), Robin builds his critique on faulty premises.[202]

Throughout Robin's scholarship, two pointed criticisms emerge again and again. The first is that the cemeteries "fail" as "artifacts of political architecture" because they are not *American* enough. In his 1995 essay, "'A Foothold in Europe': The Aesthetics and Politics of American War Cemeteries in Western Europe," Robin states:

> [T]he actual decision to erect large American cemeteries abroad demonstrated a willingness to alert the world to the presence of a new and omnipresent world power.
>
> However, the symbolism employed was self-defeating. By emulating the iconography of European culture instead of developing uniquely American symbols, the United States failed to capitalize on its contribution to the war effort.[203]

Of course, by overlooking the reality that the sites were almost entirely of the CFA's making, and that the CFA had always sought to extend the classical aesthetics of its domestic Beaux-Arts projects to the cemeteries abroad, Robin mistakenly compares the American burial grounds to the architectural designs and artistic styles of European cemeteries, memorials, and buildings alone. Robin's second major criticism is that the cemeteries' symbolism is disingenuous and irreconcilably contradictory in nature. With regard to the cemeteries' duplicity, Robin argues that, while the sites incorporate the graves of African-American soldiers, they deceitfully cover up the racial schisms of American life; that the cemeteries do not address the crucial role that modern military technologies played in the war; that the themes of egalitarianism and voluntarism erased "any sense of individuality" in the cemeteries; and, that the use of traditional architectural designs assure a sense of continuity at the cost of acknowledging "the gash of the Great War."[204] As for their incompatible physical attributes, Robin criticizes the juxtaposition of classical Greek styles with visions of the Medieval Crusades (both of which he labels as "anachronistic"); the evocation of "historical symbols to rationalize a contemporary tragedy"; and, the blatant contradiction between the sites' muted celebration of the United States' decisive role in the war and the imperious decision to establish the overseas cemeteries in the first place.[205] In the end, Robin pans the sites, describing them as "weak, inconclusive, and indicative of a naïve concept of international affairs [...] a confusing mixture of the various cultural trends affecting the American nation during the [early twentieth century]." For Robin, the cemeteries provide little more than "a small window through which we may peer at an American society coming to terms with a brave new world."[206] While certain aspects of these criticisms and judgments are not entirely incorrect, Robin has failed to take into account the domestic public discourse and the rhetorical constraints that shaped the CFA and the ABMC's aesthetic decisions and, eventually, the final visual presentations of the sites.

Seeking to set the record straight, in the following pages I will offer a visual rhetorical analysis of the cemeteries that (I believe) treats the sites more fairly and demonstrates their rhetorical power. My intentions are two-fold. First, I hope to correct some of Robin's misperceptions. Second, I hope to provide a richer analysis of the cemeteries that may be useful to interested readers and future scholarship on the subject. By no means do I claim that my interpretation will be definitive. I expect that these burial grounds will receive increased attention in the coming years, especially as the 100th anniversary of U.S. participation in the Great War is upon us. Without doubt, future scholars will conduct research, unearth materials, and publish works that supplement and, in all likelihood, challenge my own analysis of the burial grounds. Thus, one of my primary goals is to offer these future scholars a thoughtful critique that aids their own findings.

To begin, the burial grounds emulate "the iconography of European culture" (as Robin puts it) only in as far as the aesthetic principles of the City Beautiful movement, the Beaux-Arts school of design, the McMillan Plan, and contemporary American symbolism (in general) emulated the iconography of European culture. In reality, the cemeteries are not simply the material manifestations of General Pershing and the other ABMC commissioners' (untrained) imaginations. Nor are they mere conglomerations and reiterations of European cultural iconography. Rather, these sites represent and reflect the ambitions of the U.S. Commission of Fine Arts, a powerful government-funded agency that sought to extend its ideologies of neoclassical design, ordered public space, permanent architecture, and the management of citizens' bodies to the nation's overseas military cemeteries. The Greco-Roman style of the marble and limestone chapels, for instance, are in keeping with the CFA's veneration of neoclassical design (epitomized by the CFA's design of the Lincoln Memorial in Washington, D.C.). Much like the Acropolis in Athens, the Winged Victory of Samothrace at the Louvre, and the Washington Monument on the National Mall, the cemeteries' chapels, memorials, and white Italian marble headstones were constructed so as to last for all time. The uniformly spaced, standardized headstones—evenly divided between symmetrical grave plots—reflect the CFA's ambition to correct the messiness and vicissitudes of crucial civic spaces with carefully planned landscape and architectural "systems" and "compositions." The linear pathways that guide visitors through the plots and to the chapels, the directional arrows that steer one's vision toward significant sites of American battlefield glory, and the chapels (*designated venues* for contemplation and prayer), are telltale signs of the CFA's belief in establishing "flow spaces" that both shepherd visitors along planned routes and induce a particular and narrow set of experiences and rhetorical activities.[207] The seemingly endless rows of grave markers, usually elevated upon a slope, collectively address the visitor at all times and from every angle; much like the citizens and tourists who traverse the National Mall in D.C., cemetery visitors are more or less props in the respective burial ground's spacious panorama; in essence, every visitor who enters the site is transformed into what we might term 'an American pilgrim.'[208] And the cemeteries' heavy reliance on easily recognizable symbols—the Latin cross, the Star of David, the American flag, the heroic Christian crusader—help the sites amplify abstract notions of American democratic virtues and military might *and* obfuscate the complex, contradictory, and disturbing details of history that would otherwise make celebration of the dead all but impossible.

Recognizing that these national war memorials were first and foremost *cemeteries* where the remains of dead human beings would be buried, the CFA and the ABMC infused the sites with the aesthetics of familiar American gravescape designs so as to meet the expectations of grieving families back home. Carefully incorporating and synthesizing at each site the religious iconography of the memento mori gravescape (most notably the cross), the romance garden gravescape's emphases on individualism and the union of art and nature, and the epic heroism gravescape's egalitarian and spacious "lawn cemetery" scheme, the planners created *a new kind of burial ground* that nonetheless would be recognizable *as a burial ground*. ('Religion,' 'nature,' 'art,' and 'space' are concepts that readily come to mind as one encounters each site.) Functioning as *burial grounds*, these sites necessarily had to attract attention to the *soil* where the dead were interred. Transgressing their own sensibilities regarding *space* and *grounds*, the planners placed unique and relatively detailed information on the headstone of the respective soldier buried below; thus, the planners found a way to invite visitors to become addressers (not just addressees) and direct their attention to individual markers situated close to the *ground*. Likewise, gorgeous, but vigilantly manicured, flower beds, emitting fragrant scents into the air, ultimately were planted throughout the cemeteries so as to add natural beauty without distracting from the sites' larger messages. The planners also ingeniously built living quarters for a cemetery director at each site (something that no other nation did). A professional position that had become ubiquitous with the rise of the epic heroism gravescape, the cemetery director was charged with managing the day-to-day care of his respective burial ground.[209] Families of the fallen must have been glad to know, not only that an American citizen would tend to the daily maintenance of their loved ones' graves, but that an American citizen would serve as a constant guardian for their loved ones who were buried thousands of miles away.

Of course, the sites were designed to be not only cemeteries, but also *military cemeteries*. As such, they had to meet the expectations of military personnel (and perhaps most of all, General Pershing), who would insist that the cemeteries connote pro-war sentiments and celebrate the accomplishments and prowess of the modern U.S. armed forces. The prominently displayed headstones of fallen soldiers—standardized in form and situated in an almost hypnotic, mechanized, and ultra-modern scheme—immediately accomplish these tasks. As if standing at attention, the headstones signify the ultimate sacrifice that U.S. troops made for both their nation and the world. But beyond that, the cemeteries contain plaques that list the names of American soldiers who died but whose remains were never found, tributes to specific divisions (within several cemetery chapels, stained glass windows display the insignia of the divisions that fought in the respective regions), representations of Christian crusaders (those heroic warriors who fought for Europe in God's name), friezes and statues that depict stoic and noble U.S. soldiers in uniform, and depictions of early twentieth-century technologies of war (such as the carvings of cannons, machine guns, and grenades that appear at Aisne-Marne). Moreover, to reach the cemeteries in France and Belgium, one must drive through the vast regions that, at one time, constituted the Western Front; while traversing this part of Europe, one inevitably encounters numerous World War I battlefields, war memorials, and military cemeteries (mostly British, French, and German); thus, by the time one reaches any of these American cemeteries, the sites have been properly framed within the larger context of the Great War (and by deduction, war, militarism, and state-sponsored violence in general).

At the same time, it was expected that these burial grounds would suture critical, contemporary American social divides and display the dead soldier as an ideal model of the U.S. citizen (much like the cemeteries of the Civil War had done). To the first end, the cemeteries incorporate the graves of Christian soldiers (marked by the Latin cross), Jewish soldiers (marked by the Star of David), and African-American soldiers (who, for the first time in U.S. history, received somewhat equal, formal recognition of their wartime contributions and sacrifices). However, while containing the graves of black soldiers, the cemeteries fail to celebrate African Americans in any prominent fashion (a key and accurate aspect of Ron Robin's criticism of the sites). The only way one would know if particular interred soldiers were African

Americans was if the visitor knew to look for the graves of members of the 92nd and 93rd Divisions (the American Expeditionary Forces' "colored" divisions). Literally consumed into the whiteness of the marble headstones, the inscriptions of black soldiers' names fail to mark the men's racial status in the same way that their skin pigmentation had adversely marked them in life—the sites are, in essence, colorblind. Moreover, none of the plaques, friezes, or statues displayed at these sites honor black American soldiers in any discernible way. Ultimately, the cemeteries, much like the National Mall, amplify visions of American white male heroism. Thus, as Robin aptly points out, the cemeteries cover up and whitewash the great racial schisms that plagued early twentieth-century American society (from the CFA and the ABMC's point of view, however, the cemeteries adequately sutured this critical social divide). Sadly, by hiding the presence and wartime accomplishments of African-American soldiers, the cemetery planners missed an excellent opportunity to right a wrong symbolically and pronounce to the world the United States' alleged commitment to freedom, justice, and equality for all.

To the second end (displaying the dead soldier as an ideal model of the U.S. citizen), each site is nothing less than a grand shrine to the nation's citizen-soldiers. At each cemetery, the following inscription appears (usually on a chapel wall): "DEDICATED TO THE MEMORY OF THOSE WHO DIED FOR THEIR COUNTRY." And at each burial ground, at least one prominently placed flagpole displays Old Glory, which gently sways in the wind above the soldiers' grave markers (the intimate relationship between the dead soldiers and the nation is patently clear). The homogeneity of the headstones themselves is disrupted when one begins to read the ethnically diverse surnames of the individual soldiers. Baker, Fitzpatrick, Hoffmann, Jensen, Johnson, Kowalski, Levi, Libertucci, Lopez, Olson, Novak, Pavluk, Petit, Popothedoron, Toth, Zdancewicz—the heterogeneity of the U.S. population (one of the nation's most important and virtuous attributes) is poignantly on display to international visitors. Just as vitally, the inscribed names remind American visitors that every ethnic community sacrificed its men for the nation; thus, the World War is cast a great equalizer that brought previously divided and neglected ethnic communities into the country's fold.

Given the fact that these military cemeteries were to be established *overseas*, the planners had been faced with several daunting and unprecedented challenges. The first was to make the sites match (or perhaps even exceed) the monumentality and aesthetic beauty of other belligerent nations' burial grounds. But the planners could not allow the sites to extol the American nation and its citizen-soldiers in ways that might overstep the bounds of good taste; after all, American casualties of the Great War had been comparatively light to those of Britain and France, and the U.S. cemeteries would be, in a sense, the permanent guests of their host countries. Borrowing ideas predominantly from the cemeteries of Great Britain (an English-speaking state power that had established hundreds of its own World War cemeteries throughout *foreign territories*), the CFA and the ABMC successfully incorporated certain aspects of Allied cemeteries (such as the overt religious symbolism found in French and IWGC burial grounds) into the American sites. When compared to the colossal size of the Washington Monument and the Lincoln Memorial on the National Mall, the U.S. cemeteries seem to have been designed with measured restraint; the headstones, trees, memorials, and chapels (except for the one at Aisne-Marne) stay relatively low to the ground. Yet at the same time, the cemeteries (and the objects they contain) tend to be situated on slopes that elevate them above the visitor's plane of vision, a trait few European cemeteries feature; thus, the planners found a way to make the sites tastefully monumental and distinctly *American* without offending.

The second challenge was to make the cemeteries' meanings comprehensible to international audiences across time. Harnessing the talents and expertise of the finest skilled architects and artists, the planners settled on traditional (rather than forward-looking) materials (marble, stained glass, gilded iron, and natural foliage), symbols (religious, nationalistic, militaristic, and pacifist), texts (biblical quotes and lofty rhetoric written in English and local dialects), and time-tested themes (neoclassicism, democracy, and the Christian crusades) that would connote easily recognizable, if somewhat abstract, messages about the character of the United States to American and European tourists alike.

Additionally, the planners had to find ways of re-linking the cemeteries, and the soldierly remains they would contain, to the American homeland. The mere fact that the fallen U.S. soldiers are buried in, more or less, the soil where they had spilled their blood—not to mention the fact that England, France, and Belgium gave the various pieces of land to the United States in perpetuity—goes a long way in constituting the sites as *American soil*. Still, the planners found ways of reinforcing the notion that when visitors enter the cemeteries they are, in essence, walking on American territory. For instance, the planners created partitions and liminal spaces (pathways, walls, gates, and gatehouses) and erected physical objects (such as flagpoles bearing Old Glory) that effectively separate the cemeteries from the European lands that surround them. The planners also inscribed on each soldier's headstone his respective home state, thereby reminding the visitor of the relationship between the soldier's grave (on which the visitor stands) and (as in the case of Joyce Kilmer) the State of New York thousands of miles away. And in several cemeteries, the planners displayed textual inscriptions that explicitly classified the cemeteries as timeless meeting spots where Americans could commune with their heroic, fallen countrymen. For instance, the chapel of Suresnes exhibits the following words: THIS MEMORIAL HAS BEEN ERECTED BY THE

UNITED STATES OF AMERICA AS A SACRED RENDEZVOUS OF A GRATEFUL PEOPLE WITH ITS IMMORTAL DEAD.

Perhaps the most pressing task the planners faced was incorporating into the cemeteries the kind of sentimental rhetoric that had become so prevalent and (for the government, at least) *necessary* during the postwar years. To fulfill this obligation, the CFA and the ABMC planted trees and foliage (key attributes of the romance garden gravescape), as well as delicate flowers, to connote perennial thoughts and feelings of love, affection, beauty, mourning, innocence, remembrance, purity, happiness, hope, wonder, grace, rebirth, eternity, and God's presence.[210] At each cemetery, textual inscriptions couch death in the soft and gentle terms of "sleep" and "rest"; for example, a carving on the Oise-Aisne chapel reads: IN SACRED SLEEP THEY REST.[211] Grief, rather than triumph, permeates many of the sites, as statues at Suresnes and Oise-Aisne depict mourning women, and inscriptions speak (if somewhat subtly) to the suffering of grieving mothers. The planners' decision to erect headstones in the shape of the Latin cross and the Star of David indicated the government's willingness to acknowledge and represent the personal faiths and beliefs of the fallen, their next of kin, and their religious communities in these national (and, therefore, *secular*) spaces. The headstones themselves possess a particularly sentimental quality; though collectively they impart a sense of mechanical stoicism, each individual marker possesses delicate curves and tapered ends that were (and could only be) carefully hand-carved by expert artisans; when one considers these attributes, as well as the fact that someone took the time to inscribe the respective soldiers' unique information, one begins to sense just how much attention each fallen soldier received. (At the same time, however, this care and attention becomes less prominent and convincing as one retreats and sees the hand-carved headstones en masse. The delicate artistic flourishes found in each headstone's form begin to devolve into what we might term "mechanized sentimentality." Much like the telegrams and letters next of kin received during and after the war—those mass letters that, because of the unique information they contained, had an air of personal touch—the grave markers are, ultimately, reproductions masked as singular works of art.)

Finally, at each site, the planners established living quarters for a cemetery director and his family. The constant presence of this 'home' imbibes each respective burial ground with a sense of domesticity that is absent from European nation's World War I cemeteries. Serving as a manager and guardian, each cemetery director is also a host of sorts; he greets visitors when they arrive, guides them through the plots, invites them to sit and chat in the visitors' center, and generally helps them in any way that he can. In short, each cemetery director is like a friendly, ex-pat uncle who is glad to see you when you arrive and happy to tend to your physical, emotional, and intellectual needs.[212]

Most important, the endless rows of crosses that appear at each American World War I cemetery cast the violent deaths of drafted citizen-soldiers as self-sacrifice. Christians typically consider the Latin cross to be a symbol of Jesus Christ's righteous act of self-sacrificial death. In the Old Testament, an individual who offered a sacrifice did not offer her/himself, but instead offered a precious possession in substitution, such as a child (as in the story of Abraham and Isaac) or an animal. With Christ's death, the sacrificer's gift of her/himself became literal. Although Christ's alleged last words ("My God, my God, why have you forsaken me?") implied a lack of agency, it was Christ's *willingness* to die that consecrated humanity's new covenant with God—for such willingness is not easy to exert, even for the Son of God:

"Father, if you are willing, take this cup from me; yet not my will, but yours be done." An angel from heaven appeared to him and strengthened him. And being in anguish, he prayed more earnestly, and his sweat was like drops of blood falling to the ground.[213]

As the story goes, with heavenly support, in the final hours of life Christ found the will to offer himself to death to save the whole of humanity. References to these inherited Christian notions of sacrifice are made immediately apparent through the presentation of the headstones. For visitors (American or otherwise), it becomes hard to deny the swelling sense of *individual and collective sacrifice* that permeates from the numerous, harmonized rows of white cross. Every soldier's death becomes a sacrifice for the mutual benefit of the citizens of Europe, the United States, and the rest of the world—not just the American state. Taken together, it is in the eight overseas cemeteries where we see the birth (as well as most explicit and effective articulation) of the ideograph of the sacrificial, universal, modern U.S. soldier.

Ultimately, each buried soldier seems to attain salvation, his actions of war—presumably violent and against Christianity's philosophy of peace— are justified, forgiven, and wiped away. Ironically, we should note, these religious connotations far outweigh the memory of the cross as an instrument of justified torture and death used by the Roman state against its subjects (just as these religious connotations far outweigh the memory of the Great War as an ungodly act of state-sponsored militarism that took the very lives of the men buried before you). In the end, the Great War is cast not as a "human-slaughter house" (as Americans had understood it during the period of U.S. neutrality), but rather as *a battle between good and evil*.

The visual presentations of the U.S. World War I cemeteries in Europe, then, are not "a confusing mixture of various cultural trends" (as Robin argues), but rather reflections of particular historical circumstances, the ambitions of the CFA, and the rhetorical constraints that had been placed on the cemeteries' planners. Extending the CFA's aesthetic sensibilities and ideologies overseas, while also meeting the expectations of citizens, politicians, military figures, international audiences, and imagined future visitors, the planners incorporated into each site a network of symbols, texts, and objects of artistic and natural beauty that might communicate sustained messages (including the intoxicating notion of the self-sacrificial U.S. soldier) to heterogeneous audiences over time. Of course, one must possess a thorough understanding of the rhetorical foundations of the sites to come to these conclusions.

The true genius of these permanent burial grounds, however, is found in their use of what I term "the third element." Preceding questions of congruity and incongruity, logic and irrationality, harmony and dissonance, and truth and falsehood, "the third element" is the unspoken, often invisible, but always implied, relationship between any two (or more) readily perceived elements (e.g., material objects, written messages, ideas, the sight of a historically significant forest or grand battlefield monument in the distance) that exist (or appear) within close proximity of each other. By this I mean, when a visitor approaches an American cemetery and sees Old Glory flapping above a sea of white headstones, she automatically takes in a *third element*—the implied relationship between the flag and the grave markers. When a visitor directs her attention to an individual headstone, she simultaneously sees the countless other grave markers in her peripheral vision; thus, she also perceives a *third element*—the relationship between the individual soldier and the collective. When a visitor sees an inscription written in both English and French, she also sees a *third element*—the implied bond between English-speaking and French-speaking peoples. In sum, by composing physical and visual ensembles out of an expansive (if for Ron Robin *chaotic*) set of materials, symbols, texts, and themes, the CFA and the ABMC created at each site practically an infinite number of "third elements." The planners left it up to the visitors to decide which combinations of "third elements" would speak most effectively to their own minds, hearts, and guts.

Throughout the late 1920s, as the ABMC neared completion of its work on the cemeteries' final visual presentations, American newspapers and magazines issued detailed, and uniformly *positive*, accounts of the sites' appearances. The cemetery planners must have been pleased with the coverage, as it indicated to the public that the overseas burial grounds met any and all expectations Americans might have had. In a 1926 report on the work being done at the Aisne-Marne Cemetery, the *New York Times* stated: "Those who have sons or brothers lying in the 'white-shadowed' fields of France will read with grateful feelings the report of the National Commission on Fine Arts about the American cemeteries and battle monuments. Others will take patriotic satisfaction in knowing that these cemeteries will, when completed, present a 'modest, dignified and beautiful appearance quite in keeping with the national sentiment of respect and reverence for the memory of the dead.'" The article continued with the eyewitness account of Mrs. Caspar Whitney, a representative of the National League for Women's Service who had visited the site:

> We got to our cemetery at Belleau Wood just before sundown, and the beauty of the scene remains unforgettable. Our men rest on a hillside, in a beautifully kept cemetery, all green and white—green lawns and white crosses; no color otherwise, save the flag flying high above. It is majestic in its simplicity. Encircling it on three sides were fields of newly cut hay stacked in small haycocks, yellow and gold, across which the long shadows of the later afternoon fell, adding to the deep tranquility. Above, Belleau Wood, dark, solitary, mysterious, seemed to stand guard over the sleep of our men. Not a soul was in sight, not a roof to be seen, save that of the keeper of the cemetery. Here reigned the peace of God, and here one felt that God is good, and out of the sorrow and pain of the great war will come, in His own good time and way, good. Only we mustn't forget [...] I am sure that mothers and fathers, could they see where their sons lie, would feel less unhappy at having them sleep in foreign soil. Here always will the graves be cared for; never will they be neglected or disheveled, whereas I fear that many a grave at home will all too soon be neglected and forgotten.[214]

Speaking on behalf of *all* grieving Americans (most of whom would never see the sites with their own eyes), Whitney offered an account that surely brought some measure of comfort to readers whose loved ones were interred at Aisne-Marne or one of the other cemeteries abroad. Whitney's sentiments were echoed (perhaps not as eloquently) in subsequent newspaper accounts of the sites. Linking the burial grounds in Europe to the homeland, the *New York Times* described the eight cemeteries as "virtually American soil."[215] The *New York Times* also indicated that the sites functioned properly as military cemeteries—*national* burial grounds instilled with a sense of egalitarianism and focused on the heroic bravery of U.S. citizen-soldiers:

> The 30,801 headstones are ranged in military alignment. Even in death the men of the A. E. F. are soldiers. But death knows no rank; consequently there is no distinction in the placing of the graves. Officers and men lie side by side. No private monuments are permitted [...] One of the most peaceful A. E. F. cemeteries a dozen years ago was the scene of some of the most desperate fighting by American troops during the war. This is the Aisne-Marne Cemetery, which lies at the foot of Belleau Wood, a mile square patch of forest in which the marines won undying glory. They are still finding bodies in this little wood. This cemetery contains the graves of men who died in resisting the great German drive on Paris in June, 1918.[216]

In January of 1934, the *National Geographic Magazine* allowed General Pershing to publish a long article describing the visual presentation of the eight cemeteries. Replete with colored photographs, the essay provided an in-depth tour of each site. Making the most of this pulpit, Pershing overtly emphasized the themes of tranquility and maternal grief:

> To-day 30,880 [soldiers] sleep in beautiful and peaceful cemeteries in the areas where they were engaged [...] To the [mothers], to relatives of soldier dead, and to every American citizen, I can give assurance that the United States Government has kept and will continue to maintain its trust in perpetuating the memory of the bravery and sacrifices of our World War heroes.[217]

Next of kin were to be assured that Pershing and the ABMC had fulfilled their responsibilities and created proper resting places for the nation's war dead.

By the time Pershing published this article, however, thousands of American women *had* already visited the cemeteries and seen their loved ones' graves in person. Between 1930 and 1933, the U.S. government conducted what became known as the "Gold Star Mother Pilgrimages"—a federally subsidized program that brought 6,674 willing and able-bodied widows and mothers to their men's graves in Europe. Veteran A.E.F. officers, including Pershing himself, acted as tour guides for the women, many of whom were elderly and had made the long journey to see their sons' graves despite suffering from severe health issues. Shamefully, the program reflected the Jim Crow era in that African-American Gold Star Mothers were segregated from their white counterparts—a fact that undermined the cemetery planners' efforts to bring some measure of racial equality to the burial grounds. Still, grieving women of every racial and economic background were afforded the rare opportunity to visit the overseas cemeteries where their loved ones had been interred. For most of these pilgrims, the journey was bittersweet— a "wonderful, though sad" experience. On the one hand, the women were usually comforted to see that the cemeteries were, indeed, as gorgeous and majestic as the media reports had stated. "This cemetery," remarked one mother, "so beautifully and carefully tended, is worthy of the government for which he died." But despite the grandeur and tranquility of the sites, time had not healed the wounds of such profound loss. As historian Lotte Larsen Meyer tells us: "While having satisfied the desire to see a grave, the pilgrimage would never erase the pain of having lost a loving son or beloved husband."[218] One doubts that anything ever could.

NOTES

1. Once more, as opposed to the Ancient Greek conception of *chronos*, the scientific measurement and passing of time, *kairos* has been understood by rhetoricians as the "right," "opportune," or "propitious" moment for symbolic action. Much more fluid, plastic, and ambiguous than *chronos*, *kairos* represents the moment (whether a

second, minute, hour, day, year, or more) when one can use language to strike with maximum impact. As rhetoric scholar John Poulakos tells us: "Springing from one's sense of timing and the will to invent, *kairos* alludes to the realization that speech exists in time and is uttered both as a spontaneous formulation of and a barely constituted response to a new situation unfolding in the immediate present. According to this realization, time is understood as 'a succession of discontinuous occasions rather than as duration or historical continuity' while the present is conceived not 'as continuous with a causally related sequence of events' but as 'unprecedented, as a moment of decision, a moment of crisis.'" See John Poulakos, *Sophistical Rhetoric in Classical Greece* (Columbia: University of South Carolina Press, 1995), 61; and Jane Sutton, "Kairos," in *Encyclopedia of Rhetoric*, ed. Thomas O. Sloane (Oxford: Oxford University Press, 2001), 413–17.

2. Kenneth Burke, *A Rhetoric of Motives* (Berkeley: University of California Press, 1950), 13.

3. Thomas North, General North's Manuscript, unpublished and undated manuscript (given to author by David Bedford, Oise-Aisne American Cemetery and Memorial Superintendent in 2006), 1, 3, 11.

4. G. Kurt Piehler, *Remembering War the American Way* (Washington, DC: Smithsonian Institution Press, 1995), 111. The government's distribution of this 'booty' across the country revealed its desire to symbolize the national war effort, in general, and the argument that the United States had won the war, more specifically, to the American people. Whereas the outcomes and consequences of most wars fought throughout human history could be determined by material gains or losses (territory, natural resources, precious treasures, slaves, etc.), the material benefits of the United States' participation and alleged victory in Europe were not patently clear (especially to the average American citizen). But what good were decimated and captured German artillery pieces, aside from their symbolic value? For more from Piehler on the American public's uncertainty over what the war had accomplished, see page 93.

5. "Plan a National Shrine to Those Who Died in the War," *New York Times*, August 12, 1924, 1.

6. "Raise Memorials to Gallant Sons," *State* (Columbia, South Carolina), May 18, 1919, 1.

7. "Window for War Dead," *New York Times*, June 13, 1922, 18.

8. "Famous University Plants Forest for Its Hero Dead," *Dallas Morning News*, June 24, 1919, 11.

9. Piehler, *Remembering War*, 105–9.

10. "Opportunity for the Living Is Urged Instead of Tributes in Stone," *New York Times*, May 2, 1924, 18.

11. Association of the 110th Infantry, *History of the 110th Infantry (10th Pa.) of the 28th Division, U.S.A., 1917–1919: A Compilation of Orders, Citations, Maps, Records and Illustrations Relating to the 3rd Pa. Inf., 10th Pa. Inf., and 110th U.S. Inf.* (Greensburg, PA: The Association, 1920), 171.

12. Drew Gilpin Faust, *This Republic of Suffering: Death and the American Civil War* (New York: Alfred A. Knopf, 2008), 6–17, 18, 23, 25–6, 28–31, 85, 109, 124, 144, 163, 167, 174–5, 183, and 198.

13. Association of the 110th Infantry, *History*, 173.

14. Annie Kilburn Kilmer, *Memories of My Son Sergeant Joyce Kilmer: With Numerous Unpublished Poems and Letters* (New York: Brentano's, 1920).

15. Exhumations of American bodies for shipment to the United States began in 1920. The first exhumation was made at Gosport, England, on February 3, 1920, the first transatlantic shipment of bodies on February 23. During 1921, repatriation of bodily remains was nearly completed, and the exhumation and concentration of bodies for burial in overseas cemeteries commenced. Nearly every dead U.S. soldier was laid in his final resting place—whether in the States or in Europe—by the end of 1922. See U.S. National Archives and Records Administration II, College Park, Maryland, Records of the Office of the Inspector General (Army), Record Group 159, Box 772, "Brief History of Organization and Operations of Graves Registration Service from Origin to July 31, 1930," October 24, 1930, 2.

16. John Durham Peters, *Courting the Abyss: Free Speech and the Liberal Tradition* (Chicago: University of Chicago Press, 2005), 251.

17. "Taps for Our Soldier Dead," *Philadelphia Inquirer*, October 24, 1921, 12.

18. Consider the explosion of American "disillusionment" art and literature of the postwar years. Exemplified in the works of figures like Horace Pippin, John Singer Sargent, John Stuart Curry, Ivan Albright, Georgia O'Keefe, Harvey Dunn, Violet Oakley, Ernest Hemingway, F. Scott Fitzgerald, and other members of the "Lost Generation," this influential corpus of texts and visual artifacts highlighted, documented, laid bare, and condemned the violence, loss, death, destruction, futility, barbarism, and madness of World War I.

Or consider the popularity of conscientious objector and anarchist Ernst Friedrich's *Krieg Dem Krieg! (War Against War!)*. Published in 1924 and sold around the world (including throughout the United States), this shocking photographic essay unflinchingly revealed and memorialized the destructive power that World War I inflicted upon the human body, the human spirit, and Europe's physical landscape. The book is essentially a collection of roughly two hundred photographs taken from German military and medical records, most of which were banned from the public eye by government censors during the war. According to Friedrich, the purpose of the book was to provide "a picture of War, objectively true and faithful to nature […] photographically recorded for all time." Though the book's title makes plain the author's intentions, in the preface Friedrich further orients his readers for what is to follow, by dedicating it to "war profiteers and parasites," war provokers, kings, generals, presidents and ministers of all lands, and priests and other religious figures who consecrated the war in God's name. In the preface, Friedrich reveals his belief that explicit photographic images of the hideous side of The Great War would combat patriotic constructions of the war's memory and provide an aesthetic groundwork for deterrence against future wars. Citing the "inexorable" and "incorruptible" nature of the photographic lens, Friedrich writes that the frightful pictures would bear witness to the truth of war and tear the masks "field of honor," "heroic death," and other romantic lies from the gruesome face of war.

Friedrich's faith in photography's ability to tear away the mask of lies from the gruesome face of war seems reasonable, for the images in *War Against War!* retain a shocking power that can still sicken readers eighty years later. In *Regarding the Pain of Others*—an analysis of the uses and rhetorical properties of images of suffering—Susan Sontag describes Friedrich's book as "an excruciating photo-tour of four years of ruin, slaughter, and degradation." Sontag describes the pages of wrecked and plundered churches and castles, obliterated villages, ravaged forests, torpedoed passenger steamers, shattered vehicles, hanged conscientious objectors, half-naked prostitutes in military brothels, soldiers in death agonies after a poison-gas attack, and skeletal Armenian children. For Sontag, all the sequences in *War Against War!* are difficult to look at. Indeed, each page drags readers deeper into the madness of war and its destruction of body and space. Readers discover images of bloated, twisted, and disfigured corpses of soldiers and civilians alike, military executioners standing over decapitated prisoners, mass graves filled with dead naked children, and endless muddy battlefields littered with detached body parts. The essay ends with perhaps the most terrifying sequence of photographs, titled "The Faces of War," in which readers are squarely confronted with veterans who suffered massive facial wounds and other atrocious injuries. Missing jaws, bloody holes where eyes should be, burnt scalps, and amputation scars darken each page.

Every photograph in *War Against War!* is accompanied with a sardonic caption in four languages (Dutch, English, French, and German) that, in juxtaposition with the imagery, belittles and condemns nationalistic and romantic ideologies of war. For example, a close-up photograph of a soldier undergoing gruesome facial reconstructive surgery is accompanied with General Paul von Hindenburg's famous quote: "War agrees with me like a stay at a health resort." As Sontag points out, Friedrich did not make the mistake of supposing that heartrending, stomach-turning pictures would simply speak for themselves. Instead, with choice quotes and vitriolic writing, Friedrich attempted to secure the photographic essay's status as an anti-war document. For me, as for Sontag, Friedrich's anti-war book only brings about feelings of horror, repugnance, and hatred.

Of course, Kenneth Burke, in his 1933 essay "War, Response, and Contradiction," reminds us that even the most blatant of anti-war texts are capable of incurring completely unintended responses. In consideration of a public debate over Laurence Stallings's anti-war book *The First World War*, Burke argues that it is questionable whether the feelings of horror, repugnance, and hatred would furnish the best groundwork as a deterrent to war. Burke tells us that they are extremely militaristic attitudes, "being in much the same category of emotion as one might conceivably experience when plunging his bayonet into the flesh of the enemy." And they might well provide the firmest basis upon which the "heroism" of a new war could be erected. In this passage, Burke imagines an upstanding young fellow who points to photographs of mutilated bodies, and saying quietly but firmly to his sweetheart, who adores him: "See those? That is what war is. Dearie, this day I have enlisted in the service of my country." We should acknowledge that, as with any other form of communication, *War Against War!* was and is subject to interpretation, misinterpretation, and reinterpretation.

Yet it is unsurprising that governments and patriotic organizations throughout Europe came to condemn (and in some cases ban) Friedrich's book during the interwar years. By 1930, *War Against War!*, with its uncensored depictions of World War I and blasphemous, anti-nationalist writing, had gone through ten printings and had been translated into many more languages. An international bestseller popular with the masses, the book threatened to shape public opinion in a way that would undermine the legitimacy of government-sponsored memories of the war and resist the collectivistic motives for military sacrifice so necessary for future wars. Sontag tells us that in some cities the police raided bookstores, and lawsuits were brought against the public display of the photographs. This subversive, mediated representation of the war, so close to the time and place of the event itself, forced heavy-handed governmental reactions.

In short, the U.S. government's postwar, countervailing task of controlling and shaping which images, ideas, and memories would emerge from the battlefields of Europe, circulate domestically, and influence American public memory of the war was severely hampered, if not overwhelmed, by various forces, including the boom of anti-war, "disillusionment" literature and art discussed above. For more, see: Robert Cozzolino, Anne Classen Knutson, and David M. Lubin, eds., *World War I and American Art* (Philadelphia: Pennsylvania Academy of the Fine Arts, 2017); Susan Sontag, *Regarding the Pain of Others* (New York: Picador, 2003), 14–15; and, Kenneth Burke, "War, Response, and Contradiction," in *The Philosophy of Literary Form* (Berkeley: University of California Press, 1973), 234–57.

19. Piehler, *Remembering War*, 96, 114.

20. Lester C. Olson, Cara A. Finnegan, and Diane S. Hope, eds., *Visual Rhetoric: A Reader in Communication and American Culture* (Thousand Oaks, CA: Sage, 2008), 3.

21. For instance, in his thorough examination of U.S. World War II overseas commemoration projects, Sam Edwards attributes the establishment and design of America's World War I cemeteries solely to the American Battle Monuments Commission and makes no mention of the Commission of Fine Arts. See: Sam Edwards, *Allies in Memory: World War II and the Politics of Transatlantic Commemoration, c. 1941–2001* (Cambridge: Cambridge University Press, 2015), especially pages 15–29.

22. Leo R. Sack, "Association Is Formed to Lay Aside Estate in France for an American Cemetery," *Fort Worth Star-Telegram*, June 3, 1919, 12; The National Commission of Fine Arts, *Ninth Report, July 1, 1919–June 30, 1921* (Washington, DC: Government Printing Office, 1921), 39–41.

23. Establishing a Commission of Fine Arts Act of 1910, 40 U.S.C. § 104 (1910).

24. "Washington Is to Be Most Beautiful City in America," *Duluth News Tribune*, June 19, 1910, 1.

25. Developed and propagated during the 1890s and early twentieth century by influential Progressive architects and urban planners like Daniel Burnham, the "City Beautiful" movement sought to transform decaying urban centers into beautiful spaces in order to improve the lives of the poor; inspire American citizens to moral and civic virtue; and, display the young nation's greatness to the world. The Department of American Studies at the University of Virginia writes: "Generally stated, the City Beautiful advocates sought to improve their city through beautification, which would have a number of effects: (1) social ills would be swept away, as the beauty

of the city would inspire civic loyalty and moral rectitude in the impoverished; (2) American cities would be brought to cultural parity with their European competitors through the use of the European Beaux-Arts idiom; and (3) a more inviting city center still would not bring the upper classes back to live, but certainly to work and spend money in the urban areas." See Kirk Savage, *Monument Wars: Washington, D.C., the National Mall, and the Transformation of the Memorial Landscape* (Berkeley: University of California Press, 2009), 13, 18, 152, 158, and 183; and American Studies at the University of Virginia, "The City Beautiful Movement," n.d., http://xroads.virginia.edu/~CAP/CITYBEAUTIFUL/city.html (accessed April 12, 2011).

26. As Washington, D.C., approached its centennial, there was a call (by cultural and political elites) to develop the city's landscape into one worthy of a modern national capital. In 1900, Senator James McMillan of Michigan formed a small but powerful commission to work on the redesign of the city's appearance. The commission included future CFA members Charles Moore, Daniel Burnham, and Frederick Law Olmdsted, Jr., and was backed by the influential American Institute of Architects. A "war against disorder," the commission's so-called "McMillan Plan" sought to unify the city (which had been fragmented by Pierre L'Enfant's eighteenth century principle of "dispersed centers") with grand spacious avenues that would accommodate the flow of human bodies and cars. Somewhat akin to a military operation, the plan entailed the razing of slums (which were deemed unclean, unseemly, and morally corrupt); the removal of old monuments, fountains, trees, gardens, and buildings that served as obstacles to the commission's vision; and the construction of grand museums, federal buildings, and memorials designed in a neoclassical or Beaux-Arts style. The plan also involved clearing the National Mall—polluted with haphazard monuments, meandering paths, and seemingly randomly placed flowers gardens—and transforming it into a "flow of space." In 1910, Congress established the Commission of Fine Arts, which took control over the McMillan Plan. Most of the CFA's initial members, appointed by President William Howard Taft, had served on the McMillan Commission. See Savage, *Monument Wars*, 147–92; The Commission of Fine Arts, *A Brief History 1910–1995* (Washington, D.C.: U.S. Government Printing Office, 1996), 1–7.

27. The National Commission, *Ninth*, iii.

28. In 1921, President Warren G. Harding signed an executive order that extended to the CFA authority over "essential matters relating to the design of medals, insignia and coins" produced by the federal government. This edict gave the CFA virtually unchecked powers to determine the appearance of common, but symbolically significant, objects—big and small, grand and banal—that circulated and appeared in everyday American life. For instance, in 1923, the CFA declared that the American flag was "too long in proportion to its width to be artistic." As the *New York Times* reported: "In consultation with a committee of Government officials appointed for the standardization of the flag, the commission decided on a ratio of 1.67 to 1 instead of the present 1.90 to 1. The decision was reached through tests of various sized flags flown from the Arlington Amphiteatre flagpole." See The Commission, *A Brief History*, 242–3; "Plans to Shorten Our Flag to Get Better Proportion," *New York Times*, May 6, 1923, 1.

29. The sacred character, social function, and cultural meaning of a cemetery—the place where a community buries and venerates its dead—seem obvious, but should be explained further here. Religion and American Culture scholar Gary Laderman states: "How the dead body is cared for, and the practices employed for its disposal, can tell us as much about the animating principles within a given society as about how that society understands the meaning of death." Rhetoric scholar Richard Morris writes: "As fundamentally rhetorical and cultural in origin and orientation, overt responses to death reveal worldviews, cultural premises, manners of organizing, parsing, combining, interpreting, and responding to the world. When displayed in public space, they also commonly rehearse explicit cultural lessons." Rhetoric scholar Nicole Loraux has famously argued that Pericles's funeral oration (and the burial practices related to it) actually *invented* the classical city of Athens that Western society and subsequently, the United States, have venerated ever since. Communication scholar John Durham Peters argues that in the United States, "[p]erhaps even as much as money, the archmedium may be the cemetery, the place where the bodies of the dead are held in suspended animation, as the term itself suggests: 'cemetery' comes from the Greek *koimeterion*, meaning a sleeping place, quite literally a dormitory." As Peters's term "archmedium" indicates, the cemetery is, like most sacred sites, a place where the distances between life, death, and rebirth are bridged—a site where that unknowable question (the experience of death) is addressed and, at least in part, answered. History of Religion scholar Mircea Eliade expands upon this point, arguing that the cemetery is "a space where communication between Heaven, Earth, the Underworld takes place," a material space that makes possible "the passage from Earth to Heaven." According to Eliade, most societies consider the grave—a hole carved into the ground—to be an entryway to the afterlife (a provocative notion when we consider that the carefully planned graves of America's overseas military cemeteries were antithetical to the muddy battlefields of the Great War that had swallowed soldiers whole and thus denied men a safe passageway to the afterlife). French intellectual René Guénon claims that the cemetery is place where one can become a "Universal Man"—the person who effectively realizes and confronts her or his "multiple states" (pre-birth, life, death, and afterlife). Michel Foucault synthesizes the cultural and metaphysical significance of the cemetery in his famous essay, "Of Other Spaces." Foucault considers the cemetery to be a "heterotopia"—"something like [a counter-site], a kind of effectively enacted utopia in which the real sites, all the other real sites that can be found within the culture, are simultaneously represented, contested, and inverted." According to Foucault, every human society has heterotopias (like cemeteries); every heterotopia "has a precise and determined function within a society"; and, the particular function of a heterotopia can change with time as the needs and sensibilities of society shift. Ultimately, Foucault argues, the cemetery (a heterotopia) incorporates and juxtaposes things that are seemingly "incompatible" (such as life and death); allows people to step outside of "traditional time" and into a "quasi-eternity" (or sacred time); demands a certain level of decorum from visitors; and, helps organize, define, and regulate the territory of a given community. See Mircea Eliade, *Symbolism, the Sacred, and the Arts* (New York: Crossroad, 1985), 107–8; Michel Foucault, "Of Other Spaces" (1967), http://foucault.info/documents/

heteroTopia/foucault.heterotopia.en.html, n.d. (accessed April 14, 2011); René Gué-non, *Symbolism of the Cross*, trans. Angus Macnab (London: Luzac, 1958), 1–3; Gary Laderman, *The Sacred Remains: American Attitudes Toward Death, 1799–1883* (New Haven: Yale University Press, 1996), 1; Nicole Loraux, *The Invention of Athens: The Funeral Oration in the Classical City*, trans. Alan Sheridan (New York: Zone Books, 2006); Richard Morris, "Death on Display," in *Rhetorics of Display*, ed. Lawrence J. Prelli (Columbia: University of South Carolina Press, 2006), 204–24; and, John Durham Peters, *Speaking Into the Air: A History of the Idea of Communication* (Chicago: University of Chicago Press, 1999), 152.

30. Displaying the wartime sacrifices of the American people to Europeans became all the more necessary in 1924 when Belgium sought $88,000,000,000 in reparations from the United States *for the sacrifices that Belgium, Britain, and France had made in defense of the American people.* Henri La Fontaine, Vice President of the Belgian Senate, forwarded the proposal as a counter-measure to tariffs the U.S. had placed on Belgium and other debtor nations in the years following the war. "It cannot be denied that we fought for America and that we saved her," La Fontaine said in an address to the Belgian Senate. "Consequently we are entitled to expect effective help from her [...] Counting every killed soldier as representing 100,000 francs of capital destroyed, and each mutilated soldier 50,000 francs [...] this represents for the three countries one thousand and sixty-five billions." See "Says America Owes Europe $88,000,000,000," *New York Times*, January 13, 1924, 7.

31. As Savage explains throughout *Monument Wars*, the CFA and its professional and political cohorts rejected (what they viewed as) outdated Victorian and Romantic ideals of sentimentality and nature-worship. Savage states, "The reformers of the early twentieth century were cut from a different cloth. They belonged to a world organized by monopoly capitalism, where expertise and efficiency were the watchwords. It was perfectly natural for [them] to compare urban design to modern methods of military conquest and industrial production" (158).

32. Savage, *Monument Wars*, 159.

33. Ibid, 147–52, 191–2.

34. Ibid, 13–14.

35. It is safe to say that, in planting these trees, the CFA was less concerned with providing shade for pedestrians and more interested in creating designated, natural hallways of sorts that would lead people where they were *supposed* to go.

36. Savage, *Monument Wars*, 147–92. With regard to the Washington Monument's convenient and essential role within the CFA's plan to transform the Mall into a "flow of space," Savage writes on page 148: "Low horizon lines emphasize [the Washington Monument's] presence and compress the ground plane beneath it. Nothing on the monument's blank surface compels us to stop and 'read' it. The obelisk's sharp lines keep the eye in movement, at once lifting our gaze up off the ground and speeding vision longitudinally across vast distances. The monument draws us into and through space, subordinating the ground to a new compositional logic." Ironically, the CFA's transformation of the Mall from a conglomeration of flower gardens, small forests, and outdated monuments into a sweeping, wide-open space, had a major unintended consequence: it turned the Mall into a gathering space for public

assembly and social protest. Setting out to create a space that would guide and control an individual's body, the CFA had assumed that future visitors would (as Savage puts it) "follow the same genteel decorum practiced in old public grounds." However, as history has proved, the Mall would become a space for collective political behavior that is anything but "genteel." Ibid, 173–4.

37. "Purchase Assured of Belleau Woods," *Washington Post*, February 13, 1923, 2.

38. The National Commission, *Ninth*, 29. "Cleaning" became a key metaphor for supporters of the CFA, who sought to eliminate anything that polluted their vision of the Mall. As George B. Ford, a famous architect and CFA advocate, publicly stated, the CFA's plans for the Mall would help make Washington "the cleanest, most dignified, the most impressive, the most beautiful city in the world." See "Says Ugly Buildings Mar Washington," *Washington Post*, February 6, 1927, SM5.

39. The constant removal of undesired memorials served as a stark reminder that no monument is necessarily permanent. In *Standing Soldiers, Kneeling Slaves*, Kirk Savage writes: "Monuments attempt to mold a landscape of collective memory, to conserve what is worth remembering and discard the rest." By conserving useful memorials and discarding the rest, the CFA in essence dictated what would be worth remembering through the National Mall's landscape. Of course, the CFA itself ultimately designed and constructed colossal monuments like the Lincoln Memorial that would be all but impossible to remove in the future. See Kirk Savage, *Standing Soldiers, Kneeling Slaves: Race, War, and Monument in Nineteenth-Century America* (Princeton: Princeton University Press, 1997), 4.

40. According to Mircea Eliade, *shade* symbolizes many cosmological meanings that are common to most cultures. For instance, shade can represent the marking of time (embodied by the sun dial). It can signify the cosmological distortion of space, for the length of one's shadow changes with the sun's elevation angle. Shade can be understood in terms of "Cosmic Night"—a return from the chaos of the world to the safety of the mother' womb (within the context of the National Mall debates, this is a very relevant meaning). Finally, shade can imply the moment before transition from one state of being to another—the moment before one returns to the light ("Even though I walk through the valley of the shadow of death..."). See Eliade, *Symbolism*, 6–9.

41. Savage, *Monuments Wars*, 179–91. The use of the term "ground-huggers" can be understood not only as a reflection of the CFA's attack on *public grounds*, but also as a jibe against the feminine connotations of *ground* and *soil*. As Mircea Eliade states, cultures have tended to understand the soil in terms of female fertility and the womb; for thousands of years, farmers have used spades and other phallic-like tools to till the soil and plant seeds that eventually blossom into foods and grains. See Eliade, *Symbolism*, 6.

42. As Savage tells us, the CFA prevented "the forty-two individual army divisions that had fought in Europe from each erecting its own independent monument" on the Mall. Ultimately, three World War I memorials, "two of which featured long lists of names of the dead," were permitted to be built on the Mall (of course, the design plans were approved by the CFA). See Savage, *Monument Wars*, 241–2.

43. Commission, *Ninth Report*, 80.

44. Savage, *Monument Wars*, 169.

45. Savage argues that this portrayal of Lincoln as a strong but apparently worried leader responded to "a broader cultural anxiety that the United States, in its new affluence, was becoming overcivilized and effeminate." Echoing the sentiments of Teddy Roosevelt's call for a masculine return to the "strenuous life [...] a life of toil and effort, or labor strife," the Lincoln statue, Savage claims, helped advance the "ideal of unflinching commitment in the face of suffering and despair [...] the sort of 'intellectual conception' that the stock [Civil War] soldier monument lacked" (ibid, 217–28).

46. Savage argues that the Lincoln and Grant memorials' "attention to suffering opened a space for a new consciousness of trauma and victimization, even though neither monument was yet couched in the vocabulary of victimhood we have come to recognize today" (ibid, 228–37).

47. Ibid, 197–210.

48. Permanence was a key concept for the CFA, as the commission intended to create a visual ensemble that would last forever. As Charles Moore, Chairman of the CFA from 1915–1937, told the *New York Times*, "A memorial should be made to last a thousand years." The CFA, however, recognized the challenges of communicating constant and enduring messages across time. "No living person can foresee or even imagine the future of the United States in wealth and power," the CFA wrote in a 1921 report of its work on the Mall. "The utmost one can do is to build as wisely and as adequately as his limited vision will permit. No plan is final in so far as comprehensiveness is concerned. No plan will be large enough for the future." But despite these words, the CFA did attempt to create a symbolic space "large enough for the future" by erecting grand monuments that displayed abstract but discernible messages concerning democratic ideals of freedom, justice, courage, and sacrifice, and that could not easily diminish or alter with time. See "Efforts to Prevent Inartistic War Memorials," *New York Times*, March 23, 1919, 73; The National Commission, *Ninth*, 38.

49. In all likelihood, the CFA's desire to build a connecting bridge between the cemetery and the National Mall represented a hope that some of the perceived sacredness of the burial ground would rub off on the newly redesigned Mall.

50. Throughout the nineteenth and early twentieth centuries, Americans understood flowers to be "ornamental" and feminine in character—traits that the CFA generally detested. See Elias A. Long, *Ornamental Gardening for Americans: A Treatise on Beautifying Homes, Rural Districts, Towns, and Cemeteries* (New York: Orange Judd Company, 1907).

51. Ed Streeter, "Proposed Improvements for Arlington," *Washington Post*, December 19, 1920, 72.

52. Morris, "Death on Display," 205–9.

53. Ibid, 209–15.

54. Morris claims that this gravescape echoed the aesthetics and meanings of the Washington Monument, "a structure of such monumental proportions [that] announces both the dominance of the species over nature and the consequences of epic heroism" (hence the term, "epic heroism gravescape"). See ibid, 215–6.

55. Uniformly designed and presented, these gravestones were the perfect embodiments of the ideologies and practices of the age of mechanical reproduction.

56. Morris, "Death On Display," 215–21. For more on the evolving history of American cemetery design and practices, see Thomas Bender, "The 'Rural' Cemetery Movement: Urban Travail and the Appeal of Nature," *The New England Quarterly* 47.2 (June, 1974): 196–211; Margaretta J. Darnall, "The American Cemetery as Picturesque Landscape: Bellefontaine Cemetery, St. Louis," *Winterthur Portfolio* 18.4 (Winter, 1983): 249–69; Stanley French, "The Cemetery as Cultural Institution: The Establishment of Mount Auburn and the 'Rural Cemetery' Movement," *American Quarterly* 26.1 (March, 1974): 37–59; Jack Goody and Cesare Poppi, "Flowers and Bones: Approaches to the Dead in Anglo-American and Italian Cemeteries," *Comparative Studies in Society and History* 36.1 (January, 1994): 146–75; David B. Knight, "Cemeteries as Living Landscapes," *Ottawa Branch: Ontario Genealogical Society Publication* 73.8 (April, 1974): 1–55; Gary Laderman, "Locating the Dead: A Cultural History of Death in the Antebellum, Anglo-Protestant Communities of the Northeast," *Journal of the American Academy of Religion* 63.1 (Spring, 1995): 27–52; Lynn Rainville, "Hanover Deathscapes: Mortuary Variability in New Hampshire, 1770–1920," *Ethnohistory* 46.3 (Summer, 1999): 541–97; Elizabethada A. Wright, "Reading the Cemetery, *Lieu De Mémoire Par Excellance*," *Rhetoric Society Quarterly* 33.2 (Spring, 2003): 27–44; and, ibid, "Rhetorical Spaces in Memorial Places: The Cemetery as a Rhetorical Memory Place/Space," *Rhetoric Society Quarterly* 35.4 (Fall, 2005): 51–81.

57. The National Commission, *Ninth*, 43.

58. As Aristotle shows throughout *Rhetoric*—and as all contemporary rhetoricians assume—rhetoric *always* entails some degree of emotion (*pathos*). Whereas philosophy tries to limit itself to matters of reason (*logos*), rhetoric always entails the interplay of *ethos* (character), *pathos*, and *logos*.

59. Roderick Frazier Nash, *Wilderness and the American Mind*, 4th ed. (New Haven: Yale University Press, 2001), 67.

60. Ibid, 44–84.

61. Ibid, 143. The establishment of Yellowstone and the other U.S. National Parks during the late 1800s and early 1900s reflected less a veneration of American wilderness and more the necessity to defend the prestigious, untouched lands from greedy loggers, miners, and railroad companies. By the 1890s, American corporations saw the frontier less as a national shrine and more as an economic opportunity and resource for the industrial revolution. See Nash, *Wilderness*, 108–121.

62. See, especially, Edward Tabor Linenthal, *Sacred Ground: Americans and Their Battlefields* (Urbana, IL: University of Illinois Press, 1991), 1–7, 87–126, 213–17; and Timothy B. Smith, *The Golden Age of Battlefield Preservation: The Decade of the 1890s and the Establishment of America's First Five Military Parks* (Knoxville: University of Tennessee Press, 2008).

63. Smith, *The Golden Age*, 8, 19, 131, 164–5.

64. Linenthal, *Sacred Ground*, 89–90.

65. Ibid, 93. Since time immemorial, human societies have considered soil where blood has been shed (whether through war or rituals of sacrifice) to be sacred. See

Eliade, *Symbolism*, 108. Following the Great War, the belief that the blood of U.S. soldiers had consecrated Europe's battlefields became prevalent. As Charles Henry Brent, the Bishop of Western New York, publicly stated: "Bony is forever eloquent of the successful assault on the Hindenburg line on the St. Quentin Canal, where on September 29th, 1918, much precious American blood watered anew the already blood-soaked soil of Flanders." See Charles Henry Brent, "Forever Overseas," *Word's Work* 43 (December, 1921): 135–7.

66. Brent, "Forever," 105.

67. Until this historical moment, collective memories of American soldierly dead had been maintained through abstract celebrations of iconic military figures. For instance, when George Washington died in 1799, towns throughout the republic held observances and funerary rituals as if Washington's body was actually present. Through these celebrations of Washington's absent body—"a potent symbol of national unity"—communities across the country simultaneously honored the sacrifices and achievements of all the soldiers who had fought for American independence. See Laderman, *The Sacred Remains*, 16–17, 20.

68. Smith, *The Golden Age*, 21–2.

69. Linenthal, *Sacred Ground*, 91; Smith, *The Golden Age*, 33–4.

70. Marilyn Yalom, *The American Resting Place: Four Hundred Years of History Through Our Cemeteries and Burial Grounds* (Boston: Houghton Mifflin Company, 2008), 262.

71. Smith, *The Golden Age*, 32–3.

72. Ibid, 33.

73. Ibid, 35. In 1912, Congress passed legislation that shifted sole authority over the military parks to the Secretary of War. In 1933, this power was handed over to the National Park Service. Ibid, 48–9, 133–4.

74. During World War I, the American Expeditionary Forces used the battlefields of Chickamauga and Chattanooga National Military Park as training grounds. Ironically, the military severely damaged the park, constructing trenches, polo fields, golf courses, and "temporary" barracks throughout the historic property—an indication that, at this time, the military did not fully appreciate the symbolic power and sacred character of the national military parks and cemeteries. See Smith, *The Golden Age*, 73.

75. Linenthal, *Sacred Ground*, 87–126.

76. Civil War veteran Stephen B. Elkins made this statement in an 1891 official report to Congress. See Smith, *The Golden Age*, 37.

77. Secretary of War Russell A. Alger wrote these words in his 1897 annual report to Congress. See Smith, *The Golden Age*, 42.

78. These are the words of Virginia Governor Angus W. McLean, a vocal advocate for the preservation of Civil War battlefields and cemeteries. See Linenthal, *Sacred Ground*, 90.

79. These words, too, belonged to Governor McLean. See Linenthal, *Sacred Ground*, 90.

80. Smith, *The Golden Age*, 174.

81. For more on this evolution, see Jim Weeks, *Gettysburg: Memory, Market, and an American Shrine* (Princeton: Princeton University Press, 2003), 13–84.

82. As future military icon George S. Patton remarked in a 1909 personal diary entry about a visit to Gettysburg: "This evening [...] I walked down alone to the scene of the last and fiercest struggle on Cemetery hill. To get in a proper frame of mind I wandered through the cemetery and let the spirits of the dead thousands laid there in ordered rows sink deep into me. Then just as the son [*sic*] sank [...] I walked down to the scene of Pickett's great charge and seated on a rock just where Olmstead and two of my great uncles died. I watched the wonder of the day go out. The sunset painted a dull red the fields over which the terrible advance was made and I could almost see them coming growing fewer and fewer while around and beyond [*sic*] me stood calmly the very cannon that had so punished them. There were some quail calling in the trees near by and it seemed strange that they could do it where man had known his greatest and his last emotions. It was very wonderful and no one came to bother me. I drank it in until I was quite happy. A strange pleasure yet a very real one." George S. Patton, Jr., *The Patton Papers 1885–1940*, ed. Martin Blumenson (Boston: Houghton Mifflin Co., 1972), 173, quoted in Linenthal, *Sacred Ground*, 116–7.

83. In their essay, "National Park Landscapes and the Rhetorical Display of Civic Religion," S. Michael Halloran and Gregory Clark argue that the Civil War and Revolutionary War military parks that the federal government established at the turn of the century helped foster a new civic religion that combined nineteenth-century veneration of nature with the rhetorical power of military relics and memorials (which signified notions of sacrifice, martyrdom, and patriotism). Halloran and Clark point out that the Saratoga Military Park became a New York State historical park in 1927, when the Model T Ford was introducing millions of Americans to the ritual of scenic tourism; this fact explains the "tour road" that cuts through the park, along which contemporary visitors found stops marked by pictorial and textual aids meant to assist in the visualizing of battle events. The authors posit that, much like believers who participate in the Catholic ritual known as the stations of the cross, visitors of the park were encouraged to follow a narrative by moving through the actual (and imagined) landscape, pausing along the way to meditate on specific persons and events understood to be representative of Americans' collective identity. Names, labels, and narratives directed visitors' attention to whatever purportedly was significant or desirable about visually displayed objects, thus turning the seemingly ordinary—tombstones, a restored eighteenth century farmhouse, and musket balls, for example—into sacred symbols of a new civic religion. Achieving the central goals of *epideictic* rhetoric— which seeks to amplify and display the supposedly shared virtues, beliefs, and identity of the community to community members—the Saratoga Park (much like the Civil War cemeteries) afforded visitors the opportunity to undergo a transcendent and inspirational experience through their immediate and visceral encounter with symbolic representations of the ideals of the American nation. See Halloran and Clark, in Prelli, *Rhetorics of Display*, 141–56. For more on the nature and political function of *epideictic* rhetoric, see Aristotle, *Rhetoric*, trans. John Henry Freese (Cambridge: Harvard University Press, 1911); Yun Lee Too, "Epideictic Genre," in Sloane, *Encyclopedia*, 251–7.

84. In her incredibly insightful treatise on audience reception to representations of war and suffering, *Regarding the Pain of Others*, Susan Sontag argues that photographs have the ability to make previously abstract death tolls (e.g., the eighty thousand Chinese civilians killed during the Japanese "Rape of Nanking") tangible and meaningful. We might say the same thing about the individual headstones that, for 150 years, have appeared in American military cemeteries. Whereas iconic memorials, or sepulchers containing the remains of many men, condense and minimize individual sacrifices into a single representation of loss, individual headstones displayed side by side indicate a collective sacrifice that seems almost greater than the sum of its parts. See Susan Sontag, *Regarding the Pain of Others* (New York: Picador, 2003), 84–5.

85. In her ongoing study of contemporary funerary and commemoration practices in inner-city Baltimore, Maryland communication scholar Katie O'Neill has argued that when a deceased person is aligned with a particular territory, the living who align themselves with the deceased automatically become aligned with that same territory (and its meanings or symbolic values). The theory she has developed is useful for understanding sites like the Civil War cemeteries and the American World War I cemeteries in Europe, and I plan to use and build upon it throughout my future work. Katie O'Neill, "A Mournful Fashion: Form, Function, and Meaning of Baltimore's R.I.P T-Shirts," (Agora lecture, Department of Communication, University of Pittsburgh, Pittsburgh, PA, October 26, 2007).

86. I have argued elsewhere that immovable material objects placed in important civic spaces can be effective vessels for sustained symbolic action and the representation of those whose bodily presence is not otherwise possible. See David W. Seitz, "Embodying Unauthorized Immigrants: Counterhegemonic Protest and the Rhetorical Power of the 'Material Diatribe,'" in *Race and Hegemonic Struggle in the United States: Pop Culture, Politics, and Protest*, eds. Michael G. Lacy and Mary E. Triece (Madison, NJ: Fairleigh Dickinson University Press, 2014), 143–73.

87. By situating the Civil War within a longer national timeline ("Four score and seven years ago..."), Lincoln's "Gettysburg Address" effectively broadened temporal horizons in a way that would help the American people cope with the tragedies of the war.

88. Faust, *This Republic of Suffering*, 9.

89. According to cultural historian Ron Robin, the federal government and the U.S. military hoped the permanent overseas cemeteries would "dramatize [the nation's] accomplishments" in the Great War and "establish powerful and uniform symbols of the national spirit abroad." See Ron Robin, "'A Foothold in Europe': The Aesthetics and Politics of American War Cemeteries in Western Europe," *Journal of American Studies* 29.1 (1995): 55–72 (56–7).

90. See Aeschylus, *The Suppliant Maidens: The Persians*, trans. and intro. Seth G. Benardete (Chicago: University of Chicago Press, 1956), 44–5.

91. Gary Laderman shows that throughout American history, suicide has been a taboo (and, for many religious communities, a sin guaranteeing damnation). Thus, the bodies of those who commit suicide have, generally speaking, been problematic for families and communities, because, as Laderman writes, "the body of a suicide [is]

an outcast from the social order. What was once a living human being [is] now a pure and insignificant object, thoroughly desacralized and empty of meaning." Because they needed to keep numbers high, the planners of America's overseas cemeteries would incorporate the graves of soldiers who committed suicide or died of disease just as they would include the graves of soldiers who died "nobly" in action. Of course, the causes of *all* soldiers' deaths would be whitewashed and obfuscated nearly to the point where one would not know that they had died violently and prematurely. See Laderman, *Sacred Remains*, 18–20.

92. Gary Laderman describes human society's fundamental concern with proper treatment of the dead body thusly: "While most societies have turned to religious authorities and teachings to make metaphysical sense of death, confronting the reality of the human corpse has been a particularly compelling dilemma for survivors. As sociologist Robert Hertz observed, the death of a societal member 'is tantamount to a sacrilege' because society itself 'is stricken in the very principle of its life, in the faith it has in itself.'" See ibid, 1.

93. Quoted in Ron Theodore Robin, *Enclaves of America: The Rhetoric of American Political Architecture Abroad 1900–1965* (Princeton: Princeton University Press, 1992), 40.

94. Soldierly remains and unexploded armament and chemical shells from the Great War are still routinely discovered in the fields and forests of Western Europe today. For instance, in February of 2011, Canadian authorities successfully identified the remains of Private Thomas Lawless of Calgary (killed in 1917), which had been discovered by a French farmer. See "WWI soldier found in France identified as Albertan," cnews.ca, February 24, 2011, http://cnews.canoe.ca/CNEWS/Canada/2011/02/24/17396621.html (accessed April 29, 2011).

95. Lisa M. Budreau, *Bodies of War: World War I and the Politics of Commemoration in America, 1919–1933* (New York: New York University Press, 2010), 123.

96. As historian Elizabeth G. Grossman argues, the CFA was compelled to design sites that would signify that the government had been right "to induce Americans *not* to repatriate their kin." See Elizabeth G. Grossman, "Architecture for a Public Client: The Monuments and Chapels of the American Battle Monuments Commission," *Journal of the Society of Architectural Historians* 43 (May 1984): 119–143(120).

97. "American Graves Abroad," *Washington Post*, August 26, 1921, 6.

98. Newspapers offered extensive coverage of the CFA's 1921 report. See, for example, "Plan 6 Cemeteries for A.E.F. Abroad," *New York Times*, August 23, 1921.

99. The National Commission, *Ninth*, 39–41.

100. Grossman, "Architecture," 121.

101. The National Commission, *Ninth*, 41.

102. Ibid, 45–7.

103. Ibid, 43, 47.

104. Ibid, 43, 49–50.

105. Ibid, 43.

106. Ibid, 49.

107. Ibid, 44–5.

108. Ibid, 65.

109. Ibid, 50.

110. Ibid, 51–3.

111. Ibid, 49–50, 53.

112. Ibid, 53.

113. Ibid, 53–6.

114. Ibid, 58.

115. Ibid, 56–65.

116. Ibid, 49.

117. Ibid, 51, 53.

118. "American Graves Abroad."

119. "Approves Cemetery Plans," *Washington Post*, December 15, 1921, 6.

120. In time, these cemeteries would be officially named Flanders Field American Cemetery and Memorial (ACM), Aisne-Marne ACM, Meuse-Argonne ACM, Oise-Aisne ACM, Somme ACM, St. Mihiel ACM, Suresnes ACM, and Brookwood ACM. By including the term "Memorial" in each site's name, the planners indicated that these spaces were not just cemeteries, but national war memorials as well.

121. "Brief History," 2.

122. In order to instill a sense of national unity, various groups—including the Red Cross, the American Library Association, the YMCA, the Jewish Welfare Board, the Jewish Veterans of the World War, the Knights of Columbus, the National Catholic War Council, and various African-American organizations—were invited to participate in the ceremony. See Piehler, *Remembering War*, 120.

123. The Unknown Soldier was transported across the Atlantic on the USS *Olympia*, Admiral George Dewey's Spanish-American War flagship. By using *Olympia* for this purpose, the government was able to connect the Great War to the young nation's other notable overseas military venture. See Piehler, *Remembering War*, 118.

124. At the ceremony itself, General Pershing (representing both the U.S. military *and* the ABMC) gave a speech in which he made an "offering of love" to America's fallen soldiers and their mothers. As the *Washington Post* recounted: "Stressing the enormous sacrifice paid by American mothers during the late war as they reluctantly yet proudly relinquished their sons to fight overseas, Gen. Pershing pointed out that 'through memorial week exercises the entire country is happy to lay its offering of love and admiration at the tomb of the Unknown Soldier, who typifies the spirit of America [...] It is a noble and sweet thing to die for one's country.'" See "Pershing Praises Dead at Tomb of Unknown Soldier," *Washington Post*, May 27, 1925, 20.

125. "Home They Brought Her Warrior Dead," *Kansas City Times*, February 3, 1921, 18.

126. John Francis Marion, *Famous and Curious Cemeteries* (New York: Crown Publishers, 1977), 158–9.

127. "Criticizes Graves Service," *Washington Post*, January 25, 1922, 6.

128. The cemetery planners also felt it necessary to take the feelings of local Europeans into account. As one local official in the Meuse region of France told the planners: "We Frenchman cannot be expected to differentiate—Pennsylvania, Ohio, 28th Division [...] all are Americans to us. Their monuments are American monuments. And in these economically difficult times when many of our own bombed-out

people still lack roofs a Frenchman can hardly be enthusiastic at the prospect of so many monuments springing up on every side." See North, Manuscript, 28.

129. "Harding Proposes Battle Monuments," *New York Times*, March 2, 1922, 17.

130. Ibid.

131. "Proceedings of Congress and Committees in Brief," *Washington Post*, March 30, 1922, 6

132. "For Battle Monuments," *Washington Post*, January 15, 1923, 6.

133. Piehler, *Remembering War*, 98.

134. Elizabeth Nishiura, *American Battle Monuments: A Guide to Military Cemeteries and Monuments Maintained by the American Battle Monuments Commission* (Detroit: Omnigraphics, 1989), 3–4.

135. "Harding Names Monuments Board," *New York Times*, June 21, 1923, 3; North, Manuscript, 2–3.

136. Bestowed the title, "General of the Armies," General Pershing was the highest-ranking military figure in American history (an honor he held until 1976, when Congress passed a law that permanently elevated George Washington to a higher rank). Upon his return to the United States after the war, hundreds of thousands of people gathered at a New York City port to greet him. As the *Philadelphia Inquirer* reported: "On the eve of the greatest celebration in its history, New York is agog with excitement. Never before, not even when Presidents and princes were given the freedom of the city, has Manhattan Island seen the like of the celebrations planned to greet General John J. Pershing." His travels to European countries elicited similar reactions. Throughout the remaining years of his life, Pershing enjoyed a degree of international fame probably unmatched by any other contemporary. See "General Pershing is Guest of Honor in London Today," *Wilkes-Barre Times Leader*, July 15, 1919, 1; "Pershing Reception Will be Greatest in N. Y. Annals General and Famed First Division," *Philadelphia Inquirer*, September 8, 1919, 1; and, "Rest Easy: Historical Updates with Honor," *Washington Post*, August 15, 1976, 152.

137. Scholars have overlooked the essential fact that the CFA was really the brains behind this operation. Most studies of the sites begin and end with the ABMC (a point I return to later in the chapter). At best, scholars state that the ABMC worked "in consultation with the Commission of Fine Arts." See, for example, Budreau, *Bodies of War*, 149.

138. The Commission, *A Brief History*, 245.

139. North, Manuscript, 2.

140. Senator Reed was the only member of the ABMC who had any significant experience in military park and cemetery design, as he previously served on the Shiloh National Military Park Commission. See Smith, *The Golden Age*, 235. None of the ABMC commissioners, however, possessed formal training in art, architecture, or landscape design. Thus, the ABMC turned to the CFA as a student would a professor. This asymmetrical relationship commenced on October 2, 1923, when the ABMC met with CFA Chairman Charles Moore to receive firsthand the CFA's conception of the cemeteries. See Grossman, "Architecture," 121.

141. General Pershing himself took great interest in enforcing agreements between the United States and France that would prohibit the erection of unsanctioned

American battlefield monuments. Consider the following eyewitness account, as told by Pershing's personal aide, Major General Thomas North: "One day while working on guidebook business Major Eisenhower reported that a monument to the 316th Infantry crowned Cornwilly Hill: General Pershing very naturally took the position that this constituted a deliberate defiance of the governments of both France and the United States. He proposed to the French government that the monument be demolished. This was embarrassing. The matter dragged on for months, occasionally flaring up in newspapers or spoiling the day for Embassy officials" (North, Manuscript, 28). Publicly, Pershing and the ABMC defended their censorship of unsanctioned battlefield monuments by arguing that private citizens and veterans groups were not aware of how offensive their well-intentioned monuments could be to Europeans. Many battlefield monuments that had been constructed immediately after the war displayed the braggadocios remark: "We won the war." Bemoaning the apparent insensitivity of such memorials, and justifying their destruction, the ABMC stated: "It should be considered that our country was fighting during the latter part of the war only and had fewer troops engaged and lighter losses than either France, England or Italy." See "Pershing Blocks Marking of World War Sites with Merely Ornate American Memorials," *New York Times*, April 26, 1926, 1; "War Memorials Rising Throughout the World," *New York Times*, November 7, 1926, XX16.

142. Though the French and Belgian governments had agreed to allow the United States to enjoy the land upon which the cemeteries were built "in perpetuity without rent or taxation," the ABMC's ambitions often exceeded the amount of land available. Thus, the ABMC was often forced to negotiate with private landowners (who were, more often than not, unwilling to sell their properties at a reasonable price). According to General North's manuscript, the ABMC found clever ways to obtain the land they needed, including: getting landowners drunk on wine so they would sign the deeds; stirring up trouble between rivaling siblings until one of the signed away land rights to spite the other; and, working behind the scenes with local officials to pressure citizens into selling (pages 12, 14, 16, 18–19).

143. Grossman, "Architecture," 126.

144. Robin, *Enclaves*, 41-2.

145. Paul Cret, "Memorials—Columns, Shafts, Cenotaphs, and Tablets," *Architectural Forum* 45 (December 1926): 333, quoted in Robin, *Enclaves*, 43-4.

146. For more on the ABMC architects and their ties to the CFA, see Grossman, "Architecture."

147. In February of 1918, Pershing personally handpicked eight renowned American painters and illustrators to travel with him and record scenes of the U.S. military's experience in Europe. After the war, Pershing authored and published a complete history of the A.E.F's actions and accomplishments in the Great War. See "Eight Artists Commissioned for Service with Pershing," *Dallas Morning News*, February 22, 1918, 9; John J. Pershing, *My Experiences in the World War* (New York: Frederick A. Stokes, 1931).

148. North, Manuscript, 22.

149. In the media, the terms "Pershing" and "the American Battle Monuments Commission" were synonymous. Pershing was cast to the American people as a

vigilant guardian of the U.S. soldiers buried overseas. As the *New York Times* stated in 1928: "No soldier in his days of retirement, Washington to Grant, had such a task in the evening of life as has fallen to the lot of Pershing. Nothing becomes the great commander, so modest in his bearing, so generous toward the merits of others, more than his sympathy for veterans broken in the great adventure, and his solicitude that those who laid down their lives shall be fittingly honored on the fields of service." And on his 76th birthday in 1936, the *Washington Post* reported that the aging leader of the ABMC's principal interest was still "the boys who were left 'over there.'" See "Pershing Arranges for War Memorials," *New York Times*, June 26, 1927, 16; "Pershing is 76 Today with Few Signs of Aging," *Washington Post*, September 13, 1936, AA7; "Pershing Publishes Battlefield Guide for U.S. Tourists," *Washington Post*, August 21, 1917, M4; and, "Pershing's Work in France," *New York Times*, February 27, 1928, 18.

150. Pershing was never one to suppress his feelings, beliefs, or political leanings. Take, for example, his 1923 comments on "the pacifist menace": "It is the duty and should be the earnest desire of every loyal American citizen to support the War Department in its efforts [...] This support is particularly essential at this time when an active campaign against preparedness is being conducted by pacifist associations, some of which are fostered and supported, either directly or indirectly, by alien or other agencies which are inimical to our form of government." Or consider this 1923 *New York Times* report about a speech he gave to a group of Pennsylvania National Guard Troops: "General Pershing said he hoped the day would come when every American girl would demand that the man who sought her in marriage should be one who had served his time as a volunteer, willing to face every duty of American citizenship. 'I am going to say a word in the ear of our American girls for that purpose,' he added." Or, consider the fact that General Pershing accompanied fellow ABMC commissioner David A. Reed to President Calvin Coolidge's signing of the 1924 Johnson-Reed Act, a xenophobic piece of anti-immigrant legislation that that severely restricted Southern and Eastern Europeans from immigrating to the U.S., as well as prohibiting the immigration of East Asians and Asian Indians all together. See "Pacifist Menace Seen by Pershing," *New York Times*, October 23, 1923, 20; "Pershing Tells Girls to Marry Guardsmen," *New York Times*, July 17, 1923, 2; and, "President Coolidge Signing Appropriation Bills for the Veterans Bureau on the South Lawn During the Garden Party for Wounded Veterans," Library of Congress, n.d., http://loc.gov/pictures/resource/cph.3c11372/ (accessed May 3, 2011).

151. Budreau, *Bodies of War*, 122–6.

152. Robin, "'A Foothold,'" 64. This design also allowed the planners to magnify the presence of each individual soldier (an important accomplishment given the comparatively few bodies the planners had at their disposal).

153. American Battle Monuments Commission, *Annual Report to the President of the United States for the Fiscal Year 1925* (Washington, DC: Government Printing Office, 1926), 1, 13.

154. Ibid, 5, 9, 66.

155. Though the CFA often cited Arlington National Cemetery in discussions of its plans for the overseas cemeteries, the CFA was, in all likelihood, only citing

Arlington as an easily recognizable reference in reports, correspondence, and presentations to interested parties. While certain aesthetic attributes of Arlington (and Civil War cemeteries in general) would find their way into the World War I burial grounds, there is little reason to believe that the CFA—an organization that detested the characteristics of the romance garden gravescape—would hold up the nineteenth-century military cemeteries as models for the overseas projects. Ultimately, the World War I cemeteries looked and functioned much differently than their domestic predecessors. Scholars have mistakenly perceived the CFA's early references of Arlington and the subsequent "departure" from the Civil War model as the key piece of evidence that power had entirely shifted to the ABMC. I believe this misinterpretation of the CFA's intentions and rhetorical use of "Arlington" has led scholars astray—in essence, they have been barking up the ABMC's tree when they should have been barking up the CFA's. See Carole Blair, V. William Balthrop, and Neil Michel, "Arlington-sur-Seine: War Commemoration and the Perpetual Argument from Sacrifice," Sixth Conference of the International Society for the Study of Argumentation, Amsterdam, Holland June 27–30, 2006; Grossman, "Architecture," 120–1; and, Robin, "'A Foothold,'" 59.

156. ABMC, *Report*, 12, 13, 17, 21.

157. William P. Jones, Jr., "Service with the American Battle Monuments Commission, 1 April 1967 to 30 June 1974," 4, 5, William P. Jones, Jr. Papers, U.S. Army Military History Institute, Carlisle, Pennsylvania.

158. ABMC, *Report*, 17.

159. Ibid, 56–7.

160. The decision to use white marble was made not only for aesthetic reasons, but for economic ones as well. General Pershing recommended the acceptance of a bid from a quarry in Carrara, Italy, which could provide an abundance of Italian marble at a fraction of what it would cost to transport stone from the United States. The plan to use Italian stone in American cemeteries caused a minor stir in Washington, D.C., and led a coalition of "American stone men" to protest the decision publicly (but unsuccessfully). See "Favors Italian Marble," *New York Times*, June 24, 1926; "Plans for Markers May Not Be Changed," *Washington Post*, July 7, 1926; and, "Davis Acts on Headstones," *New York Times*, July 17, 1926.

161. The *Washington Post* elaborated on the notion that such religious symbolism would bring some measure of comfort and solace to next of kin: "[The Senate passed] an amendment that would insure retention in permanent form of the white crosses that now mark the graves of American war dead overseas [...] Senator Reed (Republican), Pennsylvania, who sponsored the action, said relatives of soldiers dead all favored retention of the crosses which were signalized in war poetry." See "Senate Votes to Retain Flanders White Crosses," *Washington Post*, March 23, 1924, 7. Given the demographics of the American Expeditionary Forces during the Great War, an overwhelming majority of the headstones would take the shape of the Latin cross. The image of the Latin cross itself, appearing over and over again in precisely aligned rows at each cemetery, is a well-known religious ideograph, a historical, visual symbol that signifies familiar meanings within most Western cultures. In *Signs and Symbols in Christian Art*, George Ferguson isolates the Latin cross's twentieth-century

connotations: "The cross is one of the oldest and most universal of all symbols. It is, of course, the perfect symbol of Christ because of His sacrifice upon the Cross. In a broader sense, however, the cross has become the mark or sign of the Christian religion, the emblem of atonement, and the symbol of salvation and redemption through Christianity." For Christians, the Latin cross signifies "sacrifice," "atonement," "salvation," and "redemption." In summation, the Latin cross remembers Christ's sacrifice for the collective good, the subsequent resurrection of Christ's flesh, and the journey of Christ's soul to heaven. See George Ferguson, *Signs and Symbols in Christian Art* (New York: Oxford University Press, 1959), 100.

162. For a detailed discussion of "liminal space," see Alan Wallach, "Regionalism Redux" (exhibition review), *American Quarterly* 43 (June 1991), 269.

163. ABMC, *Report*, 13, 17.

164. See Carolyn Marvin and David W. Ingle, *Blood Sacrifice and the Nation: Totem Rituals and the American Flag* (Cambridge: Cambridge University Press, 1999); "President Wilson Sets June 14 as Flag Day," *Idaho Daily Statesman*, May 31, 1916, 2.

165. Charles Moore had previously considered building a chapel at Meuse-Argonne. See Grossman, "Architecture," 121.

166. ABMC, *Report*, 17. A modest house had already been constructed next to each cemetery in anticipation of future cemetery directors and their families (the houses are still used for this purpose today). The plan to construct a chapel at each cemetery was supported by Army and Navy chaplains of the Federal Council of Churches, who publicly argued that each site needed a proper building where burial services and religious exercises could be conducted. See "Erection of Chapels for War Dead Asked," *Washington Post*, May 17, 1926, 7.

167. Gary Laderman, *Rest in Peace: A Cultural History of Death and the Funeral Home in Twentieth-Century America* (Oxford: Oxford University Press, 2003), 24–6.

168. ABMC, *Report*, 21.

169. Most of the ABMC cemeteries contain several graves of people who were not U.S. armed servicemen. For instance, Suresnes contains the graves of three chaplains, six doctors of medicine, two doctors of dentistry, two children of U.S. soldiers who died shortly after the war, eight female nurses, and two sisters (buried side by side) who died while volunteering in battlefield canteens.

170. Other proposed lists included "an alphabetical list of graves for the cemetery itself [...] a list for each cemetery by organization [...] an alphabetical list of soldiers of allied countries buried in our cemeteries [...] and an alphabetical list of naval personnel in our cemeteries." ABMC, *Report*, 58.

171. Ibid.

172. Ibid, 17.

173. Ibid, 13.

174. Ibid, 55.

175. Ibid, 13, 21.

176. Ibid, 17, 64, 74.

177. As I discussed earlier, the U.S. government allowed and paid for the repatriation of found American bodies. Because of the magnitude of British losses and the

early desire to establish symbolic "English gardens" throughout Continental Europe, the British government had no such policy. For a thorough and fascinating assessment of the IWGC's postwar policies, see Jay Winter, *Sites of Memory, Sites of Mourning: The Great War in European Cultural History* (Cambridge: Cambridge University Press, 1995).

178. ABMC, *Report*, 23.

179. Paul Fussell, *The Great War and Modern Memory* (Oxford: Oxford University Press, 1975), 70–1.

180. The ABMC experimented with the idea of letting next of kin inscribe their own words on the back of soldiers' headstones. At Suresnes, the ABMC permitted seven families to write messages much as British families had done in every IWGC cemetery. These inscriptions, which are still apparent, read: HE HAD THE POWER SUFFICIENT TO HIS DREAM; KILLED IN ACTION; TO LIVE IN HEARTS WE LEAVE BEHIND IS NOT TO DIE; A SON WHO IS THE THEME OF HONOUR'S TONGUE; KILLED IN ACTION ARGONNE OFFENSIVE; KILLED IN ACTION AT DUN SUR MEUSE; and, KILLED IN ACTION. Disturbed by phrases that spoke to the taking of life rather than the willing sacrifice of American soldiers, the ABMC discontinued the policy. As General North states: "[P]hrases such as 'Killed in Action' tended to create invidious distinctions, so the practice was abandoned." North, Manuscript, 8.

181. ABMC, *Report*, 25.

182. Fussell, *The Great War*, 70.

183. ABMC, *Report*, 17.

184. Ibid, 29.

185. Ibid, 75.

186. Ibid, 29, 31.

187. Ibid, 39.

188. Ibid, 39, 43.

189. "Pershing Arranges for War Memorials," *New York Times*, June 26, 1927, 16.

190. "Brief History of Organization," 2.

191. For more on the establishment of these battlefield monuments, the architectural principles of the cemetery chapels, and the 1937 dedication ceremonies, see Grossman, "Architecture."

192. This section synthesizes my own on-site observations (conducted over several weeks-long trips through Europe) with other scholars' descriptions of the cemeteries. While the key aesthetic attributes of each cemetery will be addressed here, the descriptions will become progressively shorter for the sake of brevity. For more thorough descriptions of each site, see Marion, *Famous*, 172–86; Richard E. Meyer, "Stylistic Variation in the Western Front Battlefield Cemeteries of World War I Combatant Nations," *Markers: Annual Journal of the Association for Gravestone Studies* 18 (2001): 189–253; and, Nishiura, *American*.

193. John McCrae, *In Flanders Field: And Other Poems*, ed. Sir Andrew Macphail (New York: G. P. Putnam's Sons, 1919), 3.

194. The chapels are decidedly Christian in nature (the term "chapel" itself denotes a small building for Christian worship). Although the ABMC eventually

placed a silver or gold menorah on each chapel's altar, there is little doubt that these designated spaces of contemplation harness traditional Christian symbolism, architectural design, and rituals of remembrance to achieve their rhetorical effect.

195. The very name of this easily recognizable tree—"weeping willow"—signifies sadness, mourning, and grief.

196. During World War II, German anti-tank guns fired at French tanks passing in the vicinity of the Aisne-Marne Cemetery. The German artillery inflicted much damage on the American burial grounds. After the war, the ABMC reconstructed what had been destroyed, but left an artillery shell hole in the stonework on the right side of the chapel entrance. This mark only serves to reinforce the masculine, violent ethos of the site.

197. Over the past three decades, public memory has become a key term and object of study across the humanities. Scholars like Paul Fussell and Pierre Nora have been credited with instigating the movement, which is to expansive to cite properly here. But some of the more relevant works include: Greg Dickinson, Carole Blair, and Brian L. Ott, *Places of Public Memory: The Rhetoric of Museums and Memorials* (Tuscaloosa: University of Alabama Press, 2010); Paul Fussell, *The Great War*; Michael Kammen, *Mystic Chords of Memory: The Transformation of Tradition in American Culture* (New York: Vintage, 1993); George Lipsitz, *Time Passages: Collective Memory and American Popular Culture* (Minneapolis: University of Minnesota Press, 1990); Pierre Nora, *Realms of Memory: The Construction of the French Past*, trans. Arthur Goldhammer (New York: Columbia University Press, 1997); Kendall R. Phillips, ed., *Framing Public Memory* (Tuscaloosa: University of Alabama Press, 2004); Kirk Savage, *Monument Wars*; and, Jay Winter, *Sites of Memory*.

198. See, for example, Suzanne Evans, *Mothers of Heroes, Mothers of Martyrs: World War I and the Politics of Grief* (Montreal: McGill-Queen's University Press, 2007); Nina Tumarkin, *The Living and the Dead: The Rise and Fall of the Cult of World War II in Russia* (New York: Basic Books, 1994); and, Jay Winter, *Remembering War: The Great War Between Memory and History in the Twentieth Century* (New Haven: Yale University Press, 2006).

199. See, for example, Richard E. Meyer, "Stylistic Variation."

200. See, for example, Blair et al., "Arlington-sur-Seine."

201. While pursuing my Ph.D. at the University of Pittsburgh, I was fortunate to win several fellowships and awards that afforded me the resources and time to conduct on-site research in Europe and archival research throughout the United States.

202. Robin builds his essay, "'A Foothold in Europe,'" on a quote taken from a 1954 article that had been written by a proponent of the establishment of World War II cemeteries in Europe. Lumping World War I cemeteries and the subsequent World War II cemeteries together, he mistakenly analyzes the World War I sites through the lens of the World War II sites. Moreover, he claims that the original members of the ABMC "acted as a rubber stamp for policies defined by" Pershing, who saw himself "first and foremost as [a representative] of the government and the military establishment rather than [a guardian] for the bereaved families." Robin proceeds to argue that the World War I cemeteries were, more or less, of Pershing's making. Unfortunately, Robin fails to cite a single piece of evidence to support these claims. Ultimately, I

believe it is foolhardy to believe that Pershing and the ABMC could have pulled off anything as artistically, architecturally, and aesthetically beautiful as these cemeteries on their own. See Robin, "'A Foothold in Europe,'" 56–8.

203. Robin, "'A Foothold in Europe,'" 71.

204. *Enclaves*, 45, 57; "'A Foothold in Europe,'" 60–5. When reading these works, one wishes that Robin had proposed some alternative possibilities for the visual presentation of the cemeteries. Regrettably, the reader is presented with only negative criticisms of the sites.

205. *Enclaves*, 58, 60; "'A Foothold in Europe,'" 60–5, 71. In his criticisms of the apparent contradictions of the American war cemeteries, Robin does not mention the fact that both war and cemeteries are, themselves, inherently contradictory in nature. While every war devolves into murder, chaos, hatred, and misery, the instigation of every war is couched in the terms of the ideology of "returning order and peace to the world." As René Guénon writes (*Symbolism of the Cross*, page 42): "From whatever aspect and in whatever domain war is envisaged, one may say that the essential reason for its existence is to put a stop to disorder and to restore order. In other terms, it is concerned with the unification of multiplicity by means which belong to the world of multiplicity itself." And I think it safe to say, that cemeteries are inherently contradictory in that visitors can become intensely aware of their own existence (of the fact that they are *alive*) when they encounter the reality of death before them.

206. "'A Foothold in Europe,'" 72. In his study of the sites, Robin makes several egregious factual errors. For instance, he states that "only name, rank, and serial number [appear] on each headstone" (he does not mention home state and date of death). He also claims that none of the sites depict weapons being used in a state of action (Aisne-Marne does). Such comments indicate that Robin may not have visited most (if any) of the cemeteries before publishing his works. See *Enclaves*, 45, 57.

207. Without fully comprehending the aesthetic strategies of the CFA, Robin criticizes this aspect of the cemeteries, stating: "The general concept was to arrange cemeteries in a formal didactic fashion which represented the views of its planners […] However casual the walkways seemed, all paths led to the chapels with their official interpretation of the war effort. The unwavering steering of visitors toward these official structures assured that due homage would be paid to the role of government in coordinating, perhaps dictating, the will of the people." See "'A Foothold in Europe,'" 64.

208. When one approaches (whether by car or foot) many of the cemeteries—particularly Oise-Aisne, Aisne-Marne, and Somme—the visitors already within the cemeteries, walking along the paths and through the rows of headstones, appear to be nothing more than little props in the grand panorama. The same can be said when one is in the cemetery proper and observes from a distance other visitors making their way through the site. This can be a little unsettling, as one can begin to realize that one too probably looks like a prop to everyone else.

209. Each ABMC cemetery director is also charged with the task of enforcing rules of behavior at his respective site. When the Tomb of the Unknown Soldier was unveiled at Arlington National Cemetery, visitors often used it as a bench or a picnic table (a common practice in the garden romance gravescape). When the American Legion complained in 1926, the government decided that the Tomb would be guarded

on a daily basis. The ABMC was sure not to let such things happen at its sites. In an oral history interview I conducted with Gerald Arsenault, Cemetery Director at the Brittany American World War II Cemetery and Memorial in St. James, France (May 10, 2006), Arsenault indicated how part of his job entailed managing visitors' behavior: "Europeans, not only Americans, consider this sacred ground. They all realize that the soldiers gave their lives for the liberation of France. I have many French families, if I have children that will run in the cemetery before I can go out to tell them to stop running, sometimes a French family will grab them by the collar and tell them, 'You're on sacred ground here, and you will behave while you're on these sacred grounds.'" For more on the Arlington controversy, see Piehler, *Remembering War*, 122.

210. Remarkably, a sense of permanence is maintained at each cemetery by keeping the presentation of the foliage (every rose bush, every tree) the same as it was when the sites opened. As Gerald Arsenault, Director of the Brittany American World War II Cemetery and Memorial told me: "And of course, as you can see, the chestnut trees, the hedges that we have, I have a planting plan, and where you see a rose bed here, you see the alignment of the chestnut trees here, you see a Douglas fir, rhododendrons, I have to follow that original planting plan. If I lose a tree I have to plant the same species and type. As you see in the cemetery today, you can visit thirty, fifty years from now, it will always be kept in this manner. And we will always have that original planting plan preserving the original vision that those architects had. Of course a lot of their work was collaborative with the Fine Arts Commission. So you visit today. Your children will visit fifty years from now, and they will basically see the same thing."

211. Mircea Eliade enumerates on the feminine undertones of the funerary rhetoric of "rest" and "sleep": "Throughout the mythology and iconography of Persephone, but above all during the Hellenistic period, the Mediterranean and Roman worlds produced certain images that show death as a deep sleep, a return to the maternal womb, a ritual passage toward a blessed world, or an upward journey through stellar space." See Eliade, *Symbolism*, 60–1.

212. As far as I know, every ABMC cemetery director has been a male who served (in some capacity) in the U.S. military—a fact that imbues the position with a somewhat paternalistic and pro-war character.

213. *The New International Version of the Bible*, Luke 22.42–44.

214. "Our Dead in France," *New York Times*, December 4, 1926, 16.

215. "Monuments to the Deeds of the A.E.F.," *New York Times*, July 17, 1927, SM14.

216. "'Row on Row,' They Await the Pilgrims," *New York Times*, May 11, 1930, 82.

217. John J. Pershing, "Our National War Memorials in Europe," *National Geographic Magazine* 65.1 (1934): 1–35.

218. Lotte Larsen Meyer, "Mourning in a Distant Land: Gold Star Pilgrimages to American Military Cemeteries in Europe, 1930–33," *Markers: Annual Journal of the Association for Gravestone Studies* 20 (2003): 31–75. For the most thorough study of the history of this program, see John W. Graham, *The Gold Star Mother Pilgrimages of the 1930s* (Jefferson, NC: McFarland and Company, 2005).

Conclusion

This book has endeavored to offer a rhetorical history of the ideographic construction of the 'modern, universal, sacrificial U.S. soldier' (as I term it). Starting from the outbreak of World War I in 1914, and ending with the final establishment of U.S. overseas cemeteries during the 1930s, this book traces the genesis of this still-influential icon. To recap ...

Between 1914 and 1917, the American public came to perceive (via graphic news reports and firsthand accounts) World War I as something akin to a "human slaughter-house"—an immoral, regressive, antidemocratic, and unnecessary mass bloodletting that harnessed the terrible destructive capacities of modern science and technology and had little to do with the interests of the United States. Essentially transforming Europe into "a vast killing field" where few fallen soldiers received proper burial and treatment, upending traditional rules of battle and notions of soldierly sacrifice, and plunging soldiers and civilians on both sides into a general state of barbarism and madness, the war seemingly entailed never-before-seen levels of mass death and physical and psychic trauma. Despite the efforts of the pro-war, "preparedness" movement during the early years of the war, the American public was generally reluctant to intervene in this horrific, *European* affair. To wit, in 1916, President Woodrow Wilson won his reelection campaign on the slogan, "He Kept Us Out of the War!" The apparent majority of Americans considered Wilson's victory to be a referendum against U.S. participation in World War I.

Shockingly, in April of 1917, Woodrow Wilson committed one of the swiftest about-faces in U.S. presidential history. Abandoning the staunch anti-war platform of his 1916 presidential campaign, he went before Congress and asked for a declaration of war against Germany. Congress overwhelmingly supported the President's idealistic call to make the world "safe for democracy" and plunged the U.S. into the Great War. The battle cries in Washington, D.C., however, did not necessarily express the sentiments of the American people. For three years, Americans had received a relatively "uncensored," if distant, view of the war in all its apparent terror, violence, and death, and many had come to see the conflict as a senseless, apocalyptic, and strictly European matter that the United States could and should stay out of.

Recognizing the antiwar and isolationist streaks that coursed through public discourse and consciousness, and comprehending the obvious incongruity between his pre- and postelection stances, President Wilson spearheaded the development of a series of wartime laws, policies, and agencies that effectively made citizen (and noncitizen) support for the war effort a matter of compulsion, not choice. Establishing an unprecedented national draft, a powerful propaganda and media censorship bureau, and a Justice Department bent on censuring and prosecuting dissenters, the Wilson Administration attempted to control the "body and soul and spirit" of every American "in the supreme effort of service and sacrifice"—or what I term "Wilson's project of motion." Within months, the people of the United States were legally and rhetorically transformed (through language, law, and force) into either "seditious" subversives or loyal, subservient participants in the national war effort. By war's end in November of 1918, roughly 117,000 citizen-soldiers would die "over there," far from the shores of their homeland.

After the war, in the United States the essential task of memorializing fallen soldiers was highly problematic. The nation had lost tens of thousands of its men in defense of territory that was not its own. Furthermore, threats to the homeland had never been as obvious as for European belligerents. Many citizens rightfully wondered for what, and for whom, had Americans died? In response to this crisis, public and private leaders began developing and popularizing through various commemorative acts (such as the eventual establishment of the Tomb of the Unknown Soldier) the now-familiar, yet then *new*, vision of the U.S. soldier as 'a global force for good'—an individual willing to sacrifice, fight, and die across the globe for Americans and foreigners alike. As this book has shown, the central component of this postwar ideological and rhetorical project was the U.S. government's unprecedented plan to establish permanent national military cemeteries abroad. Constructed throughout Europe where citizen-soldiers had fought and perished, and consecrated as *American* sites, these burial grounds would simultaneously: link the nation's war dead back to U.S. soil and the national purpose rooted there; express the nation's emerging prominent role on the world's stage; and, advance the burgeoning icon of the 'sacrificial, universal' American soldier.

The unprecedented plan for a network of overseas cemeteries, however, was highly controversial during the immediate postwar years. In order to see the cemetery project to fruition, the government needed to secure the remains of fallen soldiers; in order to secure the remains of fallen soldiers, the government needed to gain the approval of mourning next of kin. As chapter 3 of this book reveals, although many relatives simply filled out and returned the terse and non-sentimental forms issued by the War Department, others crafted messages of varied, and often poetic, rhetorical appeals to express their opinions regarding the plan to bury American war dead in distant lands. Many citizens relinquished the care of corpses to the government; others demanded, sometimes bitterly, the return of loved ones' remains to the United States; others expressed confusion, sadness, anxiety, and disenchantment. The correspondence discussed in chapter 3 reveals the complexities of the feelings, ideologies, traditions, social strata, and rights of U.S. citizens who were prompted by the death of their kin to consider both their own relation to the nation and the human costs that U.S. intervention in global affairs entailed.

Beyond capturing the sentiments of a past generation of Americans, this textual corpus also came to serve as an inventional resource for officials developing an administrative rhetoric that at once could satisfy the needs of U.S. citizens and advocate for the establishment of symbolic and monumental cemeteries in Europe. Through the process of communication in initiated with grieving families, the U.S. War Department learned to temper its highly bureaucratic and nationalistic speech with a personal and sentimental vernacular appropriated from the letters of next of kin. In doing so, the War Department was able to make a stronger public case for its controversial plan to bury soldiers in symbolic overseas cemeteries. And through this process, government and military officials came to recognize the opportunity of effectively displaying the new, generic, ideographical image of the U.S. soldier as a model of unassailable virtue, strength, sacrifice, and righteousness—that is, 'a global force for good'—that might have persuasive value for domestic and international populations in perpetuity. In sum, I argue that the ideograph of the "modern U.S. soldier" can be traced directly back to the political vicissitudes of this historical *kairotic* moment and the intimate, unnerving negotiations between the War Department and grieving American citizens and communities between 1918 and 1922.

After securing the bodily remains of roughly 35,000 fallen Doughboys, the U.S. government began a decade-long effort to construct permanent national cemeteries throughout Western Europe. Designed and established by the Commission of Fine Arts and the American Battlefield Monuments

Commission, and shaped by a myriad of powerful, competing, contemporary forces, needs, hopes, ideals, and constraints, the cemeteries ultimately came to display and advance the vision of the modern U.S. soldier as 'a global force for good'—an abstract, sanitized, and illusory, yet nonetheless potent, incalculably influential icon in which divergent emotions, memories, beliefs, and arguments of Americans and non-Americans have been poured theretofore, for better and for worse ...

Bibliography

"1871—History Repeating Itself—1918." *Wyoming State Tribune*, April 11, 1918.

"7,000 Dead Where Bodies Were Used as Rampart." *Washington Post*, September 17, 1914.

"10,000 Honor War Victim." *Oregonian*, July 25, 1921.

"30,496 A. E. F. Dead to Be Undisturbed in European Graves." *Washington Post*, April 9, 1922.

"A Woman Demands War." *New York Times*, May 13, 1915.

"A Woman's War Time Diary; When the Zeppelin Bomb Fell in Paris." *Grand Forks Daily Herald*, October 7, 1914.

"A Young Frenchman's Narrative of Trench Horrors at Fort Vaux." *New York Times*, June 14, 1916.

"Acres of Dead and Dying in Front of Trenches Along Dardanelles." *Washington Post*, October 17, 1915.

Adams, Katherine H. *Progressive Politics and the Training of America's Persuaders.* Mahwah, NJ: L. Eribaum Associates, 1999.

"Advertisement." *Columbus Ledger*, October 2, 1916.

Aeschylus. *The Suppliant Maidens: The Persians.* Translated and introduced by Seth G. Benardete. Chicago: University of Chicago Press, 1956.

"Agonized Throngs Await the Arrival of 'Forever Unfit.'" *Philadelphia Inquirer*, April 2, 1916.

"Air Pressure Kills When Shells Explode." *New York Times*, January 25, 1915.

"Alan Seeger, Soldier and Poet." *New York Times*, December 24, 1916.

"Alfred Ernst of St. Louis Is Dead." *Kansas City Star*, February 15, 1917.

"All in the Day's Work." *Washington Post*, November 5, 1917.

"Allies Gain Slowly Along Dardanelles." *New York Times*, May 17, 1915.

Alt, William E. and Betty L. Alt. *Black Soldiers, White Wars: Black Warriors from Antiquity to the Present.* Westport, CT: Praeger, 2002.

"America Is Invaded Again in the Films." *New York Times*, January 7, 1916.

"America's Dead Are Buried Near Front." *Washington Post*, November 9, 1917.

"American Barber's Grim War Story." *New York Times*, June 4, 1916.

American Battle Monuments Commission. *Annual Report to the President of the United States for the Fiscal Year 1925*. Washington, DC: Government Printing Office, 1926.

"American Couple Under German Fire." *New York Times*, October 1, 1914.

"American Flier Dead." *Washington Post*, June 25, 1916.

"American Killed at Loos; W. M. Nicholls, Annapolis Football Player, Among British Dead." *New York Times*, October 1, 1915.

"American Killed on the Mount Temple by Raider's Shot, Says Captain of Another Unlisted Victim of Moewe." *New York Times*, January 31, 1917.

"American Soldiers Killed and Wounded." *Pittsburgh Post*, November 5, 1917.

American Studies at the University of Virginia, "The City Beautiful Movement." http://xroads.virginia.edu/~CAP/CITYBEAUTIFUL/city.html.

"Approves Cemetery Plans." *Washington Post*, December 15, 1921.

"Americans, Greatly Outnumbered, Fight to Death!" *Los Angeles Times*, November 6, 1917.

"Americans Killed Must Lie in France Until War Ends." *New York Times*, November 28, 1917.

"Americans on Sunken Ship." *Los Angeles Times*, December 20, 1916.

"Anarchy." *New York Times*, March 23, 1914.

Anderson, Benedict. *Imagined Communities: Reflections on the Origin and Spread of Nationalism*. New York: Verso, 1991.

Anderson, James. Letter to GRS, November 11, 1920. "Burial Case File" (BCF) for William M. Anderson, Records of the Office of the Quartermaster General (RG 92), U.S. National Archives and Records Administration II, College Park, Maryland (NARA).

Andrews, Carrie. Letter to Adjutant General's Office, April 25, 1919. BCF for Clarence St. John, RG 92, NARA.

Anonymous. Letter to Newton D. Baker, received November 20, 1917. BCF for Thomas F. Enright, RG 92, NARA.

"Answers a Draft Wail." *New York Times*, August 29, 1917.

"Argue for Peace, But Back Wilson." *New York Times*, May 17, 1915.

Aristotle, *Rhetoric*, trans. John Henry Freese. Cambridge: Harvard University Press, 1911.

"Armenian Atrocities." *Lexington Herald*, December 5, 1915.

"Army Offenders Tied to Wagons." *Duluth News-Tribune*, December 31, 1916.

"As the Defenders of the Alamo." *Pittsburgh Gazette*, November 7, 1917.

"As Women Think of War." *New York Times*, August 23, 1915.

Association of the 110th Infantry. *History of the 110th Infantry (10th Pa.) of the 28th Division, U.S.A., 1917–1919: A Compilation of Orders, Citations, Maps, Records and Illustrations Relating to the 3rd Pa. Inf., 10th Pa. Inf., and 110th U.S. Inf.* Greensburg, Pennsylvania: The Association, 1920.

"At the Front in France and Belgium." *New York Times*, August 8, 1915.

"Attack Before Daylight." *New York Times*, November 5, 1917.

"Austrian Red Book Charges Atrocities." *New York Times*, April 16, 1915.

Ayres, Patrick. Letter to War Department, April 25, 1920. BCF for Joseph I. Ayres, RG 92, NARA.

Bach, Christian A., and Henry Noble Hall. *The Fourth Division: Its Services and Achievements in the World War*. Garden City, NY: Country Life Press, 1920.

Bailey, Thomas A. *Voices of America: The Nation's Story in Slogans, Sayings, and Songs*. New York: Free Press, 1976.

Barnett, Marie. "'Women of America, Let Us Wear No Mourning!' Cries Mother of First Sammy Slain in Action in France." *Miami District Daily News*, November 25, 1917, 2.

BCF for Lester G. Carter, RG 92, NARA.

BCF for Archibald P. Christensen, RG 92, NARA.

BCF for Hez O. De Long, RG 92, NARA.

BCF for George H. Edwards, Jr., RG 92, NARA.

BCF for Charles L. Emrich, RG 92, NARA.

BCF for Thomas F. Enright, RG 92, NARA

BCF for Frederick Wahlstrom, RG 92, NARA.

BCF for Sam J. Webb, RG 92, NARA.

Bedford, Willie Mae. Letter to J. F. Butler, March 15, 1921. BCF for Oscar Bedford, RG 92, NARA.

Beith, John Hay. "First Casualty List." *New York Times*, July 27, 1917.

"Belgians Retire From Louvain Toward Antwerp." *Wall Street Journal*, August 21, 1914.

Bell, H. C. F. *Woodrow Wilson and the People*. Garden City, New York: Country Life Press, 1945.

Bender, Thomas. "The 'Rural' Cemetery Movement: Urban Travail and the Appeal of Nature." *The New England Quarterly* 47.2 (June, 1974): 196–211.

"Berlin Denies Repulses." *New York Times*, October 16, 1914.

Beyer, Henry. Letter to GRS. June 1, 1920. BCF for Henry C. F. Beyer, RG 92, NARA.

Blair, Carole and V. William Balthrop, and Neil Michel. "Arlington-sur-Seine: War Commemoration and the Perpetual Argument from Sacrifice." Sixth Conference of the International Society for the Study of Argumentation, Amsterdam, Holland June 27–30, 2006.

Blosser, Addie. Letter to GRS, March 25, 1919. BCF for Carl F. Blosser, RG 92, NARA.

"Bodies of Heroes Sent to Homes." *Columbus Ledger*, May 12, 1914.

"Boise Boy Gets Trench Letter." *Idaho Daily Statesman*, October 26, 1916.

Bostdorff, Denise M. *The Presidency and the Rhetoric of Foreign Crisis*. Columbia: University of South Carolina Press, 1994.

Bradford, Caesar. Letter to GRS, January 4, 1921. BCF for Henry E. Bradford, RG 92, NARA.

Budrea, Lisa M. *Bodies of War: World War I and the Politics of Commemoration in America, 1919–1933* (New York: New York University Press, 2011).

Buente, William. Letter to Newton D. Baker, January 10, 1919. BCF for Howard A. Buente, RG 92, NARA.

"Braves Fire for Dead." *Washington Post*, March 28, 1915.

Brent, Charles Henry. "Forever Overseas." *Word's Work* 43 (December, 1921): 135–7.

"Brief History of Organization and Operations of Graves Registration Service from Origin to July 31, 1930." October 24, 1930, page 2, RG 159, Records of the Office of the Inspector General (Army), NARA.

Brown, Lewis. Letter to P. C. Harris, January 20, 1920. BCF for Martin O. Brown, RG 92, NARA.

Bruce, Carrie W. Letter to Charles C. Pierce, September 11, 1919. BCF for Alexander B. Bruce, RG 92, NARA.

Budreau, Lisa M. *Bodies of War: World War I and the Politics of Commemoration in America, 1919–1933*. New York: New York University Press, 2010.

Bufe, Chaz and Mitchell Cowen Verter. *Dreams of Freedom: A Ricardo Flores Magón Reader*. Oakland, CA: AK Press, 2005.

Buitenhuis, Peter. *The Great War of Words: British, American, and Canadian Propaganda and Fiction, 1914–1933*. Vancouver: University of British Columbia Press, 1987.

Burke, Kenneth. *A Grammar of Motives*. Berkeley: University of California Press, 1945.

———. *A Rhetoric of Motives*. Berkeley: University of California Press, 1950.

———. *Dramatism and Development*. Barre, MA: Clark University Press, 1972.

———. *The Philosophy of Literary Form*. Berkeley: University of California Press, 1973.

"Burn Babies to Death." *Washington Post*, September 14, 1916.

Cadzow, Hunter, Alison Conway, and Bryce Traister. "New Historicism." In *The Johns Hopkins Guide to Literary Theory and Criticism*, edited by Michael Groden, Martin Kreiswirth, and Imre Szeman, 698–703. Baltimore: Johns Hopkins University Press, 2005.

"Calls Hyphen a Failure." *New York Times*, February 1, 1916.

Campbell, Guy E. Letter to Newton D. Baker, November 21, 1917. BCF for Thomas F. Enright, RG 92, NARA.

Campbell, Karlyn Kohrs, and Kathleen Hall Jamieson. *Presidents Creating the Presidency: Deeds Done in Words*. Chicago: University of Chicago Press, 2008.

Campbell Lydia. Letter to P. C. Harris, December 12, 1919. BCF for Glenn H. Campbell, RG 92, NARA.

"Canadian Press Asks United States to Act." *New York Times*, May 9, 1915.

Capozzola, Christopher. *Uncle Sam Wants You: World War I and the Making of the Modern American Citizen*. Oxford: Oxford University Press, 2010.

"Cavell Execution Is Held to Be Butchery." *Duluth News-Tribune*, October 23, 1915.

"Censor Creel Gives Out Rules for Newspapers." *New York Times*, May 28, 1917.

Chambers II, John Whiteclay. "Conscription." In *The Oxford Companion to American Military History*, edited by John Whiteclay Chambers II, 180–2. Oxford: Oxford University Press, 1999.

"Clarence Sutcliffe First Miami Boy to Lose Life on Firing Line." *The Miami Herald*, August 4, 1918.

"Colonel Attacks Wilson's Courage." *New York Times*, October 29, 1916.

"Common Sense About the War." *New York Times*, November 22, 1914.

"Competitive-Butchery." *Philadelphia Inquirer*, February 10, 1916.

"Conan Doyle Is Converted; Famous Writer Declares He Now Believes Spiritualism." *Miami Herald,* November 28, 1916.

"Conditions in Poland Described as Terrible." *Los Angeles Times*, July 4, 1915.

Connors, Michael. "Finding Private Enright." *Pittsburgh Post-Gazette*, November 11, 2007. http://www.post-gazette.com/pg/07315/832688–109.stm.

"Convention in a Blaze." *New York Times*, June 15, 1916.

Cooper, George W. *Our Second Battalion: The Accurate and Authentic History of the Second Battalion 111th Infantry*. Pittsburgh: Second Battalion Book Company, 1920.

Copeland, David A. *The Greenwood Library of American War Reporting: World War I and World War II, the European Theater*. Westport, CT: Greenwood, 2005.

"Cosmic Bestiality of War, a Phantasmagoria of Sin." *Los Angeles Times*, October 22, 1915.

Cozzolino, Robert, Anne Classen Knutson, and David M. Lubin, eds. *World War I and American Art*. Philadelphia: Pennsylvania Academy of the Fine Arts, 2017.

Cramer, James B. Letter to Newton D. Baker. November 26, 1917. BCF for Thomas F. Enright, RG 92, NARA.

Creed, Henry. Telegram to GRS, May 17, 1921. BCF for Abraham Creed, RG 92, NARA.

Creel, George. *How We Advertised America: The First Telling of the Amazing Story of the Committee on Public Information that Carried the Gospel of Americanism to Every Corner of the Globe*. New York: Harper and Brothers, 1920.

Cret, Paul. "Memorials—Columns, Shafts, Cenotaphs, and Tablets." *Architectural Forum* 45 (December, 1926): 333.

"Criticizes Graves Service." *Washington Post*, January 25, 1922.

Cuff, Emma. Letter to Charles C. Pierce, 16 November 1920. BCF for William Cuff, RG 92, NARA.

"'Damnable!' Says Sunday." *New York Times*, May 8, 1915.

"Dangerous Possibilities." *New York Times*, May 8, 1915.

Darnall, Margaretta J. "The American Cemetery as Picturesque Landscape: Bellefontaine Cemetery, St. Louis." *Winterthur Portfolio* 18.4 (Winter, 1983): 249–69.

"Davis Acts on Headstones." *New York Times*, July 17, 1926.

DeBauche, Leslie Midkoff. *Reel Patriotism: The Movies and World War I*. Madison: University of Wisconsin Press, 1997.

"Dead Canadian Officer Impaled; Soldiers Think He Was Crucified." *Washington Post*, May 16, 1915.

"Dead Sailor's Mother Visited by Marshall." *Fort Worth Star-Telegram*, May 15, 1914.

Debs, Eugene V. "The Canton, Ohio Speech." Marxists Internet Archive, n.d., http://www.marxists.org/archive/debs/works/1918/canton.htm.

"Declaration of Principles Adopted by the Progressive National Committee." *New York Times*, January 12, 1916, 8.

Dehgan, Bahman. *America in Quotations*. Jefferson, NC: McFarland, 2003.

"Demands Vengeance." *New York Times*, May 10, 1915, 6.

Dickinson, Greg, Carole Blair, and Brian L. Ott. *Places of Public Memory: The Rhetoric of Museums and Memorials*. Tuscaloosa: University of Alabama Press, 2010.

"Died in Fleeing Kurds." *Washington Post*, April 26, 1915.

"Died Like a Heroine." *Washington Post*, October 23, 1915.

Dixon, Emily. Note to GRS, May 1919. BCF for William B. Dixon, RG 92, NARA.

Doherty, Thomas. *Projection of War: Hollywood, American Culture, and World War II*. New York: Columbia University Press, 1999.

Dooley, Nora. Letter to War Department, September 2, 1920. BCF for Frank W. Dooley, RG 92, NARA.

"Dr. Jacobi Calls for a Secretary of Peace." *New York Times*, January 23, 1916.

Dugan, Josephine and William. Letter to GRS, June 16, 1920. BCF for John F. Dugan, RG 92, NARA.

Dubose, Albert. Telegram to GRS, August 31, 1921. BCF for Will Dubose, RG 92, NARA.

Dyer, Gwynne. *War*. New York: Crown, 1985.

"'Earless Peter,' Death Dealer." *Washington Post*, July 19, 1916.

Eckert, William G. "History of the U.S. Army Graves Registration Service (1917–1950s)." *American Journal of Forensic Medicine and Pathology* 4.3 (September, 1983): 231–43.

Edgerton, Robert B. *Hidden Heroism: Black Soldiers in America's Wars*. Boulder: Westview, 2002.

Edwards, Sam. *Allies in Memory: World War II and the Politics of Transatlantic Commemoration, c. 1941–2001*. Cambridge: Cambridge University Press, 2015.

"Efforts to Prevent Inartistic War Memorials." *New York Times*, March 23, 1919.

"Eight Artists Commissioned for Service with Pershing." *Dallas Morning News*, February 22, 1918.

Mircea, Eliade. *Symbolism, the Sacred, and the Arts*. New York: Crossroad, 1985.

Ellis, Edward Robb. *Echoes of a Distant Thunder: Life in the United States, 1914–1918*. New York: Kodansha International, 1975.

Ellis, John. *Eye-Deep in Hell: Trench Warfare in World War I*. Baltimore: The Johns Hopkins University Press, 1989.

Ellis, Richard. *Speaking to the People: The Rhetorical Presidency in Historical Perspective*. Amherst: University of Massachusetts Press, 1998.

Emery, Michael and Edwin Emery. *The Press and America: An Interpretive History of the Mass Media*. Boston: Allyn and Bacon, 1996.

"Emma Goldman and A. Berkman Behind the Bars." *New York Times*, June 16, 1917.

Engelbrecht, H. C. and F. C. Hanighen. *Merchants of Death: A Study of the International Armament Industry*. New York: Dodd, Mead & Company, 1934.

"Enright Street Objected To." *Pittsburgh Post*, November 13, 1917.

"Erection of Chapels for War Dead Asked." *Washington Post*, May 17, 1926.

Ericson, Timothy L. "Building Our Own 'Iron Curtain': The Emergence of Secrecy in American Government." *American Archivist* 68.1 (Spring/Summer 2005): 18–52.

Establishing a Commission of Fine Arts Act of 1910, 40 U.S.C. § 104 (1910).

"Europe's Unmarked Graves." *Macon Daily Telegraph*, September 6, 1914.

Evans, Suzanne. *Mothers of Heroes, Mothers of Martyrs: World War I and the Politics of Grief*. Montreal: McGill-Queen's University Press, 2007.

Ezz-Eddine, Nadia. "Re: St. Mihiel Cemetery statue." Email to the author, December 11, 2008.

"Face Mending New Science." *Washington Post*, September 24, 1916.

"Famous University Plants Forest for Its Hero Dead." *Dallas Morning News*, June 24, 1919.

Farwell, Byron. *Over There: The United States in the Great War, 1917–1918*. New York: W. W. Norton & Company, 1999.

"Father Curses Germany." *Washington Post*, September 9, 1917.

Fatout, Anna. Note to GRS, May 8, 1920. BCF for Ansel Fatout, RG 92, NARA.

Faust, Drew Gilpin. *This Republic of Suffering: Death and the American Civil War*. New York: Alfred A. Knopf, 2008.

"Favors Italian Marble." *New York Times*, June 24, 1926.

Felix, Wanda. "Fatty." *Review of Arts, Literature, Philosophy and the Humanities* (Fall, 1995). http://www.ralphmag.org/fatty.html.

Ferguson, Niall. *The War of the World: Twentieth-Century Conflict and the Descent of the West*. New York: Penguin, 2006.

Fields, Wayne. *Union of Words: A History of Presidential Eloquence*. New York: Free Press, 1996.

"Fifty Lives Lost in U-Boat Attack on the Sussex." *New York Times*, March 26, 1916.

"Finds All England Alive to War Work." *New York Times*, September 18, 1915.

FirstWorldWar.com. "Primary Documents - Treaty of London, 1839." http://www.firstworldwar.com/source/london1839.htm.

"First Death in Marines." *New York Times*, August 29, 1917.

Fisher, Irving. "Ten Reasons Why I Shall Vote for Wilson." *New York Times*, August 27, 1916.

"Fists and Pacifists." *New York Times*, March 31, 1916.

"Flags Fly in All Fields." *Washington Post*, August 8, 1915.

"Flanders Front a Vast Cemetery." *New York Times*, February 27, 1915.

Fletcher, Marvin E. "World War I." In *Encyclopedia of African-American Culture and History*, edited by Jack Salzman, David Lionel Salzman, and Cornel West, 2881–3. New York: Simon, 1996.

Foner, Philip S., ed. *The Voice of Black America: Major Speeches by Negroes in the United States, 1797–1971*. New York: Simon and Schuster, 1972.

"For Battle Monuments." *Washington Post*, January 15, 1923.

"Ford Defies His Critics." *New York Times*, December 2, 1915.

Fortescue, Granville. "Entire Fort Wiped Out by Shell." *Washington Post*, December 10, 1916.

Foucault, Michel. "Of Other Spaces" (1967). http://foucault.info/documents/hetero-Topia/foucault.heterotopia.en.html.

"Four Americans Killed by Raiders." *New York Times*, September 9, 1917.

"France Prepared to Use Gas Bombs as Reprisal for Dumdum Bullets," *Washington Post*, August 26, 1914.

"France Protests against Bombardment of Cathedral." *Columbus Enquirer-Sun*, September 22, 1914.

"France Unites to Honor Its Marne Dead." *Idaho Daily Statesman*, September 11, 1916.

"France Wants U.S. Dead." *Washington Post*, December 30, 1917.

"French Atrocity Charged." *Oregonian*, September 25, 1914.

"French 'Fire Curtain' Is Deadly in Effect." *New York Times*, April 11, 1916.

"French General's Wound Fatal." *Washington Post*, January 8, 1916.

"French Machine Guns and Rifles Pour Death Into the Ranks of Kaisermen." *Macon Daily Telegraph*, March 5, 1916.

"French Officer Recites Atrocities." *New York Times*, November 21, 1915.

French, Stanley. "The Cemetery as Cultural Institution: The Establishment of Mount Auburn and the 'Rural Cemetery' Movement." *American Quarterly* 26.1 (March, 1974): 37–5.

"Frenchmen in Armored Motors Hunt Foe with All Guns Going." *Washington Post*, October 17, 1914.

"Frightful Cost of the War in Humanity." *Wall Street Journal*, April 24, 1916.

"Frost New Terror of War." *New York Times*, November 6, 1914.

"Full Text of the Address by the President to Congress." *Los Angeles Times*, April 3, 1917.

Fussell, Paul. *The Great War and Modern Memory*. Oxford: University Press, 1975.

Fuston, Mattie Lou. Telegram to GRS, December 24, 1921. BCF for Elmer Fuston, RG 92, NARA.

Gagnon, Clara. Letter to War Department, n.d. BCF for Robert E. Garner, RG 92, NARA.

Garner, Ada. Letter to Quartermaster Corps (QMC), n.d. BCF for Robert E. Garner, RG 92, NARA.

"Gen. Pershing at Soldiers' Graves." *Washington Post*, November 19, 1917.

"Gen. Wood Wants Army of 210,000." *New York Times*, January 20, 1916.

"General Pershing is Guest of Honor in London Today." *Wilkes-Barre Times Leader*, July 15, 1919.

"German Officers Joke as They Order Russians Butchered in Cold Blood." *Idaho Daily Statesman*, November 6, 1917.

"German Walls of Iron Hold 'Hell of Death' Battlelines between Arras and Ypres." *Washington Post*, June 28, 1915.

"Germans Balking at False War Reports." *Olympia Daily Recorder*, October 30, 1917.

"Germans Capture Souchez Cemetery." *New York Times*, July 15, 1913.

"Germans Raid Trench, Kill 3, Wound 5, Take 12 U.S. Men Prisoner." *Washington Post*, November 5, 1917.

"Germans Say French Tortured Wounded." *New York Times*, October 3, 1914.

"Germany Accuses France." *Wall Street Journal*, October 22, 1914.

"Germany Objects to Colored Troops." *New York Times*, September 16, 1915.

"Germany Sends Regret, and 'Sympathy', But Says the Blame Rests With England." *New York Times*, May 11, 1915.

"Germany Trains Her War-Maimed Heroes, as Well as Her Crippled Children, to Be Self-Supporting." *Washington Post*, September 17, 1916.

Gibbs, Philip. "Vivid Narrative of Great Retreat." *New York Times*, August 31, 1914.

Giffin, Frederick C. *Six Who Protested: Radical Opposition to the First World War.* Port Washington, NY: Kennikat Press, 1977.

"Girls Mutilated, Children Beheaded, Wounded Foe Drowned by Germans." *Washington Post*, September 25, 1914.

"Glory of France Revealed in Cheerful Heroism With Which Soldiers and Civilians Repel Teutonic Invaders." *Washington Post*, August 27, 1916.

Goldberg, David J. *Discontented America: The United States in the 1920s*. Baltimore: Johns Hopkins University Press, 1999.

Goody, Jack and Cesare Poppi. "Flowers and Bones: Approaches to the Dead in Anglo-American and Italian Cemeteries." *Comparative Studies in Society and History* 36.1 (January, 1994): 146–75.

Graham, John W. *The Gold Star Pilgrimages of the 1930s*. Jefferson, NC: McFarland 2004.

"Grave Danger That Soldiers of the Disbanded Armies May Scatter Epidemics Throughout Europe and America." *Washington Post*, August 22, 1915.

Graves, John S. Letter to War Department, August 12, 1919. BCF for Charles A. Bouling, RG 92, NARA.

Grayzel, Susan R. *Women and the First World War*. London: Pearson Education, 2002.

Greeley-Smith, Nixola. "Noble Women of France Give Loved Ones to Save Nation, but Do Not Weep, Says Countess DePerigny." *Washington Post*, June 11, 1916.

Grossman, Elizabeth G. "Architecture for a Public Client: The Monuments and Chapels of the American Battle Monuments Commission." *Journal of the Society of Architectural Historians* 43 (May 1984): 119–43.

Guénon, René. *Symbolism of the Cross*, trans. Angus Macnab. London: Luzac, 1958.

Hablitzel Sr., Jacob. Letter to QMC, April 16, 1919. BCF for Jacob Hablitzel Jr., RG 92, NARA.

Hajek, Rosie. Letter to P. C. Harris, May 3, 1920. BCF for Joseph Hajek, RG 92, NARA.

Halbwachs, Maurice. *On Collective Memory*. Edited and translated by Lewis A. Coser. Chicago: University of Chicago Press, 1992.

Halloran, S. Michael, and Gregory Clark. "National Park Landscapes and the Rhetorical Display of Civic Religion." In *Rhetorics of Display*, edited by Lawrence J. Prelli, 141–56. Columbia: University of South Carolina Press, 2006.

"Harding, in Memorial Day Proclamation, Asks General Homage to War Dead on May 30." *New York Times*, May 4, 1921.

"Harding Names Monuments Board." *New York Times*, June 21, 1923.

"Harding Proposes Battle Monuments." *New York Times*, March 2, 1922.

Harris, P. C. Letter to Anastaceo Rodriguez, May 1919. BCF for Juan M. Rodriguez, RG 92, NARA.

Harris, Stephen L. *Harlem's* Hell Fighters: *The African American 369th Infantry in World War I*. Washington: Brassey's, 2003.

Haste, Cate. "The Machinery of Propaganda." In *Propaganda*, edited by Robert Jackall, 105–36. New York: University Press, 1995.

Hauser, Gerard A. *Vernacular Voices: The Rhetoric of Publics and Public Spheres.* Columbia: University of South Carolina Press, 1999.

"Hayes on Battle Line." *Washington Post*, October 8, 1914.

Haynes, Robert V. *A Night of Violence: The Houston Riot of 1917.* Baton Rouge: Louisiana State University Press, 1976.

Head, Eugen. Letter to War Department, November 23, 1918. BCF for Randolph Head, RG 92, NARA.

"Hear Belgian Side Is Mercier's Plea." *New York Times*, February 2, 1916, 3.

Hicks, Mattie. Correspondence with QMC, July 21–24, 1917. BCF for Clifton R. Hicks, RG 92, NARA.

"Highlights of the War in Europe Briefly Told." *Philadelphia Inquirer*, August 2, 1914.

History Matters. "'I Didn't Raise My Boy to Be a Soldier': Singing against the War," n.d., http://historymatters.gmu.edu/d/4942/.

History of the 110th Infantry (10th Pa.) of the 28th Division, U.S.A., 1917–1919: A Compilation of Orders, Citations, Maps, Records and Illustrations Relating to the 3rd Pa. Inf., 10th Pa. Inf., and 110th U.S. Inf. Greensburg, PA: The Association, 1920.

History of the 318th Infantry Regiment of the 80th Division, 1917–1919. Richmond: William Byrd Press, 1920.

History of the American Graves Registration Service: QMC in Europe. Vol. 1. Washington, DC: The Library Office of the Quartermaster General, 1920.

Hobsbawm, E. J. *Nations and Nationalism since 1780: Programme, Myth, Reality.* Cambridge: University Press, 1990.

Hofstadter, Richard. *The Age of Reform.* New York: Vintage, 1955.

"Home They Brought Her Warrior Dead." *Kansas City Times*, February 3, 1921.

House Committee on Foreign Affairs. *Hearings on Authorizing the Appointment of a Commission to Remove the Bodies of Deceased Soldiers, Sailors, and Marines, from Foreign Countries to the United States, and Defining Its Duties and Powers.* 66th Cong., 1st sess., 1919.

"Elbert Hubbard, Alfred G. Vanderbilt and Charles Frohman, Prominent Americans Go Down with Lusitania." *Daily Herald* (Biloxi, Mississippi), May 8, 1915.

Hubert, Charles. Correspondence with War Department, August 4–12, 1921. BCF for Harold W. Hubert, RG 92, NARA.

Huelfer, Evan Andrew. *The "Casualty Issue" in American Military Practice: The Impact of World War I.* Westport, CT: Praeger, 2003.

"Hughes Praises Flag." *Washington Post*, July 5, 1916.

"Hun Airmen Deride American Victims." *Washington Post*, September 9, 1917.

"Huns Starve and Ridicule U. S. Captives." *Stars and Stripes*, February 8, 1918.

"I Didn't Raise My Boy to Be a Soldier." *Times-Picayune* (New Orleans), January 17, 1915.

"Invasion Lags in Serb Passes." *New York Times*, November 12, 1915.

Irwin, Mary. Letter to the Quartermaster Corps, November 5, 1917. BCF for Thomas F. Enright, RG 92, NARA.

"Is Perfectly Neutral." *State*, June 18, 1915.

Ivie, Robert L. "Presidential Motives for War." *Quarterly Journal of Speech* 60.3 (1974): 337–45.

Jackall, Robert, and Janice M. Hirota, "America's First Propaganda Ministry: The Committee on Public Information During the Great War," In *Propaganda*, edited by Robert Jackall, 137–73. New York: New York University Press, 1995.

"Jail Woman Heckler." *Washington Post*, October 15, 1916.

Jaires, Sarah Jane. Correspondence with QMC, April 4, 1920–July 19, 1925. BCF for Elmer J. McCann, RG 92, NARA.

Jewell, Marie. Correspondence with QMC, 1919–1920. BCF for Hewitt C. Jewell, RG 92, NARA.

Jones, Jr., William P. "Service with the American Battle Monuments Commission, 1 April 1967 to 30 June 1974." William P. Jones, Jr. Papers, U.S. Army Military History Institute, Carlisle, Pennsylvania.

Joyce, Charles H. Letter to GRS, June 4, 1920. BCF for Katherine M. Joyce, RG 92, NARA.

Kammen, Michael. *Mystic Chords of Memory: The Transformation of Tradition in American Culture*. New York: Vintage, 1993.

Karetzky, Joanne. *The Mustering of Support for World War I By The Ladies' Home Journal*. New York: Edwin Mellen, 1997.

Keene, Jennifer D. *Doughboys, the Great War, and the Making of America*. Baltimore: Johns Hopkins University Press, 2003.

———. *The United States and the First World War*. Essex, England: Pearson, 2000.

———. *World War I*. Westport, CT: Greenwood Press, 2006.

Keithan, Fred. Telegram to GRS, March 2, 1919. BCF for Frederick H. Keithan, RG 92, NARA.

Kennedy, David M. *Over Here: The First World War and American Society*. Oxford: Oxford University Press, 1980.

Kennedy, Kathleen. *Disloyal Mothers and Scurrilous Citizens: Women and Subversion During World War I*. Bloomington: Indiana University Press, 1999.

Kerby, Frederick M. "A Complete Condensed History of the Great World War." Unknown newspaper, 1920, in the John Doran Jr. Papers, Archives of the Soldiers and Sailors Memorial Hall and Museum, Pittsburgh, Pennsylvania.

Kiewe, Amos, ed. *The Modern Presidency and Crisis Rhetoric*. Westport, CT: Praeger, 1994.

Kilmer, Annie Kilburn. *Memories of My Son Sergeant Joyce Kilmer: With Numerous Unpublished Poems and Letters*. New York: Brentano's, 1920.

Kingsburgy, Celia Malone. *The Peculiar Sanity of War: Hysteria in the Literature of World War I*. Lubbock: Texas Tech University Press, 2002.

Kneale, Josie. Correspondence with War Department. BCF for Richard H. Dashwood, RG 92, NARA.

Knight, David B. "Cemeteries as Living Landscapes." *Ottawa Branch: Ontario Genealogical Society Publication* 73.8 (April, 1974): 1–55.

Kornweibel, Jr., Theodore. *"Investigate Everything": Federal Efforts to Compel Black Loyalty During World War I.* Bloomington: Indiana University Press, 2002.

Kraig, Robert Alexander. *Woodrow Wilson and the Lost World of the Oratorical Statesman.* College Station: Texas A&M University Press, 2006.

"La Follette in Effigy." *New York Times,* March 6, 1917.

Laderman, Gary. "Locating the Dead: A Cultural History of Death in the Antebellum, Anglo-Protestant Communities of the Northeast." *Journal of the American Academy of Religion* 63.1 (Spring, 1995): 27–52.

———. *Rest in Peace: A Cultural History of Death and the Funeral Home in Twentieth-Century America.* Oxford: Oxford University Press, 2003.

———. *The Sacred Remains: American Attitudes toward Death, 1799–1883.* New Haven: Yale University Press, 1996.

"Lame Marriages." *Los Angeles Times,* October 16, 1915.

Lamszus, Wilhelm. *The Human Slaughter-House: Scenes from the War that Is Sure to Come.* New York: Frederick A. Stokes Company, 1913.

"Leading Points in President's Note to Germany Demanding Redress for Attacks on Americans." *New York Times,* May 13, 1915.

"'League for Marrying of Broken Heroes,'" *New York Times,* October 14, 1915.

Le Hir, Georges. "German Verdun Drive Fails Woefully." *Los Angeles Times,* May 22, 1916.

Letter to the editor. *Idaho Daily Statesman,* October 25, 1915.

Letter to the editor. *Wilkes Barre Times Leader,* May 12, 1915.

"Lieut. G. H. Edwards Dead." *Kansas City Star,* March 2, 1919.

Linenthal, Edward Tabor. *Sacred Ground: Americans and Their Battlefields.* Urbana, Illinois: University of Illinois Press, 1991.

Lingle, John. Letter to War Department, October 21, 1919. BCF for John A. Lingle Jr., RG 92 NARA.

Link, Arthur S., and William M. Leary, Jr. "Election of 1916." In *History of American Presidential Elections 1789–1968, Vol. III,* edited by Arthur M. Schlesinger, Jr., 2245–345. New York: Chelsea House, 1971.

Lippmann, Walter. *Public Opinion.* New York: Harcourt, Brace & Company, 1922.

Lipsitz, George. *Time Passages: Collective Memory and American Popular Culture.* Minneapolis: University of Minnesota Press, 1990.

"Liquid Fire Attack Failed." *New York Times,* March 6, 1915, 3.

Lister, David. *Die Hard, Aby! Abraham Bevistein – The Boy Soldier Shot to Encourage Others.* South Yorkshire: Pen and Sword, 2005.

"Lodge Ridicules Wilson." *New York Times,* August 20, 1916.

"London Puts on No Mourning Garb." *New York Times,* April 5, 1915.

Long, Elias A. *Ornamental Gardening for Americans: A Treatise on Beautifying Homes, Rural Districts, Towns, and Cemeteries.* New York: Orange Judd Company, 1907.

Loraux, Nicole. *The Invention of Athens: The Funeral Oration in the Classical City,* trans. Alan Sheridan. New York: Zone Books, 2006.

"Louvain to Blame, Germany's Report." *New York Times,* September 22, 1914.

Luebke, Frederick C. *Bonds of Loyalty: German-Americans and World War I.* DeKalb, Ill.: Northern Illinois University Press, 1974.

"Lusitania with 188 Americans on Board Sunk by German Submarine." *Lexington Herald*, May 8, 1915.

"Mails Free to Sammy." *Washington Post*, July 27, 1917.

Malin, Brenton. "Electrifying Speeches: Emotional Control and the Technological Aesthetic of the Voice in the Early 20th Century." *U.S. Journal of Social History* 45.1 (2011): 1–19.

Manucy, Albert C. *Artillery through the Ages: A Short Illustrated History of the Cannon, Emphasizing Types Used in America.* Darby, PA: Diane Publishing, 1994.

"Many Become War 'Widows.'" *Washington Post*, October 1, 1916.

Markle, Mary. Note to GRS, July 24, 1920. BCF for Oliver Markle, RG 92, NARA.

Marion, John Francis. *Famous and Curious Cemeteries.* New York: Crown Publishers, 1977.

Marshall Cavendish Corporation. *History of World War I: Victory and Defeat, 1917–1918.* Tarrytown, New York: Marshall Cavendish Corporation, 2002.

Martens, Eggert and Martha. Letter to War Department, March 31, 1919. BCF for Charles Martens, RG 92, NARA.

Marvin, Carolyn and David W. Ingle. *Blood Sacrifice and the Nation: Totem Rituals and the American Flag.* Cambridge: Cambridge University Press, 1999.

Matsler, Leta. Letter to GRS, February 14, 1919. BCF for Seymour A. Prestwood, RG 92, NARA.

Mayes, Mary Jo, Jennifer L. Pierce, and Barbara Laslett. *Telling Stories: The Use of Personal Narratives in the Social Sciences and History.* Ithaca: Cornell University Press, 2008.

McClatchey, W. S. Letter to Newton D. Baker, n.d. BCF for Thomas F. Enright, RG 92, NARA.

McCutcheon, John T. "Pitiful Havoc is Left in War's Wake." *Oregonian*, October 2, 1914.

McDonald, Nellie. Correspondence with QMC, May 1920. BCF for Charles J. McGraw, RG 92, NARA.

McElvaine, Robert S. *Down and Out in the Great Depression: Letters from the Forgotten Man.* Chapel Hill: University of North Carolina Press, 1983.

McGee, Michael Calvin McGee. "The 'Ideograph': A Link Between Rhetoric and Ideology." *Quarterly Journal of Speech* 66.1 (1980): 1–16.

McGeough, Ryan Erik. "Endless Talk: The Purpose, Practice, and Pedagogy of the Rhetorical Conversation." In *Purpose, Practice, and Pedagogy in Rhetorical Criticism*, edited by Jim A. Kuypers, 97–107. Frederick, MD: Rowman and Littlefield, 2014.

Meigs, Mark. *Optimism at Armageddon: Voices of American Soldiers Participants in the First World War.* New York: New York University Press, 1997.

Meily, Naomi. Letter to War Department, November 1, 1920. BCF for Guy O. Meily, RG 92, NARA.

"Memorial to Private Gresham." *New York Times*, November 7, 1917.

"Men Torn to Pieces." *Washington Post*, October 9, 1914.

Meyer, Lotte Larsen. "Mourning in a Distant Land: Gold Star Pilgrimages to American Military Cemeteries in Europe, 1930–33." *Markers: Annual Journal of the Association for Gravestone Studies* 20 (2003): 31–75.

Meyer, Richard E. "Stylistic Variation in the Western Front Battlefield Cemeteries of World War I Combatant Nations." in *Markers: Annual Journal of the Association for Gravestone Studies* 18 (2001): 189–253.

"Military Training in Our Schools." *New York Times*, September 18, 1915.

"Millions Starving in War-Torn Poland." *New York Times*, July 2, 1915.

"'Missing' Men Return." *Washington Post*, September 27, 1914.

Mitchell, Stella. Note to GRS, April 26, 1920. BCF for Leon Gilder, RG 92, NARA.

Mock, James R., and Cedric Larson. *Words That Won the War: The Story of the Committee on Public Information, 1917–1919.* Princeton: Princeton University Press, 1939.

Morris, Richard. "Death on Display." In *Rhetorics of Display*, edited by Lawrence J. Prelli, 204–24. Columbia: University of South Carolina Press, 2006.

"Moslem Butchery Grows in Horror." *State*, November 27, 1915, 1.

Mosse, George L. *Fallen Soldiers: Reshaping the Memory of the World Wars.* Oxford: Oxford University Press, 1991.

"Most Hideous Crimes in the History of Civilization Have Been Traced to Germans in Invasion of Belgium." *Macon Daily Telegraph*, May 13, 1915.

"Mother Clings to Hope." *Washington Post*, September 9, 1917.

"Mother's Simple Story Proof of German Guilt, Says French Courrier." *Washington Post*, September 27, 1914.

"Mr. Wickersham Appeals for Action." *New York Times*, May 9, 1915.

"Murder on the High Seas." *New York Times*, November 12, 1915.

Myers, Alfred E. "The Courage Not to Fight." *New York Times*, May 12, 1915.

Nash, Roderick Frazier. *Wilderness and the American Mind.* 4th ed. New Haven: Yale University Press, 2001.

The National Commission of Fine Arts. *Ninth Report, July 1, 1919-June 30, 1921.* Washington, DC: Government Printing Office, 1921.

"National Rights More Important Than Peace." *Washington Post*, July 28, 1915.

"Neuve Chapelle a Graveyard." *Los Angeles Times*, April 17, 1915, 12.

Nishiura, Elizabeth. *American Battle Monuments: A Guide to Military Cemeteries and Monuments Maintained by the American Battle Monuments Commission.* Detroit: Omnigraphics, 1989.

"No Need to Fight, If Right." *New York Times*, May 11, 1915.

Nora, Pierre. "Between Memory and History: Les Lieux de Mémoire." *Representations* 26 (Spring 1989): 7–24.

———. *Realms of Memory: The Construction of the French Past.* Translated by Arthur Goldhammer. New York: Columbia University Press, 1997.

Nord, David Paul. *Communities of Journalism: A History of American Newspapers and Their Readers.* Urbana, IL: University of Illinois Press, 2001.

"Nordons Trapped by Crisis Abroad, Local Choristers Believed Unable to Return Because of the European War." *Duluth News-Tribune*, August 6, 1914.

"Norman Prince Dies from His Injuries." *New York Times*, October 16, 1916.

North, Thomas. General North's Manuscript, unpublished and undated manuscript (given to author by David Bedford, Oise-Aisne American Cemetery and Memorial Superintendent in 2006).

"Nothing to be Gained by War." *Oregonian*, May 10, 1915.

"Obituary 1 – No Title." *New York Times*, July 12, 1915.

"Obituary 2 – No Title." *New York Times*, June 24, 1915.

"Official Pictures Show Tragedies of War." *Duluth News-Tribune*, December 31, 1916.

Olson, Lester C, Cara A. Finnegan, and Diane S. Hope, eds., *Visual Rhetoric: A Reader in Communication and American Culture*. Thousand Oaks, California: Sage, 2008.

O'Neill, Katie. "A Mournful Fashion: Form, Function, and Meaning of Baltimore's R.I.P T-Shirts." (Agora lecture, Department of Communication, University of Pittsburgh, Pittsburgh, PA, October 26, 2007).

O'Neill, William L., ed. *Echoes of Revolt: The Masses 1911–1917*. Chicago: Quadrangle Books, 1966.

"On the Paths of Glory," *Kansas City Star*, March 19, 1915.

Oram, Gerard Christopher. *Military Executions During World War I*. New York: Palgrave Macmillan, 2003.

"Opinions of Others Told by Letters." *Duluth News Tribune*, December 27, 1917.

"Opportunity for the Living Is Urged Instead of Tributes in Stone." *New York Times*, May 2, 1924.

"Pacifists in Protest." *Washington Post*, February 9, 1916.

"Pacifist Menace Seen by Pershing." *New York Times*, October 23, 1923.

Palczewski, Catherine Helen. "What is 'Good Criticism'? A Conversation in Progress." *Communication Studies* 54 (2003): 385–91.

"Patriotic Spirit on Draft Registration Day Urged by U.S." *Salt Lake Telegram*, May 10, 1917.

Pancoast, Charles F., to Charles C. Pierce, April 18, 1919, BCF for Charles Pancoast, RG 92, NARA.

Patton, Jr., George S. *The Patton Papers 1885–1940*. Edited by Martin Blumenson. Boston: Houghton Mifflin Co., 1972.

"Pershing Against Removal of Dead." *New York Times*, August 24, 1919.

"Pershing and His Lads in Wonder Film 'Pershing's Crusaders' at Strand Arouses Patriotic Tingle." August 22, 1918.

"Pershing Arranges for War Memorials." *New York Times*, June 26, 1927.

"Pershing Criticises Army Literary Style; Urges Clarity and the Personal Touch." *New York Times*, April 13, 1923.

"Pershing is 76 Today with Few Signs of Aging." *Washington Post*, September 13, 1936.

Pershing, John J. *My Experiences in the World War*. New York: Frederick A. Stokes, 1931.

"Pershing Publishes Battlefield Guide for U.S. Tourists." *Washington Post*, August 21, 1917.

"Pershing Praises Dead at Tomb of Unknown Soldier." *Washington Post*, May 27, 1925.

"Pershing Reception Will Be Greatest in N. Y. Annals General and Famed First Division." *Philadelphia Inquirer*, September 8, 1919.

"Pershing Seeks a Plan to Preserve Memorials." *New York Times*, September 6, 1931.

"Pershing Tells Girls to Marry Guardsmen." *New York Times*, July 17, 1923.

Peters, Jennie. Letter to War Department, n.d., BCF for John J. Peters, RG 92, NARA.

Peters, John Durham. *Courting the Abyss: Free Speech and the Liberal Tradition*. Chicago: University of Chicago Press, 2005.

———. *Speaking Into the Air: A History of the Idea of Communication*. Chicago: University of Chicago Press, 1999.

Peterson, H. C. *Propaganda for War: The Campaign against American Neutrality, 1914–1917*. Port Washington, NY: Kennikat Press, 1939.

Phillips, Kendall R. ed. *Framing Public Memory*. Tuscaloosa: University of Alabama Press, 2004.

Piehler, Kurt G. *Remembering War the American Way*. Washington, DC: Smithsonian Institution, 1995.

Pierce, Charles C. Letter to Robert Buglune, February 1919, BCF for Arthur R. Sargent, RG 92, NARA.

"Plague of Diseases Prostrates Serbia." *New York Times*, March 20, 1915.

"Plain Burial for Zep Crew." *Kansas City Star*, September 5, 1916.

"Plan 6 Cemeteries for A.E.F. Abroad." *New York Times*, August 23, 1921.

"Plan a National Shrine to Those Who Died in the War." *New York Times*, August 12, 1924.

"Plans to Shorten Our Flag to Get Better Proportion." *New York Times*, May 6, 1923.

"Plans for Markers May Not Be Changed." *Washington Post*, July 7, 1926.

"Playground May Be Provided in Memory of Private Enright." *Pittsburgh Post*, November 13, 1917.

"Plea to Wilson for Peace After Visit to Scenes of Slaughter on West Front." December 10, 1916.

"Pope Calls War Suicide of Europe; Again Appeals for Just, Lasting Peace." *New York Times*, March 6, 1916.

Pope, F. H., to John MacIntyre, May 16, 1926, BCF for Harold V. MacIntyre, RG 92, NARA.

Poulakos, John. *Sophistical Rhetoric in Classical Greece*. Columbia: University of South Carolina Press, 1995.

"President Coolidge Signing Appropriation Bills for the Veterans Bureau on the South Lawn During the Garden Party for Wounded Veterans." Library of Congress, n.d. http://loc.gov/pictures/resource/cph.3c11372/.

"President Wilson Sets June 14 as Flag Day." *Idaho Daily Statesman*, May 31, 1916.

"Press/Censorship." Box 6127, File: "Censorship Rules of Press," RG 120, NARA.

"Press Censorship." File Number 120.290.80.35.01, RG 120, NARA.

Price, X. H., to John J. Pershing, February 12, 1925, in "Correspondence of the ABMC Chairman, Gen. John J. Pershing, 1923–45," Records of the American Battle Monuments Commission, RG 117, NARA.

"Proceedings of Congress and Committees in Brief." *Washington Post*, March 30, 1922.

"Prospect of Asiatic Hordes Being Led by Germany Into War Should Arouse America." *Washington Post*, January 4, 1916.

Prost, Antoine. *The Great War in History: Debates and Controversies, 1914 to the Present*. Cambridge: University Press, 2005.

"Purchase Assured of Belleau Woods." *Washington Post*, February 13, 1923.

Quartermaster Corps. Letter to J. E. Lowery, May 17, 1924, BCF for Robert W. Lowery, RG 92, NARA.

Rainville, Lynn. "Hanover Deathscapes: Mortuary Variability in New Hampshire, 1770–1920," *Ethnohistory* 46.3 (Summer, 1999): 541–97.

"Raise Memorials to Gallant Sons." *State* (Columbia, South Carolina), May 18, 1919.

Reager, Georgia V. Letter to QMC, September 20, 1919, BCF for Wallace C. Reager, RG 92, NARA.

Records of the Office of the Inspector General (Army), RG 159, Box 772, "Brief History of Organization and Operations of Graves Registration Service from Origin to July 31, 1930," October 24, 1930, page 2, NARA.

"Red Death in Europe." *Los Angeles Times*, March 26, 1915.

"Reports Related to the Morale of American Troops, 1917–18," Record Group 120, Box 1, Entry 195, NARA.

"Resist Huns to Death." *Washington Post*, January 21, 1918.

"Rest Easy: Historical Updates with Honor." *Washington Post*, August 15, 1976.

"Richard Hall Dies in War." *Los Angeles Times*, December 26, 1915.

Robin, Ron Theodore. *Enclaves of America: The Rhetoric of American Political Architecture Abroad 1900–1965*. Princeton: Princeton University Press, 1992.

Robin, Ron. "'A Foothold in Europe': The Aesthetics and Politics of American War Cemeteries in Western Europe," *Journal of American Studies* 29.1 (1995): 55–72.

Rodgers, E. C. "First Gold Star War Mother Hopes and Prays for Return of Body of Her Son." *Salt Lake Telegram*, May 30, 1919, 13.

Roeder Jr., George H. *The Censored War: American Visual Experience During World War Two*. New Haven, CT.: Yale University Press, 1993.

"Roosevelt Firm against Germany." *New York Times*, July 12, 1915.

"Roosevelt Heaps Blame on America." *New York Times*, December 1, 1915.

"Roosevelt Hints at Hughes for 1916." *New York Times*, July 20, 1915.

"Roosevelt's New Word." *New York Times*, July 25, 1915.

Roth, William. Letter to Senator Nicholas J. Wadsworth, April 28, 1921, BCF for Benjamin W. Roth, RG 92, NARA.

"Roundup Begins of Draft Dodgers." *New York Times*, September 29, 1917.

Roycroft, Mollie. Letter to GRS, January 21, 1919, BCF for William T. Roycroft, RG 92, NARA.

Sack, Leo R. "Association Is Formed to Lay Aside Estate in France for an American Cemetery." *Fort Worth Star-Telegram*, June 3, 1919, 12.

"Salient Points Emerging from Latest News of the Great War." *Columbus Enquirer-Sun* (Georgia), August 12, 1914.

Sanders, Mary. Letter to P. C. Harris, March 27, 1919, BCF for Eric F. Sanders, RG 92, NARA.

"Sanitary Commission Named to Purify the Battlefields in Western Poland." April 25, 1915.

Savage, Kirk. *Monument Wars: Washington, D.C., the National Mall, and the Transformation of* the Memorial Landscape. Berkeley: University of California Press, 2009.

———. *Standing Soldiers, Kneeling Slaves: Race, War, and Monument in Nineteenth-Century America.* Princeton: Princeton University Press, 1997.

"Says Ugly Buildings Mar Washington." *Washington Post*, February 6, 1927.

Schmidt, Frances. Letter to Charles C. Pierce, n.d., BCF for Ivan F. Schmidt, RG 92, NARA.

Schudson, Michael. *Discovering the News: A Social History of American Newspapers.* New York: Basic, 1978.

Schweik, Susan M. *The Ugly Laws: Disability in Public.* New York: New York University Press, 2009.

"Second Colorado Infantry Was Encamped in Pueblo Few Months." *Pueblo Chieftain*, December 30, 1917.

"Science and Spiritualism." *Oregonian*, January 15, 1917.

Secunda, Eugene and Terence P. Moran. *Selling War to America: From the Spanish American War to the Global War on Terror.* Westport, CT: Praeger Security International, 2007.

Seitz, David W. "Embodying Unauthorized Immigrants: Counterhegemonic Protest and the Rhetorical Power of the "Material Diatribe." In *Race and Hegemonic Struggle in the United States: Pop Culture, Politics, and Protest*, edited by Michael G. Lacy and Mary E. Triece, 143–73. Madison, NJ: Fairleigh Dickinson University Press, 2014.

———. "'Let Him Remain Until the Judgment in France': Family Letters and the Overseas Burying of U.S. World War I Soldiers." In *Transnational American Memories*, edited by Udo J. Hebel, 215–42. New York: Walter de Gruyter, 2009.

———. "World War I, Trauma and Remembrance: American Cemeteries and the Therapeutic 'Third Element,'" In *Speaking the Unspeakable*, edited by Catherine Ann Collins and Jeanne Ellen Clark, 71–102. Oxford: Inter-Disciplinary Press, 2013.

Sharpe, Henry G. Letter to Mattie Hicks, July 24, 1917, BCF for Clifton R. Hicks, RG 92, NARA.

Sherman, Daniel J. *The Construction of Memory in Interwar France.* Chicago: University of Chicago Press, 1999.

"Shocks the President." *New York Times*, May 8, 1915.

"Sinking Justified, Says Dr. Dernburg." *New York Times*, May 9, 1915.

"Sinking of the Lusitania." *Lexington Herald*, May 12, 1915.

"Sir James Barrie Looks for Long War." *New York Times*, September 18, 1914.

"Slacker List." Olympia Daily Recorder, October 15, 1918.

Sledge, Michael. *Soldier Dead: How We Recover, Identify, Bury, and Honor Our Military Fallen.* New York: Columbia University Press, 2005.

Slotkin, Richard. *Lost Battalions: The Great War and the Crisis of American Nationality.* New York: Henry Holt, 2005.

Smith, Timothy B. *The Golden Age of Battlefield Preservation: The Decade of the 1890s and the Establishment of America's First Five Military Parks.* Knoxville: University of Tennessee Press, 2008.

"Soldatik Interesting Views of the Fighting." *San Jose Mercury Herald,* March 14, 1915.

Somerville, Elizabeth. Note to Grave Registration Service (GRS), n.d., BCF for James Jackson, RG 92, NARA.

"Somme Offensive Described in Graphic Terms by Irish Private Who Took Part." *Washington Post,* August 13, 1916.

"Smoking Out Germans." June 27, 1915.

Snyder, Thomas D. ed. *120 Years of American Education: A Statistical Portrait.* Washington, DC: U. S. Department of Education, 1993.

Sontag, Susan. *Regarding the Pain of Others.* New York: Picador, 2003.

"Spiritualism." *Washington Post,* December 5, 1915.

"Staggering Cost of War in Human Lives." *San Jose Evening News,* October 31, 1914.

Starr, Paul. *The Creation of the Media: Political Origins of Modern Communications.* New York: Basic Books, 2004.

Stevenson, Leland C. Letter to Chief of Staff, October 18, 1918, "Reports Related to the Morale of American Troops, 1917–1918," RG 120, Record of the American Expeditionary Forces (WWI), NARA.

"Stocks Go Soaring on Wilson Speech." *New York Times,* May 12, 1915.

"Story of War Told by Lines of Crosses." *Idaho Daily Statesman,* December 14, 1915.

Streeter, Ed. "Proposed Improvements for Arlington." *Washington Post,* December 19, 1920.

"Strike against War." http://gos.sbc.edu/k/keller.html.

"Suggests a Harem for Peace Women." *Duluth News-Tribune,* October 25, 1915.

Sullivan, Anna. Letter to QMC, March 14, 1922, BCF for Richard A. Sullivan, RG 92, NARA.

Sutton, Jane. "Kairos." In *Encyclopedia of Rhetoric,* edited by Thomas O. Sloane, 413–7. Oxford: Oxford University Press, 2001.

Swain, Martha to War Department, March 26 1920, BCF for David S. J. Swain, RG 92, NARA.

Sweeney, Michael S. *The Military and the Press: An Uneasy Truce.* Evanston, IL: Northwestern University Press, 2006.

"Tabulating Butchery." *State,* May 15, 1915, 4.

"Taps for Our Soldier Dead," *Philadelphia Inquirer,* October 24, 1921.

"Tells of Austrian Savagery in Serbia." *New York Times,* May 18, 1915.

"Tells of Slaughter Near Muelhausen." *New York Times,* August 23, 1914.

"Ten Million Men Toll of World War." *Los Angeles Times,* March 12, 1917.

"Terrible Battle Still Raging in France." *Aberdeen Daily News,* April 9, 1915.

"Teutons Kill Priests." *Washington Post,* January 24, 1915.

"The Case of Edith Cavell." *New York Times*, October 31, 1915.

"The Crime Unpardonable." *Philadelphia Inquirer*, October 29, 1915.

"The Cross." *Los Angeles Times*, February 15, 1918.

"'The Human Slaughter House'—The Supreme Horrors of Modern War." *Washington Post*, August 30, 1914.

"The Kansas Spirit." *New York Times*, January 20, 1916.

The New International Version of the Bible. Colorado Springs: International Bible Society, 1984.

"The Sinking of the Lusitania." *Lexington Herald*, May 16, 1915.

"The World Loses a Shrine of Freedom." *Davenport Democrat and Leader*, July 6, 1921.

"They Gave Till They Died! What Will You Give?" *Fort Worth Star-Telegram*, May 19, 1918.

"Thousands Slain by Belgian Guns." *Washington Post*, October 3, 1914.

"To Accompany War Dead." *New York Times*, June 9, 1920.

"To Censor Every Foreign Message." *Daily Herald* (Biloxi, Mississippi), April 26, 1917.

"Torpedoes Sink 2 British Ships Life Loss Heavy." *Fort Worth Star-Telegram*, March 29, 1915.

"Tribute to American Dead." *New York Times*, May 31, 1916.

Trout, Steven. *On the Battlefield of Memory: The First World War and American Remembrance, 1919–1941.* Tuscaloosa: University of Alabama, 2012.

Turner, Kathleen J. "Rhetorical History as Social Construction." In *Doing Rhetorical History: Concepts and Cases*, edited by Kathleen J. Turner, 1–18. Tuscaloosa: University of Alabama Press, 2003.

"Truce on Dniester Front." *New York Times*, July 11, 1915.

Tumarkin, Nina. *The Living and the Dead: The Rise and Fall of the Cult of World War II in Russia.* New York: Basic Books, 1994.

"Twelve Americans Captured, Three Are Slain by a German Raiding Party." *Los Angeles Times*, November 5, 1917.

"Two Americans Killed." *New York Times*, June 26, 1915.

"Two Americans on Arabic Missing After Submarine Sinks Great Liner without Warning, Ending 20 Lives." *Washington Post*, August 20, 1915.

"Two of U.S. Army Hurt." *Washington Post*, September 11, 1917.

"U. S. Army Right Size for Good Day's Butchery." *Duluth News-Tribune*, November 20, 1915.

"U.S. Couldn't Halt Foe." *Washington Post*, October 7, 1915.

"U. S. Youth Killed in Egypt." *Washington Post*, September 29, 1915.

"Unbelievable." *Idaho Daily Times*, October 6, 1914.

"Uncle Sam Tightens His Grip on the Kaiser's Throat." *The Patriot* (Harrisburg, Pennsylvania), July 21, 1917.

"Unexpected Moral Changes Produced by the War." *Idaho Daily Statesman*, September 17, 1916.

United States National Archives and Records Administration II, College Park, Maryland Records of the Office of the Inspector General (Army), Record Group 159, Box 772.

United States of America War Office, *Regulations for the Army of the United States, 1913: Corrected to April 15, 1917 (Changes, Nos. 1 to 55)* (Washington, DC: Government Printing Office, 1917).

"Unspeakable Atrocities Committed by Germans in Belgium Premeditated." *Idaho Daily Statesman*, May 13, 1915.

"Upheld in German Pulpits." *New York Times*, May 10, 1915.

"Use Soldiers' Diaries to Answer Denials." *New York Times*, January 22, 1915.

"Veterans Back Wilson." *New York Times*, August 19, 1915.

"Victim Was Only 17." *Washington Post*, September 9, 1917.

"Vigilantes to be Organized in Every City." *Idaho Daily Statesman*, November 15, 1917.

"Villages in Ruins." *Oregonian*, December 5, 1914.

Wallach, Alan. "Regionalism Redux" (exhibition review). *American Quarterly* 43 (June 1991): 269.

"Want Referendum on War." *New York Times*, February 5, 1917.

"War—On, Beneath and Above the Waves." *Washington Post*, September 20, 1914.

"War Appears to Be Butchery, Declares Rt. Rev. M'Golrick." *Duluth News-Tribune*, October 5, 1914.

"War Brides." *Miami Herald*, March 9, 1915.

"War Cross for Enright." *New York Times*, February 4, 1918.

War Department, "Cemeterial Division Bulletin No. 10-F-W," BCF for John A. James, RG 92, NARA.

War Department to Argyle Pitman, November 21, 1919, BCF for Henry S. Pitman, RG 92, NARA.

"War Levels All Classes." *Fort Worth Star-Telegram*, July 30, 1915.

"War News from Berlin." *New York Times*, March 20, 1915.

"War's Dead for Glycerin?" *Washington Post*, May 30, 1915.

"War Silence Crazes Women; Censorship Also Has Caused Many Thousands of Suicides." *Washington Post*, December 9, 1914.

"Warns the English of Atrocity Tales," September 27, 1914.

"Washington Is to Be Most Beautiful City in America." *Duluth News Tribune*, June 19, 1910.

Watkins, Glenn. *Proof Through the Night: Music and the Great War*. Berkeley: University of California Press, 2003.

"We Salute You!" *Miami Herald Record*, April 12, 1918.

Weeks, Jim. *Gettysburg: Memory, Market, and an American Shrine*. Princeton: Princeton University Press, 2003.

Wertenbach, Fred. "World War I Diary 1918 of F. Wertenbach Co. G 111th US Infantry R.E.F.," Archives of the Soldiers and Sailors Memorial Hall and Museum, Pittsburgh, Pennsylvania.

"What Dum-Dum Bullets Are." *Wall Street Journal*, September 14, 1914.

"What Father Dakras Saw of Massacres in Turkey." *Washington Post*, November 28, 1915.

"What High-Speed Bullets Do." *Washington Post*, February 28, 1915.

"What Lipton Saw in Stricken Serbia." *New York Times*, March 23, 1915.

"What Shell Shock Is." *Washington Post*, November 7, 1915.

"What Soldiers Dream About." *Idaho Daily Statesman*, March 7, 1915.

"Where Great Britain's Ally Japan May Enter the World War." *Kansas City Star*, August 10, 1914.

White, William R. "Our Soldier Dead." *The Quartermaster Review* (May-June 1930). http://www.qmfound.com/soldier_dead.htm.

"Who Pays?" *Washington Post*, November 25, 1914.

"Wholesale Plot Arrests." *New York Times*, April 7, 1917.

"Widowed by the War." *Washington Post*, April 25, 1915.

"Wild Night Ride Of Verdun Wounded." *New York Times*, December 18, 1916.

"Will Women Rule After the World War?" *Washington Post*, August 22, 1915.

"Wilson Dope Drawn from Poetic Lines." *Duluth News-Tribune*, October 27, 1916.

"Wilson Overcome Greeting Pilgrims; Predicts Triumph." *New York Times*, November 12, 1923.

"Wilson Thanks Movie Managers." *San Jose Mercury Herald*, April 5, 1918.

Wilson, Theodore. "Training and Indoctrination." In *The Oxford Companion to American Military History*, edited by John Whitelacy Chambers II, 728–31. Oxford: Oxford University Press, 1999.

Wiltz, John Edward. "The Nye Committee, 1934." In *Congress Investigates: A Documented History, 1792–1974*, edited by Arthur M. Schlesinger, Jr. and Roger Bruns, 2735–919. New York: Chelsea House, 1975.

"Window for War Dead." *New York Times*, June 13, 1922.

Winter, Jay. *Remembering War: The Great War between Memory and History in the Twentieth Century*. New Haven: Yale University Press, 2006.

———. *Sites of Memory, Sites of Mourning: The Great War in European Cultural History*. Cambridge: Cambridge University Press, 1995.

"Woman Freed by Wilson." *Oregonian*, May 30, 1920.

"Woman Spy's Death Epochal." *Oregonian*, November 28, 1915.

"Women and Children as Shields While the Enemy Dig Trenches." *Washington Post*, November 29, 1914.

"Women of France Changed by War." *New York Times*, May 30, 1915.

"Women, Too, Are at War." *Kansas City Star*, February 21, 1915.

"Work or Fight, Warning to All on Draft Rolls." *New York Times*, May 24, 1918.

"Would Enjoin Governor in Enforcing Draft Registration." *Columbus Ledger*, May 31, 1917.

"Wounded from Russia Suffer Hardships." *Idaho Daily Statesman*, December 13, 1914.

"Wounded Left on Field to Die." September 12, 1914.

Wright, Elizabethada A. "Reading the Cemetery, *Lieu De Mémoire Par Excellance*." *Rhetoric Society Quarterly* 33.2 (Spring, 2003): 27–44.

———. "Rhetorical Spaces in Memorial Places: The Cemetery as a Rhetorical Memory Place/Space." *Rhetoric Society Quarterly* 35.4 (Fall, 2005): 51–81.

"WWI soldier found in France identified as Albertan," *cnews.ca*, February 24, 2011. http://cnews.canoe.ca/CNEWS/Canada/2011/02/24/17396621.html.

Yalom, Marilyn. *The American Resting Place: Four Hundred Years of History Through Our Cemeteries and Burial Grounds*. Boston: Houghton Mifflin Company, 2008.

Zarefsky, David. "Four Senses of Rhetorical History." In *Doing Rhetorical History: Concepts and Cases*, edited by Kathleen J. Turner, 19–32. Tuscaloosa: University of Alabama Press, 2003.

———. "Presidential Rhetoric and the Power of Definition." *Presidential Studies Quarterly* 34.3 (2004): 607–19.

"Zeppelin Bombs Fall in Antwerp." *New York Times*, August 26, 1914.

"Zeppelins Harry Fighters." *New York Times*, October 25, 1914.

Zinn, Howard. *A People's History of the United States, 1492-Present*. New York: HarperCollins, 1980.

Zurier, Rebecca. *Art for the Masses*. Philadelphia: Temple University Press, 1988.

Index

African Americans:
attitudes concerning World War I of,
xii, 163, 164;
correspondence concerning fallen
next of kin with War Department
of, 147–49, 163–67;
domestic racism towards, ix, xiv,
63n160, 83, 89, 164, 178n63, 200,
203, 204, 247, 257;
military's racist attitudes towards,
79, 129, 130, 179n67;
as "second class soldiers, first class
corpses," 163–67, 205, 207, 247,
250, 251, 272n122;
service and achievements in World
War I of, 92, 144n155, 164
Aisne-Marne American Cemetery and
Memorial, 219, 241, 242, 245,
250, 252, 255, 256, 279n196,
272n120, 280n206, 280n208
All Quiet on the Western Front, 118,
119
American Association of Advertising
Agencies (AAAA), 138n92
American Battle Monuments
Commission (ABMC), 171,
181n97, 220–57, 285, 286
American Civil War, x, xii, 17, 18,
20, 51, 96, 109, 132n2, 134n26,

144n161, 184, 187, 194, 196, 198,
201–6, 212, 250, 266n45, 268n76,
268n78, 269n83, 270n85, 270n86,
270n87, 275n155
American flag, 44, 45, 49, 54, 73, 78,
80, 91, 100, 102, 118, 159, 170,
189, 192, 194, 226, 227, 236, 237,
239, 249, 251, 252, 255, 256,
262n28
American "gravescape" designs,
199–201, 214, 249, 250, 253,
266n54, 275n155, 280n209
American Protective League (APL), 82,
83, 94
American Revolutionary War, 47, 75,
84, 96, 132n2, 134n26, 203, 206,
269n83
American Socialist Party, 49
American World War I experience:
"Americanism," 43–47, 54, 91;
disorienting impacts on U.S.
domestic life and international
politics of, xi, xii;
scholarship on, xvii, xviii
America's first combat casualties,
95–105, 142n132, 172, 173,
182n108, 184
anarchists, xii, 3, 49, 51, 63n160,
80–84, 259n18

311

About the Author

David W. Seitz is Associate Professor of Communication Arts and Sciences at Penn State University, Mont Alto. Seitz earned his B.A. and M.A. at Johns Hopkins University and his Ph.D. at University of Pittsburgh. His primary research interests include rhetorical theory and criticism, war rhetoric, public memory, and social justice. His work has been published in a range of edited volumes and academic journals, including *Cultural Studies/Critical Methodologies* and *Public Art Dialogue*.

CPSIA information can be obtained
at www.ICGtesting.com
Printed in the USA
BVHW03*0301080618
518528BV00003B/10/P